TRAVEL
IN
VOGUE

TRAVEL IN VOGUE

MACDONALD
MACDONALD FUTURA PUBLISHERS
LONDON

First published in 1981 in Great Britain by
Macdonald · London and Sydney

Macdonald Futura Publishers
Paulton House
8 Shepherdess Walk
London N1 7LW

ISBN 0 354 04600 4

Printed and bound in Great Britain
by Mackays of Chatham

CONTENTS

THE FIFTIES

THE SIXTIES

THE SEVENTIES

ACKNOWLEDGEMENTS

The people who have made this book possible are too numerous to name. Apart from all the authors whose articles are included and all the artists and photographers featured, thanks are due to the Editors of Vogue, past and present, and in particular the Travel Editors, most recently Linda McNair Scott, Jenepher Wolff, Patsy Hollis, Peta Lyn Farwagi and Paddi Benson. Special thanks to Barbara Tims whose task it was to read and sift and edit a mountain of material from Vogue files going back over sixty years. Thanks also to Clive Dorman for the design work and to Jackie Cole for coping with innumerable editorial problems.

Martin O'Brien
Vogue Travel Editor 1977–1980

FOREWORD

For over 60 years Vogue has set the scene not only in fashion, beauty and entertaining, but also in travel. It has discovered new places, reported on changing modes of travel, followed the smart set to spas and holiday resorts, published articles by far ranging correspondents and intrepid explorers and presented fashion pictures shot on location in outlandish places.

In recording contemporary styles of living Vogue has reflected changing attitudes to travel: the advent of the motor car and the pioneering journeys on untried roads, the luxurious trains, the lure of exotic places and the leisurely cruises that got you there, and of course air travel, starting with flying boats and Zeppelins and gradually shrinking the far horizons.

The material from six decades of Travel in Vogue is chosen as much for literary merit and nostalgic appeal as for historic interest and up-to-date usefulness. Vogue has always attracted the foremost writers, artists and photographers; this book presents a small selection of their work.

THE TWENTIES

"The war practically extinguished that species of human being commonly called 'tourist'," reported Vogue in 1920, "but though conditions are still unfavourable to his mode of life he is reviving daily and in large numbers. He who had the longing for strange lands has been obliged for the last five years to discover the many-sided natural beauties of England. This he has done with gratifying results. But the time invariably comes when far horizons lure the island-bound traveller, and the mystery of unknown lands calls to him across a shining sea." But at the start of the decade, a problem faced those whose "civilian journeyings" had been "temporarily suspended" by the Great War (then only fifteen months past), for in 1920 much of Europe was still "shattered by cannon, burned by gas, torn by shell, without trees, without houses — almost without ruins," hardly the kind of destination to satisfy a nation's long-frustrated wanderlust.

Vogue's recommendation in that first summer of the Twenties was twofold: to seek out strange lands untouched by war, and find "New Worlds to Conquer," or to return to the old places in novel and unfamiliar ways. In view of the prevailing conditions, Vogue opted for the former course of action.

"In Scandinavia, that country full of romance and legend, an unbelievable quiet reigns. There one may be stirred by the silence of primeval forests, by the low moaning of giant fir trees and the wizardry of the midnight sun looming low and fiery on the horizon . . . Touring Sweden in summer is one of the most satisfactory ways to spend a holiday" specified Vogue. But then anywhere that promised change, any new direction, would do the same. Apart from some tired recommendations to winter in Lisbon or Biarritz, there became evident a movement towards those places far from war-stricken Europe, a preference for anywhere "strange, remote and pristine in its picturesqueness." Scandinavia was a possibility — so too was Iceland, suitably "strange and delightfully interesting;" the Lesser Antilles "a narrow, fascinating little half-circle of islands" in the Caribbean; Trinidad farther south still; British Guiana; and perhaps the most significant of all, "the beckoning lure" of South Africa "with its colour and opulence and dazzle."

In the years that followed, this emphasis on exotic, extravagant destinations continued and Vogue spread the net wide — an indulgence easily understood given the circumstances. Twice Vogue suggested Japan "to pursue the spring all across the south, to see its beginning at the Mardi Gras in New Orleans and find it ripening into summer among the opening rosebuds of southern California . . . then to the summer shores of Hawaii and on to the clouds of cherry blossom that, in their season, are the charm of Japan;" as well as featuring Bermuda, Canada, North and South America, and "The Youngest Continent" — Australia. This was escape in its purest form, travelling to forget — not so much suggested holiday routes, but refreshing examples of alternative and undeniably tempting lifestyles.

But by 1924 the escapist rage had exhausted itself; and, anyway, conditions on the home front were now much improved. The scars of war, it seemed, had finally healed, unpleasant memories had grown hazy and wartime restrictions were now being lifted albeit "with the exception of one or two ex-enemy countries such as Bavaria and Czechoslovakia." Vogue had come full circle, favouring once again those resorts close to home and easily accessible, falling back on that second recommendation made in 1920, that it was possible to find refreshing novelty in travel by rediscovering old haunts in different ways.

July 1924 saw the first of three articles, entitled "Travel Zones of France:" "A Series of Pictorial Maps which Suggest the Delights which France has come to offer to the Summer Traveller Who is Sightseer, Sportsman and Epicure". "Happy is the holiday maker" that first article began, "whose face is turned to the pleasant land of France where he, or she, or both together, may see enchanting places, do amusing things and frivol lightly, sightsee strenuously or rusticate serenely as the spirit moves them." Not inconsiderable factors in Europe's re-emergence as an attractive holiday proposition were highly favourable exchange rates and a mounting enthusiasm for motor travel abroad, just one of the new ways of exploring old territory.

No longer was continental travel the sole preserve of the old and infirm or those escaping our own inclement weather to winter in more genial surroundings. "We go to Monte Carlo in January because of our own climate and for no other reason." That was 1920. Five years later tastes had changed dramatically.

Old favourite Deauville was now the smartest summer resort in France, its season centred around the races in early August when "all Paris and all London, all New York, all Madrid and all Buenos Aires (how cosmopolitan could you get?) gathered together on the sunny coast of Normandy amid polo, golf, riding, motoring and gambling". In the casino the new exchange rate was particularly appreciated. "At this period it is fashionable to be exaggeratedly smart and to participate in all sports. In the evening, the casino forms a brilliant pageant of gorgeously gowned women of the fashionable world and of the demi-monde, and of actresses, mannequins and couturiers, wearing the most extreme models. The same cast appears on the beach in eccentric, entertaining costumes that would be ruined, one fancies, by sudden rain", let alone a bathe! Farther along the coast, and a close rival, Le Touquet was also an excellent choice in summer with its golf and tennis tournaments. Each year it became more and more fashionable to go there. On the Riviera, Vogue reported, crowds of people were gathering for the opening of the Russian Ballet under the direction of M. Diaghileff; Cannes was rapidly becoming the social centre of the Riviera with its tennis tournaments, its sailing, golf — and new in 1926 — its Mah-jong soirées; while on the Venice Lido the spate of colourful balls in-creased each year. Any excuse, it seemed, was enough to send everyone bounding across to Europe at a moment's notice. Those who might once have basked under Lisbon's winter sun, now began an annual pilgrimage to Switzerland: "Of all the continental journeys that mark the various seasons of the year — to Mentone, to Deauville, to Paris, the Lido — that to Winter Sports' Land is perhaps the most exhilarating". With only a handful of ski lifts in operation no one was about to deny that. "Experienced athletes will probably make for resorts such as St Moritz where from the end of November to the end of March dry air, blue sky and perfect ice and snow surfaces have made a verit-able sportsmen's paradise. The fine ice rinks are crowded with skaters, curlers, bandy and hockey players, the runs are ideal for bobsleigh and luge, and tobogganists may try their prowess on the world famous Cresta Run. Everybody skis and even the most unskilful can soon learn." But Switzerland, Vogue discovered, was much more than just a winter sports' destination. For ambitious motorists, and by the mid-Twenties they were a fast growing breed, "Switzerland is perfectly charming and perfectly civilised. Surrounded by post-cardly familiar but beautiful scenery you drive your car as far removed from misadventure as you do when you take it to Brighton." Indeed, "there is nothing so glorious in the whole scheme of motor-owning as motor-mountaineering". One more destination to add to Spain, North Africa, Italy and Austria — all of which had been attracting attention in Vogue's motoring travel notes.

Vogue was also intent on promoting Switzerland, along with Morocco and Tunisia, as a desirable autumn refuge after the heat and stress of summer — that time between seasons when the summer crowds had departed and the winter ones had not yet arrived for their skiing. Among the attractions as autumn destinations Vogue made much of the glorious scenery and invigorating climate of the Bernese Oberland; the mild sunshine of cosmopolitan Vevey; the Italian Lakes and their intoxicatingly exotic atmosphere; and the health-giving waters of Baden and Bex "particularly for the English social gods tired after their season". In Switzerland, promised Vogue, "every single member of the family, no matter how widely its tastes may differ, can find something to do."

Considering the enthusiasm with which everyone, Vogue included, set about exploring holiday possibilities in Europe, always on the look-out for something new, it was hardly surprising that sooner or later, someone should discover the sun. The newcomer was an immediate success, much courted by an up-and-coming younger set, and resorts like Cannes and Monte Carlo "practically shut up in the summer" took on a new lease of life — much to the gratification of local businessmen. But in some quarters, the new arrival was greeted with less enthusiasm. On the Lido, soon to suffer at the hands of this new fad, Noël Coward writing for Vogue observed "how the blazing sun brings out the worst traits of character in all the visitors" to the extent that friends "spend hours squabbling viciously and brushing flakes of their own sun-scorched flesh from the table". Skin specialists like Helena Rubinstein and Elizabeth Arden deplored the subsequent craze for suntanning which had sprung up at all the fashionable resorts, and in 1928 a Vogue headline announced "The Burning Question of the Summer — Nut Brown Maid or Lady Fair?". But so popular had the craze become, especially amongst the young, that "the calendar has gone out of date, for no one takes any notice of time . . . the length of one's stay (and, more important, the choice of one's resort) governed only by the strength of the sun" — something the Lido was to find out within a matter of months, as the warmer Riviera grew in popularity and people discovered the charms of places like Cap d'Antibes. "Bathing from rocks is a new-found pleasure" Vogue told its readers. "Perhaps it does not sound as wonderful as it is, but when one has seen the rocks of the Cap d'Antibes, terraced as they are down to the sea with a dozen different levels, each with a little nook shaded by umbrellas under which one has cocktails, gin fizzes or tea while watching the diving; has seen the aquaplaning and the groups of people sunburned a deep mahogany, wearing the brightest bathing suits and the gayest pyjamas, it is really a scene to rival the Lido."

In the last year of the decade, as bodies blistered on the Riviera, Robert Byron looked back over the Twenties and concluded that "the most ingenious brain must find it hard to contrive a novelty". But a new decade was just around the corner, with some equally new suggestions.

BRISSAUD

IN A TUNISIAN OASIS

by ALDOUS HUXLEY

Waking at dawn, I looked out of the window. We were in the desert. On either side of the railway an immense plain, flat as Holland, but tawny instead of green, stretched out interminably. On the horizon, instead of windmills, a row of camels was silhouetted against the grey sky. Mile after mile, the train rolled slowly southward.

At Tozeur, when at last we arrived, it had just finished raining — for the first time in two and a half years — and now the wind had sprung up; there was a sandstorm. A thick brown fog, whirled into eddies by the wind, gritty to the skin, abolished the landscape from before our smarting eyes. We sneezed; there was sand in our ears, in our hair, between our teeth. It was horrible. I felt depressed, but not surprised. The weather is always horrible when I travel.

Towards evening the wind somewhat abated; the sand began to drop out of the air. At mid-day the brown curtain had been impenetrable at fifty yards. It thinned, grew gauzier; one could see objects at a hundred, two hundred yards. From the windows of the hotel bedroom in which we had sat all day, trying — but in vain, for it came through even invisible crannies — to escape from the wind-blown sand, we could see the fringes of a dense forest of palm trees, the dome of a little mosque, houses of sun-dried brick and thin brown men in flapping night-shirts walking, with muffled faces and bent heads, against the wind, or riding, sometimes astride, sometimes sideways, on the bony rumps of patient little asses. Two very professional tourists in sun helmets — there was no sun — emerged round the corner of a street. A malicious gust of wind caught them unawares; simultaneously the two helmets shot into the air, thudded, rolled in the dust. The two professional tourists scuttled in pursuit. The spectacle cheered us a little; we descended, we ventured out of doors.

A melancholy Arab offered to show us round the town. Knowing how hard it is to find one's way in these smelly labyrinths, we accepted his offer. His knowledge of French was limited; so, too, in consequence, was the information he gave us. He employed what

I may call the Berlitz method. Thus, when a column of whirling sand rose up and jumped at us round the corner of a street, our guide turned to us and said, pointing: "Poussière". We might have guessed it ourselves.

He led us interminably through narrow, many-cornered streets, between eyeless walls, half crumbled and tottering. "Village" he explained. "Très plaisant." We did not altogether agree with him.

Our guide patted a brown mud wall.

"Briques," he said and repeated the word several times, so that we might be certain what he meant.

These bricks, which are of sun-dried mud, are sometimes, on the façades of the more considerable houses, arranged in a series of simple and pleasing patterns — diamonds, quincunxes, hexagons. A local art which nobody now takes the trouble to practise — nobody, that is, except the Europeans, who, with characteristic energy, have used and wildly abused the traditional ornamentation on the walls of the station and the principal hotel. It is a curious and characteristic fact that, whenever, in Tunisia, one sees a particularly oriental piece of architecture, it is sure to have been built by the French, since 1881. The cathedral of Carthage, the law courts and schools of Tunis — these are more Moorish than the Alhambra, Moorish as only oriental tearooms in Paris or London can be Moorish. In thirty years the French have produced buildings more typically and intensely Arabian than the Arabs themselves contrived to do in the course of thirteen centuries.

We passed into the market place.

"Viande", said our guide, fingering as he passed a well-thumbed collop of mutton, lying among the dust and flies on a little booth.

We nodded.

"Très joli", commented our guide. "Très plaisant". Noisily he spat on the ground. The proprietor of the booth spat too. We hurried away; it needs time to grow inured to Arabian habits.

There are in the desert of southern Tunisia three great oases: Gabes by the sea, a little north of that island of Djerba which is, traditionally, the classical Island of the Lotus Eaters; Tozeur, to the west of it, some seventy miles inland; and Nefta, fifteen miles west of Tozeur, the starting point of the caravans which trade between southern Tunisia and the great oases of the Algerian Sahara, Biskra and Touggourt. These oases are all of much the same size, each consisting of some six or seven thousand acres of cultivated ground, and are all three remarkable for their numerous and copious springs. In the middle of the desert, suddenly, a hundred fountains come welling out of the sand; rivers run, a network of little canals is dug. An innumerable forest of date palms springs up — a forest whose undergrowth is corn and roses, vines and apricot trees, olives and pomegranates, pepper trees, castor oil trees, banana trees, every precious plant of the temperate and the sub-tropical zones. No rain falls on these little Edens — except on the days of my arrival — but the springs, fed from who knows what distant source, flow inexhaustibly and have flowed at least since Roman times. Islanded among the sands, their green luxuriance is a standing miracle.

Of the three great Tunisian oases, my favourite is Nefta. Gabes runs it close for beauty, while the proximity of the sea gives it a charm which Nefta lacks. But, on the other hand, Gabes is less fertile than Nefta and, socially, more sophisticated. There must be the best part of two hundred Europeans living in Gabes. There is dancing once a week at the hotel. Gabes is quite the little Paris. The same objection applies to Tozeur, which has a railway station and positively teems with French officials. Nefta, with fourteen thousand Arabs, has a white population of a dozen or thereabouts. A hundred

Frenchmen can always make a Paris; twelve, I am happy to say, cannot. The only non-Arabian feature of Nefta is its hotel, which is clean, comfortable, French and efficient. At Nefta one may live among barbarians, in the middle ages, and at the same time, for thirty francs a day, enjoy the advantages of contemporary western civilisation. What could be more delightful?

We set off next morning by car, across the desert. From Tozeur the road mounts slightly to a plateau which dominates the surrounding country. The day was clear and sunny. We looked down on the green island of Tozeur — four hundred thousand palm trees among the sands. Beyond the oasis we could see the chotts, glittering in the sun. The chotts are shallow depressions in the ground; at one time, no doubt, the beds of considerable lakes. There is no water in them now; but the soil is furred with a bright saline efflorescence. At a distance, you could swear you saw the sea. For the rest, the landscape was all sand and lion-coloured rock.

We bumped on across the desert. Every now and then we passed a camel, a string of camels. Their owners walked or rode on asses beside them. The women folk were perched among the baggage on the hump — a testimony, most eloquent in this Mohammedan country, to the great discomfort of camel riding. Once, we met a small Citroën lorry, crammed to overflowing with white-robed Arabs. In the Sahara, the automobile has begun to challenge the supremacy of the camel. Little ten horse-power Citroëns dart about the desert. For the rougher mountainous country, special six-wheeled cars are needed, and with caterpillar wheels one may even affront the soft and shifting sand of the dunes. Motor buses now ply across the desert.

The hotel at Nefta is a long low building, occupying one whole side of the market square. From your bedroom window you watch the Arabs living; they do it unhurriedly and with a dignified inefficiency. Endlessly haggling, they buy and sell. The vendor offers a mutton chop, slightly soiled; the buyer professes himself outraged by the price, which would be exorbitant if the goods were spotlessly first-hand. It takes them half an hour to come to a compromise. On the ground white bundles doze in the sun; when the sun grows too hot, they roll a few yards and doze again in the shade. The notables of the town, the rich proprietors of palm trees, stroll past with the dignity of Roman senators. Their garments are of the finest wool; they carry walking sticks; they wear European shoes and socks, and on their bare brown calves — a little touch entirely characteristic of the real as opposed to the literary East — pale mauve or shell-pink sock-suspenders. Wild men ride in from the desert. Some of them, trusting to common sense as well as Allah to preserve them from ophthalmia, wear smoked motor goggles. With much shouting, much reverberant thumping of dusty, moth-eaten hides, a string of camels is driven in. They kneel, they are unloaded. Supercilious and haughty, they turn this way and that, like the dowagers of very aristocratic families at a plebeian evening party.

Sitting at our window, we watch the spectacle. And at night, after a pink and yellow sunset with silhouetted palm trees and domes against the sky (for my taste, I am afraid, altogether too like the coloured plates in the illustrated Bible) — at night huge stars come out in the indigo sky, the cafés are little caves of yellow light, draped figures move in the narrow streets with lanterns in their hands, and on the flat roofs of the houses one sees the prowling shadows of enormous watch dogs. There is silence, the silence of the desert; from time to time, there comes to us, very distinctly, the distant sound of spitting.

by SACHEVERELL SITWELL

This is the time of year when the interval between tea and dinner is so dark and long that the electric light has a strange and cat-like fascination for one's tired eyes, and so it is difficult not to sit with head tilted back looking at it, which induces the kind of dazed tranquillity of mood that one can obtain by looking intently into a fire. It is a relief to break this spell by getting up and walking to the window. The public house opposite is as bright as any aquarium with those elaborate brass rails and the steamy heat upon the windows. Occasionally the door is flung open and out comes one of those nearly extinct specimens with bonnet and ragged feather-boa, of which the public houses seem to be the last preserves — as it were, the National Park. Yes! It is London, the land of Congreve — and of Phil May. Such figures emerge, as though spilt, from their retreats; they come out into the street on a sort of yellow flood of light, like the fly that you might spill from a tea-cup on to the tablecloth; and they crawl off, dripping and bedraggled, into the darkness.

So much for our National Colour — unless you like to add a few pearl-buttons, or an extra depth of grime from the coal-mines; but none of us have ever doubted that lands which have a more liberal allowance of sun possess different advantages. Those beams of light fall upon and improve what we should consider in England a flimsy, if pretty, building with just the same magical charm with which we set our mock-suns to work in a theatre. They rush suddenly into the darkness of space and throw an indescribable halo of beauty about a face or figure that would be depressing if invested in its customary mackintosh. One arc-lamp even, as Marinetti has said, can make the moon hide its face with shame. When we think, then, of a modern theatre with all its contrivances for throwing forward and intensifying, thinning and retreating, or throwing a steady, clear radiance, we must admit that the pale, old fashioned spectre is decidedly out of date.

Old, perhaps, but still full of ideas; and the sun and moon are not Academicians for nothing. According to the formula of an anonymous wit — can it have been Mr Raymond Mortimer? — "every Oxford man has his Cambridge moments", and we may suppose that our two luminaries, in a determination to forestall modern developments, had, ready prepared for use, a country in which every effect was set out in order to exhibit the potentialities, the possibilities, of lighting. Hence Spain, and hence these beautiful photographs.

We are trying, then, to dispel the English fog, and keep off the rain for a bit by this dizzy and crackling solar virtuosity, which keeps up a kind of sustained note where there is a flat level surface of wall, and then hits out all the ornament like the playing of a rippling scale. White walls (and walls, somehow, seem generally to be white) are so many perfect back-cloths for the appearance of those earringed and be-handkerchiefed banditti that we must expect, and manage always to find.

The real authorities on Spain will tell you that Andalusia is nothing, and that every fine building is in the North, where few travellers venture, for the year has only two seasons, broiling summer and a biting winter. I believe their verdict is true with regard to those who have visited Spain more than once, but certainly, at first experience, the Alhambra and the Alcazar of Seville must evoke some sensation in even the most vapid and blasé of travellers. Perhaps, then, the learned critics are really right, and this art is a form of almost Jewish exuberance, a delight in detail for detail's sake, for this gifted

17

Oriental race have played a large part in Spanish history. All the ornament of the Alhambra, for example, has been impressed with a variety of stamps or dies, and the whole affair is stucco. It is therefore hand-made, and yet not hand-made; like music, not played on a pianola, but on a piano that is made to sound like a pianola. We will name no names.

After these stalactites and honeycombs it is interesting to turn to the other photographs, where the component material should be more simple. But no, the Spaniards have never yet been able to leave well alone, and they cannot resist a bit of decoration. Look at these two Renaissance doorways, and ask yourself what more could they do! In truth, they have left not a stone unturned.

Spanish Gothic is not illustrated here, except, perhaps, for the one photograph of a fine arched doorway, and this is rather a pity, because nowhere is Gothic found in such diversity and profusion as in Spain. I suppose there are no buildings of this date that are as perfect in every detail down to their jewelled treasuries and vestments as the cathedrals of Leon and Burgos. The pilgrim whose footsteps we are following makes straight from the Moorish to the Plateresque, and this latter word may need a line or two of explanation. This style of building is so called because of its resemblance to jewellers' work, and more especially silversmiths'. The ornament is repoussé off a flat surface, that is to say, and the Spaniards, as we have remarked, were not sparing in decoration. The date of this style roughly corresponds with the period of Henry VIII in England. Armed with this information, and not needing to glance into our Baedekers, we can pause, therefore, with our pilgrim in front of this Plateresque door with its huge hooded porch, and can take a good look at it while he sets up his camera. It is a fine dramatic affair, which, like everything else in this country, has been beautifully planned for the arrival of the photographer. It is a little late, though, rather past the best period of Plateresque and running into the days of Baroque.

Look up at that tower, now, and see the grass growing there above the pairs of twisted pillars. In another moment we shall be round the corner, in front of the façade, and forewarned and on the look-out for twists and spirals. Here it is: a great double storied and pedimented doorway with a couple of those spiral pillars on the first floor. We are a

long way now from the Plateresque. Dealing in specimens, we may say that we have left behind the Guadalajara Palace and the House with the Shells of Salamanca (these two being the best examples of the former style) and are on our way now to the days of that neglected architectural genius, Churriguera, and, to name two typical instances, the Cathedral of Murcia and the Cartuja at Granada. We are shown a lovely little convent courtyard with grilled windows, as the new sign of our times.

In Spain it is a little of everything, some French Gothic, as at Leon, even a little English here and there, and every variety of German, Burgundian and Flemish Gothic. Then we have Moorish work, lots of Jewish work at Toledo, heaps of Italian, one of the great geniuses of painting, El Greco, from Crete, quantities of French 18th century at the Palaces of La Granja and Aranjuez near Madrid, and eventually all the Spanish music-game, with Rimsky-Korsakoff, Glinka, Ravel, Lalo, Chabrier, Debussy, Lord Berners, down to our latest Spaniard, Arthur Rubinstein. Anything may happen at any moment. Do not be surprised, then, if we end up with a view (is it of Avila or Segovia?) — a Romanesque church of imposing and monastic severity, and a Roman aqueduct. We might add, only space forbids, a Greek temple and a watercolour by Sargent, or, *tempora mutantur,* a fine drawing by Picasso. It is all there, waiting to be seen, and to be viewed leisurely from the windows of a double-gauge train. A comfortable train, too, but one which might be coaxed out of what Mr Firbank terms a "stately trot" into some more amenable swiftness. You can walk, if you like, and indeed you may win on the train in the end, but other alternative there is none; for motoring is almost completely impossible, save between dreary San Sebastian and dusty Madrid. Something tremendous must be done about it all, and the Swiss hotel managers should be implored to collect their energies and attack this difficult terrain!

In the meanwhile the Labour report on Spain, recently issued, says Spain is no land of Romance, because 50 per cent of the population are illiterate and have no profession, and because of the imposing figures that he quotes about infant mortality and the lack of drainage. I am sure anyone who sees these photographs will reverse this decision, and agree that it is these defects that constitute a land of Romance. All the same, it may be rather uncomfortable for the Spaniards!

19

Adieu à la Neige

by COLETTE

You leave Paris at night, and lose your heart, a willing victim, to the first glimpse from the train of a screen of cypresses outlined against the dawn, to the first inlet of the Mediterranean, a watery axe that splits two hills asunder, to the first orange-tree and the first rose. But the winter sun has nowadays a rival, the unsullied, lasting snow, shot with blue from the sky that it reflects.

We are not old friends, the snow and I. Nor am I yet familiar with its ways, as the children are that I see on it, gaily dressed and shod, it seems, with lightning, or mounted on skis, with which they play about the lower slopes and cross the purple-shadowed valleys. But the air above the snow has the delicate, frozen scent of peppermint and with the first deep breaths that filled my lungs I knew its power. You call the snow a country or a climate? Say, rather, a planet. Before it the invader stays his greed, and starts to dream. Only upon the snow can every people meet in friendliness. Peaceful and shapeless, it welcomes all strangers alike, and they forget to be haughty or patriotic or grown-up. It is contact with the earth, with its vitality and smell, that makes man savage, sentimental and piratical; and this snow hides the earth away.

Only upon the snow can very old and very young sit together on the same small wooden toboggans, to slide down the same gentle slopes, smiling at one another from the excitement that they share. The bobsleigh does not rouse their envy, as it rushes past, noisy and meteoric, scything the air and spraying splintered ice. To the luge also belong the wide spaces and the steeper slopes. Two reins of rope it requires to guide it, but the little toboggan has no need of them. But a phantom steed races in front of each of these magic coaches, and surely there is a mare made of transparent ice round whose neck the luge's cords pass to hold the bit while, making ten leagues an hour, she gallops down. The fairy-mare I drove knew well her passenger's love of poor earthly pleasures. Each day she threw me in a somersault to the ground, stopping short just at a chàlet's door, where kippered herrings frizzled above a fire of cones, and cheese, steeped in brandy and hot wine, melted in great tear-like drops on top of a succulent joint. Then there was a white wine, watery-looking but treacherous, and cold as the snow in which it had been iced, and our greed made a domestic poem of the sizzling pan, the smoke, and the hot blue breath that came from the mouths of us hearty mountaineers.

Innocent, dangerous and everlasting is your kingdom, Snow! A merry child you make of man, attentive only to his energetic leisure. You have invented a new pleasure, making of enjoyment a duty in this anxiety we feel to live only for our bodies: they grow stronger and more alive with every hour we consecrate to you, they gather fresh force from every fall. You see your devotees leave the hotel early each day, when the dawn lets the foot of the mountains still drowse in violet sleep, though it silhouettes the peaks against the blue sky in a hard, burning and metallic orange. Our skis, tied like long wings, upon our shoulder, and a stick in either hand, we set out. And we might be ten-year-old children, so solemn we are, and so well-behaved.

Last night we chose our goal, some invisible and arbitrary spot: the peak of a mountain, or some châlet concealed beneath its snow-laden eaves. One place or another, what difference does it make, so long as we achieve an instant of intellectual and physical exaltation, so long as we reach a happiness which we shall keep for ever secret, standing somewhere marvellously high where the firmament hangs heavy and dark above the mountains, and we must needs open wide our hearts and arms to take in this, our Paradise. At mid-day we return, our bodies smoking with heat and happiness, and little bright blue shadows follow at our feet. Or we do not come back till evening, perhaps, slow with fatigue, and silent. And our silence seems lyrical: we have ceased to think. We are lovers, Snow, that you have satisfied. We have seen nothing, we have possessed nothing, save you, since daybreak, and you have sufficed. We have seen the mountain grow smaller, the landscape larger, beneath our steps. When we stopped, it was to sit upon an unsullied fold of your robe, sweet Snow, and we sat back to back because of the sun that scorched our shoulders. But hunger made us feel light and empty, and we foraged in our pockets; then ate with faces turned to the sun, gathering our crumbs with pious carefulness. Then on to our feet we strapped once more our wings, and set forth upon our flight down the valleys. Sometimes we marked great circles on the untouched fields of snow, and leaping to right or left, watched a hollow bowl of land approach, depart, and yet again approach. We grew iridescent from our falls; and we dived head first into drifts that glittered like sequins in the sun with all the colours of the rainbow.

Contests we have held with one another, of boldness and of speed. But we have not pursued or killed the harmless birds or beasts. We have not thought of the love of women, or coveted our neighbour's goods. For you require us that are your lovers, mighty Snow, to be pure, and pure you render us. At night we sleep like children, long and soundly, and even in our dreams we are faithful to you. It is still you that we see in our sleep, and we feel ourselves in still finer flight than in our waking hours. Our windows are open wide for your silence to come in by, and nothing stirs in your domains, not even the wind, but only the quivering fire of the stars. And if we forget for a few hours in our sleep the passion we have vowed to you, you fall, jealous Snow, like autumn leaves, flutter and hesitate around our rest, pouring before our beds the gentle homage of your flakes — feathers in armfuls, flowers, precious stones without flaw, that vanish like the bounty of a dream, as the first footsteps of the day.

LEPAPE

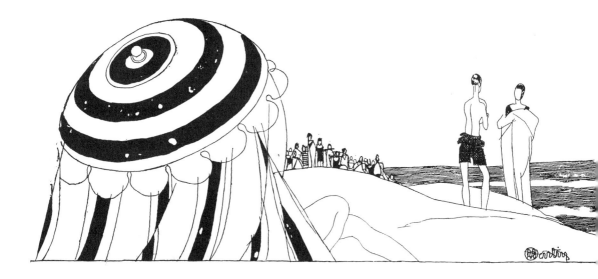

THE LIDO BEACH

by NOEL COWARD

For a few months in every year, a fierce and relentless sun blazes down upon Venice — winsomely, if a trifle superficially, described as "The City of Beautiful Nonsense". Enthusiastic steam launches forge raucously up and down the Grand Canal, causing perspiring tourists to clutch the carved wooden seats of their gondolas as they bounce up and down in the wash and swirl away from slippery green steps at the precise moment that somebody is attempting to get into them.

Hordes of earnest women, with pince-nez and Baedekers, rush spiritedly through austere buildings to converge ultimately, wearing expressions of weary triumph, upon the Piazza San Marco, where, for a few brief moments, they relax and consume ices and cakes preparatory to gathering themselves together for renewed onslaughts upon the wistful remnants of further beautiful nonsense.

Flocks of unembarrassed pigeons are photographed incessantly with a charming disregard of social distinctions, perching upon the more vulnerable anatomical points of minor European royalties and self-conscious American matrons, and, all through the long, scorching days, clouds of effusive superlatives are wafted up and over the shrinking domes and spires of what was once the most graceful and dignified city of the world.

It is not altogether surprising, therefore, that the wealthy exclusive nucleus of cosmopolitans, self-designated as the "sheik set," migrate with a slightly uncalled-for air of superiority to the Excelsior Hotel on the Lido. Here, for hours on end, the placid shallows of the long-suffering Adriatic are peppered with bobbing and gesticulating figures. There can be but small consolation for it in the knowledge that it is being ravished by the best people — salt water is a notorious leveller of class differences. Every square inch of fine, powdered sand is churned up by the passing of unnumerable toes and dented and depressed by recumbent sun-blistered bodies of various nationalities.

Perhaps the most astonishing deduction to be drawn from the Lido Beach as a pleasure resort is the tragically demoralising effect that it has upon character. Pleasantly innocuous people who, during the larger portion of the year, lead useless but well-meaning lives, arrive at the Excelsior without so much as a harsh thought even for their best friends — suffering a little from inevitable traveller's fatigue, following a hot and dusty train journey — and desiring only peace and idle hours of languorous tranquillity. Usually, a day or two passes before the first signs of moral degeneration begin to appear in varying forms of irascibility — sudden, violent quarrels at bridge or an unreasoning desire to frustrate the most harmless plans suggested by casual acquaintances in the worthy cause of general enjoyment. In the case of more dominant personalities, a few hours only are necessary in order to bring forth those treacherous impulses and revoltingly primitive desires, which, if we are to believe Monsieur Gustave Flaubert, are firmly embodied in the most charming natures.

For the benefit of the mercifully uninitiated, it would, perhaps, be well to describe this Gomorrah of frowzy splendour. An undecorative and incomplete wooden pier wanders listlessly for a few yards into the sea and stops short abruptly, as though discouraged by its own unattractiveness. An amazingly hot strip of sand is semicircularised by two rows of *cabañas*, or bathing huts, intersected by narrow planks that scorch the soles of the feet unless some person has flung down a wet bathing-dress and left a damp patch of grateful coolth. A wider board walk leads from the centre of the beach to a majestic flight of steps culminating in the terrace of the Excelsior Hotel. It is not considered etiquette to penetrate as far as this unless comparatively clothed. Within the lounge an air of well-ordered civilization soothes the senses — one or two of the bridge players actually seem to be enjoying themselves, unlike their scowling friends on the beach, who spend hours squabbling viciously and brushing flakes of their own sun-scorched flesh from the table.

The visitors who live in Venice and come out to the Lido only for the day have more chance of ultimate salvation. By the time that they have reached their hotels in the evening and have dressed and dined, the sour lines have been eradicated from their faces and their sanity of outlook restored. They begin to chatter and laugh again, sublimely unconscious of the pit from which they have escaped. They glide about peacefully in gondolas and watch marionette-like figures jigging about on lantern-hung *Serenatas*. The lights on the Piazza are lazily extinguished. Dim couples wander through the shadows, occasionally speaking Italian — until, at last, for a few hours, the crowd-racked city succumbs to the weary sleep of gently decaying beauty.

MARTIN

FLORIDA

by VIOLA TREE

There are two physical ways of approach to Florida which may affect your mental approach. You may love it more or you may like it less if you approach by its land way than its sea way but you will like it differently.

By its land way you will pretty certainly have seen New York first, have been broken in, shocked, stunned, by its hospitality — and then flung into a train, when you will be again broken in and stunned by the vastness of everything, the terrors and hairy hideousness of the forests, the miles and miles where nothing has ever happened, chaos, with this thin line of civilisation rushing through it.

You will know why all things in America are so different. You will compare your going with a journey, for instance, from Hull to Kent.

From Hull to Kent is perhaps about six hours; from New York to Florida about three days. When you are in that vast country, time and space when travelling take on different values and the difference between Hull and Kent and New York and Florida are about the same in your mind. You will think of the tiny orchards, brown villages and hares on little hills of your own country, of the prettiness and the poetry of Lovelace and Suckling — then look out of the window on the grey, vast, untrodden lands and think of Whitman; suddenly the country changes as you get into that miraculous belt of sun and you are in the Everglades (a beautiful name for the everlasting palm and hibiscus, palm and hibiscus and bougainvillea to the heart's content — they know no other plant), the train stops, and "So this is Palm Beach!"

The sea way is different. You are more like Christopher Columbus; you are discovering America from your own country, or from Marseilles or Havana, where you may have embarked.

The amazing thought — I am to touch this long peninsula which is part of America! A place called Key West greets you; officials so foreign and so cruel, so unlike anything but Bedlam, rob you of your honour by trying to find spirits in your hot water bottle.

Then you are flung into a train over a chain of islands threaded like beads on to the steel thread of the line. A scientific triumph, pictorial in itself — chemical, wonderful, mechanical.

You are flung out then at what all must believe me when I tell them is the gateway to Florida (from the sea) — Miami, pronounced, now be careful, "Miammah." There is no station; they have not had time for one. You are just set down, everything in the making and on the make. The railway line crosses the main street, Flagler Street. Never forget Flagler Street; if you are here long it is to be your life. It never begins. But this is just where it ends — in the cul de sac made by the sea. There has been no time to clear away the dead bodies of the palms — those exquisite pillars bearing, as their Ionic or Doric capitals, coconuts in green or brown clusters. A white light is on everything: the light of a magnificent and permanent sun.

A very tiny area has the present town itself. Flagler Street is nothing but eating shops, real estate offices, and a few Riviera shops for pretty clothes, stockings and bags. The big hotel never ceases to charm you by the iced water which you drink out of cups you throw away, and the high average of prettiness in the girls who serve the soft drinks, and

24

in those you meet in the street.

The hotels are skyscrapers and the town has no beauty of any kind. But, then, you take a motor over the giant causeway and go to Miami Beach, the Margate of Florida, which can't help being beautiful because of the palms and hibiscus. Miami is one of the places that was a wild forest of palm, and that the first lucky settler bought for a dollar or so an acre; but now! Millionaires can hardly buy the land and the "real estate" boom goes on from one end of the island to the other.

Coral Gables, on the Dixie highway, which, they say, goes right through to Montreal, is perhaps the most booming of the booms. Once this was the land of grape-fruit industries, now ruthlessly cut down to build tiny bungalows worth a million dollars. Huge lakes and golf links are planned and placed where once there was only an Indian trail. All because the air is like wine and the soil a miracle of fecundity.

How nearly we bought a "Venetian Island" on Golden Beach for five hundred pounds! And how rich we should have been now if we had. There was no island then, only water—the canal that led, I believe, to the Hudson! We just had to point "There!" and a huge machine we watched pumped up an island out of the glorious reproductive mud and sand — and on that one built a house!

The worst of this Utopian scheme is that no one cares how the houses are built. You can have the worst type of Spanish or a Gothic tower, or a corrugated iron garage — no one stops you.

Palm Beach, a few hours away by train or motor, is a different idea. Made again from wild swamp of palm or pine, it is a dwelling place for the rich, made by the rich; it is not widely populated. There are only a few houses — mostly large.

The really beautiful colonial architectural hotels, called the Breakers and the Poinciana, with pale lemon painted wood and green shutters, are like the delicious cool grapefruit that grows there almost like blackberries. These hotels are rather despised by the inhabitants because they are uninsured, on account of being wooden, and because they are neither skyscrapers nor the hideous pseudo-Moorish architecture affected by the Americans. But the Americans are having their way; one (the Breakers) was burnt down last year.

If someone said to me "How does Palm Beach look?" I should shut my eyes and describe: "Well, the Solent on one side, the sea on another, between it a glorified Sunningdale, dotted with palms instead of pines, the women flitting about like a musical comedy beauty chorus, the men with much the same aspect, only that they are serious and the girls are laughing. There are sedan chairs—that is to say, basket armchairs, borne along by a coloured man on a bicycle — thousands of them, they are to be hired at the big hotels. For the rest, everyone has motors, and walking in the true sense of the word is hardly counted as a means of progression; the nights are as rich and glorious as the day, when the sun is like our July sun, sometimes greater but never less; a cool breeze may sweep by from some far-away mountain of stream, a few drops of rain may shake the leaves, but you are safe in summer clothes; nothing hot or dark need ever come out of your suitcases and a gay look tends to a gay mind."

25

REGATTA WEEK AT COWES

by NANCY HOYT

So many of the choicest spots in the world seem to be islands that the conclusion drawn must be that human beings like a beautiful place which is hard of access better than an equally lovely one more easily visited. There are Capri and Brioni, and there are Skye and Iona, those jewels of the western seas, and finally the Isle of Wight, toy kingdom and playground of English royalty for many centuries. The Isle is perhaps forty miles long and twenty miles wide. There are no spectacular views and rather less of historical interest than one would find in the same amount of territory on the mainland, but, somehow, the sun shines more brightly, the grass is a shade greener, and life takes on a pleasant touch of ease and laziness.

For eleven months of the year, the Isle of Wight is the quietest place imaginable. The little town of East Cowes has the daily excitement of the arrival of the ferry to Southampton, and occasional steamers take trippers in masses to Ryde and Hythe, where they debark into enormous "charry bangs," from which no place seems sacred.

But, a sudden change takes place each year at the beginning of July. The harbour is filled with small yachts, new arrivals slip into moorings each day, ship-chandlers and sailmakers begin to take an interest in life, shutters come down from shop windows, stewards rush through the streets reprovisioning their pantries. The tiny higgledy-piggledy town is galvanised into violent activity. Up incredibly narrow streets, not so wide as alleys, huge cars begin to move, backing almost into the sea to let others pass. Caviar and canvas espadrilles, Paris scent and Basque red berets can be bought in a few moments. The post-office hums with cables and telegrams. "Speed boats" and fast motor launches rush back and forth from Southampton Water to Cowes.

People make up trips to bathe at Bembridge. The black pirate ship of the Guinness family, a beautiful eighteenth-century brigantine turned into a luxurious yacht, is in the harbour ready for the annual house-party of super-bright young persons. The big cutters are, perhaps, still racing elsewhere, but, as the month goes on, they come sailing along, too beautiful to be true. Seen from an incoming yacht, the Royal Yacht Squadron lawns are dotted with colour. Neither love nor money can get you a room at the Gloucester Hotel; most of it is booked up from year to year. Marconi's *Electra* is arriving with the great inventor and his pretty wife aboard. It is to be hoped that the *Sans Peur* is not off cruising this year, for no one wants to miss the sight of the beautiful Duchess of Sutherland striding up the wet Squadron jetty in a white pleated skirt and scarlet jacket.

Mrs Peter Thursby, Mrs Reggie Fellowes and three swains in white flannels and yachting caps drop in before lunch for a cocktail with the inimitable Rosa Lewis, who has descended on Castle Rock for a couple of weeks respite. Lord Birkenhead, smoking the inevitable cigar, comes up the road with Lady Eleanor Smith. Americans are there in masses. A bronzed Dutch youth and two French yachtsmen discuss the ocean race to Fastnet. Four Harvard boys who have come over alone in a Gloucester fishing schooner are asked everywhere. All the boring panoply of formal entertaining in tow disappears.

But curiously enough, smart frocks are almost a rule. A daytime uniform, pleasantly varied by individual wearers, consisting of a pleated skirt, a jersey jumper or a double-breasted reefer, and a yachting cap or beret, is worn from eight in the morning until seven at night. The most beautiful evening dresses of the great French designers are dispatched by aeroplane to London in time for Cowes. It is an extraordinary thing that women living aboard, with one small cabin for themselves and their wardrobes, arrive at dinner-time in exquisite frocks cut very low, strung with perfect jewels, and perfectly *soignée*. Those staying in the town achieve an equal miracle, for space in the little old-fashioned place is limited, and one pays thirty pounds sometimes for a tiny back bedroom which the rest of the year remains empty.

But Cowes must be expensive, for it has only a brief season in which to overcharge frivolous Mayfair. All this is forgiven it for the fact that only there can one see a princess and a duchess, dressed with more than Oriental splendour, happily attending a rather slow charity ball in a funny little town hall.

MORGUE

Le Touquet

by JOHN McMULLIN

ERICKSON

Picture a little town by the sea. It nestles in the sand dunes with its tiny villas, crowding each other along the plage as though to get a better view of the sea, sleeping in the spring sunshine and waiting the magic touch of the great world to come and wake it from its long winter sleep and turn it over-night into a scene that resembles the first-act of an elaborately staged musical comedy with a Normandy setting. That is Le Touquet. The fringe of villas along the sea is called Paris-Plage, while Le Touquet proper is that part of the town which retires back into the woods along the fringe of the golf course, where the more elaborate villas are hidden away among the silver birches and the forests of pine.

On Thursday morning before Easter the first signs of life appear when a blinking shutter here and there opens to the world like a sleepy eye of a child. By noon there are more shutters opened, doors are thrown wide, shop windows unmuffled and chocolate Easter eggs, tied up with huge blue and pink ribbons, are put out in the windows of the sweet shops. The fruit vendor displays a box of peaches luxuriously lying on cotton and fills his window with small boxes containing six cherries each presented to look like a collection of rubies in a jeweller's shop. Taxis cruise along the streets and the little red-jacketed boys from the Casino are seen flying about on their bicycles with the air of important messengers. The late afternoon trains arrive and suddenly the little town is filled with people, lights blink from the hotel windows, the Casino is illuminated and Le Touquet has come to life. As darkness descends the curtain goes up on a stage of brilliance and gaiety which has completely transformed the little town.

By midnight everyone is at the Casino and the real show begins. Dinner is very late at Le Touquet, never before half-past nine or ten, and the crowd that assembles later at the Casino has been dining in small groups at the Hermitage, the Westminster, the Forêt, which is the new restaurant at the gate of the Casino, or at the little villas tucked away in the woods. But wherever one may have dined, the Casino is the next objective and there everyone assembles to look everyone else over. One has the sensation of being comfortably installed in the first row of a theatre for the opening night of a big revue. There are no end of people to look at. Lord and Lady Portarlington have just arrived with Lady Bingham. Wilfred Egerton and his brother, Lord Ellesmere, are sitting in the bar having drinks with friends. Miss Bridget Chapman, the daughter of the popular "Bill" Chapman, who is secretary of the Travellers' Club in Paris, is there, with a party of young people, looking very chic in a dress of apple-green and white satin which reminds one of a jockey's colours. Mrs Allen Horne is sitting at one of the gambling tables looking like a dark Gladys Cooper and particularly lovely in a flame-red Vionnet dress with a golden scarf. Miss Doris Delavigne, who has the reputation of being one of the great beauties of London to-day, is certainly looking the part in a white dress from Irfé and wearing the most lovely diamond pin from Cartier which suggests the Marble Arch modelled in long slits of diamonds with little diamond urns inset in the arches. It is really one of the most beautiful pieces of modern jewellery one could see and everyone is discussing it.

Miss Nancy Cunard is wearing a gold dress with many barbaric gold bangles and long earrings. She is looking very unusual but quite lovely, like a portrait by one of the most modern of the moderns. She has made her eyes up in a new way which on first sight makes her unrecognisable to her best friends. Mrs Somerset Maugham and Lady Cheetham are wearing two beautiful wraps which they keep on during the evening. Mrs Maugham's, from Molyneux, is made of emerald green velvet lines with chinchilla and Lady Cheetham's of flame gold and pearls.

There is no better setting for beautifully dressed women than a brilliantly lit Casino. It is the place where everyone is on the stage and in the audience at the same time. The

spectacle could not fail to thrill the most sophisticated, for who is ever tired of looking at different types of people, watching them play and speculating on their thoughts, which now and again are visible for a fleeting moment behind the masks worn on the faces sitting round the magic circle of the gambling table. Large sums of money are lost and won again. What are they all playing for, who for gain, and who for the excitement of the thing? Strolling from table to table one is alternately thrilled, depressed, amused and sometimes frightened. A beautiful woman covered with jewels goes "banco," but if she wins or loses her expression is apt to be the same. But what of the man at her shoulder who is silently watching her play? What does he think, and which of them cares? These are the unanswered riddles, and one is consumed with curiosity.

Indeed, it is a better show than one can see at the theatre. In fact, it is more like a three-ring circus with its side shows — the people dancing in the ballroom and the crowd collecting about the bar — but best of all is the centre ring, the most important table, which is roped off, at which the big gamblers play and where the crowd is thickest. Around this table the watchers are twenty deep fighting for a place to see the next move of Miss Jenny Dolly, who is the centre of all eyes. She is wearing a white dress, three beautiful strings of pearls and long pearl drops in her ears. On her finger is a wonderful diamond ring and before her is a pile of fresh bank notes wrapped in packages of ten thousand and bound with elastic bands. There is something thrilling about this complete disregard of money.

The shaded globes throw a brilliant spot on the dark table and on the strange, silent people sitting within the ring of light who no longer seem to be the human beings among whom we live, but rather figures in a pantomime acting behind their masks. The hour grows late but the atmosphere becomes more intense. Fewer people are strolling about, for groups have collected at tables in the bar and the serious gamblers appear to be glued to their places at the tables. It seems as though the night would never end for those who are keeping a silent vigil round the tables where the croupier in a low voice keeps repeating himself, and with a long spade automatically collects the drawn cards and deposits them in the little slit in the table. But one knows the morning must come, and visions of the golf course, the tennis courts or an early walk to the sea eventually lure the casual onlooker to the waiting motor, and so, through the quiet woods one speeds back to a slumbering villa and to bed.

IN SWITZERLAND

by B. LUNN

To those of us who have the habit of Switzerland the name conjures up visions of sparkling snow, sleigh bells jangling on the air, and a miraculous, if only temporary, capacity for enjoyment, which functions for twenty out of the twenty-four hours.

But the really excellent quality of the life at the winter sports centres in Switzerland lies in the fact that whatever one's tastes, sex, age, nationality, height or colour of hair and eyes may be, one is positively not permitted to be bored for a single moment. The days are never long enough, the nights all too short. If you are too young and innocent for the cocktail hour at Hanselmann's, there is always the village luge run, with the delightful possibility of bumping an aged soap king, or of picking off the heir to the latest mid-European monarchy; and if you are so jaded that even the most exigent ski run has lost its thrill for you, you can still try your luck on the Cresta, with the reassuring knowledge that the kind ambulance is waiting to pick up the pieces.

If you go to such places as Murren, Pontresina or Maloja, you must go prepared to face the fact that, willy nilly, you will be ski-ing, and what is more, ski-ing quite respectably (that is to say, going on short expeditions), at the end of five days. You may even by that time be considering the question of going in for a test, for you cannot breathe the air of any of these centres without imbibing a certain amount of keenness.

You must not, however, be allowed to run away with the impression that life in these places consists entirely in getting snow down the back of your neck. After five o'clock we all become human again, and remember that such pleasures as bridge, dancing, and the wearing of pretty frocks still exist.

Morgins is known as the last stronghold of English skating, and there you may see stern-faced old gentlemen who have only just discarded their Dundreary whiskers solemnly circling round an orange at the word of command. But English figure-skating, enthralling though it may be to the performers, has, like writing with a quill, something of the flavour of an anachronism, and for skating as we know it now, that is to say, Continental skating, you must go to Villais or St. Moritz, where you will have the opportunity of emulating the finest performers in the world.

Klosters is, I believe, entirely inhabited by people who have done the Parsenn run and all its variations, and want to do it all over again; by people who have never done it before, and want to add it to their repertoire of great runs, and by people who are working up to their first-class test, and want to get in all the running they can for the least possible amount of uphill work. It is the classic ski-ing run, for it offers about seven thousand feet of downhill running for three thousand feet of climbing.

I suppose what gives the Swiss winter centres of the St. Moritz, Adelboden Grindelwald type their peculiar charm is the unique juxtaposition of sophistication and sport, — emphatically not *le sport*, but the kind of sport which is a real test of courage and endurance.

Tailing parties, bobbing parties, ski-ing parties, cocktail bars, thé-dansants, jumping competitions, international ice hockey matches, are the order of the day, while the night offers an infinite variety of *bals fantaisies*, Lido balls, balls on the ice rinks, cotillion balls, to say nothing of what the Americans call high-balls. Perhaps nowhere else in the civilised world do you see such a riot of colour, for winter sports give men as well as women an unparalleled opportunity for indulging their secret sins and suppressed desires.

IRELAND

It rains, they say. Of course it does. If the Irish were better showmen they would advertise the rain. They themselves know how sweet and soft it is, and how to enjoy it. "A soft day, thank God," they say to one another in deep satisfaction when there comes the drizzle that spangles all the cobwebs on the furze bushes, but never comes through an Irish hand-woven frieze coat (rhyme, please, with "prize" — not "freeze"), not, that is, if it is the real thing, still holding the natural oil. They know what green gardens, what apple-blossom skins, the rain brings. Besides, it doesn't always rain, and in between the "soft" days there are glories of colour and clearnesses of atmosphere that dry countries never know.

Ireland might have been especially designed for holidays, for, unlike England and most other countries, she keeps her best scenery all round the edges. Mountains and sea nearly all the way. Cliffs like those of Clare, grand and unforgettable, standing up stark out of the Atlantic. Pointed mountains, like Slieve League in Donegal, with their feet in the sea, staring, as it were, straight across to America — how far would you go in any other direction for sights like these?

If you are a little weary of the Corniche roads you might try the coast drive from Belfast to the Giant's Causeway, which is as beautiful as any of them with the purple Mull of Cantire seen across the Moyle and the five blue heads of Antrim stretched before one, fold on fold of loveliness. Not so hot as the Corniche, not quite so flowery, except in spring, when there are primroses in the very cart tracks, and in late summer when the heather blooms and the fuchsia hedges are gay in the glens. But who would change this strong deep sea with its peacock blues and greens for the lazy Mediterranean, or this air that is like food and wine for the flatter, weary airs of the South. Here, just past Cushendall, is Moira O'Neill's glen, and at Cushendun the white house she lived in, with Shane O'Neill's grave in its garden. It was hereabouts that the ancient house of Red Branch stood in the old times, and the child Deirdre was reared to the beauty that brought its doom. On a clear day you can see across to Alba, where Deirdre wandered with the sons of Usnach.

Not that interest in these parts is dependent on Celtic twilightery. There is much vigorous bathing, fishing, golf and tennis. You can do all these things with the liveliness of a town about you, as at Ballycastle or Portrush, or you may go farther along the top of the map, as it were, and find them in the exquisite silences of places like Portsalon on Lough Swilly. The name of Lough Swilly suffers in Anglicisation as so many Irish names do, and really means Lake of the Shadows — partly because it was the setting for the Flight of the Earls, and partly because of its changing skies. And there is Rosapenna and Dunfanaghy, where there are miles of shining gold sands, where you can see Tory Island like drifting castles on the horizon, and which is the station for Horn Head. Dunfanaghy is a place to which you must never take people who are especially keen on birds, because they often, I believe, to refuse to come home again. Now you are at the top left-hand corner and may proceed down the west coast through unimaginable loveliness of bogland and mountain among a peasantry still living in an almost Homeric simplicity. Here you can pretend the industrial age has never been. Here you may be called "a European" by some polite hostess of a mud hut — and how far east from London do you have to go before any such thrill could be found again? Just round the corner you may come on the Silver Strand that Lord Leighton came to paint for his Greek composition — still clear and Hellenic as ever.

There is Galway with its Spanish tang, from where you may sail to the Aran Islands in the wake of Synge and many another. There is Clonmacnoise with its delicious, far-off, brooding melancholy, for those with time to reach the Shannon plains. For the more hurried there are the Mountains of Mourne, with gold and gaiety at Newcastle.

Killarney everybody knows about, but not everybody knows Cahirciveen and other marvellous strands in the deeply indented parts of Kerry, Clare and Cork. The city of Cork still shows melancholy signs of the "troubles," but the natural beauties of the harbour remain. One can see the Rock of Cashel on the way back to Dublin through Tipperary. One may loiter in Wexford for the fishing, one can do nothing else but loiter in Wicklow, so soothing are the glens, so alluring the serpentine roads that wind about the mountains.

Dublin takes itself rather more seriously now, but let no tourist fear that there is still not a sufficiency of enchanting hackney side-car drivers who will pretend that their marvellous vehicles are called "jaunting cars," who will "lave it to your honour" when asked the fare, and even say "Begorra" and wish "the top o' the morning" to you if they think you like that kind of thing. There are still sunsets on the Liffey, still charming blue-eyed girls shopping in Grafton Street, still an infinity of parties attended by dark-eyed poets for those with half an introduction to the intelligentsia, still the polite charm of urban Georgian architecture.

Good hotels may be rather far apart, but that does not matter so much in these motoring days. Good cooking may be rare, but in most places the food itself is so good that it cannot be spoiled. And nowhere else in Europe are there people so highly articulate as the Irish. This is not to say that they are easy to understand, but it means ease and charm to their guests.

Don't expect to come away without some stirring of your heart. It isn't done. The Wicklow peaks and the brave head of Howth see to that as you sail out of Dublin Bay. You will never be quite so impatient again of Irish blether, of Irish exile affectations, of very minor Irish verse. You may find yourself presently engaged in all three.

OAKDEN

A FORTNIGHT /PENT IN ·JAVA·

by PRINCESS ACHILLE MURAT

STEICHEN

Nobody possessed by the demon of travel should go to the Far East without visiting the wonderful Dutch Indies, only thirty-six hours from Singapore. You cross the Line between two showers, and Java, the "scented island," lies before you. The first vision of docks at Tanjong Priok is unattractive, but a rapid drive along a Dutch canal takes you to Weltevreden. This, the fashionable annex of old Batavia, is a charming town, spacious and airy, with pretty houses surrounded by large gardens. I do not want to sound like a guide-book, but I can not help saying, try the Hôtel des Indes. From all points of view — comfort, food, and cleanliness — it was certainly one of the best hotels we had come across in the tropics, and it was a delightful change, coming as it did after a few less agreeable experiences.

Sheltered by a huge banyan tree with dozens of hanging branches which take root as they reach ground, the hotel stands near the Kali Besar, the river that runs through the town and is, on a sunny morning, one of the prettiest sights in Weltevreden. The brown women of Java, with their many-coloured skirts reaching from armpits to ankles, come down to the water's edge and splash about, washing themselves, their linen, and their teeth most unconcernedly.

These ladies, in common with all Eastern women, feel extremely annoyed if they remain childless after a few months of married life. In fact, they are still imbued with the antiquated idea (that would, I am afraid, make a few of their white sisters scream with horror) that a woman's chief rôle in the world is to perpetuate the human race. In the middle of a square of the old city of Batavia lies a sixteenth-century bronze cannon covered with flowers and paper offerings. It is here that the women who have not been blessed with a baby come and pray for one. They purchase, from the guardian, flowers and paper toys to decorate the cannon, then sit on the breech while burning a stick of incense. I do not know what mysterious power dwells in the old bronze — perhaps, the cannon feels sorry for the destruction he has been responsible for and wants to repair it.

34

All I do know is that I have myself performed this quaint pilgrimage and been successfully rewarded.

Pens better qualified than my own have called Java "the Garden of the East" and have described its many points of interest and beauty. I shall not attempt the task, but should like to relate a few personal impressions that I have carried away from that beautiful and attractive country. And uppermost in my stock of reminiscences comes the remembrance of the hearty hospitality that was bestowed upon us. We had hardly arrived at Weltevreden before we received an invitation to go to a party, which turned out to be a very holy affair. Dutchmen are busy all the week, at office or plantation works, and recreation is left for Sundays. The day starts early, owing to the drowsy atmosphere of the hot afternoons. Religious duties are over by nine o'clock, and, at ten in the morning, we were already dancing in a charming old house, tastefully arranged with bits of ancient Dutch furniture and native curios. A big swimming pool occupied the middle of the garden, and we were soon enjoying a long swim and a game of ball in the delightful warm water. After that, bridge and mah-jong tables were laid out in the covered veranda that ran along the front of the house, while cocktails and ice-cream were handed around to the sound of native music accompanying an amusing Javanese dance. The dancers were hidden inside two huge, grotesque-looking giant dolls, which they conducted through a series of comical steps and gestures. By this time, it was nearly two o'clock, and our amiable hostess took her thirty guests to the open-air dining-room to partake of the delicious native dish which has been adopted by all Europeans in the Dutch Indies, the famous *rijstafel*. It consists of a big plateful of rice on which you heap a little of the contents of twenty or twenty-five dishes, presented by a file of bare-footed, white-clad native servants. The result is a monument built on rice and made of meat and eggs, several varieties of fish and fowl, boiled, dried, or roasted, vegetables and coconut shreds, with spiced and peppered sauces and pimentoes hot and innumerable. The *rijstafel* is very tasty if you have a good appetite and are prepared to fast for the next twenty-four hours.

Our stay at Java unfortunately coincided with the Mahometan New Year festivities, during which time the sultans of Djodja and Solo cannot entertain strangers. So we did not see these interesting courts and the "Serimpi" dances we had heard so much about. Owing, however, to the influence of some very kind Dutch friends, a relative of the Sultan of Djodjakarta, Prince Pakoe Alam, asked us to spend the evening at his palace to see his boy dancers. Two of them danced for us; they were the Prince's own son and one of his nephews, both about fifteen years old. The sight was extraordinarily interesting. The two handsome youths wore queerly shaped gilded helmets, and their bright silken garments were copied from those of the Hindu warriors on the Boroboedoer bas-reliefs. What they danced was the representation of a single combat, the challenge, and the long fight with swords and bows and arrows till one boy fell to the ground. It was as if two young gods had stepped out of an old legend. Their painted faces moved no more than twin masks, but their long, supple limbs worked into the strangest and most unnatural, yet fascinating, positions, with as much ease as if they belonged to the well-known disjointed Javanese dolls. The orchestra consisted of twenty singers and musicians squatted on the floor; the instruments were mostly gongs, a few big ones and several sets of small ones arranged as keyboards on boat-shaped gilded wooden frames. Each gong gives forth a different sound, and the result is truly beautiful, with its insinuating rhythm, and the soft bell-like tones changing into weird minor, almost discordant strains, and ending in the clash of cymbals. The pantomime of the dancers was explained (in Javanese, of course) by a man sitting near the orchestra and reading, or rather chanting, in a sing-song tone and text of the legend they were acting. He impersonated the dancers, speaking the parts which they played and changing his voice in a suitable manner.

Prince Pakoe has a very intelligent face. He speaks Dutch, English, and French, although he has never left Java, and it is even whispered that he is a Freemason, which sounds somehow rather surprising. He wore the native "sarong", a skirt made of cotton with batiked flowers and various designs in sepia tints, a short black cloth jacket with gold braid, and, on his head, the national handkerchief arranged like a turban and matching the sarong. He also had a beautiful chiselled *kriss,* or Javanese sword, stuck into a diamond-studded belt. His wife looked extremely pleasant, but, as she only spoke Dutch and her own language, our conversation was limited to smiles. She wore the sarong and a blue satin jacket and earrings, necklace, and rings with diamonds of amazing size and brilliance.

We all sat in Louis XV gilt chairs, in the middle of a great bare room without any particular style. It was a three-sided room, one end of it entirely open, overlooking the garden, and we could dimly distinguish a silent crowd of natives squatting in the distance and watching the dancing, which took place between them and us. They formed an interesting background, their eager faces showing up dimly in the half-light. When the entertainment was over. a file of servants, each one carrying a glass of lemonade and followed by a parasol bearer, literally crawled to Prince Pakoe's feet. Etiquette reigns supreme here, as elsewhere. Our glasses and those of our two hosts were covered with gold lids, while those given to non-princes had only silver ones. Before we left, our host showed us some old Javanese manuscripts of which he was very proud. The pages were of parchment and covered with exquisitely illuminated architectural designs and garlands of flowers with birds and animals. He then accompanied us to the flight of steps that descended to the garden, and we took leave of him, charmed with our interesting evening.

We spent a delightful fortnight motoring all over Java. The countryside, often very mountainous, is always beautiful, whether it be covered with rice-fields, rising in terraces with a border of palm-trees, or sugar, tea, or coffee plantations. Hardly an inch of the fertile soil has been left uncultivated, and the country is so densely populated that often for miles on each side of the winding roads stretches an uninterrupted line of picturesque villages. The men go trotting along to work, wearing huge straw hats and sarongs and carrying on their shoulders long bamboo poles each with a load attached to the extremity. The women are often pretty. I remember particularly two sunburned smiling girls who were extremely attractive. They were sitting, with three or four other women, on the edge of a lake, each holding a pair of musical instruments made of hollow bamboo sticks that knock together when shaken. The instruments are of various sizes and produce different sounds. When they are handled by experienced musicians, such as these girls, the sounds produced are quite lovely and constitute real harmony. They drifted to us like a melody of tinkling bells as we were being rowed across a lake in a somewhat original manner, our boat being a platform surmounted by a roof and resting on two small canoes, each manned by two women. It looked exactly like a floating house.

On another day, we had been wandering through the magnificent botanical gardens at Buitenzorg when somebody happened to say: "I imagine the garden of Eden was like this; what a pity it is we shall not meet a tame lion speaking to Eve". "Well", replied one of our Dutch friends, "I am afraid I cannot produce the lion, but Eve will not be very difficult to find. Prepare your cameras". He went up to a group of pretty girls, spoke to them in Malay, and gave them ten cents each. They straightway slipped out of their sarongs and four brown and smiling little Eves stood in the sunshine amid the flowers! Happy, unsophisticated country!

GO WEST, YOUNG DUDE, GO WEST

Today when one disappears after the ardours of a London season it is no longer inevitable that one's destination is either Scotland, the Riviera, South Germany, or the Dalmatian Coast. One may vanish from the European scene altogether, leaving "effete" civilisation far behind, and sail out into the west as did Columbus to discover unknown lands, stopping only overnight, in such ordinary places as New York and Montreal, then travelling swiftly westwards towards the open spaces. For now, like the younger sons who went out in the 70's, we have become ranch owners.

We have our own cattle for our own cowboys to "wrangle", or we have ranch-owning friends. No longer is any trip to the United States or Canada complete unless it takes us west — "dudes" though we are! With joy we seize upon any invitation to "rough it" in the wilds, we wangle one, or simply plead traveller's rights and descend upon any friend we find, thanking heaven for Western hospitality. No longer are we islanders, no longer are we even Empire builders, the pursuit of health and sport takes us now 5,000 miles from England before we can travel another 2,000 miles by rail, twisting to and fro across the Rockies from Canada to the United States, from Wyoming to Saskatchewan, with only a sign-post to tell us we have passed an an international boundary. Ranching is the thing, and since we are barred from being ranchers by reason of our pursuits and customs, we are content for a few weeks to be visitors from Europe, termed "dudes" by good-natured, weather-beaten cowmen with amazing skill for knowing horse and human nature, and performing feats with the English language.

No longer in these wildernesses is a horse something that one rides in the hunting field, or sees flashing past a white post on the green turf, nor are riding habits tailored in Cork Street and Savile Row. Elasticity of body and mind — both qualities which have little to do with age — are the prime requirements for this westward venture.

Even those who have never undertaken the adventure before know more or less what to expect — for fortunately we have the cinema always with us, and what about the extraordinary "Gunpowder Thompsons" and "Tex Austins" of the Rodeo which descended upon London some three years ago? What we can't know in advance, however, is the effect of mere altitude on our British sea-level spirits, and what early rising, much exercise, constant sunshine, can do to our sea-level appetites. Ordinary food takes on the quality of ambrosia. Ordinary coffee — and, by the way, this means most extraordinarily good coffee — is the sublimest nectar. Ordinary beds seem something to be looked forward to at the earliest possible hour with gasping joy and hopped out of the next morning, having shed ten years in a night.

During the first week the absolute tenderfoot may feel a bit out of the picture, particularly if she or he is not used to a cowboy saddle — stiff things that make you feel like a sack draped over a horse and tied into place. The second week, one comes alive — soreness gone, blisters peeling, sunburn turned from red to brown. After that the mere fact of existence is something to be greeted with joy. Small wonder that winter, back in our London house, finds us sentimentalising over a snapshot that shows our conventional selves impossibly attired in blue-jeans at a dollar and a half — a shirt at even less, and a smile that could not be found in all London.

MOTORING IN THE BALKANS

by LORD CARDIGAN

To travel by road from one end of Europe to the other is, even in these days, not an adventure to be lightly undertaken. Two things, in fact, are required before such a trip can hope to meet with success. One is a car of unusually solid construction and of unfailing reliability, the other a strong sense of humour on the part of the passengers and driver.

A reliable car is a rather obvious necessity, yet it is almost impossible for people in England to realise how arduous are the conditions under which mechanism is expected to function in out-of-the-way parts of the world. To speak of a pot-hole, for instance, as being three feet deep sounds like a ludicrous exaggeration, if not a complete fiction. Nevertheless, that is precisely the sort of thing that we encountered in the more remote districts of Europe.

As for a sense of humour, no traveller should venture so far afield as Turkey or Greece without one. How else is it possible to maintain a cheerful countenance while watching a perplexed frontier official fritter away a valuable hour of daylight in filling in a tryptique, or while the entire population of a village turns out to superintend the complicated business of supplying a stranger with a few litres of benzine?

Our route between London and Constantinople took us through Holland, Germany, Poland, Czechoslovakia, Austria, Hungary, Rumania, Bulgaria, and Greece, so that our motoring experiences extended over quite a considerable part of the Continent. In all, we covered something like 8,000 miles, nearly a year's average running within the space of two months.

The best roads that we met with were in the Rhineland district of Germany; the worst in Greece, Bulgaria, and Poland. The Polish roads must have been, at the time, quite reasonably good, but they have been allowed latterly to fall into a most deplorable state of decay. They are now definitely very much inferior to the country cart tracks which in many districts run parallel to them. It is nearly always possible to drive in top gear along a Polish cart-track, the surface being sufficiently smooth to permit speeds of 10 or even 20 m.p.h. to be indulged in without undue discomfort. The main roads, on the other hand, are so badly knocked about that for miles at a stretch it may be necessary to drive over them in third or second gear, averaging rather less than five miles per hour.

It was only after we had been ferried across the Danube at Rustchuck that civilisation really began to wear rather thin. The costume and appearance of the Bulgarian peasants is far more Eastern than European. Motor cars are a rarity, roads vary between indifferent and bad, and hotels where clean and comfortable lodgings can be obtained are usually several hundred miles apart.

Herein lies the chief difficulty that faces the motorist in the Balkans. It is impossible to keep up a decent average speed while "pot-hole dodging" takes up the whole of the driver's energies and attention. On the other hand, one is faced with the choice of making long and exhausting runs or of forfeiting that great and glorious luxury — a clean bed to sleep in at night. Thus it was that on three separate occasions between Bucharest and Athens we were on the road for about twenty-four hours at a stretch — determined to find civilised quarters before making a halt. On three other occasions we stopped at local hotels when night came on, but it was an experiment which, though interesting to look back on, we regretted at the time!

In Greece the roads are really atrocious. They are actually nothing more than glorified cart tracks, and may be anything up to a hundred yards in width. This is due to the prudent custom of the local carters, who prefer to cut new tracks for themselves during the rainy season rather than follow in the ruts made by their neighbours.

Maps are unreliable, and signposts non-existent. The scenery is certainly glorious, but it is mostly wasted upon the unfortunate driver, who, for safety's sake, dare not take his eyes from the surface of the road ahead. There are holes in which a man can stand upright up to his waist; there are ravines where torrents have swept across the road during the winter; there are places where landslides have carried away embankments, and bridges which have been allowed to tumble down. Many a time did we drive down into the dry bed of a river, and climb out as best we could on the other side. Hairpin bends are numerous, and the mountain roads frequently climb in spirals for many thousands of feet.

The result is that a 200 or 250 mile run is a fairly strenuous affair, and may easily occupy all day and half the night. If a frontier intervenes and causes the usual hour or two of delay, the car may very well be on the road for a full twenty-four hours. Hardships such as these, however, we were able to laugh at after a day of rest in Athens. The only adventure which left a permanently disagreeable impression in our minds was of a somewhat different nature — namely, an encounter with a swarm of locusts and other insects which took place in one of the mountain passes.

Attacks by insects are, of course, not unknown even in England. We are accustomed to hear of hundreds of flies, or even of thousands of mosquitoes. Locusts, however, can only be numbered in tens of millions! They cover the ground in a solid mass, and may easily take complete possession of a full five miles of road.

Driving through a locust swarm is a revolting experience. The car leaves behind it two long trails of squashy corpses, the tyres and wheels become encrusted with them, while the running boards are soon black with those that still live and crawl. Nothing is sacred to the creatures. They penetrate even under the bonnet and and into the engine. Those that fly come flopping down inside the car, and cause panic and confusion among the passengers upon whom they descend. So thickly are they massed on the road ahead that it is possible to observe the strange phenomenon of stones being apparently on the move. Actually, this illusion is caused by a living river of insects flowing past the stones in the opposite direction.

In the midst of these tribulations came the crowning disaster — a puncture, and the necessity for descending into the road to change a wheel. Of the ensuing horrors I will not speak. It was the only occasion on which I regretted having undertaken an otherwise successful European tour.

PLAT

ON THE ROAD

FISH 1923

"All Paris thronged to the 'Salon de L'Automobile' at the Grand Palais in 1920 to see, for the first time in five years, luxurious models in private cars." In these new cars "long lines blended with curves that recall Greek sculpture; there were quiet colours, and with them was the restrained richness of beautiful grey and beige upholstery with here and there a touch of bright metal work like highlights on an artist's canvas". There was an appearance of lightness in them and "an amusing tendency towards yacht lines in the torpedo models... everything done to keep the lines unbroken". The following summer Vogue declared that "there is no motorist so jaded whose pulse will not quicken at the sight of the distinction of the new cars, the ingeniousness of the new luggage and the temptation of newly opened roads". In America there were "seven million pleasure-seeking, mile-eating motor cars . . . and in the summer about half of them are seized with the wanderlust or a sight-seeing fervour and are off to somewhere over the best roads they can find".

In England it was the same story, with Vogue considering "the best way to arrive on the Riviera, whether easily by train or adventurously by motor," and despite problems en route "to be on the Riviera without a car is a condition we do not care to imagine".

On the Continent "everywhere the engineers of the French and Italian armies have been at work. New tracks are made, ancient highways vastly improved and many of the more considerable dangers of travel removed. Such work, executed for the soldiers' purpose, must now serve that of the civilian."

Vogue soon had a regular motoring column "Round and About the Car", loaded with practical advice on maintenance and possible destinations, with illustrations and summaries of the latest models. There were reports from Sweden, North Africa, the Riviera, Switzerland and Spain, Palestine and the Balkans, where the roads were "less familiar than the Corniche and the Amalfi Drive but no less lovely". By 1934 Vogue was even driving across Sumatra. For the less adventurous, there were features on motoring tours through the Home counties; in Devon — "after cream the motor car is probably the next essential to the proper enjoyment of the county;" and into Shakespeare Country where "a hot day of motoring over the Cotswolds is a perfect summer's journey".

Motoring, declared Rosita Forbes, was a magic carpet awaiting the traveller "provided with six cylinders and forty horse power and under its wheels the roads slip smoothly." But is was a magic carpet that belonged more than anything else to the Twenties, the first symbol of acceleration that took us from veils to goggles. Much eclipsed by cruising and air travel in the Thirties, and greatly restricted by petrol rationing in the Forties motoring in Vogue soon became an all-too-familiar accessory to travel, slipping comfortably into the background — always there but rarely featuring.

"This business of eating outdoors
is the simplest thing in the world
when a table, that unfolds
to just the proper height,
discloses a service
for six, neatly packed
in its two drawers"

1920

"There is no motorist so jaded that his pulse will not quicken at the sight of the distinction of the new cars, the ingeniousness of the new luggage, and the temptation of newly opened roads"

1
B.S.A. LIGHT SIX
SPORTS SALOON

2
STER 18 SALOON

5
THE HUMBER SNIPE

3
AUSTIN RUBY SALOON

6
FORD V8 TOURING CAR DE LUXE

7
BENTLEY DROP HEAD COUPÉ

DAIMLER DROP HEAD COUPÉ

FROST
THOMPSON
4

43

VERNIER 1965

44

THE THIRTIES

"My theme is the triumph of speed over space . . . During the last few years the spirit of acceleration has been such that we have now discovered — irrespective of time limits — that the world is our oyster and that we can be, in Ralph Hodgson's lovely line: 'Last week in Babylon, last night in Rome'." Lesley Blanch writing for Vogue in the early summer of 1937, an enthusiastic hymn in praise of the new travel — so distant in temperament and outlook from the gloomy forecast made by Robert Byron in Vogue at the end of the Twenties that "there is scarcely any more travelling to be done". With the new decade came a new generation rediscovering their parents' old haunts for themselves, finding new ones on their own, but more important still, having the resources to do so within the narrow bounds of the average holiday period; having what Lesley Blanch described as "the spirit of acceleration", to speed them on their way.

Though commercial airlines had been operating successfully for more than a decade at the start of the Thirties, few had foreseen the rapid progress and increasing popularity of air travel, let alone thought to consider the attendant stimulus and sense of competition it gave to railway and shipping companies. Never had the world been more our oyster and the pearls therein so easily accessible: "By taking wings over Europe and Asia we can take tiffin with memsahibs on India's Coral Strand in less than a week . . . the forbidden frescoes of Pompeii are now supplanted by those of Ajanta, in India. We can range tropic or Arctic zones with equal ease . . . adventure the lush tropical swamps of the Amazon . . . explore the foothills of the Atlas Mountains . . . wander in the gardens of Shalimar among the ruined Moghul palaces, or stay in one of the modern house-boats on the Jhelum River . . . go by the Flying Clipper ships to Hawaii . . . and on to Manila . . . Shanghai . . . and home by the Trans-Siberian Railway." And the cost? While admitting that some of these suggestions were "not bargain lines in holidays, and even Maharajahs might hesitate to do them often", Vogue pointed out that suddenly such trips were now possible thanks to "the triumph of speed over space". For those who didn't care to fly to these destinations, or perhaps couldn't afford to, Vogue was only too ready to recommend alternative means — cruising, for instance, "one of the world's purer joys and most tantalising torments . . . one of the pleasantest ways to see the world," which enjoyed mounting popularity during the Thirties: "Formerly the Vanderbilt millions could not bridge the Atlantic in less than seven days. Now we can do it in four, for £20. We can reach the Arctic Circle, in five days, for £12, or North Africa in about three days, for £5 — by travelling cheaply, of course, but by no means uncomfortably."

But then, in the enthusiastic scramble to travel that typified the Thirties, "to wander where the spirit wishes," who was not prepared to accept a little discomfort on the way? For those who were not, Vogue admonished "The craven who travels with one eye on the drains and the other on the local fauna (and selects to stay only in those places that have installed the first and removed the second) must abandon all hope of seeing many of the loveliest places left in this fast-changing world."

As for other travellers, two distinct types emerged as the decade progressed: "those who rush furiously to a chosen spot — and then relax, and those who relax en route for the chosen spot — and usually do not reach it". Cecil Beaton, in 1932, preferred the former style and warned his readers: "do not expect a daring travel article of rifle shots in the jungle, of encounters with warlike tribes and sheiks, for we have no hankerings to don burnous and travel into parts unknown, or to dig for undiscovered treasures; we wish for sun, for certain of the nice faces that we know, for an occasional building of beauty, in all to spend a pleasant holiday". Elinor Mordaunt wasted little time replying "Travel is a wonderful thing, but it must by no means be the mere shifting of one's body from one place to another, where we meet the sort of people we know, eat the same sort of food . . ." Vogue travel articles in the Thirties ranged from expeditions into remotest Kurdistan to pleasant weeks spent in small, newly discovered fishing villages like St Tropez, one of many the younger set had discovered along the Riviera. Though both camps railed vigorously one against the other, the magazine itself showed no preferences and reserved any editorial judgement. The important thing was to get up and go, no matter how, no matter where.

But whatever the reader's destination, by whichever means he chose to arrive there and no matter how he wished to spend his month's holiday, the Thirties saw Vogue assert itself, not only as a guide but counsellor in the more mundane matters of travel. When it came to luggage, Vogue showed a preference for practicality combined with good looks and recommended "the Vuitton 'Butterfly' trunk. It lies flat and opens in a straight line that makes it very accessible. The diminutive Vuitton library trunks are indispensable for all the history and reference and guide books and maps with which the ordinary tourists surround themselves. They have, too, all sorts of compartments for the necessary writing materials, can be opened out to serve as a desk and may be carried as a suitcase."

To fill such trunks, Vogue was, not surprisingly, well-informed. Cruising back from Egypt, warm, comfortable woollen sports clothes were recommended "with a change into something sleek, black and Parisian at tea-time". In addition "a good travelling rug, like the one from Schiaparelli, with a corner that turns over and has a slide fastening forming a pocket for chilly feet". In Greece "be sure you include a hat with a stiff brim wide enough to protect the back of your neck and don't forget a pair or two of well-fitting dark glasses". In India, "gloves you will not wear much — one pair with a tweed suit, one with afternoon outfits and garden party frocks, and one or two above-elbow length pairs for evening are all you need (!) . . . at least one pair of walking shoes to wear with tweeds, another to wear with washing frocks, a smart pair of shoes for afternoon, several pairs of sandals for morning, several pairs to go with evening dresses, bedroom slippers and shoes for sports". With such a seemingly endless list of travel essentials it is hardly surprising to read of John McMullin's arrival in Bombay with two companions and more than fifty pieces of luggage!

But when it came to travel tips, Vogue excelled itself with ceaseless recommendations and almost matronly warnings. On the question of eye shades for tennis in Kashmir, "the sort that has a white band at the back should be avoided. When you get hot the band gets dirty. Need more be said?" while "straw hats are useless in the sun, and they travel so badly, and nothing looks worse than a brim bent in the wrong place". Certain dress material fared little better: "avoid georgette, which is apt to split and rot easily, gold and silver tissue which tarnish in the sea air and heat, and tulle, which does not stand up well to packing;" "your topee," insisted Vogue, "must, of course, be a Khaki one. Never be persuaded to buy one of those disguised affairs which looks like an inverted soup tureen covered with felt". Finally, a glorious precautionary note for those about to embark on a cruise: "No need to worry about sea-sickness . . . if you feel apprehensive, wear a tight belt or corset; the support will prevent that weak sensation in one's middle"!

Like a seasoned traveller reporting on his experiences abroad, Vogue made much of the specialised attractions of travel. For the gourmet: "the best lobster in the world is in Chile . . . the best crabs, with lime and mayonnaise in Colon, Panama . . . the best meat in the world is roasted over live coals in the Grill room of the Plaza Hotel in Buenos Aires . . . Lacti del Mari — in other words minute whitebait fried in butter — is a Sicilian triumph . . . at the Restaurant Verdun in Marseilles, your mackerel is singed over a fire of broken twigs before you at the table . . . and at the Lorelei (an enchanting hotel hanging over the sea near Sorrento), something you'll never forget: raisins soaked in the dregs of all the liqueurs, mixed with a little chopped lemon peel, then rolled in lemon leaves, and baked for a few moments in the oven." Or for the golfer: "the very good course at Ginga in Uganda, where large signs are posted at the club-house to inform you that 'Any Ball Falling in the Footprint of a Hippopotamus May be Moved' . . . the fabulous hole at the links near Colon, Panama, which requires shooting across the torrent of the spillway from Gatun Lake and where a nice bit of research on international profanity could be done . . . and the Sporting Club Course at Mount Agel above Monte Carlo. You must literally wait till the clouds roll by to play the ninth hole." For the motorist: "It is a pleasure to take the road again in Italy, for all are superb and all beautifully marked by posts and signs, men being constantly at work even in the highest mountains". Even in Sumatra, motoring could prove immensely pleasurable if only for the fact that "there is only one main road — a road that continually stupefies you by the magnificence of its engineering work and the changing panoramas revealed to your amazed eyes." For shoppers too, Vogue pictured the world as one vast, fascinating marketplace: "Wait till Java, for batiks . . . wait till Singapore for kimonos . . . brasses and silver bracelets in Madras . . . star sapphires and rubies, moonstones and zircons in Ceylon . . . Zanzibar for amber and ivory."

Many of these suggestions appeared in Vogue's first regular series of travel articles, introduced in 1936 and entitled "Vogue's Travelog", each one featuring "new places, new people, new ways of doing everyday things . . ." and each intent on widening the reader's travel perspective. But by 1939 "with Europe in its present unsettled condition it is not altogether easy to decide where you can laze in the sun without being called upon to leave precipitously". Already Vogue had observed "the lawns along the Champs Elysées . . . gashed to install bomb-proof shelters and in the basement of the Louvre are packing cases yawning to receive treasures to be whisked away to safety".

With the first shivers of concern, the immediate reaction had been to recommend away-from-it-all places like Australia and the South Seas, but by Easter 1939 it was suggested that readers "think, instead, about Worcestershire orchards, Warwickshire towns, the Fens, the Peaks, the Lakes, the Yorkshire Moors, the Scottish Highlands", the same natural beauties that had sufficed during the last Great War.

A few weeks later, in May 1939, Vogue added the further cautionary note: "After a winter in which nerves have been frayed by recurrent crises in international politics, and even at weekends it has been difficult to get away from broadcast news of threatening speeches, troop concentrations and anxious diplomatic activity, wise people are planning early summer holidays" in those places "where the shadow of the Berlin-Rome Axis does not fall and Europe's troubled politics seem blissfully remote". Remote they would not remain for long and wise indeed were those who took their summer holidays early in 1939. It would be many years before they could do so as easily again.

MAIDEN VOYAGE

by CECIL BEATON

The year was at its best in England. The new leaves sufficiently light and delicate to permit the architecture of the trees to be seen; the May trees in blossom. All roads to Southampton were busy with a stream of cars speeding to the *Queen Mary*. On the dock, a large yellow caterpillar, the awning gangplank, led to the new monster ship, where a Hieronymus Bosch inferno of activity, so strangely in contrast with the bucolic scene outside, assumed an almost terrifying unreality.

Here, in the electric light, it could be any time of the day or night in any country, for the crowds, swarming like excited ants to inspect the vessel, were of every nationality, and the backgrounds of stained woods gave no indication of being British. Along, up, down, the crowds bustled, while stewards shouted, "Keep moving, please". Streams of people were winding in curves against the general tide. To spread pandemonium among the ants, sirens went off, hooters and fog horns were blown, bells clanged, and after the hurried leave-takings, the boat was launched on its historic career.

Aeroplanes roared above, the pearl-coloured funnels rent the very earth with their hoots. The photographers clicked their lenses and the cinema men ground the wheels of the "eyes of the world", while the thousands on board waved to the greater thousands on land. The fluttering handkerchiefs subsided, while the black and gold uniformed band clashed out the anthem — *Britannia Rules the Waves*.

Gradually the boats in the sea dispersed and became distant specks, and comparative calm gave to the vast crowds aboard opportunity to move in droves seeing the beauties and magnificences of England's latest pride and joy. Reminiscent of the unhappy day when, for the first time, one inspected the new school, the school that was to be one's prison for so many weeks, now a cursory tour of inspection was made of the new, strange surroundings that were to become gradually so familiar and be for the next few days one's home.

The crowds swarm round the swimming pool, into the vast lounges, in cocktail bars, smoke rooms, children's playgrounds, dog kennels, private dining-rooms, drawing rooms, massage and writing rooms. Eventually, exhausted from their long trips of discovery, they settle down to rest and while away the time as on any other Atlantic crossing. The men bring out out their pipes with a vengeance, women their shorts and sailor trousers. Everyone eats enormously, socialises a lot, and there is leonine prowling of the decks and greed for exercise, since this is a British boat.

On this particular trip there is never a quiet moment, every public room always filled to overflowing. The writing desks are never innocent of souvenir collectors, and after the second day the company's supply of 25,000 postcards is exhausted. The ink runs low in the wells, and stamps give out entirely. At night, the betting on the run of the ship reaches great heights; the value of the pool reaches four figures.

When constructing a boat, even a luxury liner, the English do not consider their women very carefully. There are hardly any large mirrors in the general rooms, no great flight of stairs for ladies to make an entrance. The decorations have a monotony without uniformity; there is too much woodwork. The effort at being modern is decidedly forced, and the Wadsworth surréalism does not look well in close juxtaposition with the bronze pilasters of renaissance knights in the smoking lounge. The Verandah Grill, however, is by far the prettiest room on any ship — becomingly lit, gay in colour and obviously so successful that it would be crowded if twice its present size. The cabins are beautifully equipped and more refreshingly decorated than on any other boat. There are less paper-cap galas than on a French boat, and sportsmen are taken greater care of with squash-racket courts, pools, deck tennis and the excitement of the afternoon horse-racing.

Below, in an underworld of turbines and boilers, a new world is inhabited by efficient workers who are responsible for the running of this vast new city that has been built for the sea. It is incredible that one human mind can understand so vast a mechanism as this. How it could have been evolved is a miracle. The *Queen Mary* is a great and magnificent ship, fast, smooth-running. There are many small rooms in which it is possible to hide from the onslaught of fellow passengers.

The approach itself to New York was historic and emotionally deeply moving. Aeroplanes roared past the portholes of the cabins. Stewards fidgeted about the luggage.

As in the millennium, the air became uncanny with the screams of hooters, roars of engines, cheers of humanity and the clash of bands. The aeroplanes above swooped with alarming ferocity and deafening noise to drop roses. A Versailles grands eaux effect was produced by the fountains of fire boats. From every window kisses were blown and handkerchiefs waved, and the cheers reverberated down the caverns of the skyscrapers, which belched forth paper fluttering as though flocks of doves had been released. The air was filled with confetti. Every available inch of roof space was crowded. Along the Battery, the crowds had been standing since daylight, forty deep. New York, most appreciative of all achievement, gave a magnificent welcome to the *Queen Mary*.

EATON

51

THE PLEASURES OF INDIA

by ROBERT BYRON

The machinery of travel in this pear-shaped continent is mountainous. Having arrived by air, my original luggage was necessarily restricted. And though swollen by the suit of evening clothes without which it is scarcely possible to obtain a biscuit after eight o'clock, and which I had immediately had constructed of white drill by a bearded Karachi Mussulman; though bulging with winged collars of such devious shapes that I hope to place the collection on loan at the British Museum early next year, I was confident that a Revelation suitcase and a kitbag would see me comfortably through a month's tour of the South of India. Yet a fortnight later, examining the luggage of myself and of a friend who had joined me, I noted the following necessities: 1 kitbag, 3 suitcases, 2 holdalls of bedding containing sheets, blankets, mattresses, pillows and towels, 1 leather-lidded wash-basin rattling with soap, 1 striped bundle enwrapping our servant's bedding, his brass food-pot, 1 white ice-chest shaped like the Baptistery at Pisa, 1 despatch case, 2 cameras, 1 canvas dirty-clothes bag, a spare topee, and a mechanical bird in a wire cage, which latter caused the Ceylon customs considerable embarrassment on its being officially declared. Beside this pile, the servant, Nazibullah, stood erect in a brown surtout; on his head a white puggaree twined round a basket cone and dangling to his shoulder-blades; on his face a Victorian moustache and an air of painful, though dignified, resignation. From his wrist dangled a massive, permanently unfurled umbrella. This instrument, formerly the adjunct of royalty alone, is now the emblem of self-respect among all classes during the monsoon season.

Thus armoured against discomfort, we entrained at Bombay. After two nights on the Karachi steamer, spent in clinging to the bunk with the grip of a trapezist, the prospect of an Indian broad gauge carriage, labelled externally with its prospective inhabitants' names, was one of Elysian repose. There confronted us a kind of square lodging-house parlour, denuded, it is true, of china dogs and the wedding group, but so familiar in its twin horsehair couches, resplendent mahogany and bevelled mirror that it seemed as though a forest of aspidistras must soon evolve out of the very smuts. Other doors disclosed the "usual offices", the bathroom having a nickel-plated shower and mosaic floor. Our belongings were disposed on the racks; our brushes laid out as on a dressing-table; bottles of soda water were in readiness; the fans were set in motion; the Edgar Wallaces selected; and we rolled off into that permanent nineteenth century which is the hallmark of the British genius in India.

Darkness fell, and the guard, poking his head through the window, announced that dinner would be ready at the next station. Owing to the prevalence of railway bandits, Indian trains are furnished with neither corridors nor outside steps. When the next station arrived, the servant came to guard the carriage. We dined; and at the station after that, returned to find the beds made. The carriage was now transformed into a fortress. The doors were locked, and each of the eight windows heavily shuttered with wire or wood.

Hotels in India are fortunately few. Such as exist are Gothic, charge £1 a day for small, squalid rooms, serve their nauseating victuals with unlimited pretension, and double their prices and their incompetence during the winter season, when mothers arrive to marry off their daughters and Americans come to inspect the other Anglo-Saxon achievement. For the most part the traveller stays either in dâk bungalows, pleasant little houses in gardens on the outskirts of towns, where the charges are small and the food plain and eatable, or else in the station retiring-rooms, in which case meals are taken in the station restaurants.

For weeks together our home was in stations, among the puff of vagrant engines and the crowds that sleep permanently on every platform. There we gulped enormous cold whiskies and sodas after days beneath the boiling sun, fell into conversation with other travellers who were always insurance agents, and gnawed through menus that never varied.

Whereas the North of India has been eternally the prey of new settlers, and its architecture, typified in the Taj Mahal, is no more than a Saracenic importation, in the South the traveller is confronted by an aboriginal, homogeneous race, and by buildings of a native style, organically sprung from the land around them. These are the Dravidian temples, whose convex towers, great jungles of ornament rising two hundred feet and more against the colourless, shadowless glare of the Indian sun, are usually condemned as the ultimate degradation of the builder's art. Yet in these towers, so strangely divorced from the understanding of nineteenth century criticism, there is apparent precisely that ingenious principle of horizontal and vertical recession which is now transforming the American skyscraper from an industrial into an architectural form. Artistically, they form undoubtedly the most interesting province of India. At Ramesvaram, the remotest of the temples, situate on that spit of land which just fails to reach Ceylon, we discovered a native wood-sculpture, strongly reminiscent of that West African style whose masks are becoming an integral feature of modern decoration. It was very hot, as we chose our statuettes among the booths at the temple entrance. And the sound of the sea gently rippling the shore beyond called us to bathe. Some way along its edge there appeared a convenient shelter, on to whose floor, a raised platform some four feet above the ground, we climbed to undress. We bathed, and having no towels, were lying outstretched beside our clothes to dry, when a boy came up, and said: "You know what this is?" "No", we answered. "It's the burning-ghat. Here (pointing to me) they place the bodies of the Brahmins; there, the common people". Descending on to a soil composed entirely of human ashes, we dressed in the sun.

Eventually we arrived in Ceylon, where the trains provide their own bedding, and the atmosphere, despite the survival of the Dutch Burgher community, is overpoweringly English. Both in Colombo and Kandy, the hotels are better than those in India; their waiters wear tortoiseshell tiaras, stuck backwards into buns of uncut hair, and furnished with two diabolical horns in front. The chief features of Colombo are the old Dutch church, with its fine carved pews, and the new War Memorial. To see the buried cities, which lie towards the north of the island, it is necessary to take a motor. But more interesting than these enormous expanses of ruins are the Buddhist frescoes of Sigirya. This astonishing sixth century fortress, with its baths and conduits perched on an overhanging rock 700 feet above the level of the surround plain, and festooned with wild bee's nests, is now approached, thanks to the Archaeological Commission, by a stairway of comparative safety. Unfortunately, the frescoes are contained in a diminutive cleft some thirty feet above it. Access is by a rope ladder, which slopes outward towards the top, so that as the wind shakes it the venturer is swayed to and fro over a drop of 300 feet and a view of fifty miles. But the paintings are worth it. To discover, in this region of acute formalisation, a freedom of drawing and a delicacy of modelling reminiscent of the Italian Renaissance, makes the traveller realise how little he knows of the civilisation that once flourished here. But now, let us be thankful, there are Wesleyan chapels instead.

GOING SOUTH IN ENGLAND

by MRS. JOHN BUCHAN

GLENNY

We had always intended to go for a short trip abroad this winter, but patriotism and the temporary dowdiness of the British pound forbade this, and one day we took our seats in the Penzance train instead.

For some time we remained gloomy and disappointed. We surveyed the triumphs of the jerry builder at Didcot and Swindon with aversion. But we raised our heads out of our books to look with glad surprise at a city set upon hills whose colour was that of old ivory, and whose name proved to be Bath.

We then laid our books aside and gazed down on to farms and cottages and streams and upon distant hills. One specially delightful picture dwells in my mind. We looked as we passed into a deep green lane, full of startlingly white geese, to a farm with a brown high pitched roof. The adjoining little station bore the charming caption of Puxley-on-the-Worle.

Our train which had begun with haughty pride as one of the fastest of expresses, now slowed down to the gentle pace of a local train, and began stopping at every station. Country women got in and out, energetically retailing local gossip to each other.

That evening we slept at the Queen's Hotel, Penzance, the sound of the waves beating like a Bach fugue through our dreams. Next morning in sunshine we looked out on a blue bay and St. Michael's Mount, a little fairy mountain rising suddenly out of the water.

Penzance has the immemorial charm of the seaport — the rows of little houses, the small streets of tiny shops, sailors, ropes and nets everywhere, in the best traditions of romance. A huge mass meeting of sea gulls on the top of a fish market, crying imperiously for offal, completed the picture.

As we walked towards Newlyn a small bus passed us bearing on its brow the one word "Mousehole". We smiled, but soon found that Mousehole was no invented name, but a delightful reality; a tiny harbour with houses close together all around it, full of black and blue boats laid up for the winter — and with the harbour walls hung with long black nets.

I have so many impressions in my mind that they confuse me as I write: Land's End, where we looked down on to a sapphire sea framed between rose coloured rocks; the expanse of sea broken only by a lighthouse and these small groups of rocks, and a tramp steamer burying its nose in its own foam.

Then Porthleven, a lovely unspoilt fishing village hugging its little harbour and sands. We walked along the cliff and saw the largest inland lake in Cornwall. It is separated from the sea by a bar of shingle — but what shingle! Not the usual large grey stones so painful to the feet, but myriads of tiny polished oval pebbles, polished down the ages by the sea. There was no wind, and the hills looked as if they had been sculptured; the trees were motionless, each stem catching the light. It all looked so magical and unreal that when I was told that Tennyson had cast the last scene of the *Morte d'Arthur* there, and that Excalibur had been flung into those ruffled grey waters I felt no surprise at all.

We motored over to St. Ives — and fell in love with its harbour of mouse-coloured houses with the little blue and black boats drawn cosily up for the winter. The underclothing of the population of that part of St. Ives, hanging out on lines, supplied brilliant patches of colour and completed the picture very well.

Par, the junction for Fowey and Newquay, has a most attractive little Cornish harbour. Near by one can see something of the china clay industry. It has its own curious beauty in the snowy-white cone-shaped mounds of china clay which decorate the landscape and contrast with the surrounding green countryside.

From Cornwall into Devonshire is but a step, and to spend a day or two in Plymouth is a very interesting experience. Plymouth for all its imposing sea front and widely flung harbour is a seaport plus a moderate sized country town. It has been said that in every house in Plymouth there is a freshly gathered bunch of flowers, some new butter and cheese or a bowl of clotted cream, the fruits of a country outing or an offering from country friends. I am always much attracted by the fish and flower market at Plymouth and was especially fascinated when on a visit there by the Cornish snowdrops with the elongated blooms.

For those to whom sunshine in the winter is a necessity, Torquay is a haven of refuge. For Torquay has an unequalled record for winter sunshine. The dark red rocks in the little coves, sharply outlined against a blue sea, the tiny cyclamen growing in the grass in the months when everywhere else gardens are bleak and bare, makes Torquay unique in charm. It is even possible to sit out and doze in a deck chair on a January morning.

Totnes has a red sandstone church with a fine perpendicular tower and a curious porch, also an interesting old Guildhall and castle. It is also a centre for many expeditions, and the Seymour Hotel lays itself out to make its visitors comfortable and to advise them what is most well worth seeing in the neighbourhood. It is famous for its cyder.

Devonshire — the name alone brings to our minds such marvellous pictures. We conjure up visions of exquisite little villages and orchards, picturesque market towns, wide views and distant gleams of sea. The reluctant British sun is kind to Devonshire and beams at the sight of her charming landscape. Travellers in Britain cannot do better than go there to be thawed and renewed in health and vigour by the sunshine.

CALIFORNIA

by LOUIS BROMFIELD

For all of us, there are certain corners of the earth which seem to possess a peculiar attraction and sympathy. It is one of the joys of travelling that we suffer the indignities of trains and motors, ships and planes in the constant expectancy of finding just round the next corner a country which holds for us a new romance and beauty. Sometimes, it seems that the new land is really an old one which we have always known and to which we have returned: for native towns and communities are like relatives, they are wished on us without choice, and sometimes late in life we discover the spot which spiritually is our native land.

There are spots in the world which I find it impossible to do without — most of Spain, London, Broadway, New England in October, the high Alps in winter, and lately a new country which is within the borders of the United States, but which even to Americans must seem a foreign land.

The sense of its foreignness begins, I think, at the moment the westward-bound traveller opens his eyes and witnesses the glories of the sunrise over the painted deserts of Arizona. In a country so solid and rich and prosperous as America, the disorderly colour and extravagance of the scene seem foreign. There is so much space.

Its extravagance is not that of money made and thrown away again lavishly in the open-handed gambling American way, but the extravagance of a colossal wasteland. It seems odd that no American has thought of some means by which this useless magnificence can be transmuted into something material and profitable. Real-estate operators have tried to plant towns here and there on the fringe of the splendour, but, like most real-estate developments, the result has been a failure and the attempts appear unkempt and seedy. This magnificent desert and the country sloping westward to the Pacific seem, after the neatness of the mid-West, quite out of hand. And it has done something to the character of the Americans who have settled there. It is a country which imposed itself upon the character of a people, their architecture, their thought, and even upon their policemen, for even the policemen in this country are different from policemen in the rest of America. Beyond this desert lies Southern California, and crossing the desert is like crossing the ocean — it seems to separate the United States from a foreign country.

Anyone who knows California understands its vast size and realises the great distance that separates Northern and Southern California. It is of Southern California I am writing — the rather fantastic California of Agua Caliente, Hollywood, Santa Barbara, Palos Verdes, Bel Air, and a dozen other communities. It is a country where the architecture is inclined to fantasy, the flowers and colours to extravagance. Its very landscape has the agitating quality of an El Greco. The tempo of living is slower. One laughs more frequently. Worries fade away, and even the process of thinking becomes lazy and careless.

After a few months in this strange country, you come magically to slip into the native point of view. Everything in California is so different, and there is always the eternal sunshine which withers old worries and stifles potential new ones. One wakes in the morning filled only with a desire to be out-of-doors. The staunchest Babbitt suddenly betrays a liking for scarlet neckwear and no hat, and gayer spirits suddenly appear in berets and red silk shirts; and the odd thing is that none of your fellow-citizens seem to resent the change or regard the gay clothing as ridiculous. In Hollywood, the process of

PLANK 1927

LEPAPE 1918

LEPAPE 1918

change has come to have a name. It is called "going native", a phrase which, in itself, implies the foreignness of California.

It is a bad country for the intellectual and a superb country for the athlete. That is the fault of the sun, for profound thinking belongs to countries of fog and rain, and physical animal beauty to countries of the sun. One has only to visit any public beach on the Southern California coast to notice the difference in physique between Californians and the inhabitants of the Atlantic coast of America. In California, a grotesque physical specimen is the exception. In the East, it is likely to be the rule. And the sun lures the Californian into an extremely un-American disregard for clothing. Young people drive about in motors, clad in the lightest of bathing-costumes, and no one objects. On the beach, the sun is worshipped and most of the body is frankly exposed in order to acquire a fine mahogany tint. One soon becomes aware of the Californian's lack of prudery and false modesty, a quality which extends even to policemen and officials. And love-making quite open and unashamed is in evidence to a degree which is Latin.

Once, at a dinner, I expressed the opinion that in the end the perpetual sunshine might change the whole character of the Americans who chose to live in California. I suggested that these fortunate Americans might gradually acquire the qualities of gaiety and perhaps even the charm and the careless moral attitude which distinguishes the Mediterranean peoples. But the Californians present were still American enough to resent the suggestion, because it implied also that they might come to have an un-

American dislike for hard work and that Californian labour would be less efficient than labour elsewhere in America.

Someone has described Los Angeles as six suburbs in search of a city, and I think no one will dispute the statement that, in its present stage, Los Angeles is a sprawling American boom city not yet quite organised and settled into a genuine city pattern. It is still in the hands of optimistic real-estate operators who have spread their city rather thinly over a too large territory. But, by the same token, it is in one sense the most modern of America's great cities. It has grown up since the advent of motors and is built for them. The roads and streets, save in the very heart of the city, are so wide that a motor travelling at twenty-five miles an hour gets underfoot. Distances are immense. One's office is twenty miles from home and one's golf course fifteen miles in another direction, but distance is, after all, measured by time, and fifteen miles in Los Angeles is less than two miles in Long Island City. Los Angeles, like most of Southern California, has accepted the aeroplane, and everyone travels by 'plane.

One becomes aware gradually of a new people living in a new country who are building for the future, unhindered by any great conservatism. In Los Angeles exists, I think, perhaps the most beautiful shop in the world — a great branch department store known as Bullock's-Wilshire, which stands on the edge of the city a dozen stories higher than any other building. It is modern to the last detail. It is built for the future. It is beautiful, and, oddly enough, no one finds its extremely advanced type of decoration and lighting either bizarre or startling. It is accepted as a creation for the future when the city will have grown up to it. It rates in beauty with the famous Hollywood Bowl, where the planting and orchestra stage are at once modern and Greek. Here, thousands of people may gather under the night sky to listen to music and watch ballets, seated comfortably, smoking, at ease. And they may arrive and leave without traffic troubles, because the place and the roads leading to and from it are built for the future.

But, if the city itself is sprawling and American, it possesses five or six suburbs — Beverly Hills, Pasadena, Santa Monica, Westwood, Bel Air, Palos Verdes, set in a glittering chain, which are, perhaps, the loveliest suburbs which exist, flower-girded and exotic, with homes which fit into a landscape more Spanish than American. Indeed, to the first exploring Spaniards the first sight of Southern California must have been singularly sympathetic, for the landscape is for all the world like the flat valleys, plains, and mountains of Spain itself, lacking only one of the beauties of Spain — that curious violet evening light which one finds in Spanish pictures. The houses, white and grilled, lean against hillsides surrounded by camellia-trees and hedges of geraniums. To the younger architects of Southern California must go a colossal credit for understanding the close affinity between the Californian landscape and the white-walled, red-roofed Basque and Spanish houses. There are spots like Bel Aire and Montecito which seem a glorified Spain, where knowledge and taste have improved an architecture born in Spain. In Palos Verdes, with its self-contained life of sport and sunshine, one has the impression of entering a Paradise designed by the Spanish for the anointed of Heaven.

The population is the most colourful and strange which exists in America. It is composed of native Californians, Filipinos, Chinese, Japanese, Indians, and Mexicans, with a rich mixture from Iowa, Kansas, and Nebraska and other Mississippi states. Watching them, one feels that here, more than anywhere else in America, the individual is all-important. Character is allowed to run rampant. One sees Japanese families, grandfather and the grandchildren working side by side in fields of flowers. Chinese and Filipinos pad about to wait on you. Even the emigrant native Americans have turned colourful. I have seen hard-boiled surveyors at work enjoying the sun in a nakedness that extended to the waist, and I have seen them working in scarlet jerseys.

VOYAGE TO VALPARAISO

by HELEN BROWN NORDEN

"In *my* country", said the Ecuadorean Colonel, "we are very quick with the machete. At feasts, the men always have machete fights and slash each other's teeth out. It is very funny to watch".

"How they amuse themselves in Ecuador!" said the Argentine lady.

"*Caramba*, yes!" he said. He was the only man I had ever met in real life who said *caramba*, just like the Mexican villains on the stage.

It was the *Santa Lucia's* third day out at sea on her South American run, and the passengers had passed that preliminary stage where they walk about all day, eyeing one another with guarded eagerness. We had started out complete strangers, shoving one another against the rail as we threw confetti at our friends and relatives wishing us god-speed from the dock below. (Of course, since the wind was blowing the wrong way that day, the confetti all curled back in our own faces, but then, we had made the gesture.) But after three days of open sea, scrambling like mice over the beautiful ship, dawdling by day in the big pool on the sun-deck, dancing and going to the movies by night, we had settled down to that curiously unreal and stimulating family life that is characteristic of long sea cruises.

We knew all the incipient romances and most of the gossip: the blonde girl who was going to Chile to marry a man she had met in China; the well-known American woman who was travelling under a false name, to forget her last divorce; the lady missionary headed for a post in Ecuador's lonely mountain district. Certain salient personalities had begun to stand out against the background of cruise passengers, school-teachers, society women, explorers, and the large number of successful business men, with mining or other interests, who are always on South American ships.

The ship's first stop was at Cristóbal, where you can either stay on the boat and go through the Canal, or you can get off and take the train over to Panama. Most of the passengers stayed on board, to see the famous locks.

All my life I have wanted to go to Panama — or at least ever since I saw Carole Lombard in "Swing High, Swing Low" — because I had fondly pictured it as a fascinating and glamorous centre of slightly sinister night-life. The Peruvian purser on the ship had described it in stirring terms, so I was just a bundle of nerves when I went down the gang-plank. Since it was nine o'clock in the morning, the colourful night-life of my dreams was not immediately apparent. I was with the Colonel, who was met by still another Ecuadorean Colonel. The latter was very gallant, and, unlike his friend, he spoke English.

59

"Would you like a shake?" he said.

I must have looked a little startled. "I beg your pardon?"

"Well, maybe later", he said. "They make very good shakes here in Panama. I suppose you dance the fox?"

"Oh, yes", I murmured, and followed him into a taxicab elaborately furnished with crocheted white curtains at all the windows and an Oriental rug on the floor.

Between them, they took me on quite a tour. They took me to meet the Governor, who gave us a pass on the railway; and to meet the President, which was fine, because all the soldiers in the Palace stood at salute when the two Colonels went by. They took me through the jail. They took me to the military barracks. They took me to the air base. They took me miles out in the country to see a pile of old stones where, so they informed me, came Balboa once upon a time, saying, "How *pacific* are your waters!" They took me to see all the public monuments. They took me through two hospitals, in the newer of which, as a grand climax, they showed me in the operating-room the hospital's first operation: a lovely tumour in a glass jar. I was impressed. I was also exhausted. By the time night came, I was still muttering doggedly, "What about the nightlife?" but it was without any real heart. We wandered dazedly past a dance-hall, filled with sailors in uniform and pretty hostesses of various colours. At the entrance was a lively party of people we recognised as being from the *Santa Lucia*, the women looking very fresh and gay in their smart summery evening gowns, the men, spotless in white dinner-jackets.

The next day none of the other passengers showed up on deck till afternoon. When they did, it was with glowing reports of the gaiety of night-life in both Colón and Panama City. "Ah", they said, "there's nothing else like it in the world. Exotic! Colourful! Glamorous! Exciting!"

"I'll bet", I said, and went back to sleep in my deck-chair.

From that time on, we stopped at a different port almost every day, and, at every one, we all trooped off, armed to the teeth with our deadly cameras, our sun-goggles, and our relentless quest for post-cards.

The first Peruvian port reached, whichever it is, is the signal for a llama hunt. Since llamas no longer roam Peru in abundance, someone or other — possibly the ever-thoughtful Grace Line — usually has the wit to see to it that at least one is on display, so that the tourists can cluster round the frightened thing, shouting, "Is *that* a llama?" and buying picture post-cards of it, on which they invariably write: "This is a llama. When they get angry, they spit at you. Love from Mabel".

The ship stops overnight in Lima, or, rather, in Callao, the port, which is about twenty minutes drive from Lima; and here everyone buys curious and sometimes very beautiful objects made of the famous hand-wrought Peruvian silver. Everyone also gets very drunk on the equally famous Peruvian *pisco*, which, taken alone, is a foul and fiery potion, but, mixed in a Pisco Sour at the Bolivar Hotel or at Lima's attractive Country Club, is quite palatable.

After each shore trip, we all came back to the boat to compare purchases and impressions. The school-teachers were disappointed in Lima because it wasn't tropical. "Imagine!" said one of them. "They have *dandelions* and *petunias* growing all over the place! Peru indeed!"

In Manta, Ecuador, we anchored out in the ocean and watched the dozens of tiny sailing boats skimming out like water-beetles to meet us, filled with dark little men who scampered up the ship's ladder and followed us all over the boat, holding out great piles of Panama hats and chattering incessantly. One of them had a honey-bear with him — a funny little tan thing with a bare pink nose and a plaintive voice — which he was also trying to sell, but the bear kept jumping on passengers' shoulders and scaring the wits out of them, so finally they had to put him in a basket and shove the lid down to keep him quiet.

The first sight of Chile is pretty exciting. After the austere grandeur of Peru's coast-line, the friendly trees and flowers of Chile are like a WELCOME mat to the passengers. In Arica, you have the bougainvillea flaming forth its scarlet flowers all over town; and in Antofagasta, the dock is lined with violet-coloured rowing boats, whose handsome proprietors yell "Goodbye, baby!" at you when you leave. By the time we reached Valparaiso, after eighteen days, almost everyone felt as if he had come home, at long last. The skiers got happily off to go about their ski-ing in the fabulously beautiful lake district, and on the snow-covered slopes of live volcanoes. The blonde girl got off to marry the man she had met in China. The half-dozen or so one-way passengers, including the American Ambassador who had come aboard at Antofagasta from a fishing trip, got off to go on to Santiago. And the rest of us, minus the Colonel, whom we had dropped in Ecuador, got off to wander round Valparaiso, to buy tremendous bunches of Persian violets — looking like small orchids — and *yunkos,* which have a piercingly sweet fragrance similar to narcissus, to gamble in Viña del Mar's world-famous Casino, and to eat *chilemoyas,* a fruit which looks on the outside like a green baby porcupine, and on the inside like a pear with lots of little brown seeds.

I was staying in Chile, but I went to the boat to see it sail. By the time a ship starts back for home, the original cruisers all know one another as well as if they had lived together for fifty years with never a cross word, so the new passenger getting on at Valparaiso is apt to feel for the first few days like a new boy at school. I could spot a few of these standing shyly apart on the deck. The remnants of the original family group stood in a solid phalanx, busily taking last minute snapshots of Valparaiso's harbour. We who had broken away from them had done so with a great exchange of cards and addresses, although we knew that we would never see them again. It is a strange feeling. For weeks you live together in family intimacy — you who were strangers at first and who will be strangers again. And at some future date, showing your snapshots, you will be heard to say, "This is me in Chile. That? Let me see now. We were together all the time on the cruise. I think she came from California. Her name was Klinks. Or was it Plinks? Well, anyway, we were together on the cruise".

∫PAIN AGAIN

by H. W. YOXALL

The wonderful thing about Spain is that it is so Spanish. Everything that you have ever read about it, or imagined. Mountains snow-tipped in summertime, and great tawny plateaux. White houses shimmering in African sunshine, and shady gardens where fountains and nightingales sing to each other. Orange groves growing right up to the *patios* of cathedrals, and great castles or Roman monuments rising sheer from the countryside . . . Men really do wear tall black hats and tight trousers, women grace themselves with the mantilla. Church treasures make those of northern Europe look like Woolworth's. Noble houses are descried behind superb grilles. Women out of *Carmen* gather with shapely water-jars at the village cisterns. Caravans of asses wind between cacti and cork trees. Flights of storks hover above Moorish ruins. Herds of goats tinkle in and out of the city gateways. They couldn't do it better, even in Hollywood.

And yet in this most ancient, most foreign country of western Europe, there are all the comforts. Madrid, Barcelona, Seville, Granada and the *plages* have magnificent hotels. Burgos, Toledo, Valencia, Zaragoza, Ronda, Salamanca, Cordoba have excellent ones. And there are those delectable inns, the *paradores* of the *Patronato Nacional del Turismo,* set to break motor journeys previously too long; for instance, at Merida, between Madrid and Seville, at Manzanares between Madrid and Malaga, at Baillen between Cordoba and Granada. Charming buildings, their architecture and furnishing a clever blend of modernism and the regional styles, spotlessly clean, where you can have a room and bath and simple meals for next to nothing.

Perhaps the most delightful of all these *paradores* is at Ciudad Rodrigo. It is built in the citadel of this walled town, high above the river and the Portuguese plain, and the great stone dining-room is the old stable where Wellington stabled his horses in the first Spanish fortress captured in 1812. But it is rather out of the way unless you are going or returning from Lisbon, when you could take it in via Salamanca, the only university town on the continent which has anything like our Oxford or Cambridge colleges. It is, by the way, a sensible thing to do to make the journey either there or back by sea, and so cut out one of the tiring and costly overland trips. If you are doing Spain by train, it is best to sail to Gibraltar. If you are taking your car, Lisbon is perhaps more convenient, for it enables you to make a big swing round and take in something of both the east and west, whereas if you are working north from Gibraltar you have to commit yourself to one side or other. Both passenger fares and car freights are remarkably inexpensive to either port. Should you not be going until the autumn, so that you want to travel southwards in Spain, you can get a boat to Santander, Vigo or Coruña: or, of course, go down through France and return from Gibraltar.

You know the show places to go to, of course: Seville, Cordoba, Granada, Toledo, Burgos and the rest. But on no account miss Avila and Segovia, within easy motor rides from Madrid over the magnificent Sierra de Guadarrama, with its 6,000 feet pass which the lightest car will easily take, so well are the gradients engineered. If you want to stay overnight at one or the other, Segovia has a comfortable, unpretentious inn.

Avila surely wins the first prize for walled cities in Europe, ahead of Dinkelsbühl and Visby, with Aigues Mortes fourth and the over-restored Carcassonne also ran. An eleventh century *enceinte* unbroken save for the ten city gates, with eighty-six towers and the battlemented apse of the cathedral built into the fortifications as a special bastion on the most exposed side . . . The silhouette of Segovia is the apotheosis of the picturesque. It is like a great ship in sail, with the steep-pitched turrets of the Alcazar for canvas, the cathedral campanile as mast, and the majestic Roman aqueduct at the other end, striding majestically away like a rolling wake. Near by is the palace of La Granja, with fountains which eclipse Versailles (find out in advance when they are playing). And speaking of the northern gardens, do not miss Aranjuez, a little way the other side of Madrid, where the valley of the Tajo (our old friend of geography lessons, the Tagus) makes an oasis in the dusty plain of Don Quixote's La Mancha, and where the strawberries and the asparagus are outstandingly good.

And now that we have descended to such material things as food, here are a few practical tips. . . . It is difficult to get dinner before eight, and nine is the usual hour; if planning to shop in the afternoon remember the native (and sensible) habit of the *siesta*. . . . Should you have a long drive ahead and there should chance to be no *parador nacional* en route, ask the head-waiter to pack a picnic lunch. They do it very well . . . *Agua de Solares* is a pleasant, unmedicated table water. If you are not of a strong stomach, perhaps it is better to avoid fresh salads and unpeeled fruit, even those Aranjuez strawberries. . . . Do not ask for Jerez when you want sherry, but for a Tio Pepe, a Manzanilla, etc., according to the type you prefer. . . . The roads in the towns are as confusing as those in the country are clear, and it pays to take on the running board one of the numerous boys who will charge out to meet you, and let him guide you to your hotel. Fifty *centavos* (3½d.) is a generous tip for this service . . . You may drive thirty miles between petrol pumps, so don't let the tank get too low. . . . If you go to Seville for Easter, don't, because of all the processions, overlook the *Seises* in the cathdral. Ten little choir boys in plumed hats and 17th-century costumes, singing and dancing with castanets before the high altar. You can also see this unique spectacle at Corpus Christi and at the Immaculate Conception. . . . At Cordoba, after you have seen the mosque, buy some *turrones* at the cake shops in the Calle Libreria — delicious nougat cakes which elsewhere it is hard to get except at Christmas. And the Montillo wine here (our Amontillado) is delectable. . . . However much you have seen of the Alhambra by day, climb the hill one night, stand by the parapet in front of the Palace of Charles V and listen to the voice of Granada coming up from the gorge below, as you look across to the fires flickering in front of the gypsy caves on the opposite hill. Never have I known the soul of a city more vocal. . . . At Toledo see the greatest of the Grecos, in Santo Tomé, by morning light. . . . Remember at Madrid that the Prado, in summer time, is only open in the mornings.

Finally, now that they have padding on the horses, only the determinedly sentimental can take offence at a bull fight. And for the others, what a magnificent spectacle — how characteristic of this strange and beautiful country.

LET'S GO TO RUSSIA

by DENISE ÉMILE-SCHREIBER

Brass buttons, like marine officers, are polite, even amiable, if we are to judge by their smile, for we do not understand a word they say. Luckily, all notices concerning Customs and the exchange of money are translated into German, English and French.

Our luggage once stamped and closed, inspection is made of our pocket-books, which are filled with dollars, the currency most appreciated by the Soviets. We go into the Exchange Office and receive two roubles for a dollar, at stabilised exchange. Not wishing to look like capitalists, we prepare to carry our own luggage, but porters appear and relieve us of it. Russian trains are comfortable and clean. The food served in the dining-cars is not remarkable for its excellence, but, after all, one could hardly expect to find French chefs in Russia.

Here we are, then, on Soviet soil, on the road to Moscow. Everything, until now, seems to have worked out well. The train startles us with a bellow, but we shall get used to this noise, for, instead of a whistle, Russian trains have a muffled siren which is both profound and impressive. We pass a comfortable night, and, as the sun rises, we see a country of great immensity, the horizon pushed back beyond its normal limits. There are no roads, only sandy paths on which curious horse-drawn wagons come and go.

When we arrive at the huge station now under construction at Moscow, two charming young women, neatly dressed, await us on the platform. They are the interpreters that "Intourist" delegated to receive us. Far from being treated as strangers, we are welcomed as guests of the Intourist — the Soviet Tourist Agency — which aims to make our stay agreeable and to ensure our leaving the country satisfied that we have had an opportunity of seeing everything in which we were interested.

Leaving the station, we make our first contact with the Russian crowd. It is not at all what we expected. We pictured rags and bare feet; and here are people dressed much as any crowd of workers emerging from a factory. All in the crowd are workers, all are cheaply, plainly dressed, but their feet are in shoes which, while neither fashionable nor of particularly good quality, are, nevertheless, shoes.

Moscow, famous for its many fine hotels before the Revolution, now has only four or five first-class ones. Only the biggest and most modern have been preserved for foreigners. We stop at the Grand Hotel and are given, my husband and myself, an immense bedroom with a salon of equal size. The bathroom is impressive; except that the hot-water tap is broken and all the enamel is chipped off the bath. The furniture, overladen with gilded bronze, appears to be rarely cleaned, but the beds are all right, and there are fresh towels at the wash-basin.

Our young guides allow us little time for getting settled. It is half-past ten, the breakfast hour, and we must go down to the dining-room. There isn't much to say about the gastronomic pleasures of Russia. Rarely fresh, the food is prepared in too rudimentary a fashion for the palate of a French gourmand. The service is slow and clumsy, but, during our entire trip, we shall have plenty to eat. Only one drink is possible — tea. Beer and wine are undrinkable and outrageously expensive.

We begin our survey of Moscow in a comfortable sightseeing bus. (There are, by the way, very few motors, and all are in Government service.) We go through miserable streets lined with houses from which the plaster is falling, when suddenly there arises before our eyes a group of workers' houses of the handsomest modern architecture. These contradictory first impressions are repeated during the entire trip. The Soviets preserve and repair nothing. Whatever building they do is begun from the ground up, but the task of restoring this immense territory is not yet completed.

Our days are passed in visiting factories, workmen's clubs, organizations for the protection of children. By observation and questioning, we begin to get the trend of Soviet life; we begin to understand what is taking place in this fabulous social laboratory.

The Russian woman works like a man. She can have the highest position and play a great rôle in the immense machine that the Soviets are trying to put in motion, but which still creaks a good deal. I visited some marvellous maternity homes where the women are kept only six days and where no visit to the young mothers is allowed; great posters in the entrance hall give the families whatever news they can have.

No distinction is made between legitimate and illegitimate offspring; all children — legitimate or illegitimate — have the same rights, the fathers the same responsibilities. I saw a great number of day nurseries. All are clean and intelligently arranged; they play, besides, a great rôle in Russian life; the women, since they are all working, leave their children at the nurseries in the morning and reclaim them in the evening.

Large parks for sports, tennis, football, and other sports are installed near all settlements. On coming out of the factory, the Russian workman — who is, in general, badly lodged — resorts to the clubs, where he may indulge in sports, read books, or simply dream in restful armchairs. Life might be most agreeable if it were not for the obligation to stand in a queue, for hours, before the State Co-operative stores, in order to buy all the things indispensable to life. The Russian worker nearly always takes his meals in immense co-operative restaurants, where he is fairly well nourished for a very small sum. In the U.S.S.R., there is no private commerce. Everything is State Co-operative, even the Torgsin, or tourists' store, where all purchases must be made in dollars. There I bought, at a very reasonable price, astrakhan skins which I could never have found anywhere else for the same sum. Besides furs, there are also jewels and antique art objects — some of which are very beautiful — formerly belonging to noble families.

Needing a manicure, I was greatly surprised to learn that there were several beauty shops in Moscow. All over Russia, it appears, there are many women who have had their nails manicured and visit the coiffeur. But I have the impression that I should not care to put my hair in the hands of the coiffeurs I saw.

The Russian women are not pretty, but they are strong, healthy types. They wear very short skirts, almost to the knee, and, in the summer time, many wear socks instead of stockings. Handkerchiefs tied round the head are the usual form of head-dress.

There is not a club, a theatre, a museum, a nursery, not even a street where one does not see large red banners, bearing in gigantic letters flattering inscriptions on the Revolution or on the Five-Year plan; not a single work of art is turned out that has not propaganda as its aim; not a book is allowed to be published if it is not in favour of the formidable enterprise which is carried on according to the most modern methods of this immense country.

I came back much impressed by this extraordinary and perfectly easy trip. It was made possible for me to see so clearly and at first-hand this remarkable experiment — in which the advantages and the faults are of equal importance, so that one could, according to his own tendencies, describe either one or the other. And that explains why the reports of a trip into the U.S.S.R. are so contradictory.

A JOURNEY TO PRAGUE

by LESLEY BLANCH

I have yet to find the lonely mountain pass or the wild uncharted moor which will be more difficult to cross than London once proved itself, on our departure for Prague, after too good a farewell dinner party. Most of the first night was spent circling the Crystal Palace in an attempt to reach the Dover Road.

However, Dover achieved, an early start was made by all except the engine, which resulted in our crossing on the midday boat, and reaching Ostend in time for an alcoholic tea. Our route lay through Bruges and Ghent, cities of indestructible calm beauty, to Brussels, where we indulged unrestrained, in Belgian patisseries, a particularly Gallic music hall, and the Musée Wiertz. Heading for the Ardennes, we went through Namur and Dinant to Château d'Ardennes, a perfect hotel, in perfect surroundings, high among the wooded mountainous gorges of the Ardennes, where placid rivers wind through the rocks, and pink and yellow villages offer omelettes and trout.

Next, we headed for Strasbourg, the City of the Stork, full of quaveringly old red gabled houses, an exquisite pink Gothic Cathedral, bi-lingual Franco-Prussian inhabitants, pâté de foie gras, market squares and glimpses of storks nesting among the chimney-pots in the best German fairy story manner. All next day was spent wandering through the unspoiled villages of Alsace-Lorraine, sampling the local pastry, such as Quiche Lorraine and other Alsatian delicacies — tarts with a custard base, which include cheese, walnuts and onions in their ingredients. So, over the frontier to Germany, and on through the *unheimlich* groves of the Black Forest, to a small inn full of platinum blonde storm troopers, and rather beefy mädchen, in uniform black velvet bodices and puffed muslin sleeves. Augsburg's mediaeval enchantment was too strong to be withstood; we lingered there at the expense of Munich, whose treasures we were forced to gulp with true tourist dispatch. The marionette theatres and the superb bookshops linger in my memory; also our earnest rehearsals of the fashionable Nazi salute, in front of a triple mirror.

We spent one day at Nymphenburg, though a lifetime would be too short for this paradisical palace, I feel. Then on, through Landshut, a strange unspoiled little town, to the Czecho-Slovakian frontier, which was crossed *cosily* rather than officially. A pleasing absence of formality was *de rigueur* here. The douane was crowded with toothpicks, last week's calendar, flowers, amiable officials and an over-fed chocolate coloured dog. We drove on through lovely rolling open country, stretching away to the High Tatra mountains — over fine roads, past pink-washed villages, white oxen, and huge sunflowers tied up in bandannas, to catch the seeds, which are used for oil, and are the local equivalent of chewing gum. The peasants appeared literally in the pink wearing bunchy crimson skirts, scarlet stockings, pink shawls, and red tasselled bicycles (I suppose this is the Czech version of the Neapolitan horse tassels, worn to ward off the evil eye). The language problem was solved by my smattering of Russian and my companion's German; but we regretted not having brushed up our Czech, for we wished to talk and laugh with these childishly gay and beautiful peasants.

Through Pilzn, or Pilsen — of lager fame, to Prague, a sort of Polyglopolis, part Paris, part Rome, part Russia, an architectural mixture of Renaissance, Baroque, and L'école de Corbusier. A mediaeval German geographist in his Cosmographia, described Europe as a noble lady, with Spain as her head, Italy and Jutland her arms, and Prague her heart. So, today, "Zlatà Praha", Golden Prague, is a paradise for the historically in-quisitive visitor. More than any other place I have known, I would call Prague a *vintage* city. It is so mellow, so subtle; all of the wine merchant's adjectives apply to its warmth and richness.

Dark, sinister, "Student of Prague"-ish arcaded streets, narrow ways, full of drama, such as the famous "Street of the Necromancers": wide, brilliantly lit boulevards, all cafés, shops and chic: lovely open air restaurants and swimming pools on the islands of the Vlatava, looking across to the castle of Hradčany, the monasteries and palaces on the heights. The streets are full of good-looking people, with the perfect teeth and dark slanting Tartar eyes of the South Russians. Many of the women, beautiful and soignée, have the romantic habit of carrying bunches of carnations in their hands, which is more effective than any boutonnière.

The men, wearing long, fluffy overcoats, drive high-powered cars at high speed, and play cards with packs of such decorative beauty and traditional quaintness that, as a mere beholder, I longed to "cut in". At the street corners, top-booted old peasant women were selling peculiar knobs of varnished mahogany, which turned out to be a treacly cheese.

Far on the outskirts of the city lies the little house at Betramka, in which Mozart wrote *Don Giovanni*. Now a dilapidated and pathetic museum, its broken shutters flap dismally in the wind which rustles through the tangled overgrown garden. Inside the villa, with its tarnished gilding and faded panelling, the salon where Mozart worked is left much as it was during his visit.

That night, we went to the "Theatre of the Estates" in the centre of the city, still in its exquisite original pink, gold, and crystal frivolity of eighteenth-century taste. It was here that *Don Giovanni* was first performed, but alas! on the occasion of our visit, there was a bedroom farce, called, I think, *Darling*.

Prague is justly proud of its Opera House, its singers and their repertoire. It is true we noticed a preponderance of Bartered Brides on the season's programmes, but that is not altogether unexpected, since Smetana was a local product.

We also saw beautiful productions of *L'Espoir*, and the classic *Brothers Karamazov*. Tairov and his company, from the Karmeny Theatre, Moscow, were playing to packed houses, while obscure music halls proved as entertaining in central Europe as in central London. The Museum-minded, amongst whom I personally rank, should not fail to visit the National Museum which stands at the top of the Wencelas Boulevard, the principal street, and named after that Good King. Once inside the Museum, forsake all, and make for the mediaeval apothecaries' shops, which have been saved from demolition, and reconstructed, a miracle of accuracy, full of retorts, and burners, stuffed crocodiles and astronomic globes, old herbals, occult books, and reminders of demonology and witchcraft.

Go, too, to marvel at the fabulous jewels and gold plate at the Loreta Monastery, where, in the cloisters, you will find a chapel containing the curious figure of a bearded lady, in panniered skirts, crucified. She was a saint, and her legend will be told you by the monks, who relish its ghoulish mixture of cruelty, naïvety and piety. See the famous little smiling Infant Jesus, the "Miraculous Jesus of Prague", a tiny doll-like waxen figure, covered in pearls and laces, tassels and brocades, worldly, yet strangely beautiful.

In short, go to Prague, and stay there as long as you can.

A VISITOR TO SHANGHAI

by BEATRICE WELLS

From Peiping to Shanghai by train is a matter of a thousand miles and some fifty-two hours on the Shanghai Express (which turns out to be an ancient and halting conveyance, musty, mouldy and moth-eaten, and not even vaguely Pullmanish). However, once arrived in Shanghai, life becomes glamorous, gay — and steeped in iniquity, or so they tell us.

At the Cathay — where everyone stays — you'll find your suite is modern and deliciously comfortable. And once you're nicely settled, with your cabin trunk open wide and your favourite frocks swishing in the racy breeze that blows in from the Bund, you'll be thinking what a heavenly sensation it is, after all these weeks of endless sight-seeing, to tell yourself that you don't need a *Baedeker* and you don't need a guide; because there is nothing you *have* to see in Shanghai. It is one of the few cities in this world of ours that are still free from charabanc coaches and all things "trippery". All you really *have* to do is to have a gay, enchanting holiday.

But you will want to do a little exploring on your own these first days; so after the usual Shanghai breakfast of orange-juice, luscious little crescent rolls, honey and coffee, you will go for a walk along the Bund, which faces the crowded water-front of the Whangpoo. It's proud and imposing and amazingly clean, this avenue they call the Bund; and if its shining whitewashed legations, banks and residences were two dozen stories high, instead of six or under, you might almost believe you were on Michigan Boulevard in Chicago, instead of in a Chinese city.

But by now you're probably eager to begin your shopping, for musical bracelets and malachite rings and all the other enchanting things that one can buy in China; so hail a slant-eyed 'ricksha boy in tattered pants and a twisted cotton turban and take out your little notebook with your pidgin-English phrases (remember — "chop chop" means "hurry"; "maskee" is "never mind"; and "man man" is "stop"). And go jogging like mad down Nanking Road, out Kukiang way towards the Old City, till you come to a rag-tag little byway that's called Pig Alley, where you will find the most intriguing things you've ever seen in its tiny musty shops. An ostrich made of jade . . . a gilt Buddha, loot from a temple . . . an ivory house and a blackwood man . . . earrings made of kingfisher feathers, all blue and blinking in the morning sunlight. An hour's pleasant bartering, and the lovely things are yours. And all for a pocketful of *"mex"!*

But it must be time for *tiffin* (lunch, to you) now, so run up to the Astor House, which is always gay and amusing; but don't stay any longer than half-past two, because there are still so many things you *must* buy in Shanghai, or you will be sorry ever after.

First of all, after tiffin, step in to The Jade Store on Nanking Road, because you must take home with you a pair of earrings, shining leaves of emerald jade, hung by a slender thread of diamonds. Then go over to Laou Kiu Luen's and order a tailored lounging-robe of heavy delft-blue moiré, with a lining and your monogram worked in palest lemon-yellow. Two guineas will be the top, and so also will your dressing-gown. The Sea Captain's Shop, which is also on Nanking Road, is next on your list; and if you go stark, staring mad over smooth jade cocktail cups (at a guinea a dozen!) that will keep your Manhattans cold as ice, you can put the blame on me. Oh, you'll be wanting to shop tomorrow and tomorrow and tomorrow in Shanghai. For a mandarin coat of scarlet and blue — for a little jewel-tree in a cloisonné bowl — for a three-quart silver cocktail shaker, emblazoned with a dragon!

About four in the afternoon, you'll be slipping back to the Cathay to change into something long and sleek for tea-dancing at Le Cercle Sportif Français (French Club, for short) — because Shanghai is formal rather than casual at tea-time. And on the way over, perhaps you will be able to wheedle your escort into whisking you, in his long, shining Rolls, through some of Shanghai's crooked, funny little streets; past some of its enticingly reeky markets, where wrinkled yellow merchants offer lacquered ducks as red as cinnabar, sharks' fins that glisten in a drab and jaundiced jelly, drying octopi and eggs that have passed the century mark these many years. Then wend your way through cobbled lanes — thronged and noisy as Piccadilly Circus at midnight on New Year's Eve — where roadside barbers are cropping Chinese pates, and ear-cleaning establishments do a whacking business.

And then, only minutes later, your car will be drawing up under the wide, imposing porte-cochère of the French Club, and you will be ushered into that fabulous ballroom where the maple dance floor is a shining oval set on springs. Look round and watch the interesting crowd for a little; because, although it will be primarily French, you'll see a smattering of at least a dozen other nationalities. Rye high-balls, Scotch-and-sodas, and absinthe-drip frappées will be much in evidence, but the favourite always seems to be the "Caresse Cocktail", a speciality of the house. You make it with a liqueur glass of cherry brandy, a wine-glass each of gin and curaçao, one half of a wine-glass each of cognac and lemon-juice, and one third of a glass of grenadine.

About eight you'll be going back to the Cathay for a brief nap and to dress, for you'll be dining formally at ten at the perennially popular Little Club. Dinner there will be a sumptuous affair from the large sweet prawns, fresh from Nagasaki, to the "Kaffé Royale", a brew that smacks subtly of apricot brandy, cognac, coffee and a drowsy little café in Cordoba.

And in between times everybody will be telling you what fun it is to live in Shanghai; because besides all that Shanghai itself offers, you're so near, you know, to Kyoto, to Canton and Macao and a dozen other fascinating places. And while we are on the subject, we'd like to suggest that, if the length of your stay in the East will allow it, you take a week and run down to Manila — even if you can stay for only a day! But take along a cherry coloured evening dress and white jade clips for your hair, because there will be red hibiscus and white orchids on your dinner-table at the Polo Club.

At midnight — we're back in Shanghai now — everyone decamps for the clubs. Only, whatever you do, don't let your escort — especially if he's a Russian — take you to the little club they call the Casanova. Because always, forever after, no matter where you go — whether you're lingering over a sherry cobbler on the tiny grey terrace of the hotel at Angkor, where the stars slip down almost to the causeway at night; or whether you're dancing in an ambassador's moon-drenched compound at Chiengmai — always, the sight of little tables round a polished dance floor, the sound of laughter and of dance music will take you back to a glamorous little club in China. A club they call the Casanova, where the tables are crowded with Frenchmen, Egyptians, Russians and Turks; where a small Hawaiian orchestra plays *La Cucaracha* hauntingly, disturbingly; and where you found yourself wishing that a square of polished dance floor were the length and breadth of the world.

MORRIS

/HADE/ OF JO/EPHINE

by THOMAS KERNAN

Life in Martinique is a delicate *pousse-café*. At the top of the glass is a thin *crème de la crème* . . . French officials, French Line officers, a few plantation families that have rigorously preserved their race. Next is the *café au lait* society of rich and cultured creoles. Here are the most beautiful women, educated in French convents, sharing the pride of another mademoiselle from Martinique who also went to France and into history . . . the Empress Josephine. The business of the port is in the hands of the creole men, who meet the men of the white world on equal terms; they do not meet the women.

Below the *café au lait* is the *café noir* — the world of little shopkeepers, housekeepers, down to the most delightful of all castes in Martinique — the dou-dou girls. These are the waitresses, the barmaids, the market women, the portresses, who wear the native costume of bright calico dress and the brilliant bandana tied into an elaborate headdress, according to each one's fantasy. Gold hoops pierce their ears, and white teeth are always flashing into a smile. They are impudent, friendly, humorous, and you will love them always if you see them first, as I did, at carnival time, at the dou-dou ball. What does dou-dou mean? It is the patois for *douce-douce* — sweetheart, sweetheart. All the friendliness of Martinique is implicit in this symbol, that a gentleman will refer to the barmaid as sweetheart, or a woman scolding her servant will still call her dou-dou.

For five nights in February the city of Fort-de-France is given over to carnival. And although the native of Martinique is apt to move in his own stratum of the *pousse-café*, the stranger may always claim wider privileges.

Let us start, one night, at the dance at the Lido Club. Here is a transplantation from the Riviera. Broad roofs, open balconies for dancing, the gardened terraces down to the beach; it is hard to realise at first that this is Anse Colas, and not Antibes. Cyril is behind the bar, making frosty miracles with rum buccanier and a twist of lime-peel. White, too-pale women drift in wearing Lanvin's or Schiaparelli's latest model, of net, or organdie, or organza, for in this country silks and brocades do not wear well. It is cool, for the trade winds blow always in the evening. The men wear white dinner-jackets; the naval officers from the French cruisers are in white uniform. You might well be at a most correct party on Long Island, except that unfamiliar stars over-hang the black bay, and strange perfumes drift up from the garden. And then the music of the negro musicians begins; and although they start by playing a conscientious tango or foxtrot, they soon desert whatever white influences lurk in their tawny skins and enlist under the rhythms of their black ancestors. A tango with a negro accent, a carioca, a rumba consume the night.

In Fort-de-France, five miles away by car, a huge ball is taking place at the "Sporting Club". Here the creole world forgathers. Here the gowns are equally smart but run to more colour. The dancing is a little less correct, the musicians make little pretence of playing American jazz and make direct for their own heritage. Many of the dancers seem as white as any European; their presence here alone betrays them. But in Martinique to be coloured is no crime; the white man is the relic or the parvenu. The creole women wear their emeralds with an air, in this country that their race has made.

But towards three o'clock in the morning, many of the dutiful wives and fiancées have been taken home in that uncomplaining way that French wives have the world over, and the bachelors, and many young husbands of the town, drift towards the river. Here are the dou-dou balls.

The girls are all in island costume, and looking down from the balcony the floor is an unbelievable calico of every brilliant hue. The full skirts are tucked up, to one side, under the girdle, showing an expanse of starched and embroidered petticoat. The bandana may be water-melon-pink with yellow dots; the skirt and bodice pea-green with yellow stripes; the girdle yellow. All have gold earrings, gold chains against their dark throats, and they move with the grace of women who carry great baskets on their heads for miles without fatigue. They have been drinking raw white rum, and they are dancing the *biguine*. When I saw the *biguine*, I blushingly retreated to the balcony, from which nothing could dislodge me.

After the carnival, the year's great festival, the island settles down to the routine of a busy country where life must be gained, and the sugar must be ground.

For sugar is the god of Martinique. Every valley between the volcanoes sways with cane. In a single year, the exports have been a quarter of a billion francs of rum and sugar. France is her customer, and, in return, every shirt and shoe, every awl and gimlet on the island comes from France. The genius of the French is present, too, in her civic economy. In Martinique, the world in the streets and roads is well-fed and happy, clean and good humoured. And beautiful.

To the still infrequent visitor, the hospitality is overwhelming, and one cannot attend one lunch or dinner without being invited to two others. In addition to living comfortably in their open, veranda-ed houses, the people of Martinique eat exceedingly well. The cuisine is spicy, with lime-juice, garlic, pimento and cloves. All green vegetables are abundant at any time of the year, and, while meats are not fine, the amazing fruits of the sea make up for the loss. The great clawless lobsters, the flying fish, the dolphin steaks, the fresh tuna.

Good roads permit you, with leisure, to go to all parts of the island. The sun on the beach at the Lido through lazy mornings . . . fishermen hauling their seines at dusk on to the beach of some little village . . . the trees with orchids on every branch, as you drive through the high jungle . . . these are memories that Martinique holds in store.

And there will float down your memory the refrain of a song that your French nurse doubtless sang:

> *À Martinique, à Martinique,*
> *C'est ça qui est chic,*
> *C'est ça qui est chic.*
>
> *Pas de veston, de col, de pantalon,*
> *Simplement un tout petit calecon,*
>
> *Y'a du plaisir, du plaisir, du plaisir,*
> *Jamais malade, jamais mourir,*
> *À Martinique, à Martinique.*

AT SEA

FISH 1928

From a summer cruise in 1923 through the Norwegian fjords, to Cunard's Pacific jamboree in 1978 from Hong Kong to San Francisco, the pleasures of cruising have never palled for Vogue.

Cruising was more than just a means of getting from one side of the Atlantic to the other. "Taking a ship means taking your time. No rush or bustle, no packing and unpacking every other day, no timetables to follow, no promises to keep — except the one to yourself, to get away from it all. Just you, the ship and over 140 million square miles of sea." It was "a cushioned, comfortable and pampered world" where "one gets rest, constant change of scene without fatigue, luxurious accommodation, sports, amusements and companionship if one wants it — solitude if one prefers. And the best of it is that all these desirable things are at a moderate cost." In 1935 Vogue suggested a ten-day cruise on the 16,400-ton SS *Montclare* to Casablanca, Tangier, Gibraltar and Lisbon for only nine pounds.

"Of the three elements of cruising — ships, passengers, ports — ships take pride of place." A ship was "the most masculine of triumphs . . . a great jewelled hulk waiting to be freed . . . heading towards mystery," "a white towering marvel, lights glowing through portholes, shadow silhouettes of people strolling about . . ." and "every year new inventions, new refinements of technique in shipping or decorating are adapted for the further comfort of the passengers." Vogue was less charitable towards passengers: "They fall into two classes: the Few and the Many. The few are, of course, charming people like ourselves, who hate those awful tourists and love pottering about in out-of-the-way places, and can't stand organised tours (though, of course, they are useful aren't they, when it's a question of Vesuvius) . . . The Many: fanatics and fat women." As far as the ports were concerned "the choice is almost as wide as the world," from the Holy Land to the East Indies, to the South Seas and Australia, to China and Japan, to Egypt, India and Penang — and all these "at a pace not too quick, a pace not too slow". In 1936 Vogue reported that "everyone goes cruising and the trouble is not to find a cruise but to choose from the numberless, almost equally alluring cruises that are most suited to one's particular fancy" whether you wanted to cruise in winter or summer; in the Tropics or Arctic; a fly cruise or a cultural cruise. Whatever you wanted — cruising had it. "The least that a ship does is to take you to places. The most it does is to free you," reported Vogue. Could there be a better recommendation?

1926

FISH 1928

"The younger set goes in gaily for the Three-legged Race which forms more affinities and breaks up more family steamer parties than any other diversion"

"The Master-at-Arms' stern duty is to drive late lovers out of the lifeboats"

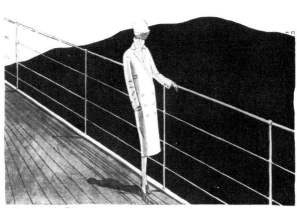

BOLIN 1926

CRUISE 1934

Here is the world laid out flat for your inspection. Each of these lines is the furrow some ship ploughs on its way from port to port, and why should not you go with it? Have you only time to sprint into the sunshine and back? Then follow the track of the Cunard boat *Laconia* which circles the Mediterranean. Do the West Indies seem to you the best refuge from January winds? The Orient Line sends out the *Orontes* to visit these islands. How about two other famous islands, St. Helena and Tristan da Cunha, with a further voyage to Rio de Janeiro? Or if you are so far afield why not as far as Australia? The Royal Mail and the P. and O. are the people you ought to see about these.

This map also illustrates a weakness common to all travellers. You may set out with your mind on the ruins of the Parthenon but you come back with an absurd doll. You forget high matters like history and architecture and remember a series of vivid trivialities. You cross thousands of miles of sea to Honolulu—and bring back a wooden bowl. No use saying "You could have got one just like that in London." It wouldn't have been the same at all.

So here is the world to roam in and the steamship routes to take, and scattered over the continents the exciting childish things you bring back.

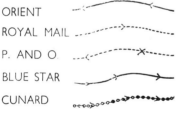

ORIENT

ROYAL MAIL

P. AND O.

BLUE STAR

CUNARD

REIGNANUM

74

What they bring back

BEATON

PASSENGERS AT ONE OF THEIR FAVOURITE OCCUPATIONS

75

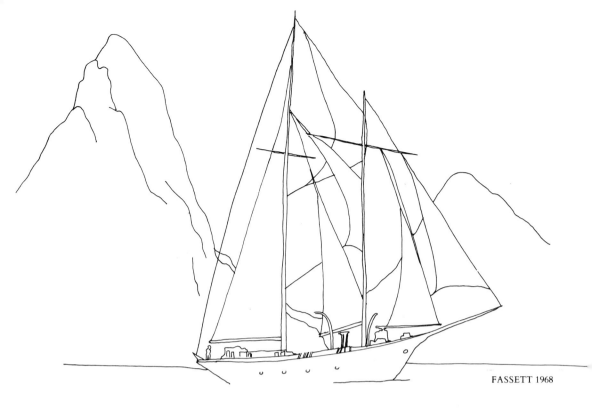

FASSETT 1968

1963

1947

COFFIN 1

THE FORTIES

If one was no longer free to travel, one was still free to read, and Vogue set about satisfying a nation of armchair travellers with a series of war reports that conveniently doubled as travel features. In issues, now considerably thinner due to paper rationing, came news from Greece, for instance, where "the women are all organising themselves to give courageous aid to their country;" from China, where "young and enthusiastic students were ready to sacrifice all for their country;" or from Bermuda "a vital Atlantic base where our forces are always on duty;" and more frequently than ever before in Vogue, regular reports from across the Atlantic where, "remote from the tanks and minefields of modern warfare," Americans were anxious to learn how they could help with the war effort. "In New York everyone wears an emblem representing either the British War Relief, Bundles for Britain or some other aid to Britain." Several thousand children had been evacuated to the U.S.A. and every day more and more would-be foster parents came forward to offer their services. "All over the country, people take inventory of their houses, their grounds, their means; of how many children they could take if they added a sleeping porch here or put central heating into the house that is only used in summer." News like this, good or bad, whether from peacetime America or war-torn Europe, greatly relieved the feeling of isolation.

For the duration of the war, despite enormous censorship and paper rationing, Vogue continued these reports from overseas, one of the most frequent contributors being Cecil Beaton, whose services had been enlisted by the Government. "It sounds like some magic carpet tour, or pre-war millionaire's holiday," wrote Mr Beaton after a three-month Ministry of Information tour to Takorudi, Cairo, Kano, Teheran, Baghdad, Palmyra and Baalbec in 1942. "But no; I was sent by the Government" — the same man who, ten years earlier, had warned his readers not to expect any daring travel articles, who had maintained that his only interests when travelling abroad were the pursuits of fine weather, friends and the occasional building of beauty!

Now he took us with him to Tunisia with "its striped awnings, its jalousied windows, blue-washed walls and wafts of spiced, aromatic smoke drifting down the narrow alleys where silent groups sit huddled in the thick folds of their Arab burnouses;" to Turkey where "the iron discipline and visionary concepts of Kemal Ataturk have bred a new people in a new land;" to Bombay "the most cosmopolitan and emancipated European city in India today;" and, on his way home from a tour of the East, to New York where "after the shabbiness of the last four years I was struck greatly by the smartness everywhere, the new paint, the alluring window displays, the crocodiles of taxis, the long, hot baths, the long, cold drinks, the succulent dishes".

His reports, and those from Vogue's war correspondent Lee Miller who, as well as being the first woman journalist into France after the Normandy landings, "thumbed a ride to the siege of St Malo . . . went down the Loire and saw two sensational German surrenders . . . went through the campaigns of Luxembourg and Alsace . . . bumped and rattled and ground into Brussels . . . entered Cologne on the heels of the capturing forces . . . and saw the war end in a plume of smoke curling up from the remnants of Hitler's mountain retreat", were eagerly awaited by Vogue readers.

"Dear, snubbed, neglected English countryside: we are rediscovering it in those short snatches of respite which may come our way. For the word 'holiday' has dropped from our vocabulary. We look no further than a long week-end . . . go where we can when we can, and triumph as in an achievement when we bring off that brief break so necessary to strength."

It was almost a year since the declaration of war and here was the first indication in Vogue that all was not well. For ten months it had been the Phoney War, or as Vogue called it in lighthearted Thirties fashion, the "Bore War," the inevitable restrictions it placed on travel generally accepted as only a temporary inconvenience.

Vogue contented homebound readers with encouraging reports from Paris where, after the first flurries of precautionary activity — bomb shelters on the Champs Elysées and packing cases in the Louvre — life was back to normal: "The lines of taxis are back on the Champs Elysées, the crowds are back in the darkened cafés, you see children playing in front of the doorways and maids coming from their morning marketing with full provision bags."

This initial return to normality in the French capital almost certainly accounted for Vogue's blithely optimistic prediction in May 1940 that "this summer you can still bake yourself a golden brown on the beaches of the Riviera, see the superb scenery of the Pyrenees, stay along the Côte Basque, at most of the Atlantic sea-board resorts, in Brittany, or just be a gastronome at the village inn which, you hope, is going to remain your own discovery". In the circumstances, there was little chance of that. Within weeks, the British Expeditionary Force was pushed back to the beaches of Dunkirk and the Phoney War was over.

"New values bring new vision," declared a chastened Vogue a month after the retreat. "Our present danger illuminates, like lightning, the familiar English landscape, making it vivid, strange and new . . . nowhere in the world, in such small compass, will you find such changing scenes as in the trifling length and breadth of England." Which was just as well since there were few alternatives. Pages once reserved for the delights and details of foreign travel were now, in the first full flush of patriotism, dedicated to "the country we are shy of naming and slow to praise; but to whom we turn now with deep content . . . a country which, perhaps, we have taken for granted, but now, in snatches of leisure, see with fresh eyes".

But it was a "New England," and even Vogue was forced to admit that "in spite of the soft yellows and browns of the Downs and solitary honey-coloured haystacks against the rich chocolate plough, and the whole countryside bathed in the pale light of a watery winter sun, one cannot help being aware of the war . . . Blue mountains, green valleys, endless stretches of sand — all are still there but no holiday makers disturb them this year". Petrol was rationed, the manufacture of cars had ceased and Government posters, pinned up in waiting rooms and pasted onto billboards, demanded "Is your journey really necessary?" Even if you could get away for that long weekend, accommodation was hard to find — "no tourist or casual visitor can get a room for love or money" — all available space quickly filled by billeted troops and the crowds of evacuees being bundled out of London.

A month after Germany's unconditional surrender and six years after the outbreak of war, Vogue drew up and published a list of items under the title and headings "What we want to keep, to get rid of, to have back". In the last category, sandwiched between "real slap-up wedding cakes" and "ice-cream sundaes" was "easy, inexpensive world travel facilities". "For six slow-passing years every country was, for its own nationals, a concentration camp. Travel for travel's sake was an obsolete activity. How nostalgically did we not look forward to the day when, once again, we should be free to saunter into a travel agency, to turn over a pile of folders and negligently remark "Yes, I'll go there this summer."

But though hostilities had ceased in Europe, travel in the immediate post-war years was by no means the easy proposition everyone had hoped for. Petrol rationing continued into the Fifties except for a special Holiday Allowance introduced in 1949 — which prompted Vogue's first motoring feature in more than a decade, while stringent currency regulations controlled the amount of money that could be taken out of the country, thus limiting the choice of holiday and destination. "Though it is now more than two years since the last shot was fired," wrote Alec Waugh, "Europeans are still tied within their frontiers. A Briton can only set foot outside his Empire (substantial despite rumblings) for business reasons. An iron curtain lies across half the world. Two thirds of such shipping as is still afloat is commandeered. Air passages are expensive. Indeed, in the entire globe there are few places where it is practical for an Englishman to take a holiday".

But the prospect was not that bleak. In December 1946 Vogue celebrated the first peacetime voyage of the RMS *Queen Elizabeth* after its years of war duty — ferrying passengers now rather than troops — and the following month started a new year with the optimistic report that "one by one the ships are slipping back to port, and months later, like Queens recrowned, return to sea shining in their bright new paint. Ocean travel is slowly shedding its ghost-like quality and is once again becoming the most luxurious way of going places. To sit back and relax, waited on, drinking in the tang of the salt air, glorying in the clothes hanging in your stateroom; this was a dream — but this dream is back." More than anything else, the reappearance of these great liners in their original role seemed to confirm the world's gradual return to normality and Vogue ensured its subsequent travel features were equally encouraging. There were shopping and beauty hints for the traveller and although many of the more popular pre-war destinations remained out of bounds for some years there was still the Sterling Area with "a choice of exciting out-of-the-usual places". Included within its economic boundaries were the West Indies (rarely a hardship!) "with everything to offer in the grim winter months between January and April — rum and sun and lazy days;" Iceland, an alternative destination for ski-addicts whose favourite Alpine runs were momentarily closed to them; and Cyprus, of course, where, as Osbert Lancaster observed, "a new wave of Anglo-Saxon invaders has arrived. Winkled out of the plages of the South of France and villas of Capri by the currency restrictions, a stream of displaced good-timers has descended on this, the last outpost of the Sterling Area in the Mediterranean".

Even the currency restrictions were not initially as forbidding as they might have seemed. In 1948 Marghanita Laski and her husband holidayed in France and returned with a list of recommendations on how to make the most of a summer holiday abroad for £35. "The first essential is to buy everything in sterling before you start, so that not a penny of your foreign currency is wasted on unnecessary purchases. Cigarettes up to the maximum allowed, face creams and tooth paste are the obvious things to pack. An even wiser precaution, if you can bring yourself to it, is to ask the price of everything, even down to the odd cup of coffee."

How distant these considerations seem from the spirit of acceleration and carelessness that typified the Thirties, how dramatically our values had changed in the space of a decade. But as the war had taught us only too well, it was simply a question of making do until the situation improved.

On the way out

OFFICIAL PHOTOGRAPHER

by CECIL BEATON

Takorudi, Cairo, Kano, Teheran, Baghdad, Palmyra, Baalbec: these are some of the places I have visited during the last three months. It sounds like some magic-carpet tour, or pre-war millionaire's holiday. But no; I was sent by the Government to collect certain records and to take war photographs, and my jobs brought me to many historic sights of the East. During the airplane trips, or on ships or trains I wrote some notes in diary form. Here are some extracts from them:

Somewhere in North of England. We were taken out in a launch to what seemed, in the pearly Whistlerian haze of the first spring day, to be a craggy theatrical looking coastline, with pointed white precipices surmounted by a fairytale castle. This proved to be the vast camouflaged warship that was to be our home for the next weeks at sea.

Once on board, the element of time ceases to exist: the days fade into one another; the sea becomes bluer as the sun's rays become stronger. One finds oneself doing exactly the same things at the same time each day.

A submarine is sighted, depth charges dropped; a conning tower seen for a moment: it is possible that the U boat, badly shaken, may have got to its base, but . . . The ship's company now appear in tropical white kit. Flying fish are seen. The presence of an enemy armed cruiser is reported — a destroyer leaves the enemy in pursuit — our course is altered again — false alarm.

A signal arrives for the Captain and the Commander: "You will arrive day after tomorrow at 0900".

The convoy manoeuvres into position for entry into harbour. Through the scuttles we see a pale misty strip of land floating by. Land! and covered with thick lush tropical vegetation. Natives, incredibly black, come alongside, in spearlike canoes, to sell — of all magic things — bananas.

Ashore. The women, carrying mountains on their turbaned heads, walk with downcast eyes, and the dignity of queens. The audacity of their clothes is something even Paris could never attempt. Colours are blended with intuitive artistry: dark liver colour, forget-me-not blue, indigo, crimson, black, and lemon yellow are some of the dyes chosen for their draperies, printed in Manchester with designs of cricket bats, Red Cross ambulances, parachutists, winged hearts or sewing machines. The English colony wear dark glasses and solar topees.

We fly over the coast. From this height the tropical trees are like a carpet of Irish moss or spinach. A few clouds have broken away from the cumulus ceiling, and float over the jungle carpet below like wads of cotton wool.

At the end of the day, we welcome a surprising American meal of sweet and salty goods all mixed together. Then we sleep for eight hours in the centre of the African Desert.

Tobruk. We pitched camp in a Wadi near the sea: a most surprisingly fertile spot — almost an oasis — with fig trees, flowering cacti, a lot of wild flowers and wonderful birds. The adjutant had posted a sign "No shooting. By order". Cooked a good stew for dinner "M & V" (meat and vegetables) but too much Worcestershire sauce.

The gunfire like thunder storms: as soon as it was dark we went to bed: a nice sensation, going to sleep with the expiration of the day.

El Hacheim. Feel healthier than I have in years. Don't mind dirt or discomfort. Am only sorry to leave forward areas and regret returning to base. Have little appetite for Cairo or Alexandria now, but that is where much of my work is to be done.

The journey back through the scrubland of desolation was as eventless as a sleep without dreams — a drab, mottled recession of dun colour, stretching in all directions.

The aircraft lost height, banked, and we saw in the centre of this purposeless, uncompromising emptiness the oasis of Siwa with its minarets, towers and unexpected richness of trees. When we arrived, the adjutant welcomed us: "The colonel expects you to lunch at 1 o'clock — here is transport and a driver — until then the oasis is yours!" He pointed to the magnanimous gift of palm trees, date and apricot trees — pomegranates in flower — to the emerald green streams, Cleopatra's pool, the Temple of Jupiter Ammon and the old crumbled city, the apotheosis of all children's mud castle cities.

Alexandria. As we sailed past Admiral Vian's flagship we saw General Smuts in a topee, waving a baton and haranguing the sailors lined up in spotless white. A grand old man who always does more than is asked of him. This speech was unexpected and impromptu. The men tremendously heartened and thrilled.

Iraq to Iran . . . They are horrible mountains to fly over, especially in the late afternoon, when the heat pockets bang you about a lot. Since my attacks of "Egyptian Stomach" I find I am more sensitive to bumpings in the air. At last we landed — Teheran. Rows of

A woman of Lagos

A native of West Africa

A Palestinian beggar

American bombers were lined up. The American White Star will be painted red when the aircraft are flown over by Russian pilots to Kuibishev. A further convoy of bombers arriving while we waited to get our forty-four pounds of baggage out of the hold.

Woke early to a radio playing Iranian music for "setting-up" exercises — not much pep called for, but pretty. Outside, the Persian garden was disappointing — not at all romantic — with a lot of sand-coloured caked earth, cement and concrete. The Shah's Summer Palace, modern as the latest cinema, two huge silver sphinx as bastions to a flight of marble steps. Modernistic lights and furniture and furnishings — maroon-coloured geometric patterns and squashed strawberry and chutney colourings. The Queen in poison green — with knee-length skirts. The snow-striped mountain range above. The water gushes down through the streets of Teheran. The Persians — very beautiful, especially after the Egyptians — drink this water, throw their rubbish into it, bathe in it; with the result that ten per cent get terrible boils which take a year to cure.

Baghdad. As the aeroplane circled I saw Stuart Perowne hurrying down the steps to welcome me and take me off to the King. At the Palais des Fleurs, a crowd of guards clicking their bayonets and stamping their feet like horses in a stable. The Regent, a direct descendant of Mohamed, like a Marie Laurencin drawing, brought in the King by the hand. The King wore white shorts. He is seven years old. A great child, but not a precocious child. Grave and responsible but gay too. Perfectly brought up. I think the credit lies largely with Miss Borland, the nice, grey-haired young Scotswoman who sat there knitting a khaki scarf.

Jerusalem. The Russian Convent on the Mount of Olives gives you the impression that 500 years have suddenly rolled away. Against a cyclorama background of Jerusalem glimpsed through cypress trees, the old women were "playing up" almost too theatrically, bringing out the samovar; one sitting reading a 16th century Bible looked like Rembrandt's portrait of his mother.

Transjordania. As the evening sun was sinking slowly and casting long blue shadows on the desert scene we came across another car. Glubb, in a khaki-coloured tajrifa (head-dress) was returning, with a colonel and two highly coloured Arab henchmen in the back of his car, from the camp a few miles on. He looked baffled and miserable at the sight of me, but thanks to him, we had a thrilling evening being entertained by the Arab Legion in their scarlet, pink and khaki uniforms — sitting in a circle around a charcoal fire. Slept in a wooden hut under a mosquito netting — this a grand fortress against the cockroaches and the large spider I had seen last thing before turning down the lamp. The heat of the desert turns to wind at night, and three times I had to brave the insect world to shut the door which blew off the latch.

H.Q. The R.A.F. are doing as many sorties as ever they were in the desert, though now they have comparatively few landing grounds. German aircraft never seen by day, and we have aircraft that dive on tanks, firing a gun as big as a Bofors. When these "Tankbusters" score a hit the tank is not just damaged: it is obliterated.

En route for Home. The skipper of our aircraft had achieved almost a record run covering the distance that before, on the way out, we had taken three days to conquer. We cut through the bright sky at tremendous speed at such a height it would take us nearly a hundred miles to descend slowly to the jungle below.

It was a new sensation waking up at 1.30 a.m. to shave and start the day. We got into a flying boat and took off in the blackness of night. Difficult to tell at what point we were airborne. Silk-lined walls, arm chairs like Pullmans, various compartments for eating, sleeping, smoking — this is the aircraft that took Churchill to America. How much longer the return journey seems — how grateful I am to be among the lucky ones on the last lap for home.

ABROAD IN EDINBURGH

by AUDREY STANLEY OF ALDERLEY

Crossing the Border now is as interesting as crossing the Channel was before the war; and I must confess I was astonished to find, after having travelled about the world much, that Edinburgh, with its conglomeration of architecture, good and bad, remains one of the loveliest cities in the world.

It reminded me of a foreign city, not of any particular one, but a medley of memories of almost all. Its wide boulevards with statues at all four corners, reminded me of Washington; the squares and crescents, of Bloomsbury; apertures in narrow streets, revealing deep stairways and unexpected vistas, recalled Southern Spain. The tall granite houses, with wynds like deep incisions dividing them, and the shabby shopsigns in Candlemakers' Row, down by the old Grass Market, reminded me of parts of Paris.

Princes Street, however, could not be anywhere but in Edinburgh. Its commercial façade of stores, tartan shops, bakeries and confectioners (all now as bare as Mother Hubbard's cupboard after noon) and opposite, close enough to throw a biscuit, the castle, 240 feet above, on a level with the church spires. The whole enshrouded in a Scotch mist, which about mid-day lifts to reveal — as a romantic back-drop to the scene — the Pentland Hills, silhouetted against the sky-line.

This historic city, so scarred by former battles, at first sight appears little changed by this war. Princes Street is packed with people admiring the shop windows and enjoying a little well-earned leisure for 48 hours. Canadian troops have a saying "The farther north and the colder the climate, the warmer the hospitality". This is probably the reason why Edinburgh is such a popular place for leave. The shortage of servants and fuel has brought people from the country into the town.

I climbed to the top of the castle, through the seven gateways, each one famed in Scottish history. My fellow sight-seers were Dominion troops. The men all know 121A Princes Street, the Victoria League Club, and treat it as their home. It is run by Lady Wallace; Harriet, Lady Findlay, and her brother Admiral Backhouse. They serve 30,000 meals a month, provide beds if accommodation is needed, and find private hospitality.

The W.V.S. in Scotland is headed by Lady Ruth Balfour and five Regional Administrators. They run Emergency Food Vans for air-raids. In a lull, these vans are used for hot meals for war workers, and for residential schools, financed by the "Save the Children Fund" from America. They have set up an Allied Information Bureau where twelve languages are spoken. Czechs, Poles, Frenchmen flock to it; in fact, so many foreigners visit the city, that a page in French, headed "Pour Nos Alliés" has been incorporated in the new Guidebook to Edinburgh.

The W.V.S. also pack vegetables for mine-sweeping crews in East Lothian and form the personnel of the efficient Guide Service which directs the forces on arrival, and copes with their problems. There are countless other jobs to do.

The Lord Provost, Will Y. Darling, true to his name, is one of the most beloved personalities in Edinburgh. I saw him in his shop, wearing his top-hat, from which he is never parted. He told me, with pride, of the activities of the town. He pointed to the public parks, partially given over to Food Production; to the Citizens' Advice Bureau, which is never stumped by any question; and took off his hat to the Church of Scotland, which runs canteens and cinemas to military outposts.

No wonder people like Edinburgh for their leave.

GOING DOWN
TO THE SEA AGAIN

by ROSE MACAULAY

To a thoughtful mind, remarked the *Brighthelmstone Ambulator* in the eighteenth century, the ocean is always an interesting object; and never did this journal print a truer word. So much salt water all together in a vast expanse, beating or lapping on the edges of the land — no wonder it has always excited the minds, both thoughtful and thoughtless, of mankind. After all, we lived and breathed in it once, more million years ago than we care to count; it is our aboriginal home. Now it seems strange, fantastic, intimidating, alluring, a magical element, a romantic adventure. We leave, when we can, the prose and comfort of cities, brave the turbulent anguish of trains, in order to spend a week, a weekend, a month, beside this chill and romantic waste of waters sliding and tossing up and down delightful shining sands.

Five years ago, the sea round our island became a war casualty; access to most of it was forbidden; it was hedged off behind barbed wire of the most alarming nature; mines were sown in its sands; everything was done to make it forbidding to invaders and forbidden to ourselves. In the event, all these arrangements proved unnecessary; but Hitler had not informed us that he was not going to arrive. And perhaps, but for all that intimidating wire and those buried mines, he might have had a shot at it, who knows? Anyhow, the effect of making our sea unapproachable by us has given it the extra burnish of a forbidden dream country; and now that we are free of it, it will burst on our astonished eyes with new and stunning strangeness; we shall exclaim "Is this the mighty ocean? Is this all?" with the fervent astonishment of childhood.

Thousands of us will, in fact, be actual children. They will perhaps have seen the ocean in pictures, moving and still: they will have been told of the great blue wilderness with its tossing white flowers; they may know how south sea islanders leap and dive into it, how white people lie beside it cooking themselves in the sun. They will have a shock at first, when they see that the sea that girdles their native land is not blue and warm and smooth, but grey and cold and rough; they will have a worse (possibly a fatal) shock when they enter it; but, should they survive, they will toughen and harden, and after the first day or so should be enough acclimatised to enjoy it. After all, they have no standards to measure it by. Their elders may be dreaming wistfully of warmer, better seas, "beside a pumice isle in Baiae's bay", seas in which they could swim and float all day, shores on which, coming out, they could lie and bake, whereas here, like Milton's smooth Adonis from his rock, they run purple to the sea, swim out through cold waves, splashing as they swim to avert cramp, and emerge more purple than when they went in. But to children it is just bathing; they know no other, and it is a superb adventure. So, even, is paddling. So is running over the glistening sands whence the tide has ebbed leaving behind it illimitable treasures — seaweed, pink shells, star-fish, old tins.

They follow the sea out, they build sand castles where late the ocean flowed, they retire from its advancing flood with shrieks of pleasure. The sand may be three parts mud, into which the feet deliciously squelch; it may be pebbly; it may be wriggling with sea-worms, oozy with sea foliage; it may be hard, glistening brown sand; best of all, it may be rocks. Best, because where there are rocks there are pools, and where there are rock pools there is green water, anemones, crabs, shrimps. Armed with a shrimping net you can wade among these evasive beings, hunt among the crevices and seaweed for crabs, fright the shy anemone, dip your net for shrimps; should you catch one, you bring it back for tea.

If you are not a hunter, you can sit by the pool and dabble, and watch the sky and clouds in its green shallows. The tide laps in, wave over wave; it brims and over-runs now one pool now another; at last it lies heaving and lapping over all the spur of rocks. It runs on into the cave behind, splashing and hissing as it enters, then, when right inside those dim depths, "voiced like a great bell swinging in a dome"; if you have been playing smugglers there, it is more than time to flee.

Perhaps, instead, you have been playing pirates. But for this you need a boat. You can then maroon someone on a lonely rock, or on a cannibal-infested island or coast. All the things that can be done with a boat need no suggestions. You can bathe from it; whether you can climb into it again is another matter.

But most of us have no boat; we must bathe from the shore or from the rocks. If we are on a rocky part of the Cornish coast, we undress on the rocks and dive straight from them into deep green cold water. If we can swim, we swim out into the cove and beyond, and look back at the little fishing town on its cliffs, clinging there as it has clung for centuries. Outside the little cove the sea is gurly and grey; inside, beneath the shadow of rocks, it is clear deep green; the cove is pebbly, it smells of fish; stretched on the sands to dry are brown nets and painted fishing boats.

If you are a good swimmer, you can swim out beyond the throng, who are mostly coast bound; swim and swim, until, far out, you are alone with heaving green waves and crying gulls, and the human noises reach you only faintly from the shore.

But even if you cannot swim at all, are too cold to wade, too old or lazy to scramble about rocks, there is still the sea. You may watch it through a whole day, and find it never for five minutes the same. It will have the sheen of a pearly floor; it will change to iris, violet ringed with silver-grey like a pigeon, softly lifting smooth wings, with gentle murmurs and coos; the silver will be shot with golden lights; a wind blows, ruffling up flecks of white flowers, that swell to cauliflowers in a green heaving field; green, grey and indigo, the cloud shadows and the currents race before the wind; the clouds go, the sky clears, the wind drops and the white flowers sink into their beds: the sea is steel blue. Not the crystalline blue of the summer Mediterranean; never that; but blue. Evening falls; the blue grows dimmer, purer, more exquisite; night steals over it, and it is a purple waste. Never still, never the same; whatever may disappoint you at the seaside, the colour of the sea will not; unless you are of those who long always for Mediterranean blue and will not be comforted by all the other colours of the rainbow. But in that case you will be wiser not to spoil your vision of the sea by visiting the English coast; cherish it against a better day when we are free of better seas.

For those not thus enspelled by what songs the sirens sing abroad, the British seas can offer much, alike to the brave and hardy who go completely into them, to those who only wade, and to those who do neither, but sit in deckchairs, braving only the risks of the mined beach, reading their books, smelling the seaweed and fish which compose the mixture known as ozone; and to those who lie lulled and entranced, staring throughout the day at the "dragon-green, the luminous, the dark, the serpent-haunted sea", which they have reached again at last after five years of absence; and all they hope is that no one will bring in shrimps for tea. Those little pink, whiskered beings — they were never designed for human food. But that is another point about the seaside — people will eat anything there.

R.M.S.
QUEEN ELIZABETH

This was her sixty-first ocean crossing but she felt young, for it was her peacetime début. She wore a bright new dress of black, white and red, very different from the drab grey overcoat of the six war years, worn thin by travelling some five hundred thousand miles through submarine-infested waters. (The "Queen" always travelled without an escort.) She had carried eight hundred thousand service men to and from battle fronts.

Now leaving Southampton, she was surrounded by swarming tugboats, motor yachts, racing boats and excursion steamers all whistling and flagged, all loaded with farewell waving crowds. The bluish-grey, misty English Channel sky was full of roaring planes of all types: nosy little helicopters, fighters and bombers. Hydroplanes stood lined up for parade, and finally fireworks closed the performance. The "Queen" was left alone, quiet and steady, listening to the deep, steady hum of her engines. She felt lighthearted and lightheaded, with only twenty-two hundred passengers; she had made one trip carrying a whole division of fifteen thousand men in battledress. Their initials were still carved on her handrails. But now those days were past and there were lights and music and pretty women aboard. This was a celebration, a refresher course in luxury, leisure, and how to enjoy them. The passenger list was so packed with great names that sixty reporters demanded daily press conferences. This was a curtain raiser, the come-back of a much missed star known as pre-war luxury.

Confronted by so much, people realized suddenly that it was hard to relax, to laugh and be light-hearted all day for five days. In the evening the women consciously dressed down, most of them in long black sheaths with few jewels in evidence. (They looked far more dashing during the day in their magnificently cut tweeds.)

There was little organized fun. There was nothing to do, and that was enough to keep everyone doubly busy. Busy as twenty-one hundred creamy plastic telephones buzzing with the day's plans. Whether to have a facial or a shampoo or was there time for both? Whether to play deck tennis or indoor squash. Or bridge in one of the two winter gardens. Which of the six bars to meet in before lunch.

There were quantities of fresh flowers everywhere. Quantities of food but no caviar. Quantities of liquor and superb service. There was a glistening sense of overall newness. Twenty-one thousand spanking new pieces of furniture filled her cabins and public rooms. Not a chair had ever been sat in before this trip, nor a glass sipped from. There were new gadgets. The world's largest windshield wiper to throw off rain and snow from the vital wheelhouse windows. A fog-horn toned down to two octaves below middle A could be heard growling ten miles at sea, but to passenger ears it never rose above a whisper.

At night the "Queen" was ablaze with jewels — thirty thousand electric lights all lit — gave her a make-believe look. But she was very real as she steamed into New York. Her arrival was as jubilant as her departure. Fireboats, tugs, motor launches and more helicopters followed her past the prow of Manhattan. When at last she tied up at her flag festooned pier even the customs officers in their blue uniforms were grinning a greeting. The "Queen" had come to town.

HOLIDAY IN FRANCE

by MARGHANITA LASKI

We are sitting on the terrace of a pub in Provence under a canopy of wistaria. The air is heavy with lilac and narcissus and apple-blossom, and sweet-scented purple iris are growing at our feet. At the next table a large party who have come up from Marseilles for the day in a lorry are singing a sentimental ballad about a poor girl who lived in Paris and every Sunday bought roses, white roses for her mother. The sky is blue all over, the olive-trees are swaying silver in the breeze; the countryside to the south is covered with puffs of blossom, pink and white and deep purple peach; to the north rise the grey mountains of the Luberon smelling of lavender and rosemary and thyme. We have just lunched off *pâté* and asparagus and *andouiettes* and a dish made of biscuits soaked in sweet white wine, covered with chocolate and topped with grapes-in-brandy. In the distance a small hill is crowned with a sand-coloured Provençal village, an old stone castle four-square beside it. To my left, a little waterfall splashes into a deep black pool.

And all this for two guineas a day for both of us.

I must admit that when we started from Boulogne with forty pounds and the car, we didn't really think we'd get as far as the "Paradou" at Lourmarin. On the Autocarrier, people were saying how it cost a packet even to set foot in France and what with French dirt and incompetence and lack of coffee — well, they were just going to dash through to Switzerland as quickly as ever they could.

But we didn't feel that way. We have never thought the French either dirty or incompetent; rather a people who prefer not to spend their money communally or on outward show. And then we love France, holding it to be, in its infinite variations of countryside, the most beautiful country in the world. And since we had, before the war, reckoned that two pounds a day would see us anywhere in Europe with a car, well-fed and with a sufficiency of comfort, we thought we'd see how far forty pounds would take us now.

Where to go for the night was our first problem. Paris, we knew, was financially out of the question, what with temptations of one sort and another when one got there. To go south-east to Rheims or due south to the Verneuil area meant that the whole of our first day would be on dull roads we had driven too often before. After prolonged study of the appropriate Michelin map — which thoughtfully and reliably marks the pictures-que roads — we decided to make for that part of the Seine that lies about fifty kilometres to the west of Paris.

As far as food went, we had an inauspicious start. We stopped at a café in Montreuil and asked for a snack which turned out to be stale sandwiches and a cup of tea or that appalling *mélange* that passes for coffee; still, it only cost a shilling, which was hopeful. Then we turned off the dreary pit-holed N.I. just before Abbeville and immediately were in lovely country, little hills and streams and meadows dotted with huge scentless cowslips.

We drove into Les Andelys just before dinner. We weren't really expecting a *very* cheap night, being so near Paris, and when we saw the "Hotel des Fleurs", we knew we wanted to stay there; gaily painted; scarlet flowers in its window-boxes, a pretty old house as nicely decorated inside as out. Still more surprising, its proprietor was an Englishman.

Over a glass of Calvados he gave us some good advice. He didn't believe, he said, that two people could get far in France on three pounds a day, of which nearly a pound would go straightway on the car whenever we were travelling. Still, if we were really determined to try, one thing was essential, *always to ask the price of everything, even down to the odd cup of coffee, before we agreed to take it.* Then we walked across the dark tree-shaded square among the old houses to the tow-path by the Seine and watched a great barge slip by in the twilight.

Next day the sky was entirely blue and we started to drive south. We were making for Chartres — to see the windows again — and to Orleans to change some money. Soon we got hungry, what with a general sense of happiness and being unaccustomed to small breakfasts, and pulled up before a little café-cum-épicerie-cum-dairy in a small town.

We could have coffee and bread and butter, the fat proprietress said. It didn't sound very promising and, mindful of our instructions, we asked how much it would be. Fifty francs, she said (which is about two bob) and we couldn't be bothered to go further so we agreed.

Huge bowls of coffee, she brought us, soup-bowls of real coffee and milk and sugar and table-spoons to drink it with; she brought us a long loaf of crisp fresh bread and a great slab of butter and there we sat gorging in the sun.

After that, you won't be surprised to hear that our lunch was a small one, ten bobs' worth of *potage* and steak-and-chips and beer and cheese and coffee. It wouldn't have cost so much if we hadn't forgotten to ask the price of the coffee first.

We came that night to Hérisson — which means "hedgehog" — a little walled village beside a river off the main road from St. Amand to Montluçon. The inn was called the "Petit Pierre", and they fed and slept and breakfasted us well for about seventeen-and-six.

Next day we were driving over the Massif Central. My husband had a feeling that we *must* see Le Puy which someone — but he'd forgotten whom — had told him was the most beautiful town in France.

It isn't! But it's such a joke that it's worth a brief visit. Le Puy, by some eccentric dispensation of nature, is dotted with great needle-like monoliths of rock and on each of these the French, with a really majestic sense of incongruity, have erected an outsize religious monument, on one a chapel, on another a Virgin. Alas, it's one of those visual jokes, and it loses in the telling.

After Le Puy, we were deep in the mountains of the Massif Central, tall, strange and remote, our road hair-pinning among peaks and deep shadowed gorges. We spent the night in an ugly modern pub just outside a mountain village south of La Bastide. We had got into the region of six-course meals now, and for the first time wine was included in the price. There was, of course, nowhere to sit after dinner but the hideous dining-room or the equally hideous café across the hall. There never is in these small hotels, but what the hell! You can wander round the village, you can go to bed early, or you can sit and drink with the *patron* and his wife and talk about rationing and Communism and listen, a pleasure that never palls for me, to their little cries of horror when you explain that the English like mutton with mint sauce.

Soon after we left that inn, we slid down over the last hairpin bends — and we were in Provence, once more after seven years, back in the most lovely, most satisfying countryside in the world. We drove through Nîmes and Arles and Tarascon and Avignon, that crowded, dusty, gay, sunny city. We drove east to "the Paradou" at Lourmarin and here we have been for a week, fishing ineffectually for tench, making little excursions to see the Mediterranean, climbing the hills, talking, and lying in the sun. We have had two baths and eleven days of our holiday and we have spent twenty-seven pounds. Tomorrow we start for home.

WINTER AT HOME

by JOHN BETJEMAN

Now comes the time when gardeners have given up trying to sweep away leaves. We have taken the honesty out of the top shelf in the linen cupboard and stuck it in the brass altar vases of the village church. Last Sunday the last of the Michaelmas daisies were too frost-bitten to be conducive to public worship. Now England, having got rid of tourists and those who feel they must seek sunlight, settles down to be herself. With any luck there will be fogs in November and December so that the sky will not be poisoned with aeroplanes and a quiet of eternity will be about us, just the drip drip from wet branches and smells of woodsmoke and fungus in the lanes. The Women's Institute will take on new life with a revival of basket making; more leather-work purses will be made than there is money to put into them, and even Mrs. Hutchinson's talk on her visit to Rhodesia will seem interesting although the magic lantern is certain to fail.

Ah! the sweet prelude to an English winter! For me it is so infinitely a more beautiful season than any other, which is just as well since it goes on for most of the year. It is a time when there is more colour in the country than there was ever before. Ploughed fields take on a look like a farming scene in the initial letter of a mediaeval manuscript. Bricks are an intenser red and Cotswold stone is more golden, the limestone and granite of the north is more silver, bare branches are like pressed seaweed against the pale blue sky. Whatever remains green is more deeply, richly green than it was before. This waiting, intense stillness is generally a prelude to a storm. The smallest sound is easily heard. Cocks are continually crowing, ducks quacking as though they were happy, and even across three miles of still, misty fields, it is possible to distinguish all six of the church bells as men practise method ringing in the oil-lit evening tower. But this night there is not one of those gigantic winter sunsets and the house is more than usually full of spiders, huge hairy ones which cast a shadow twice their own size on the drawing room carpet. And then, in the night the storm begins. Will the trees stand it, this gale which makes them roar and creak and roar again? Will the earth ever be able to soak in these torrents which beat the house, brim the water-butts and swish on grass and gravel? And has anyone remembered to shut the upstairs window?

Winter is the one time when I feel I can indulge myself in reading what I like instead of what I ought to read. Time stretches out a little more and I stretch myself with it. Slow books come back and I try to forget our jerky modern novels. While the storm shakes the shutters, I re-read Scott, generally starting with *The Heart of Midlothian.* And as the great rumbling periods, as surely and steadily as a stage-coach, carry me back to Edinburgh, the most beautiful city in these islands, I feel an *embarras de richesse.* There is too much I want to read, too many memories I wish to experience.

Winter is the time for reading poetry and often I discover for myself some minor English poet, a country parson who on just such a night, must have sat in his study and blown sand off lines like these, written in ink made of oak-gall:—

> "Soon as eve closes, the loud hooting owl
> That loves the turbulent and frosty night
> Perches aloft upon the rocking elm
> And halloes to the moon."

And here they are, these lines, widely spaced upon the printed page and hundreds more, by the Reverend James Hurdis, D.D., Incumbent of Bishopstone, Sussex, printed a century and a half ago, some of the most perfect descriptions of an English winter that were ever written in English. And you and I are probably the only people in England who are reading Hurdis. The smell of the old book is like a country church when first you open its door, the look of the pages is spacious like the age in which it was written and the broad margins isolate the poetry as Bishopstone must then have been isolated among windy miles of sheep-nibbled downs.

There is no need only to escape into the civilised past, which is more easily done in winter than in any other time of the year. Even modern barbarism becomes almost human, especially in places which make their money out of summer visitors. Am I wrong in thinking that the blonde with a handkerchief wound round her head and a cigarette in her mouth, is a little politer now when she refuses to sell me the cigarettes I know she has in hundreds under the counter? Do I perceive a mood less casual in the bar-attendant at the grand hotel? Is it possible that when I ask for a room at the reception desk, I will actually be accommodated instead of being sent away with a scornful refusal? Maybe this is all imagination. But of this I am quite certain, when I receive my fee for describing to you these joys of winter, I shall indulge in the greatest winter joy I know. I shall take the train to the coast and spend a night by the sea.

The train from London will be fairly empty. By the time evening has set in there will be hardly anyone in it at all, for the larger towns on the way to the sea will have taken off most of the passengers. What started as an express, will have turned into a local train, stopping at oil-lit stations while the gale whistles in the ventilators of empty carriages. Standing out white on a blue glass ground, will appear the names of wayside stations and reflected in a puddle, the light of a farmer's car in the yard will sparkle beyond the platform fence.

Then we will go into the windy dark until at last there is a station slightly more important than those we have passed, lit with gas instead of oil and that is mine. I will hear the soft local accent, smell the salt in the wet and warmer air and descry through the lines of rain that lace the taxi's windscreen, bulks of houses that were full and formid-able in summer and now have not a light in any of their windows.

And then I will see the village of my youth and of my holidays. There will be cigarettes in the post office, no one about but the old friends who are permanent residents. And before I see friends or buy cigarettes, I will run down the lane to the sea. Feathery tamarisk weighed down with rain drops and black against the night sky, noise of lapping waves and smell of seaweed, soft crunch of sand under my shoes and there, all to myself, faintly visible under a watery moon, the cold and spreading beach. No vestige of picnics now, no cars in the car park, no lovers on the cliff path, no bathers, golfers, sports girls or sand castles, nothing but shadowy cliffs and the ever faithful sea.

Thump-umph! I will hear the breakers sucked and shot away from the blowhole and in the little moonlight, the rollers will be, to my imagination, more mountainous than ever they have been before. And safe in bed, I shall listen to the gale beating the window and hear, above the wind, the plunge and roar of the breakers against the cliff.

"They come — they mount — they charge in vain,
Thus far, incalculable main!
No more! thine hosts have not o'erthrown
The lichen on the barrier-stone."

With Parson Hawker's poem *The Storm* in my head, I shall switch the light out for one of the long, deep country sleeps of winter.

WEST INDIES

by ALEC WAUGH

For six slow-passing years travel for travel's sake was an obsolete activity. How nostalgically did we not look forward to the day when, once again, we should be free to saunter into a travel agency, to turn over a pile of folders and negligently remark, "Yes, I'll go there this summer."

But though it is now more than two years since the last shot was fired, travel has by no means become the easy proposition we had expected. Europeans are still tied within their frontiers. A Briton can only set foot outside his empire for business reasons. An iron curtain lies across half the world. Two-thirds of such shipping as is still afloat is commandeered. Air passages are expensive. Indeed, in the entire globe there are few places where it is practical for an Englishman to take a holiday. In recompense, however, it can be safely said that those few places are among the pleasantest that the world has to offer to the traveller, particularly in the case of the West Indian islands.

The West Indies have, indeed, everything to offer in the grim winter months between January and April. They provide every kind of sport: cricket and golf and tennis; fishing, shooting, riding. Fruit and fish are plentiful. Rum is a *vin de pays,* and when the sun is shining there is not a great deal to spend money on. By day you idle on a beach, in the evening you sip cocktails on a veranda. One day becomes the next.

Nor could the climate during those three months be better. It is hot to the extent that a man wears ducks or Palmbeach clothes by day and a white dinner jacket in the evening. He would feel overweighted by a flannel suit; but there is no equivalent for the overpowering dry heat of Iraq or for the exhausting damp heat of Malaya. Trinidad is the only island that has a sticky climate, but even in Trinidad there is a cool breeze at night. There is very little malaria, and mosquitoes are rarely troublesome. There is a certain amount of rain. But the showers though violent, are brief. You are quite likely to get soaked, but you are very unlikely to have your plans for a whole day ruined.

The way of life there is as gracious and congenial as the setting. In whatever island he may choose to visit, the routine of a traveller's day will be very similar. He will wake shortly after six, in a large bare hotel bedroom. The sunlight, striking through the shutters, will be designing a zebra pattern on the walls and ceiling. He will throw back the shutters and walk out on to his balcony. The sun will be warm upon his cheeks, but a cool breeze will be blowing from the hills. Across the road an untidy garden will be bright with yellow cassia. The road below will be narrow and uneven, on the one side climbing into the mountains in whose shelter the town is built, on the other side running down into the port. Above grey-tiled and corrugated iron roofs he will see the grey blue stretches of the harbour. Square-sailed fishing boats will be tacking near the shore. A launch carrying coastal cargo will be chunking its slow way between them. Shadowy on the horizon is the outline of another island.

An expedition to one of the estates will probably have been arranged for him. He will be driven, by a mounting, circling road, into the hills. The valleys will be bright with sugar cane. The bush will be dotted with wattle and corrugated iron shacks. Here and there he will see the ruined masonry of an aqueduct or a gateway, relics of the old plantation days.

94

In Trinidad and Grenada he will be taken to see the working of the cocoa. He will watch the trampling of the seeds for polish in large circular cauldrons by laughing, sweating labourers, with their trousers rolled above their knees. In St Vincent he will be taken to see an arrowroot plantation. The factories are as clean as dairies. In Antigua and in Barbados he will watch bundles of sugar cane crushed between rollers till the last drop of juice has been extracted.

He will be back from his expedition in time for a pre-lunch swim. Nowhere in the world is there better bathing. There is none of the coral against which in Tahiti you have to be so much upon your guard that it is foolish to bathe barefooted. The water is fresher and has more bite than the Mediterranean's. There is no reason to be afraid of sunstroke, and the precautions that you take against sunburn on the Riviera are adequate in the Caribbean. An hour on the beach sends him back with a good appetite to lunch, and in need of the hour of siesta that will follow it and from which he will wake refreshed for the strenuous period that follows tea.

That period is the most pleasant of the day.

The social life of the island is concentrated upon the next few hours. It is then that the tennis courts are crowded; that stumps are pitched on the cricket field, that caddies are summoned to the links. The heat has lessened, a breeze is blowing from the hills. There seems to be more colour in the flowers; the leaves and grasses that by day had become polished surfaces to reflect the sunlight, resume their own fresh greens. All day one has walked at the pace of a slow motion film. At last one can move with freedom. One has the sense of having one's limbs restored to one. And later, in the swift fallen dusk it is with a contented feeling of languor that one sits out on the verandah of the club over one's punch or swizzle.

How often, during the war, when evening fell upon bomb-scarred London, or the brown burnt wastes of the Syrian desert, have I not wished myself back on to a small West Indian island.

CYPRUS

by OSBERT LANCASTER

Few among the various remote and improbable dependencies which, during the course of the eighteenth and nineteenth centuries, the British Crown rather absent-mindedly acquired, have so extraordinary a history or so fantastically mixed a culture as Cyprus. Tucked away at the extreme eastern end of the Mediterranean, the Cypriots were from the earliest times exposed to the conflicting influences of powerful neighbours and consequently developed a remarkable facility for compromise and understandable inability to make up their minds. Hovering uncertainly between Europe and Asia, they have always alternated between an Oriental fatalism and a passionate philhellenism, and have never, for more than a single century, controlled their own destinies.

An inhibiting dualism is reflected even in the landscape of the island. Along the North Coast opposite Asia Minor there stretches a thin chain of limestone mountains of fantastic, but not unfamiliar beauty; save for a subtle difference in the quality of the light, one might be in Euboea or Crete. By contrast, the vast plain which lies to the south, and occupies most of the island, has about it nothing of Greece nor of Europe. Dead flat, dusty-red in colour, and intensely cultivated for a short period in the year, it stretches monotonously away to the sea on the south and east, and to the foothills of the Troodos on the west.

All across the variegated landscape are scattered buildings of the most exotic and unsuitable character, of which the Troodos holiday camps are only the most recent examples. Of classical antiquity little enough remains in the way of architecture, a loss which the execrable bad taste of most of the details which have survived forbids us to deplore, but Byzantium is better represented. It is true that there exists no single church that can compare with the best in Constantinople or Greece, but the monastery of Antiphonitis, set in a high cleft of the northern range, does not owe its charm wholly to the beauty of its setting, and certain of the strange little wooden-roofed churches, tucked away in remote valleys of the Troodos, though provincial, have great character, and their wall paintings constitute what is perhaps the best-preserved and least studied corpus of Byzantine pictorial art that exists anywhere.

At the beginning of the Third Crusade, Cyprus was enjoying, or perhaps more accurately undergoing, a period of temporary independence. An obscure member of the imperial family had recently declared himself the sole sovereign of the island, which he proceeded to misgovern and exploit to his heart's content. His arbitrary actions were resented but uncontested, but when he was so misguided as to try to interfere with certain members of the Third Crusade, Richard Coeur-de-Lion reacted forcibly and at once. In the course of a short campaign, he overthrew the tyrant and annexed the island which, for the next four hundred years, remained an isolated outpost of European feudalism, surrounded, after the fall of the Latin kingdom of Jerusalem, on all sides by the Mussulmans.

It is the visible remains of this period which lend to Cyprus its peculiarly exotic, almost surrealist, quality. The most immediately remarkable are perhaps the three great castles of Hillorion, Kantara and Buffavento.

Hardly less moving, although in a different style, are the churches and the cathedral of Famagusta. In an almost abandoned area, enclosed by the circuit of vast Venetian walls, are the remains of more than a hundred churches, of which at least twenty are considerable ruins. Rising above groves of palms and fringed by dilapidated Turkish houses built from mediaeval rubble, these towers and pinnacles, flamboyant windows innocent of glass, but still retaining their elaborate tracery, create the most extraordinary impression.

Nowhere is this feeling of being in two totally different worlds at once so strongly induced as in the cathedral itself. Nave, choir, triforium, vaulting. Gothic piers still provide a framework of Western Christendom, upon which is superimposed a wholly Moslem surface. Coats of whitewash, rugs orientated to Mecca and cutting diagonally across the main line of the aisles, mihrabs and mimba, and the monotonous intoning of the turbaned imam all combine, with only limited success, in a determined effort to expunge from the mind of the beholder every remembrance of the origins of the shrine.

The Turks, who held the island from the sixteenth to the end of the nineteenth century, apart from adaptations, made, and still make, their presence felt in a number of ways. A few original mosques, as opposed to converted churches, one of which shelters the remains of the Prophet's aunt who was so unlucky as to fall from her mule and break her neck on the shores of the salt-lake near Larnaca; cemeteries in which turbaned tombstones are visible above the tamarisks, testify to their past activity. Today, though vastly outnumbered by the Greeks, they still present their individuality and national characteristics. The women, though usually unveiled, retain their bright blue or black all-enveloping shawls, the men their fezes, turbans and cummerbunds. The muezzin still calls from the minarets, the hubble-bubble is still part of the equipment of every coffee shop.

The British, who have administered the Island since the '80s of the last century, are not as yet commemorated by quite such striking monuments as the Crusaders, but have nevertheless stamped their image on the face of the land in a number of characteristic ways. All over the island one encounters dogs in which various features clearly indicate a fairly direct, though by no means unmixed descent from the original pack of fox-hounds brought in the last century by British sportsmen. Places of worship in a robust Victorian Gothic, less pure in style but every bit as exotic, as the churches of Famagusta, provide a weekly rallying place for a vintage collection of retired Indian Army colonels and colonial administrators in curious Panama hats and striking club ties, together with their determined and energetic women-folk. After service, all will repair to the country-club to enjoy the feeling of superiority engendered in a land of ouzo and arak by the consumption of pink-gins. Such, until very recently, was the pattern of life of the ruling race, but since the last war a subtle change has come about. Not only is the dominant position of the retired, and none too generously pensioned, colony of soldiers and administrators threatened by the rising cost of living, but a new wave of Anglo-Saxon invaders has arrived; sail-cloth beach slacks and espadrilles now jostle neatly-pressed flannels and shantung imprimés in the club, and the sound of the cocktail shaker is heard in the land. The two groups are engaged in a struggle of which the issue can hardly be in doubt. The newcomers have youth, money and a twentieth-century ruthlessness to which the old brigade can only oppose their tenacious belief in a standard of behaviour which, even in the land of its origin, appears outmoded. But it would seem unlikely that their triumph will prove very long-lived; in the world of the Cominform and Hiroshima the "Rockpool" itself takes on an old-world twentyish air. It may well be that this island, the very name of which was in antiquity synonymous with pleasure, will prove the still centre of the coming hurricane and may thus be privileged to catch the last dying echoes of the swan-song of the roaring 'twenties.

ICELAND

by JAMES WHITTAKER

The worst thing about Iceland is its name: yet the average difference in temperature over the whole year when compared with the British Isles is only four degrees. Winter in New York is infinitely colder than in Iceland. In January, which is the coldest month in the year, the average temperature is 33 degrees Fahrenheit. The name Iceland conjures a vision of glacial coldness and arctic desolation, yet it would be far nearer the truth to call the country "Fireland," for there is visible daily evidence of immense volcanic forces at work over large parts of the land.

If you want to head away from the beaten track, away from the usual tourist routes, and away from all the irritant evils that develop on such routes, then Iceland is the place for you. Here is an unspoiled land of immense distances and brilliant skies, colourful mountains and singing rivers (none of which are navigable), vast volcanic deserts comparable only to the surface of the moon, beautiful fjords and distant snow-capped peaks rising above mighty glaciers. . . . Here is a land, 40,000 square miles in area (a fifth larger than the whole of Ireland), lying halfway between the old and new worlds, with its head cooled by the Arctic Seas, and its feet bathed in the warm currents from the Gulf Stream. Here is a land which offers nothing but itself in terms of colour, peace and serenity under the most brilliant and luminous atmosphere to be found in any inhabited part of the globe. Here is a land that was once remote; now it takes five hours from Prestwick.

Ski-ing in Iceland is nothing at all like ski-ing in Switzerland, where winter sports are highly organized, with beginners' slopes everywhere and instructors on hand day and night, and mountain railways up every mountain. In Iceland, ski-ing, mountaineering, tramping, camping is very much an individual business and an individual's own concern. True, help and tuition may be had, and advice will be freely given by Icelanders who have skied from an early age but, all in all, the delight, excitement and adventure attendant on Icelandic ski-ing depends entirely on what the individual cares to expend.

The almost indescribable charm of Iceland lies in its purity of atmosphere: the winds that blow from the north come across the Arctic Seas — the winds from the west race across Greenland's mighty ice-cap — the winds from the east have passed over the polar seas and the north of Norway — whilst the winds from the south have crossed the broad Atlantic.

The colour of Iceland goes right across the spectrum-band: it is both the delight and exasperation of the traveller, artist, and painter, that no-one short of a genius can adequately convey the vividness of this northern land. The tremendous visibility sharpens and intensifies all colour so that the land, to the foreign eye, looks as though Matisse had been let loose. This brilliant colouring, bright over great distances, ranges from the intense green of the coastal plain (brighter than the famous "Emerald Isle") to the light jade green of the fjords, to the grey, black, browns, reds, purple and maroon of the mountain slopes, with mountain peaks here and there dazzling in sulphur-yellow. And above the lower mountain slopes glitter and glimmer the blue-white, green-white and amethyst-white of the glaciers and ice-caps. . . . . It is in Iceland that the greatest icefield in Europe may be seen: this is the Vatnajokull, an ice mass extending for something like 5,000 square miles. . . . Yet as if to emphasize that Iceland is indeed a land of contrasts and more truly a land of fire than of ice, in recent years volcanic eruptions have taken place in the Vatnajokull area breaking clean through ice that is a thousand feet thick.

In many parts of Iceland — particularly in the south-east about Reykjavik — there is plenty of evidence of volcanic activity. There are innumerable hot springs, geysers, both large and small, pools of boiling mud, warm rivers, vents from which superheated gases and steam blow and roar all day long. Reykjavik is the only capital city in the world largely heated from volcanic sources.

There are numerous cafés and small restaurants, most of them extremely modern, all clean, and all offering a wide range of excellently produced meals. One thing may be emphasized for foreign visitors — the visitor will find that all Icelanders and Icelandic habitations are extremely clean.

Towards the end of August, the displays of the Northern Lights begin, and it is both breathtaking and awe-inspiring to see great skies full of shimmering, dancing sheets of iridescent light (in all patterns and forms), ranging through all intensities and through all colours with pale pink, gold, silver-yellow, moon-blue, deep purple, pink, green, gold and sheet amethyst. These displays are, of course, intermittent, and last from late August to February and March.

Icelandic is not a dialect, as foreigners often imagine, nor is it a corrupt language. It is the sole remaining pure language in Northern Europe, and has remained virtually un-changed since the great Saga Period — say, back to Anglo-Saxon times. Once upon a time, the language that is now current in Iceland was spoken and understood throughout Norway, Sweden, Denmark, parts of Northern Germany, Holland, Belgium, and in large parts of the British Isles.

Most Icelanders understand English — and a very large number of them speak it to perfection. Icelanders are, without doubt, the best-read and the most literate of all white races. The number and excellence of their bookshops will astonish British visitors. There they will find shelves crammed with Goethe, Shakespeare, Balzac, Dickens, Galsworthy, Shaw, Ibsen, Wells, Cervantes, Tolstoy, rubbing shoulders with the best works of living contemporary writers of all lands.

There are no railways in Iceland, but modern buses connect most of the inhabited areas. An excellent network of modern planes covers the greater part of the island. Away from the coastal plain, where the bulk of the population lives, the only means of travel is by the adorable and trustworthy Icelandic pony — not "ponies" in our sense of the word, but the small medieval horse illustrated so often in ancient MSS. They are excellent beasts, strong, never vicious, and provide an easy ride. There is a great sense and feeling of classic grace and abandon in watching them running in herds with their long, golden, untrimmed manes and tails flying in the wind.

Visitors going to Iceland — even in winter — need not equip themselves as if facing Mt. Everest. Iceland's climate in general is akin to that of the Scottish Hebrides — which means that a visitor should think more of raincoats than of overcoats!

Outwardly the Icelander is rather reserved, which leads strangers to assume that he is "cold." This is far from the truth. In some ways, the Icelanders are rather like certain northern Scots: once you are known to them, and once they accept you, you will find yourself a target for generosity and hospitality. They are exceedingly kind and generous.

Some years ago, that eminent traveller and world-famous publisher, Stanley Unwin, had this to say of Iceland: ". . . it is a paradise for anglers, bird-lovers, botanists and geologists . . . above all it appeals to those who love an open-air life and are fascinated with the thought of riding scores of miles on indefatigable ponies through wild and sometimes desolate country, confident that when they finally arrive at some isolated farmhouse they will be given the most friendly and hospitable welcome."

IN FLIGHT

References to flying in early issues of Vogue were restricted to oblique mentions of "aviators", sometimes with an accompanying picture, the subject suitably moustachioed, leather-helmeted and begoggled. The Great War changed all that, accelerating the natural process of technological advancement and turning "improbable things into mere commonplaces". By the end of the war the aeroplane had evolved from an eccentric curiosity into a highly efficient "machine", an advance that Vogue, in 1920, suggested "wasn't dreamable before the war, unless you'd been reading Wells".

Science fiction was suddenly a fact of life, dreams a reality. In the Twenties aviation became an adventurous hobby, a social pastime, a thrilling and happy departure into the future, far, far removed from worldly considerations. "Click goes the safety belt. Click goes the throttle too. Then down goggles, a last wave toward the poor stay-at-homes and off you go . . ." More than anything, aviation offered escape not only from the ground but from the past, triggered off a hitherto unknown enthusiasm and zest for life, evoking a deeply physical and emotional response in the participants: ". . . a lift of the heart, a catch of the throat, a drumming roar in your ears that chants 'I knew it — I knew it!' This is what I've always wanted. I was born for it. I can never do without it again". Flying became glamorous too, if only because it served to stress the difference between those on the ground and those in the air, widening the gap between the adventurous and the dull.

Aviation was at once daring and youthful and the element of risk, so attractive on one level, prompted Vogue to suggest that "the woman who doesn't care for thrills had better wait for a year or two".

The second world war was a great stimulus for aviation, making possible in months what would normally have taken many years. The progress was astonishing: advanced electronics, radar, jet propulsion, unmanned missiles — Vogue had seen the world "shrunk to the size of a football by the aeroplane". The "spirit of adventure" had never been stronger, never so easily and variously satisfied. Airlines opened new routes, serviced new destinations, developed and operated new aircraft, while the pages of Vogue filled with their rival advertisements.

The magic carpet of air travel became available to all, making the world as compact as a single small country of fifty years ago — countries which used to be holiday destinations were becoming feasible for a long weekend.

MADAME,
THE AEROPLANE WAITS

As Surely as the Woman of Yes-
terday Was Born to Ride in a
Limousine, the Woman of To-day
Was Born to Fly in an Aeroplane

H 1920

IRIBE 1920

AIRWAYS
LINKING EUROPE'S
CAPITALS

HELGOLAND
WESTERLAND
WESERMÜNDE
BREMERHAVEN
WANGERROOGE
BORKUM
NORDERNEY
HAMB
BREMEN
HANNO
AMSTERDAM
KASSEL
LONDON
OST·ENDE
ANTWERPEN
ROTTERDAM
DORTMUND
LE TOUQUET
ESSEN
ERFUR
BRÜSSEL
DÜSSELDORF
KÖLN
FRANKFURT a/M
SAARBRÜCKEN
HEIDELBG
MANNHEIM
LUDWIGSHF
PARIS
KARLSRUHE
STRASSBURG
STUTTGART
BASEL
BADEN BADEN
BARCELONA
MARSEILLE
GENF
KONSTANZ
MADRID
LAUSANNE
MAILA
ZÜRICH

MOURGUE 1932

FRISSELL 1941

BRUEHL 1937

102

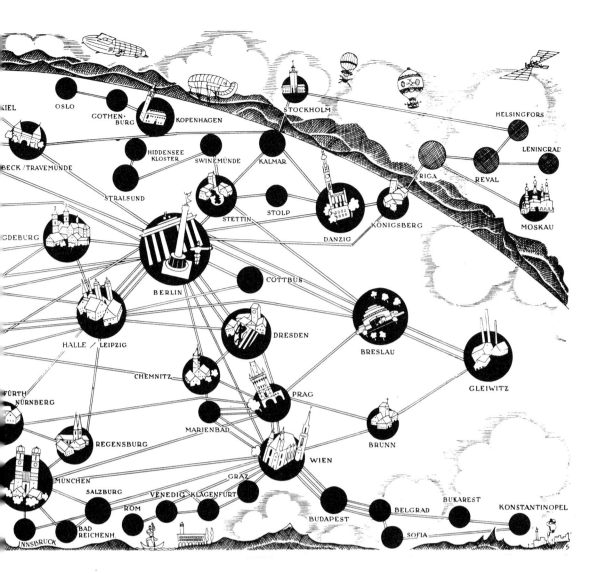

KIEL OSLO GOTHEN-BURG KOPENHAGEN STOCKHOLM HELSINGFORS LENINGRAD BECK/TRAVEMÜNDE HIDDENSEE KLOSTER SWINEMÜNDE KALMAR RIGA REVAL MOSKAU STRALSUND STETTIN STOLP DANZIG KÖNIGSBERG GDEBURG BERLIN COTTBUS HALLE / LEIPZIG DRESDEN BRESLAU CHEMNITZ GLEIWITZ FÜRTH NÜRNBERG PRAG MARIENBAD BRÜNN REGENSBURG WIEN MÜNCHEN GRAZ SALZBURG VENEDIG KLAGENFURT BUKAREST KONSTANTINOPEL RÖM BELGRAD BUDAPEST SOFIA INNSBRUCK BAD REICHENH.

LEE MILLER

ARROWSMITH 1

NEWTON 1967

THE FIFTIES

There was little cause for celebration at the start of the new decade. Petrol and food were still rationed, currency restrictions played havoc with holiday plans while the country's initial post-war optimism and enthusiasm vanished in the face of increasing austerity. As Vogue had predicted five years earlier: "The war is only half over; the second half may be no less bitter."

Recovery proved to be a slow process — a fact few had bargained for. "If you are escaping from the police, or merely a pleasant person escaping, then by all means come here," advised Truman Capote in Tangier. There was a lot to escape from. Indeed, to be "swallowed in the mists of the Casbah," as he suggested, was a tempting alternative to life at home where rationing in the early fifties was at its most severe since the end of the war.

After an absence of ten years Vogue's Travelog reappeared, its original brief to find "new places, new people, new ways of doing everyday things" redefined. Now its energies were channelled into the search for those destinations outside the Sterling Area but inside the bounds of a holiday allowance, in the Fifties fluctuating between an all-time low of £25 in 1952 and £100 in 1959. Among its many suggestions there was the small principality of Andorra where one could live comfortably for about £1 a day; Majorca, a sensible proposition "now that Spain is generously giving us so many pesetas for our pound"; Copenhagen where "good hotels are not expensive, even the Hotel d'Angleterre, which is probably the best in Scandinavia, will be within the reach of most visitors (a single room costs from 15s. to 30s. a day). Those who want to economise will find the Hotel Vestersohus exceptionally reasonable; "a friend and I paid 25s. a day for two (breakfasts included) for a handsome apartment: two bed-sitting rooms, a bathroom and a large balcony"; farther north in Finland though, "hotels are generally good but rarely cheap, and a room without bath is likely to cost 25s. to 30s. a night without service; there are no steaks under 15s. apiece, and coffee in some hotels is 7s. 6d. a pot. However, one full-sized Finnish meal is likely to satisfy an English appetite for two days". Even those able to afford the passage to South Africa were advised that "by crossing the bridge at Victoria Falls from Southern Rhodesia to Northern Rhodesia, you save 10d. a packet on the local popular brand of cigarettes".

For those who preferred their holidays at home and an unrestricted holiday allowance, Vogue was ready with directions to "corners of the British Isles as strange and different as a visit to the Balkans". Within this category were the Orkney and Shetland Islands: "a visit to either or both a rewarding and certainly not a humdrum experience. Fishermen will find the island a paradise with plentiful sea-trout and loch fishing . . . serious ornithologists will be interested to learn that the present proprietor of Fair Isle has established a bird sanctuary and a hostel where bird watchers can stay. If you are a natural explorer and sightseer you will find enough on the island to occupy a month of Sundays. For those who like pottering amongst ruins, there are many ancient Viking monuments . . . with beautiful walks along flower-covered, gull-haunted cliffs". If all this sounded too bleak, there were the southern counties "in their colour and customs, history and houses, infinite variety", and Mr Churchill's "dear Channel Islands"— the oldest dependencies of the Crown and sufficiently French to give visitors from the mainland, as the islanders always call Britain, the agreeable illusion of having "gone foreign" with none of the attendant currency frustrations.

There was one other institution which also remained virtually untouched by such restrictions. "Even in those not-so-distant, almost-forgotten days of unrestricted foreign currency and full value for the pound, cruising was a popular way of spending a holiday. In the uncosy light of today's economic facts, it is the simplest possible exercise to add a desire for foreign travel in leisure and comfort to an inelastic twenty-five pounds and arrive at a cruise (simply because one paid an inclusive price in sterling before departure). Which is why you may have difficulty in translating theory into action. Most cruises of average holiday length, unastronomically priced, tend to be heavily booked and unless you anchor your hopes to a cancellation you should plan several months in advance."

By the end of 1954 "the uncosy light of today's economic facts" had brightened — if only by a glimmer, but it was enough for Vogue to welcome in the New Year with probably the most encouraging travel coverage since before the war: "Here you open a twenty-page section collected to help you to lay your 1955 holiday plans. The ground? From Asia Minor to Deauville, from festivals to lazy beaches".

"In Sicily, it is easy to become a temple addict . . . in Turkey, the eye, the tongue, the light of the Orient, it is impossible for the most frivolous tourist, downing a Martini at the Park Oteli bar, to remain unaware of the texture of history all around . . . In Switzerland, there's alpine climbing, fishing, sailing, golf, swimming, strenuous walks, mild walks, lazing in beautiful surroundings, music festivals, historical places, tourist spas and health centres. You can even pick your language". Emphasizing the glamour and attraction of these destinations, pages and pages of fashion photographs on location. "In the sun that strikes through the pillars of the Temple of Juno at Agrigento — a playsuit in blue poplin." "At the rector's Palace, Dubrovnik, which now houses the city archives . . . in a white cotton playshirt printed with coral dandelions." And also in Norway, Scandinavia and Denmark — "Clothes fresh in the shops flown on a holiday preview".

The following year and for the rest of the decade it was the same exuberant story: Galicia, in Northern Spain, "an ideal place for a quiet sun drenched, unsophisticated holiday — swimming, lazing in the sun or exploring the pinewoods . . . excellent bathing where you are unlikely to be troubled by Spain's stringent bathing costume regulations, although the bathing police from Vigo may swoop down once a year and impose a few small fines". In Malta "a riviera in the Sterling area . . . you can swim in the bay where St Paul was shipwrecked, and picnic in the cave where tradition says Calypso lured Ulysses". In Kashmir the more ambitious "can shoot red bear and snow leopard, play golf in summer on a course surrounded by snowy mountains and hire a houseboat instead of a hotel room".

After the bleakness of post-war austerity "This is the time to give winter wings — to look ahead to summer coming up over the frost-rimmed horizon". Vogue's Travelog was now Vogue's Portfolio though the aims remained the same: "To help launch holiday plans, we present new thoughts on themes of where to go . . . how to get there". There were "Holidays with a Difference" in places like the Aeolian Islands, still almost unknown and completely unexploited but as a result "not recommended for those in search of sophisticated luxury, or even moderately civilised comfort". Or for those to whom ten years of post-war restrictions had been more than enough "only twenty flying hours away, if you go by Britannia", there was South Africa "from November through April, a gay and sophisticated holiday life is in full swing. Hotels are lively and good, the sun shines and the hardest work is keeping up with your suntan"; for "Travellers looking for new worlds to explore, Australia is crackling with brand new sophistication", and "now that we have dollars with which to bless our British name, people are turning their attention to South America". In the winter of 1958 you could ski in France, Italy, Germany, Norway, Switzerland and Austria, and when these better-known resorts became too crowded "it is possible to escape to less familiar ski terrain which offers the additional excitement of being in a country you may never have visited" — like Czechoslovakia, Poland and Lapland. In 1958 too, Spain's Costa del Sol began attracting attention in Vogue, as an ideal destination for young people "who have seldom, if ever, been abroad for a holiday before", and of course for winter holidays: "There is no place in Europe where winter warmth and sunshine can be guaranteed. But the place where it is most likely to be found is the Costa del Sol". Late the following year the travel allowance was increased from an all-time Fifties high of £100 to £250 a year. But that was announced in November 1959. It would be the next decade that benefited.

ROSOMAN

TANGIER NOTES

by TRUMAN CAPOTE

BEATON

Tangier? It is two days by boat from Marseilles, a charming trip that takes you along the coast of Spain, and if you are someone escaping from the police, or merely a pleasant person escaping, then by all means come here: hemmed with hills, confronted by the sea, and looking like a white cape draped on the shores of Africa, it is an international city with an excellent climate most of the year. There are magnificent beaches, really extraordinary stretches of sugar-soft sand and surf; and if you have a mind for that sort of thing, the night-life, though neither particularly innocent nor especially varied, is dark to dawn, which, when you consider that most people nap all afternoon, and that very few people dine before ten or eleven, is not too unusual. Almost everything else in Tangier is unusual, however, and before coming here you should do three things: be inoculated for typhoid, withdraw your savings from the bank, and say goodbye to your friends — heaven knows you may never see them again. This advice is quite serious, for it is alarming the number of travellers who have landed here on a brief holiday, then settled down and let the years go by. Because Tangier is a basin that holds you, a timeless place: the days slide by less noticed than foam in a waterfall; this, I imagine, is the way time passes in a monastery, unobtrusive and on slippered feet; for that matter, these two institutions, a monastery and Tangier, have another common denominator: self-containment.

One spends a great deal of time sitting in the Petit Soko, a café-cluttered square at the foot of the Casbah. Offhand, it seems to be a miniature version of the Galleria in Naples, but on closer acquaintance it assumes a character so grotesquely individual you cannot fairly compare it with any other place in the world. At no hour of the day or night is the Petit Soko not crowded: Broadway, Piccadilly, all these places have their off moments, but the little Soko booms around the clock. Twenty steps away, and you are swallowed in the mists of the Casbah; the apparitions drifting out of these mists into the hurdy-gurdy clamour of the Soko make a lively show: it is a display ground for prostitutes, a depot for drug-peddlars, a spy centre; it is also the place where some simpler folk drink their evening apéritif. The Soko has its own celebrities, but it is a precarious honour, for the audience is excessively fickle.

The Petit Soko is also something of a fashion centre. One innovation that is regrettable is the passion for dark glasses that has developed among Arab women, whose eyes,

110

peering just above their veiling, have always been so provocative. Now all one sees are those great black lenses embedded like coal-hunks in a snowball of cloth.

Of an evening at seven the little Soko reaches its height. It is the apéritif hour, some twenty nationalities are rubbing elbows, and the hum of voices is like the singing of giant mosquitoes.

At the end of June, and with the start of a new moon, Ramadan begins. For the Arabs, Ramadan is a month of abstinence. As dark comes on, a coloured string is stretched in the air, and when the string grows invisible conch horns signal the Arabs to the food and drink that during the day they cannot touch. These dark-night feasts emanate a festive spirit that lasts until dawn. From distant towers oboe players serenade before prayers; drums, hidden but heard, tomtom behind closed doors, and the voices of men, singsonging the Koran, carry out of the Mosques into the narrow moonbright streets. Even high on the mountain above Tangier you can hear the oboe player wailing in the far-off dark, a solemn thread of melody winding across Africa from here to Mecca and back.

Sidi Kacem is a limitless, Sahara-like beach bordered by olive groves; at the end of Ramadan, Arabs from all over Morocco arrive at Sidi Kacem in trucks, astride donkeys, on foot: for three days a city appears there, a fragile dream city of coloured lights and cafés under lantern-lighted trees. We drove out there around midnight; the first glimpse of the city was like seeing a birthday cake blazing in a darkened room, and it filled you with the same exciting awe: you knew you could not blow out all the candles. Right away we got separated from the people we'd come with, but in the surge and sway it was impossible to stay together, and after the first few frightened moments we never bothered looking for them; the night caught us in its hand and there was nothing to do but become another of the masked, ecstatic faces flashing in the torch-flare. Everywhere little orchestras played. Voices, sweet and sultry as kif moke, chanted over drums, and somewhere, stumbling through the silver, floating trees, we got smothered in a crowd of dancers: a circle of old bearded men beat the rhythm, and the dancers, so concentrated you could put a pin in them, rippled as though the wind were moving them around. According to the Arab calendar, this is the year 1370; seeing a shadow through the silk of a tent, watching a family fry honey-cakes on a flat twig fire, moving among the dancers and hearing the thrill of a lonely flute on the beach, it was simple to believe that one was living in 1370 and that time would never move forward.

Occasionally we had to rest; there were straw mats under the olive trees, and if you sat on one of these a man would bring you a glass of hot mint tea. It was while we were drinking tea that we saw a curious line of men file past. They wore beautiful robes, and the man in front, old like a piece of ivory, carried a bowl of rose water which, to the accompaniment of bagpipes, he sprinkled side to side. We got up to follow them, and they took us out of the grove onto the beach. The sand was as cold as the moon; humped dunes of it drifted toward the water, and flickers of light burst in the dark like fallen stars. At last the priest and his followers went into a temple which it was forbidden us to enter, and so we wandered down across the beach. We counted the shooting stars, there were so many. Wind whispered on the sand like the sound of the sea; cut-throat figures outlined themselves against the kneeling orange moon, and the beach was as cold as a snowfield. From high on a dune in a blue, almost-dawn light we saw below us, spread along the shore, all the celebrants, their brilliant clothes fluttering in the morning breeze. Just as the sun touched the horizon a great roar went up, and two horsemen, riding bare-back, splashed through the surf and swept down the beach. Like a lifting curtain sunrise crept toward us: and we shuddered at its coming, knowing that when it reached us we would be back in our own century.

JAPAN

by VINCENT SHEEAN

First and last, during my drives through the streets of the sprawling city of Tokyo, my most vivid impression was of the children. Carried papoose-style on the backs of elder relatives — not only on the backs of their mothers, as it was when I first saw the city in 1927 — they looked out of their cocoons with such round and rosy faces that it was impossible to think how a terrible period of war and devastation could have produced them. Of course, all the ones I saw were the children of a post-war period, when the American occupation had greatly lightened the hardships of the people, but they looked so well-fed and sturdy that it must be truer among the Japanese than among others that the children get the best of the food available.

And although it is most difficult for any westerner to see far into the Japanese mind without years of study, the priority thus given to the children would fit very well into what I was able to understand of it. It seemed to me that the Japanese to whom I was able to speak thought of the future and of the past, chiefly, but relatively little about the present. A Buddhist philosopher of distinction told me that all Japanese were Buddhists. When I asked him how many were Shintoists he said: "All Japanese are Shintoists too." This is perhaps the key to the matter, although it does not harmonize in the least with the official statistics under which the religions of Japan are tabulated; from Buddhism the Japanese learns to look far into the past and far into the future, since the soul is reborn innumerable times on its pilgrimage; and from Shintoism he learns that his own soil is sacred, his race and culture divine, and his descent from the Sun-goddess made manifest in the national archetype, the Emperor. Although the two beliefs do not seem to me to go together well, they have long since merged in the Japanese consciousness.

The result of this combination is to produce a people capable of almost any sacrifice for the general cause, since rebirth is certain and patriotism a religion. The American occupation has changed many of the forms of Japanese life, made labour unions important, and broken up the big feudal estates. However, it has gone on long enough to make these novelties deeply a part of the people's life. They still show in many small ways the persistence of faiths held for ages, customs and observances that come from the depths. Most of them still bow in the direction of the imperial palace, where the representative of the Sun-goddess lives, and most of them would avert their eyes from him if they should see him.

The Emperor's divinity was abolished by his own decree of January 1, 1946, in which he declared that his relationship to his people does not depend upon "mere myths."

You would think that so much bombing from the air would have made the Japanese hate the Americans. However, I saw no evidence of any such thing.

Their attitude towards war, and particularly towards the last war, was what interested me most. I could get only a clue here and there, since many things are firmly sealed up in the Japanese mind and cannot be reached by a foreigner speaking a foreign language. (This was even more so in the old days before the warlike period began.) One of the oddest cases I encountered was that of a young man who was chauffeur to the American family in whose house I was staying. He had been trained as a suicide pilot and the war had ended just as he was about to take his flight to the next life. Through the barriers of language I gathered that this eventuality (the single flight of the suicide pilot) had not perturbed him. Rebirth is certain, immediate, and, in such cases, an improvement. He

TOPOLSKI

seemed to have no feeling whatever of hostility to the Americans and was delighted to be working for them. And yet it seemed likely, from the tone so far as I could get it, that he would not hesitate to do the same thing again. This is the product of some thousands of years, and a few years of democratic doctrine and parliamentary frameworks could hardly touch such a spirit.

Flowers and bombings, waste land and new shacks — these are still the impressions of the Tokyo streets. The wonderful colours of the kimonos on a bright day, the sudden outburst of coloured umbrellas when it rains, give the streets of the city — that is, outside the centre — an air of being gardens themselves. This is especially true if you ascend a street without traffic on a day when all the umbrellas bend in the same way against the wind, pushing against the climate to which the Japanese have so strangely not adapted themselves. They are not an adaptable people: their spirit is too single, too old, too indifferent to time.

I think they must have been originally a people from the South Seas who in some adventurous pre-history set off in sampans, perhaps towards the east, and found themselves blown at last upon these shores where the climate did not suit their habits. Perhaps the reason why they worship the Sun-goddess and claim descent from her is precisely this, that the race remembers its origin in a sunnier clime than that which is now allotted to it.

In a sense they would therefore be the children of the Sun-goddess, exiled in time and space. They are still a southern people too far north for their nature, reaching towards the sun for their posterity as for their ancestors.

113

A YOUNG SMUGGLER'S GUIDE TO THE CUSTOMS

by PETER USTINOV

Just as facial expression can suggest a person's character more faithfully, and certainly more profoundly, than lengthy conversation, tinged as that is with prejudice and a desire to conceal, so that the Customs House can provide a glimpse of a nation's soul before the traveller has time to lose himself in the confusing bustle of national behaviour in the streets. The British Customs, for example, provide an accurate foretaste of what the visitor may expect beyond the barrier, at the same time crystallizing all that he will have experienced on departure.

There is, over here, a sense of slightly unimaginative order, of obedience to the clumsy letter of the law, which is calculated to inspire confusion in the heart of the smuggler; the officers study the voyager with the unswerving and unsettling gaze of a well-trained Alsatian, so that he feels that one false move, even if it is only to take a handkerchief from his pocket, will occasion a warning growl. A degree of Emmetish surrealism in the language of the Excisemen is yet another distracting influence on the mind of the man with his underwear full of diamonds, and his shoe-leather ticking away peacefully in a solid Swiss way. I am thinking especially of the solemn warning on the wall at Dover, which promises hideous penalties for the undeclared importation of parrots, and indicates that a considerably heavier price will have to be paid if an attempt to import a motor-car secretly (presumably in the traveller's pocket) is discovered. Such awe-inspiring legislation leads automatically to a full confession of not only dutiable purchases, but also valueless knick-knacks, and even details of one's private life.

The promise of the Customs House is not belied by subsequent adventures in this land of splendidly ornate legal loopholes and self-conscious discipline.

The French Customs are more difficult to epitomize, as they are so frequently on strike, thereby affording a Liberal like myself an unexpected glimpse into the glories of Free Trade. When they are on the job, they are patently not terribly interested in it, and stamp away at their documents, thinking all the while of deeper things, and trying desperately to keep the spiralling smoke of their Gauloises out of their eyes without actually removing the blackened stubs from their mouths. They know very well that if a man is bursting with wrist-watches, he is taking an absurd risk, and his courage deserves every assistance they can provide. And, in any case, it is not the confiscation of a bagful of chronometers which will stop the rot in the Lower House. The trouble is at the top, not among the hunted ranks of the petty criminals.

The only danger the smuggler runs is when he comes face to face with a female officer, who is evidently a direct descendant from the knitting-women of the Revolution, and who crouches behind her splintered counter like the concièrge of Hell, wrapped in a knitted shawl, and demanding the head. These ancient Mariannes have a bitter knowledge of life, of its possibilities, and of its harshness, and consequently seem possessed with an overt desire to strip everybody. They are the superannuated muses of

Toulouse-Lautrec, who have outlived their client, and now practise their intransigence on the innocents of less civilized lands. Even if there are no diamonds on you, they must be found, and your caitiff attempt to desecrate the Tricolor, Verdun, Solferino, and all Citoyens must be exposed, and all this with a glitter of onyx eyes and a fearful twitching of the mouth.

The Italians mix their officers shrewdly. Some are very ferocious-looking gentlemen with fast-growing beards and grenades exploding dramatically on their caps, while others are very old men in shirtsleeves, who have some difficulty in hearing, and even more difficulty in speaking. The shrewdness of his arrangement lies in the fact that the ferocious gentlemen invariably have hearts of gold, as they are eager to welcome the visitor to a land of historical monuments and ultra-modern *turismo,* while the old civilians, uninhibited by such considerations, plough patiently and indiscriminately through piles of luggage, murmuring to themselves, and finally signing suitcases with a flourish of such assurance that they might be Titians making their marks on their greatest achievements.

Should an irregularity be discovered, however, the administrative excitement is surpassed in no other country that I know. In England, they know the rules, and fine you. In Italy, they rush to read the rules, and each man interprets them according to his conception of power, humanism, Christianity, honour and expediency. While one will accuse you of an assault on the very roots of the young republic another will admonish you in clerical cadences for your lack of faith in your fellow men, and a third will just shout. Eventually they will become more interested in each other than in you, and it is at a point when the conversation has turned into an evaluation of the Partisans' resistance on the Adriatic coast that it is quite safe for you to leave, with your contraband, naturally.

The Spaniards are far less reassuring. The calm is not the calm of Heathrow, the calm of the hospital corridor — this is the austere reticence of the Inquisition. The procedure is akin to a ghostly pavane, danced in the shadows of a bleak, comfortless shack. No language but Spanish seems to be spoken, and if you are unable to answer the questions, that is the first black mark against you. In an oppressive silence, the white-gloved official indicates with choreographic gestures the objects he wishes to examine. The mime is hypnotic. Prostrated by the sheer weight of the true faith, you demolish your careful packing, and lay bare the innermost secrets of your shaving-kit. When the ordeal is over, you are shot a smile of unexpected playfulness, which you have not the confidence to answer, and an imperious hand waves you towards the mystery of the horizon. It requires a nerve of iron, and a deep faith in the things of the spirit, to import even an undeclared tin of condensed milk into the land of the Catholic kings.

As for the U.S., well, we are all cops and robbers, and Japanese torpedoes are approaching from all directions. The Marines fix bayonets and charge through your personal belongings. You are innocent till you are proved innocent, and guilty till you are proved guilty. No time to think or make your excuses. The G-men are after you, and how d'you like New York? Get these guys out of here, and get the next lot in, and what's in that vanity-case?

Here there are no rules. The smuggler must talk faster and louder than his interrogator, and show a healthy interest in the baseball scores. That, if nothing else, will prove his innocence.

I hope that these few sketches may be of use to those thinking of taking up an ancient art professionally, and that it may facilitate the free distribution of goods the world over. One word of advice. Don't try to run before you can walk. Don't begin your career by concealing a Macaw in your umbrella at Northolt.

Frances Rose

CORSICA

by DOROTHY CARRINGTON

Seen from a distance, Calvi looks sleepy and idyllic. It is neither. But the first sight of it is bound to be deceptive. There it lies, at the tip of a long crescent-shaped bay as deserted, it seems, as the coasts of Central Africa. The ochre houses are packed together by the little fishing port; above, on a rocky promontory, rises the historic citadel, enclosed by ancient ramparts, crowned by a baroque cathedral dome. Here, you imagine, is the ideal hide-out from the anguish of civilization: here self-exiled poets and painters create masterpieces while the simple indolent inhabitants dream their dreams. No poet or painter I ever heard of has ever created anything in Calvi; the inhabitants are neither simple nor indolent and they are not given to dreaming. As one of them, a lorry driver, said: "We Corsicans never dream because we realize our desires."

No sooner do you enter the village than this first impression changes. Whether you come by boat or bus or plane or train you are bound to arrive in the evening, and this is the crucial moment in Calvi life. Crowds of tourists and Corsicans are promenading the port, not casually, but with the tense expectancy of people about to take part in a battle of wits or a test of physical endurance. The continuous string of cafés lights up, rivalling the crimson sunset glow seen between the forest of masts of visiting yachts. Into the air, tropic and erotic, exotic with the incense of the *maquis* — the sweet-smelling scrub that grows all over the island — gramophones, accordions and guitars pour heart-stirring tangos, javas and *valses musettes.* They will be heard all night, while the moon makes a silver picture-postcard view of mountains and sea, and later, when the sun blazes up over the jagged crest of Monte Carlo and the cafés are serving black coffee laced with *eau de vie* — a vodka-like spirit — for breakfast, Corsicans and tourists will still be dancing as though life itself were at stake.

For the "season" is not only Calvi's main source of revenue, but only source of amusement. From June to September the population is more than doubled and everyone is busy making money, spending it, and relishing what the Cosicans aptly call *la vie vérit-able* — the real, or true, life.

As much in evidence as the foreign holiday-makers are the Corsicans: American business men from the Continent, Corsicans on leave from civil service, army or police in Morocco, Tunis, Algiers, Indo-China and Marseilles. Corsicans, like the Irish, emigrate from their poverty-stricken island to achieve success or fame abroad. Local tradition has it that Christopher Columbus was a native of Calvi under the Genoese occupation and his ruined house is shown on the heights of the citadel. Many of these Corsicans come home on holiday every year, for however unaffording the island may be to the ambitious — and most Corsicans are ambitious, would-be Columbuses and Napoleons — it keeps its hold over its people. They "languish" for Corsica, they tell you, as indeed does nearly every tourist who has once visited it. And many will stay, for some

116

days at least, at Calvi, though their homes may be elsewhere: in the pine and chestnut forests of the mountainous interior, or on the southern and eastern coasts.

This is because Calvi provides the only good time Corsica has ever known. Poor and rocky, with a grim history of invasion and oppression, guerilla warfare and war, Corsica is austere. In the stony villages, where the houses are furnished with little more than a bench, a table and the guns hanging on the walls, there are no amusements, no cinemas, no dances. Hard-working, proud, passionate and possessive, the peasants observe a stern code. Young men do not go out with young girls — cannot, indeed, for fear that the girls' fathers and brothers will demand immediate marriage on pain of death. There is no social life beyond christening and wedding parties; the shadow of the vendetta still broods over the remoter villages. But to Calvi comes the yearly invasion of foreigners with more sophisticated customs; and to meet them come not only visiting Corsicans but bus-loads and lorry-loads of Corsicans from the interior, to *profiter de la vie* as they term it; in other words, to enjoy themselves.

Sheep-breeders from the high Tibet-like plateau of the Niolo stalk into the port, ruddy-cheeked, in checked shirts and tight-legged corduroy trousers and scarlet cummerbunds, carrying their guns and followed by their mongrel dogs. They mingle with Calvi's fishermen and labourers, swarthy as Red Indians, with the Continental ladies floating off yachts in Paris evening gowns, with the campers and tourists in shorts and pirate costumes. During the high peak of the season in mid-August the roulette tables, set up in red bunting booths along the port, are permanently crowded with dark, intent faces, for Corsicans are addicted gamblers; fireworks cascade green and violet stars into the bay; Chez Tao, the night-club on the ramparts, keeps open all the twenty-four hours. There Corsicans and tourists dance like dervishes in the basement chapel of a fifteenth-century bishop's residence where Napoleon once hid escaping from a rival Corsican faction; there fishermen sing melancholy Moorish-sounding songs of love and death and revenge between the tangos. On the fête of Saint Marie the same Corsicans are to be seen in white surplices carrying the Renaissance statue of the Virgin from the cathedral round the cobbled canyons of the citadel, led by the village priest, followed by a procession of chanting pilgrims.

Many places in the Mediterranean are as beautiful as Calvi, though it is impossible to think of this when you have fallen under the spell of its peacock-blue bay and theatrical back-drop of pinnacled mountains; most have as good a climate and very many are more luxurious. What gives Calvi its incomparable allure is the vital quality of its local primitive life. It is an oasis of gaiety, hectic with the relaxation of nerve-strained city tourists and the ferocious zest for life of pleasure-starved Corsicans, who are out to pack as much experience as possible into that brief time before the last visitor has left, before the icy winds drive down from the Alps, and there is nothing to do after the rough day's work but play poker huddled round the stoves of half-empty cafés.

ROSE

117

VENICE

by HENRY GREEN

Venice, where no ice is, and green has never been, at dawn the fishless stinking sea milk white, a pink palace domed into a sky of milk and towards which one black gondola is being poled; Venice where the only horses must be statues and they have yet to put up motor cars in stone, oh Venice with no bicycle bells but with a Bridge of Sighs and Casanova always on a roof — the sun in rising must bring azure to your roads of sea, tideless with a steadily rising stench, Venice where Proust thought to travel and never did, Venice they somehow missed when bombing, Venice which is still here but for how long, and will it be too late soon, the pigeons, St. Mark's, a populace standing under colonnades angrily arguing prices, the sun at noon too sharp striking light off marble, the brazen horses hot and dry to touch — up in that dormer window on the lead roof a maid stretched in black, snoring on the bed with skirts up about her mouth, the natives poling spaghetti down, Venice which is too hot because she never freezes — where do they get their drinking water or do they strike this like oil, are there derricks to gush it from the ocean into those old palaces past which the motor boats must not speed in case they bring the places down.

Venice, for the honeymoon, cushions at the rear in a little moving room, the gondolier who does not look back, but no he would be pushing from the stern — we would be stretched out before him — so what, do they have shades on that little backward looking window through which his envenomed eyes at the corners of which two bluebottles sip brighter than jewels, the gondolier appraising our love-making, can you then draw a blind to exclude him or can he go to the bows to pole and not look over a shoulder, to stare into sun with his wounds of eyes while I wound you, my love, on cushions white like rice to the lap lap of water . . .

Venice, the lions of St. Mark's in stone — did one such lion on a great afternoon swim in from blinding yellow sands every yard from the South, its home — an orange head athwart the azure sea, with salt encrusted nostrils, eyes red, a white fish impaled on the claws of one forepaw all the sad way from Africa towards which Venice ever leans — did they then who live there catch its sobbing breath, the dark despair of effort a sounding band about the heart oh Venice of marble, my love unvisited, my honeymoon unspent . . .

Or is it at dusk when each emerald within the sea will rise to take the surface air, when light winds from the Bosphorus, the Golden Gates, waft from the East to cool the palace windows even now lighting against dusk and the sky is gold, when pigeons clap their wings to take evening flight in air that now is eyelid pink and the stench subsides, when those blue stoned walls can breathe and saints in stone do stretch to sigh for another day that is done in five, six hundred years, then, is it then, Venice, time for lovers in that darker dusk within the little room that glides while the gondolier hums . . .

Hanging to his bars the prisoner at his cell will see this evening dove flight, the maid in black and on her bed will yawn at them then draw her skirts down along fat legs, the lovesick girl will droop on doves as they find their way, as the sea must fade, the sunset before they roost on an old statue's taut right arm, the marble shoulder, or on bronze imperishable ever folded wings of angels standing on a corner to await the daily death of Venice . . .

And the rising moon. Above a sea turned dark as night on which Venice ever leans her tresses the disc emerges apricot gold and every small wave set with diamonds, fanned by her desert breath, takes on an Afric sunshine only cold as death as dolphins come in out of the wide sea to Venice. For she is wedded to the sea. Her rulers the Doges, when each in his turn came to office, had this custom by which he was rowed out on to the main where he let drop a golden ring to sway criss-cross down into the ocean, to gleam, for Venice is wed to the sea called Mediterranean . . .

And the dolphins at night drive in from the sea. With their brief sigh as they come up to breathe, they are quicksilver in moonlight over Venice and in their play they do sigh for lovers adrift in that moonlight lane from Venice . . .

And these lovers, as they are urged by no action of their own into this old enchantment, leave behind as they must in their care for one another, marble with blood in its veins under midday heat, now classically turned blue blooded in the moon, blanched, carved into a living identity with its statues that live for ever on the buildings of Venice which does not sleep at night. Here too the noonday blaze which stunned Venice, which drew her stench up to freight the air with living, has cooled, has turned as cold as silhouettes where the gondola cuts its own outline where no other vessel is and where, in one another's arms, cut off in our shade from the gondolier, we voyage more than ever by ourselves away from the cold marble forehead of Venice in which doves now swoon on statues and the night holds still and we, bereft in one another's warmth by the sheer moonlight, in one another's nyloned skin, each gently haloed in the other's breath, and silenced she and I, are silenced as we draw out from Venice . . .

For silence is best where we, while idly talking, might disagree under the clear stars, alone, the gondolier forgotten. Nor is it safe for lovers to more than murmur in Venice, even out at sea. For behind them they have the storied pavements, great lives in mosaic, and above those fabled women swathed in marble idleness over great niches set in silken covered walls, there are ceilings dimmed now by night, unreflected by moonlight through the wide windows, there are heroes drawn over stretched motionless ceilings to vast designs which were painted to show each in his greatest moment and, thus painted, become the thieves of time; these are for us, in the city we have left behind, which our gondola has sunk beneath the skyline, these are the epitome of all love stories, in mosaic, in statues and in great painting to bring us mortals down to little more than ghosts, but warm, off Venice . . .

So it is perhaps we should be chary of a honeymoon in or off the seaborne city. It may be too much has gone on or is pictured there. There could be frailty in our lives not to be endured under that magnificence. We might be found wanting. How then can the inhabitants live through such a challenge? The answer must be they are so used to riches that they no longer feel, or else they live in cross-eyed blindness . . .

Can one then have the heart, the impudence to visit Venice? Is that the reason Proust would never go? For against this, if it might be too hot by day or the stench then too great, by contrast it would seem only too easy to set out by moonlight so that no couple, if given the miraculous chance, could fail, intent on their two selves, to sink Venice, as can be done tomorrow by the gondola covering of a moonlit lane of sea. Yet to leave her thus is but to come back to bed in Venice. The dawn is always chill, better met between sheets. The sun, in first rising, is not warmer than the loved one's arms. So, in returning over the sea, in seeing that fabled city rise out of the ocean under moonlight, first one dome then another, and the gold crosses paled to white, next the roads of water between

black shadows — oh here then must be who knows what of the great myths of the world that each one carries within him, Venice by moonlight, all the whole literature of the world that every human being, the heir as we all are to each beautiful line created, is born to and holds in a molten casket in his heart for Venice . . .

For Venice is everlasting, lives by a life that cannot die except by bombs. It may be she is too strong for mortals, that we could feel too human to submit our will to hers. But sure as day follows night the morrow's sun will rise on Venice, the stench, if you will, return. But the doves must come down from up the palaces, dawn will find her great statuary eyes wide opened. Prisons, palaces and churches will smile again as they have through centuries, and the people of Venice will go on unregarding. And while she is here still, through her and under her will continue to drift brave pilgrims from the West. Then, as day closes yet once more, Venice will clothe herself for the moon. And, when that reflection rises from Africa in the moon's triumph over men, that is the time for all the world's lovers, living their lives over again (their lives perhaps to be) in the photographs and pictures of Venice; a city for ever wedded to the sea that there is no one does not carry by him and which each one of us lives by, despite himself, his inward eye fixed, perhaps it would best be not in, but rather trained upon Venice . . .

120

ELBA, HAPPY EXILE

by SIRIOL HUGH JONES

We left the Paris-Rome train at Campiglia. Our fellow-passengers, with whom we had shared cushions, mineral water, ham rolls from station trolleys and tired copies of English newspapers, stuck appalled faces out of the carriage window and cried "Where are you *going?*" "To Elba. We hope", we said faintly, suddenly feeling as deserted as Captain Bligh, and watching personified mute alarm, frozen in time like a news photograph, whirling off towards a sensible Roman destination. There we were, unable to say more in Italian than "Ah, ye courtiers, vile race accursed", or "It is thus that Tosca kisses!" and other handy operatic passwords, with a phrase-book that honestly said "Send the bales by the next steamer". Our bales were our own concern. Even the Emperor, one supposed, reached the island of exile with someone to see him safe to the door.

But once embarked on the single-gauge local train to Piombino, we began to feel more like explorers than exiles. And at Piombino we even succeeded in finding a local inhabitant whose French, fast and frenziedly Italianate though it was, stretched as far into our understanding as to convey that if we were to hire one of the horse-drawn carriages standing outside the little station, we would — after a dignified amble — reach the steamer for Elba.

And so, just as the sun was setting, we did. Among the blandishments of the newsvendors selling a wonderful mixture of illustrated magazines and crime stories with marvellous jackets, the cackling and crying of crated fowls and pigs being loaded aboard, and the enthusiastic persuasion of a kindly longshoreman who wanted to direct us to those Elba resorts which attracted most English and German visitors, we installed ourselves in the spotless bar and began to learn how to order a drink and how to pay for it.

Elba at sunset looks like an eighteenth-century traveller's concept of romantic land-scape — thickly wooded, dramatic, at once smooth and precipitous. Less savage and outlawed than Corsica, it looked to us like *Toteninsel* on the horizon, brooding a little, contemplative, very peaceful.

We had no notion of where we wanted to make landfall. Twice the ferry stopped to drop travellers into little local cockleshells, full of baggage and the starling-chatter of relatives. We settled, in the gathering darkness, for Porto Azzurro, because we liked the name. It proved to have only one hotel that we could immediately discover, on the little quay itself, cleanly tiled and unpretentious, but alas, packed to its open doors. We moved on to spend the night in the back bedroom of a house in the village, amid spotless cleanliness, a good deal of lace-work, tinted photographs of family occasions, holy pictures, and much kindness from a family clearly accustomed to a mixture of operatic phrases and sign language.

The next day we discovered the superb Elba bus service. Great monsters of buses, extra comfortable, hurtle along the roads, with no nonsense about room for five standing only. Everyone piles in until the bus is full, and at the next stop a lot more pile in and the bus is much fuller. Simple and optimistic, and in Anglo-Saxon experience comparable only with the Marx Brothers making a confined space nice and cosy. The incredible thing, to us, was that the buses run on time to the minute, that the timetable is clear, accurate and understandable, and the whole island well-serviced.

121

Napoleon's villa

We were deposited at the island's hub, Portoferraio, a town of iron-works, huge ruined Medici fortifications, a Moorish-looking waterfront, white and dazzling and shadowless, a vast hotel, and a popular local cinema. Over Portoferraio still lies the great blessing-bestowing hand of the Emperor. You become conscious of golden bees, Imperial Eagles, and the ubiquitous letter N. Here he landed, set up his headquarters, instantly set about creating new roads, a theatre, a little fleet, a cadet's school, public works of all kinds. From here he told the adoring islanders to be good children, promising in exchange to be a good, if rather impermanent, father. And inland, in the mountains at San Martino, they built him a summer villa.

You reach the Villa Napoleonica by bus (of course) from Portoferraio. We were stunned by great gates, a long approach to a gigantic stone façade topped by rampant Imperial Eagles, watchful in stone. Even for an exiled Emperor, fresh from Fontainebleau and earlier glory, this seemed excessive. The grandiloquent façade turned out to belong to a post-Napoleon museum, built on to the villa itself, and containing the most incredible, crowded brantub of exhibits, a Canova, lots of "school of" paintings, and a great many that the baffled guide-book merely describes as "artistic".

Back and above the museum, the villa — very simple, small and infinitely touching, and, like the birthplace in Ajaccio in Corsica, speaking somehow more of its occupant than all the triumphant Paris relics. Here his exile had not yet begun to be great and tragic, and the villa is hardly touched even by melancholy. Probably only the sentimental prefer minor masterpieces and little rooms left behind by great men in defeat — and perhaps it is even more sentimental to see irony in the charming, elegiac simplicity of this pretty, rustic villa, still so alive, and the pomposity of that pastiche-façade, all Eagles and *la gloire* and dustiness.

122

The villa is cool as a breeze and bare except for occasional pieces of the original furniture, the walls decorated charmingly with Italian *trompe-l'œil* murals, pale and gentle, with draperies, doves and *nœuds d'amour,* sunset-clouds in sugar-pink (tactless, one would have thought) and a dear little Egyptian Room, all hieroglyphics, camels and palms and signs of the zodiac, tenderly intended, one supposes, to be a comforting memory of past glories to a repenting tyrant.

Even the Egyptian Room, and a visit from Marie Walewska, did not keep him to enjoy the green hills and the simple life. From the long windows one can see out to the Bay of Portoferraio, and that way he went.

Portoferraio is good to get to know because you can reach everywhere, including the mainland, from it — the bus depot is magnificent, with a bar and a huge timetable which is a miracle of complexity and reliability. But don't stay there. We chose to move on to Marina di Campo, a straggly little village with a quay as big as a diving board and a beautiful shallow arc of a bay.

Out of season, it is as quiet as a prolonged eternal siesta. The sun shines for ever, small mulatto-brown French, Swiss and Italian babies spout and roll like flying fish in the shallows, the big bright-coloured umbrellas lean drunkenly out of the white sand towards a violet sea. Life becomes so complete a capitulation towards laziness — there being no art treasures or historic buildings to nag one's conscience into Baedeker-activity — that we came slightly to resent the fact that, drugged with sun, we had to stagger quite a way from our umbrella through warm sea to reach deep water, and couldn't simply flop straight in from dry land.

To break the exquisite monotony we earnestly practised Italian in the afternoon-delivered morning paper, and made walks into the well-kept, vine-covered hills behind the village, every inch cultivated, passing lonely little pink-washed houses, bare and scrubbed and swept, with vine-grown steps and terraces and geraniums in pots. We climbed to San Piero in Campo, once a Roman village, now a huddle of strange, straight alleys, crazy houses, stray chickens, and an immemorial square of stone and green leaves that one comes upon suddenly, a place of great quiet, where a few people sit in the shade under one gigantic tree and a little bar with a bead curtain sells beer as cold as ice.

The Elba climate is never harsh, almost always fine, especially in spring. Last year, when almost all Europe had hardly seen the sun, Elba was green, blue and golden. It is an industrious, active island, heavily vineyarded — especial local products, *aleatico* and *muscato,* dessert wines of a gentle, refreshing sweetness, that hold a true taste of grape. There are wonderful deserted beaches, overhung with smoothly wooded hills, perfect swimming and I gather good fishing.

The cliffs and pinewoods have that character peculiar to Mediterranean islands — they seem seaborne, and still to shelter a local god, a *genius loci.* Here it is a good spirit, with none of the blackened fires, the sudden rage, the awful drama and the grief of the Corsican landscape. Past ages are present, amicably and with no feeling of awe. We discovered a magnificent building of great dignity and antiquity on a hill above Porto Azzurro, which turned out to be the penitentiary, very monastic and peaceful-seeming. And on one of the gates of Portferraio a stone is inscribed in memory of the great Cosimo de Medici and the fortress he built here — *"Templa, moenia, domos, arces portum Cosmus florentinorum Dux a fundamentis erexit A.D. 1548".*

If you take a car, the ferry boat from Piombino will ship it as well as you. And Napoleon and Mussolini, both of whom cared passionately about roads, seem to have left the island a good legacy for motorists. But if you go without, the bus service takes you everywhere — or within easy walking distance.

WHITTAKER

ſCOTLAND IN AUGUſT

by ERIC LINKLATER

Every year, when August broke through the calendar, Scotland used to be invaded by a prosperous, well-uniformed, magnificently armed international force intent on killing that handsome and succulent bird the Red Grouse. From England and the United States they came, with princes from India and millionaires from the Argentine, all attended by their loudly talking, clear-eyed, confident and betweeded women; and the remnant aristocracy of Scotland — those, that is, who had failed to let their rivers and their moors and forests — assembled in turreted castles or white-walled lodges their cousins and their creditors, their brokers and their bachelor uncles; and on the glorious 12th made common cause with the invaders, and on a thousand windy hillsides manned the butts and waited for the birds.

The 12th of August was to Scotland — or, to be accurate, to that part of it which had the means and the leisure to be interested in shooting — what the 4th of June is to Eton, or the 4th of July to America, or the 14th of that month to Republican France. It was a day of serious festivity, of ritual rejoicing; and throughout the loneliest and loveliest parts of the land, from the glens of Angus to the moors of Caithness, on the great slopes of Perthshire and the river-glinting lands about the Dee and the Don, the shooters went plodding up their chosen hill, and the red grouse called from the heather: "Go back, go back!"

But when evening came the grouse were hung in the larders of the shooting-lodges — grouse counted by the hundred brace, brought down by expensive 12-bore guns from the rushing sky — and the shooters with their confident women were full of a physical and spiritual contentment, and the keepers and the gillies (if the day had gone well) full of whisky. The 12th had been honoured; the grouse that had been hatched for sport had been killed in a splendid ritual, and a vast pleasure had been reaped from barren hills.

But times have changed — times change their linen as regularly as if they had been well brought up — and though the 12th is still a well-regarded date in the calendar, and grouse delectable on the table the 12th has lost its social importance, and grouse moors no longer contribute much to the economy of Scotland. The world of migratory sportsmen has shrunk; and nowadays the majority of August invaders who cross the Border carry not cartridge-bags and double-barrelled guns by Purdey or Holland & Holland; but concert programmes, the score of a Beethoven quartet, or Arnold Haskell's latest guide-book to the ballet. There are still invaders, and they still come in August; but the Edinburgh Festival is their objective, not grouse.

If, however, I were visiting Scotland for the first time, and had only August for my visit, I would divide my month into three, and in the first third drive about the Border country with a copy in my hand of Scott's *Minstrelsy of the Scottish Border,* or the Oxford *Book of Ballads.* Though from sea to sea — from Berwick-on-Tweed to the Solway Firth — is only about eighty miles, those rolling hills have the secret of enormous space, and in their hollows and gentle valleys are the gloriously ruined abbeys of Melrose and Kelso, Dryburgh and Jedburgh, Dundrennan and Sweetheart Abbey; where time has preserved a savage history in broken but still soaring beauty, in exquisite vacant windows and noble choirs half open to the sky. The abbeys and the ballads and the rolling hills go well together, and they should, I think, be deliberately mixed.

Then I should drive northward to Stirling, and from the high castle contemplate a Highland tour. A little painless history could be imbibed, and the first expedition should be to the Trossachs — but very early in the morning, for in a holiday month the Trossachs may be obscured by tourists, and their charm requires solitude. Then (with averted eyes for some part of the short journey) I should drive by Balloch to the west side of Loch Lomond, where a winding road offers enchanting views, but may carry too much traffic. (I myself prefer sight-seeing in winter, when the roads are empty and the weather is often delightful.) From Loch Lomond the road goes by Crianlarich and Tyndrum (look at a map) to the Pass of Glencoe, where really bad weather may be an advantage, for the impending hills acquire a fearful gloom in which the famous massacre seems all too credible. Then, at Ballachulish, there is a ferry across a turbulent stream and the road runs through the Great Glen; the great divide that almost makes an island of north-western Scotland. At Fort Augustus the road crosses the Glen, and a few miles farther on, near Castle Urquhart, the motorist must be very careful of other motorists, few of whom are watching where they go. And why? Because they are watching the long, deep loch that lies below the road, in hope of seeing the Loch Ness Monster. But if an accident is avoided, the traveller will arrive in Inverness, which is called the capital of the Highlands.

From there he would be well advised to go west again, to Kyle of Lochalsh, to Gairloch and Lochinver — to the broad beaches and the enormous hills and the sudden little mountains of the wildest part of Scotland. He should go as far as stamina and his tyres endure (the roads are not very good), for here are the noblest views in Scotland: the Seven Sisters of Kintail, Skye over the water, Loch Maree, the Summer Isles and Suilven . . . But it is time to turn again, and the road to Edinburgh lies through Aviemore, Drumochter Pass, Pitlochry (there is a summer theatre there) and Perth, where one can linger with pleasure.

Then, for the last third of the month, the Festival. And if, as so often happens nowadays, I — a devotee of the arts, a glutton for culture — have a great burly, thickly muscled wife (or mother, or sister) who prefers exercise to aesthetics, why, I should pack her off to play golf at Prestwick or Muirfield or St. Andrews; at Carnoustie, Aberdeen, or Dornoch. The east coast of Scotland is almost entirely composed of golf courses, and rain makes no difference to a golfer on sandy soil.

125

BELGIUM

by PENELOPE GILLIATT

It is easy to be enchanted by the unknown, a thousand miles up the Orinoco, or trekking across Turkey alone with a history of Byzantium and a motor bicycle; but a place familiar by the proxy of books or films or hearsay starts off at a disadvantage, like someone saluted with "I've heard so much about you." The way that education has of sending us abroad with rhythmical mutters in the memory about esparto grass and tunny fish and warm-wet-winters is fairly calculated to blunt delight.

Belgium is a near neighbour and relative of ours, so that the British go there even for the first time with a long acquaintanceship (Blunden, Maeterlinck, the Waterloo of *Vanity Fair,* Emile Cammaerts, soldiers' tales of Brussels on leave, small smatterings of Napoleonic history and the 1830 aftermath). Perhaps it is the least annotated part of Belgium, the Forests of the Ardennes, that turns the unexpected face and makes one begin again at the charmed beginning.

The Ardennes are one of the most beautiful places in Europe for a holiday, but known as little as our own wild and lovely Northumberland. Such unconstrained reaches seem paradoxical in the country that can proverbially be crossed in a tram ride; these really are forests, sizeable enough still to harbour red deer and wolves, run through with dark streams and rivers brittle in the sun. *Châteaux* at the turn of a river or the prow of a hill gather round them a manor house, a farm, a family church, in the feudal way. Withdrawn and recollective as wooded places often are, the Ardennes have their own mystery, and that is perhaps what marks them out from many another holiday site with equally fine fishing and walking and cooking. This is the ground that raised grunting boar as stupendously unlikely as the pterodactyl; they saw the *Princes-Évêques* build bastions of power around their cathedrals which no comer could storm; that sheltered the sustained, devoted scholarship of the mediæval schools-men and the sudden flowering of the *vagantes* after the Dark Ages.

Any stranger to Belgium should certainly spend a day or two in Brussels *en route* for the Ardennes. It is a spacious, uncontrived city, with too much of its own colour to deserve the less-pretty-twin-sister comparison with Paris that many rapid travellers have made: historically evocative and contemporarily energetic. Its new blocks of apartments on high broad boulevards, like those outside Lisbon, are purposefully modern and unselfconscious about it. The Musée d'Art Ancien has a motley collection, some very fine things amongst it: there is a charming, dim little Maes called *La Lecture* and a bigger one, *La Songeuse,* beautiful studies of the withdrawal and the fitful alternation of waking and sleep that mark old age; there are several examples of Franz Hals, de Hooch, Van Dyck, Rembrandt; a collection of fifteenth-century tryptychs from this part of Europe that makes an interesting comparison with Giotto: and an exquisite little Crucifixion framed in velvet, attributed to a Franco-Flamand master of about 1400, with the poignant, boneless curves of the body that expressed the mediæval sense of tragedy.

In Namur, we were at the gate of the Ardennes. It is a lovely city, spiritually as old as the hills even though scores of sieges meant that it was largely rebuilt in the eighteenth century. (To this very day no fewer than nine of the oldest British regiments have Namur's name on their regimental flags.) It stands at the confluence of the Meuse and the Sambre, looped round with a citadel that embodies parts of the original castle of the

Counts of Namur; from there, the view of the roof-tops is as model-perfect as the Thames scene at the opening of the film of *Henry V*. By city law, all roofs in Namur must be in the same bonfire-smoke blue-grey.

Namur is an expert hostess. It has good hotels (we had lunch at the excellent, picturesque Hospice d'Harscamp, converted from a convent of 1750), a casino (a rather regrettably neo-Riviera note in an old city, but every tourist *venue* in Belgium has one), the astonishing grottoes of Han quite close, and a Théâtre d'Été that mounts opera in the open summer air. The main bridge across the Meuse is eleventh-century, and one can find little roads in the old quarter that are not a great deal younger: the rue des Brasseurs, the rue Marcelle, the rue de Fer, with little Madonnas in their wayside niches of which one at least is fifteenth-century.

The Hôtel de Groesbeeck de Croix, built in 1750, is now a museum. It is well worth a visit, this private house of two hundred years ago, perfectly preserved. It is decorated in the Louis XIV and XV manners, with a long vaulted passage from front to back paved with red and grey marble, an elegant oak staircase with a snow sleigh left oddly at the foot, and an Ionic domed rotunda at the head, that hides ingeniously within a square lantern tower, and a kitchen—often the room most immediately evocative of the life a house once harboured—lined with priceless Delft tiles.

Go south from here, and at once you climb into the forests and brook-veined plateaux of the Ardennes. We went first to Spa, the town that gave its name to the whole group of watering places. Its eggy-smelling waters were first noted by Henry VIII's Venetian physician; among the famous who came were Montaigne, Madame Récamier, Wellington, Peter the Great, Joseph II and Disraeli. In spite of the honour roll, though, it has now an extraordinary ageing pettiness, ghosts of illustrious rheumatics in an atmosphere grown obsessive and very ordinary, preoccupied with health in a way that to the fortunate hale and hearty is contradictorily unhealthy. The baths themselves witness the wealth that must have poured into the place: one comes up steps like the Capitol's and into a foyer as neo-classical as a casino, with founts of the waters at each side and air like a damp warm flannel over the face. The baths themselves are given in copper, the one material which the waters do not corrode—all but the mud baths, primeval ablutions in a wooden bath-trolley filled with thick black slime like kidney-soup. "Very healing, and it washes off quite easily," said our guide. And later, proudly, "In all the history of the bathestablishments" (making a word of two in the Germanic way) "only two persons have died in the baths."

Dinant, gallant, entrancing little town on the Meuse, is only a few kilometres farther on. It has a terrible history of battles, from the first sacking by Charles the Rash in 1466 through two hundred assaults and seventeen sieges to the American bombardment of the last war. Before the Great War it was entirely a mediæval town; all of its ancient stance in myth still remains and much of the old architecture, along with the traditional brass and copperware (hence *dinanderie*) and intricately wrought gingerbread and loaves. It presses close on the river with rocky mountains at its back, a town of frail-seeming cottages that hardly balance on the slope and a church with a tower like a shallot hung by its root (Victor Hugo called it a *pôt-à-eau*). The fishing on the Meuse here, and on the Lesse, a walk away, is famous: for trout, for instance, that may come deliciously to the table *à l'amande* or *à la crème*. The place of Dinant is altogether in time with *la pêche*: there is a casino, and a *piste de danse,* but nothing can stir the exquisite stagnancy of the place. To gainsay the gentle monotony, though (because then it is so good to submit to it again), one should brave the *télésiège* that swings spider-like on a thread up to the Tower of Montfort, and certainly see the extraordinary grottoes and caves beneath the town's very feet.

LOURENÇO MARQUES

by ALAN ROSS

To the South African, Lourenço Marques is an image, adapted to the sub-tropics, of the Europe he dreams about, but may not know — a lush, pear-shaped windfall from the continental tree that, despite its long descent, its bruised African rottingness, secretes still some of its original flavour. But it is an experience, as well as an idea; gastronomic, visual and giving off a slight but enticing illusion of sin.

You can drive out of Johannesburg at dusk, the hollow of Alexandra Township filled with the smoke from thousands of braziers, the veld flooded with saffron and green light, and soon urban Africa, with its dwindling flickers of neon, is drowned in the darkness. The long, flowering grasses smell sickly-sweet over the red earth; as the sun slips like melting ice over the horizon the ox-carts hang out their lamps, searching a place for the night's outspan, and an African, his loosely rolled umbrella slanted like a rifle on his shoulder, bicycles away beneath the brightly nailed Southern Cross. The road, gently humped over the plains, runs straight as a ruler eastward for nearly four hundred miles. Near the Mozambique frontier, the scaly hills of the Eastern Transvaal flatten out and for the best part of the hundred miles to the coast the narrower Portuguese road is without incline or curve. The sun splashes through the groves of fever trees, their branches like luminous, pale green coral, and one notices, a second sign that the Union has been left and Portuguese territory entered, that the skins of the Africans working along the roads are blacker—a blue-ebony colour.

The Portuguese treat their natives sternly but less self-consciously than South Africans—they may discriminate, but do not legislate against them. But few people visit Mozambique to compare racial attitudes: they go largely to eat, though there are other, as interesting, and valid reasons. For example, the architectural styles of Lourenço Marques, which, ranging from the sugary Manueline to the ultra-modern, are as various, experimental and, on the whole, graceful as anywhere in the tropics. Though the future of Lourenço Marques as a commercial port was virtually underwritten in 1895, when the railway line was run into the Transvaal, the city has really only come into flower in the last ten years. The architects, who work together with the civic authorities, have therefore had a new town to play with. They were provided with a wide bay, a river, and a backcloth of intersecting hills sloping out of forests almost flush with a string of sandy beaches. They had room, and they had approval to indulge their fancy.

So that, driving down the wide boulevards of the city centre, one is conscious of sunlight and space, of tall honeycombed buildings and deep-set, glass-fronted shops, of trees and sea, and striped mosaic pavements imposing their marine curves on the eye. Liners come almost into the main square, their sirens hooting over the herds of fishing boats, each one bearing large painted eyes on its bows, that thrust their masts up behind the planes and palms like a further row of trees.

From the port, looking uphill, the eye is taken by the verticals that seem to be cut out of the green headland at their back: the cathedral, consecrated in 1944, soaring lily white and cool from its heart-shaped pedestal; the Hotel Girassol, a circular tower, an un-leaning version of the tower at Pisa, the vast Rádio Clube, home of Lourenço Marques radio, which feeds its dance music into the radios of automobiles parked late at night by the sighing beaches.

But the truly exciting architecture of Lourenço Marques, which, more than anything else, should make it develop into the gayest, as well as most harmonious of African cities, is domestic. The majority of the private houses now being built are more imaginative and spectacular than anything one can find in Europe. Parts of Lourenço Marques in fact resemble rocket-launching sites, the houses themselves—cone-shaped, with tubular chimneys, some like linked lighthouses, others like groups of bottles. Their forms are essentially sculptural: smooth flowing, unresistant to wind. They are mobiles invented for a climate, giving a sense of movement and exhilaration, as if they might suddenly take off. The "flatted house" is a particular feature of Lourenço Marques: from a ground-floor entrance opening into a garden, the flat spirals up three or four storeys, the top floors of nearly all of them looking over the coconut palms of the Avenida Trigo de Morais to the blue water of the Baia da Boa Paz.

Several of the newer blocks of flats are perched either on huge cantilevers, or mounted on pillars: the central space underneath serves as garages, and the air is able to circulate freely, rather in the manner of the stilt-supported Queensland houses in Australia. The external finish of the flats produces the effect of an abstract painting, by Miró perhaps, or Mondrian, small or large rectangles of dove grey, coral pink, black and cinnamon-coloured paint laid against each other, both horizontally and vertically.

There are various subsidiary leisure activities in Mozambique: you can hunt wild game around Panda and Mapulanguene, buffalo, impalas, jackals, and lions for example, but you may not shoot giraffes, gnus, ostriches, vultures or serpent-eaters: you can watch bulls being fought in the giant new stadium (the Portuguese exhaust, but do not kill their bulls, and the bulls each enter the ring only once in their lives): you can see cool and brilliant soccer played in heat and before heated audiences, and you may observe, in the football close season, the energy and passion devoted to the national sport of basket-ball. There is good sailing and fair underwater fishing, a lavish supply of beaches.

But when all is said and done the major pastime, for the unsated visitor anyway, is eating: the eating of prawns and chicken, the drinking of Portuguese wines, the *vinho branco verde* especially.

Nearly everyone in Lourenço Marques eats their prawns and chicken *piri-piri*; that is to say, smeared with lemon and chili, cooked over an open flame and basted lavishly with butter. The sauces are of two kinds, hot and very hot. You will not get better prawns or chickens anywhere.

The best places for prawns and chicken are the Cervejaria Coimbra and the Galo de Ouro: they are eating-houses rather than restaurants, with nothing fancy in the way of décor to distract the customer. The radio blares, the floors are tiled, and they bring you hot rolls and butter to absorb the saliva while you are waiting. When you begin to sweat, they know the *piri-piri* has been satisfactory, and after you have torn two chickens apart in your hands — a knife and fork is a gentility the Lourenço Marquino rarely bothers with — the African waiter will bring you a tin bowl of warm water, some slices of lemon and a towel. You feel very much like a boxer at the end of a gruelling round. There is scarcely any talking in these eating rooms: the atmosphere is genial, but self-absorbed and ritualistic. The service is scrupulously attentive.

Generally, one drinks a Portuguese white wine, a *vinho branco,* and the ordinary *vinho da casa* is both cheap and adequate. Less cheap, but quite excellent, is the Casal Garcia, a white *vinho verde*—green, as opposed to the *maduro,* the matured wine. It is on the narrow delicate frontier between dryness and sweetness, very faintly sparkling, and as charming to drink as it is to look at. (The "green" wines can, of course, be either red or white — Casal Garcia is made from the must of black grapes as well as from white grapes.)

If you stick to prawns or chicken, you will probably settle for Casal Garcia,

Montanhez or the very dry Quinta da Aveleda. If you care for steak à la Portugaise, fried with egg, tomato, pimento, and garlic, then you can drink the red Vila Real, an admirable cheap wine of youth and virility.

The prawns are caught mostly by the fishermen of Catembe, a small fishing community on the right bank of the Espirito Santo estuary, where at various times between the 16th and 18th centuries the Portuguese and Dutch established bases among the mangroves. Catembe is primitive, poor and romantically beautiful: the prawn boats come in with the tide, and the heaped baskets of grey prawns are hauled up the mud flats to the wooden huts, built on stilts, that line the long deserted beach. On the dead, white branches of fallen trees the nets are hung out to dry, and the sea laps up to the edges of the huts and around the sand-filled carcasses of ancient ships that litter the shore. Behind the mangroves, remains of the first European settlement — broken columns, dilapidated archways, crumbling architraves and pediments — slowly settle in the rising undergrowth. The lapsed grandeur of an old town, the perennial struggle of a fishing community that is both old and new, are symbolised here in dwellings beaten to their knees by time and the elements.

And across the bay the dazzling white shapes of a city spreading its wings, take flight into the future. A whiff of life, a whiff of death. Meanwhile, the chickens sizzle on the grills, the prawns grow pink as sunrise, and the knowing sailors, land-hungry, life-hungry, make bee-lines for the Penguin, there, in the drumming smoke, to be solaced according to their needs.

THE GREAT TOM OF ABYSSINIA

by THOMAS PAKENHAM

My Ethiopian friends in Addis Ababa were curiously reticent when I said I was going to make a trip this spring across the remote and romantic highlands. "It's all right now," said one, "but just wait until the great Tom." But he did not enlarge on this. "I don't envy you off into the wilds with the great Tom coming on," said another. I refused to be put off. I had long planned a trip across a slice of the Abyssinian plateau that has never been properly explored, though once the seat of a medieval Christian empire. It was said that there might well be rare manuscipts lying unrecognised in the remote churches of the interior. I decided to go and see, Tom or no Tom.

I made no preparations beyond planning my route, hired two sinister-looking guides and a spavined mule (all I could get) and set off gaily for the interior. On the day we left the road and struck out into new country it was explained to me that the Tom was not a person at all, but the great Lenten fast of Ethiopia, which was just beginning. For forty days all animal products are forbidden, while vegetable foods may only be eaten from midday to midnight. The news appalled me. I had brought no food at all with me, telling my friends that I would live off the country. My worst fears were quickly confirmed. The great Tom dogged our footsteps as we marched, haunted us as we ate, and kept us awake in the long hours of the African night. It seemed to bedevil everything: the mule fell sick and I was forced to walk all the time instead of riding at intervals; and the guides lost their way, so we wandered about in circles pursued by mosquitoes at low altitudes, and fleas at high ones.

Now there were no baskets of eggs and legs of mutton pressed on us by hospitable peasantry. After much haggling we would get in each village a handful of beans and *berberi* (the ferocious red-peppers of these parts), pound it away with a pestle and mortar and then cook the result in some reeking black stew-pot that an obliging lady of the village would (for a price) lend us for dinner. We plodded gloomily over the interminable plateau. The sick mule brought up the rear and brayed sadly at frequent intervals.

On the eighth day we reached a church which was obviously of a great age. Its round thatched roof had probably been repaired many times, but the original timbers could be seen holding up the eaves of the roof. A particularly fine tiara of ostrich eggs (remains of a pre-Christian egg-cult common to Egypt and Ethiopia) glowed like fairy-lights on the top of the roof.

We sat down under a bamboula tree (the African sycamore) to wait for the priests. In a few minutes they would be with us, the carpet would be spread with the most delicious of vegetarian banquets, and at the end of the meal, like a glass of rare liqueur, would be brought in the books I had come for. Weak with hunger and excitement, I dozed off with my back to the bamboula tree and with the apron of my jitterbub (I was in full Ethiopian dress) as a serviceable parasol.

I was rudely awakened. A furious argument was going on between my guides and a number of turbulent priests. No, the *ferangi* (or Frank) could not stay—there was no food; it was the great Tom, the time for prayer and fasting, not sight-seeing. In vain my guides showed my letters of introduction, my firman from the governor-general telling every headman and priest to help me. In vain we cried that we would go at once if we could see the manuscripts. There were none, they replied scowling, and even if there had been we could not have seen them. There was nothing for it; we had to shake the dust of Georghis off our feet and plod on.

In the next few days the going became even more difficult. We were now at an immense height, nearly 11,000 feet I calculated. The ground was very soggy as their little rains were just ending. My white suit became caked in the rich black boggy soil and I wondered why I had brought the absurd outfit.

With the height came the cold. Even at midday, with the African sun almost vertically above, it would be chilly inside a stone hut or a church or under a bushy juniper tree. But at night the cold became unbearable. Coupled with the cold were the fleas. Never have I encountered such a ruthless army of under-fed fleas.

The twelfth night was the worst. Ahead of us lay the spine of Mount Abuna Josef, a frosty blue line that disappeared in patches of cloud blowing across the plateau. We were invited in by the *shum* or headman of the district, whose house was one of the largest in the province of Dalanta. It was oval, not round, with a double thickness of stone walls, and small annexe for the sheep. The roof was well thatched and reinforced with poles like the sprouting spokes of an umbrella. There was only one aperture, the door, through which passed to their resting-place the *shum* and his family, also their dogs, the *shum's* horse (a fine Arab), his wife's mule, their much-prized cow and their flock of sheep. There was, of course, no window or chimney to let in unnecessary light or let out the smoke. We coughed and choked in the darkness while the *shum's* wife was gracefully preparing the inevitable vegetable stew.

After dinner there were the usual questions: why had I come without guides and soldiers like other Europeans? And if my mule was ill, why didn't I hire another? Above all, why did I travel in the great Tom?

Gradually conversation became easier. We talked about the harvest: it had been a terrible year, they said, with the rains breaking too late. We also talked, as one always did in the country, about the glories of Addis Ababa. Then we began to talk of old manuscripts. Gourds of honey-wine were passed round and I presented the *shum* with a thimbleful of Remy-Martin that I had kept in readiness for just such a convivial evening. It was late before the *shum* rolled the great round door to the mouth of the hut, a huge block of wood like the stone which sealed Polyphemus' cave. As he did so the *shum* added with a laugh: "Tomorrow I can take you to Gischon where there may be some old books."

I was light-headed with the news and well primed with alcohol. But the night was bitterly cold. I wondered where to sleep. The *shum* and the *shum's* wife slept behind an arras, the family huddled round the embers of the fire and the various animals had selected other choice sleeping places. Eventually I curled up in a goatskin rug and lay awake shivering, while from far away on the plateau came the faint chuckles of hyenas foraging for carrion.

Next morning the plateau was in a dense cloud, which gradually cleared, revealing to the south a monotonous grassy plain receding to the horizon. Every couple of miles were the fungus-like clusters of huts, hardly worth the name of village. To the east the plateau disintegrated alarmingly. Great gorges interposed between one piece of plateau and the next, deepening as the rivers they carried left the watershed behind. It was to the east that the *shum* had directed us, sending his son as guide. He himself with the cunning of his race had stayed behind.

Ahead of us the great massif of Gischon gained stature as we descended. On the summit, said the *shum's* son, the church of Gischon Mariam had been built to be safe from the infidel. Did I not know, he added, that after the First Crusade the true cross had been brought there for safety?

Soon we began to climb. The mountain rose some three thousand feet in natural terraces, covered first with scree and euphorbia, then with wild olive trees. We toiled up past numerous patches of plough. The plough men stopped to ask us where we were going, and on being told, repeated like a Litany: "Gischon, Gischon". I was off to Gischon — poor, mad *ferangi* — and in the great Tom, too! they laughed hugely.

The church of Mariam, when we finally reached it, gave no signs of being old. But, of course, it could still contain an old manuscript. I sat down under the usual bamboula tree and waited. The *shum's* son had disappeared into some hut and was obviously drinking arak. My own party were far behind, coaxing or pretending to coax the wretched mule up the nearly vertical path. There was no sign of any welcome from the priests. The silence was ominous.

Then came, as in a dream, a gorgeous procession from the church of Mariam. Ahead trooped boy deacons dressed in purple and gold and carrying huge processional crosses of beaten silver. Behind came three priests magnificently arrayed, each with an acolyte beside him who carried a sort of golf umbrella. All sang soothingly and harmoniously. In the rear came a fourth priest even more splendidly decked than the rest. He carried a great book which I easily recognised to be of the best style and period.

I was inarticulate with surprise and delight. Luckily my party had arrived just in time over the crest of the hill and instantly engaged the priests in conversation. "Look at him," they cried pitifully, "he has come all the way from London just to see an old book with pictures. He has walked hundreds of miles"—only two hundred actually but I was grateful for the exaggeration—"through terrible bandit-infested country because he is a Christian and likes Christian books. Now he begs you to show him yours. Yes, he has come to see this one book, and in the great Tom, too." My guides broke down, overcome with emotion as was customary when they made this moving little speech.

But for once the speech had the desired effect. To my amazement the priests greeted me politely, and at the mention of the great Tom the high priest smiled. Was the *ferangi* then a Christian? I pointed to the pectoral cross that I wore as an ostentatious sign of my faith. And had he kept the great Tom like one of them? It was unheard of, they all cried. There was a chorus of congratulation which I rather sheepishly acknowledged. Then the book was given me to study.

It was a 15th-century Book of Gospels with nearly seventy illuminated pictures. No finer Ethiopian book of this period exists. I was struck at once by the force and originality of the artist. There was special vitality even in conventional scenes like the Annunciation with Mary spinning and the Angel Gabriel saluting her. But there were also many charming details which other manuscripts lack: the stone before the tomb like a vast megalith dwarfing the centurions, the Magi holding out their gifts like Bath buns, and the Shepherds pointing to a dream of the Nativity floating over their fields like a huge balloon. Most amazing of all was the excellent condition of the manuscript. It had survived not only the invasions of the 16th century, but centuries of the abuse which all manuscripts suffer. Yet the pictures themselves were as glowing and fresh as they must have been on the day they were painted: their colours were the brilliant translucent colours of Chinese lacquer-work.

As we left the church the priests were still muttering to themselves "and in the great Tom, too, and in the great Tom." Who can tell: perhaps it was my folly that won them over?

BY SEA TO AUSTRALIA

by CYNTHIA NOLAN

"It's really a weird show. The country has an extraordinary hoary, weird attraction. As you get used to it, it seems so *old*, as if it had missed all this Semite-Egyptian-Indo-European vast area of history, and was coal age, the age of great ferns and mosses . . . A strange effect it has on one."*

Australia remains a weird show, even to someone born there, and after many years spent abroad I still feel the pull of this far-away place. A part of Asia, yet full of English suburbs; geologically fantastically old, yet with new, experimenting people; a landscape fragile as a fairy tale, yet menacing. And light—light as though nothing *but* light had ever existed. And then deep black nights descending with the rapidity of Newton's apple.

As you will not be sailing from Newgate, and are free to choose your date of departure, I would suggest that the best seasons for visiting the greater part of the Antipodes are either autumn — April and May — or spring — September, October — which flickers with wild flowers and the first bright cotton dresses. In January and February the summer temperatures in Sydney may reach one hundred degrees, but it is chiefly the high humidity that some visitors find tiresome, although evening always brings a refreshingly cool sea breeze. Melbourne is hotter and dryer, and correspondingly colder in winter. Yet in both cities one has winter sunshine, and in Sydney we have eaten our lunch on the veranda during July.

Gibraltar, your first port of call and a few days out from Southampton, can be depended on for sunshine and wine. Now you are really away, basking through the Mediterranean to Port Said. It is worthwhile to leave the ship and drive down to Cairo, a teeming, flat, dun-coloured city with violet shadows. Cairo's Museum is one of the world's greatest, and stuffed with gold and lapis, treasures from Tut-ankh-amen's tomb. The old bazaar is still a maze of booths where craftsmen sit cross-legged, in an atmosphere of intrigue and secrecy, softly tapping their hammers on metal. Along the dusty bank of the Nile, women shrouded in black, as they were in Biblical times, pass by with their donkeys and small tattered children.

And so on again, through the high-pitched ochre landscape, to go on board at Suez; perhaps to call in at Aden; and then the warm journey to Ceylon. It will certainly be hot and damp on land, but fifteen minutes away there is comfort, air conditioning, cool drinks, and a view of white sands and palm trees at the Galle Face Hotel. One can swim lazily in some small secluded cove or, in the city, bargain for semi-precious stones, ebony elephants, tussore silk, and antique silver jewellery.

Make the fascinating day trip up to Kandy, passing palm-roofed native villages and at least one group of elephants bathing each other in the shallows of a river. If you are lucky you may strike festival time in Kandy, when religious rites are observed with processions, splendour, music and dancing. In any case there are the great temples with their orange-clad, shaven-headed, dignified priests moving through the scented shadows.

As the days on board slip peacefully past, one settles down to cross the Equator, and after eight to ten days at sea there is the real landing at Perth, the city which Sir Kenneth Clark once compared to a René Clair film. And indeed there is an off-beat lyricism about it, perhaps due to the absolute clarity of the light on the shabby Victorian

*From *The Letters of D. H. Lawrence* (Heinemann).

134

architecture, and tram-cars with perambulators obligingly strapped at their backs. This, combined with the scent of dry grass, birds' song, heat tightening the cheeks, and the sudden sight of verandas on every house, is apt to choke up returning Australians who glance mistily at each other, exclaiming "We're home!"

Perth is perhaps the slowest and gentlest of Australian state capitals. And Western Australia is the state for wild flowers. In and around Perth bloom the famous and extraordinary lime, scarlet and brown velvet "kangaroo paws," waratahs, grevilleas and wild boronia.

The choice is now to continue on the ship, or take a plane east. I prefer to fly over the fantastic treeless Nullabor plain which forms the desert bridge to Adelaide, a well-laid-out city of churches and University buildings set among olive and wine growing hills. From there a little train makes the sixty-hour journey to Alice Springs, a town which possesses an almost medicinal winter climate of bracing sunny days and frosty nights. En route, cinnabar-coloured sand dunes and mesquite trees form a landscape so arid, delicate and vivid, that one thinks one must be dreaming.

Alice Springs is virtually the centre of the Continent, and from here one can go by bus into the multi-coloured exposed geology of curious gorges, and across spinifex deserts to water holes beneath purple mountains. For the more venturesome there is the magnet of the world's greatest rock. Pink and mighty, Ayers Rock lies like a stranded whale in the midst of a staggering plain. (Formerly almost inaccessible, the journey to the rock can now be made by plane or truck once permission is granted by the appropriate Government Department.) Standing beneath the rock shelves, naked stone-age men still paint their tribal symbols on the walls of the monolith, for centuries a meeting place and a centre for their ceremonies.

Interesting country extends for a thousand miles in all directions from Alice Springs, and there is an excellent internal airline which enables tourists to fly from the strange, dry, silent desert where camels, kangaroos and emus roam, to the jungle in the north inhabited by alligator, buffalo and water-birds. Back in Adelaide you can again choose sea or air for the next step to Melbourne. This city at the tip of the Antipodes has, surprisingly enough, a magnificent van Eyck in its National Gallery. It also has a hard core of business, an unlimited enthusiasm for horse-racing, well-laid-out parks, the River Yarra, and inexplicable drinking laws. Intellectually Melbourne is perhaps the most lively of all Australia's cities.

At Sassafras, Olinda and other small towns thirty to fifty miles away, are fern and eucalyptus gullies where one hears liquid bird calls and sees the fabulous lyre-bird singing and dancing on its mound at dawn. This disconcerting bird can imitate almost any sound, including train whistle and the sobbing of a hurt child. Here lives the rare and shy platypus, the web-footed mammal which lays eggs — so startling, biologically, that when first shown, stuffed, in Europe, it was dismissed as a taxidermist's practical joke.

Somewhere further to the north-east lies the Kelly country which the famous outlaw Ned Kelly and his gang rode and ruled for a brief period during the 'eighties. Those interested in myth and folk heroes can take a tram-ride in Melbourne to the Aquarium to see the iron armour which Kelly constructed out of plough shares, and which for a time preserved his life.

Tasmania, the southernmost state, has also had her share of bushranger-highwaymen, and some of her most beautiful mountain ranges and peaks are named after them. I remember one in the north, Brady's Lookout, which towers over rich flats where clovers and grasses hide the legs of the red Herefords who stand, switching their tails against the flies, in the shade of willow trees growing beside shallow, fast-running trout streams. In Tasmania can still be seen a few fine examples of Georgian Colonial architecture. The antiques are somewhat over-prized, but there are the most beautiful private gardens in Australia. Little evidence now remains of the legendary brutality of the convict settlement at Port Arthur, nor of the clash between early settlers and aborigines which led to the latter's extermination.

Five hundred miles north of Melbourne (if you have decided to continue by ocean) is Australia's largest city. Sydney is eccentric and volatile and perhaps most typical of Australia. Certainly cosmopolitan, it relates to some earlier period of America. The vast flow of emigrants has profoundly altered the once all-pervading English flavour. Already food, clothing and the arts are showing the benefit of this influx.

Almost on the doorstep of the business section are the great surf beaches which have helped to form the Australian outdoor personality. Unending sun and the challenge of the vast, crashing Pacific Ocean have produced hundred per cent literacy in swimming, and the superlative skill of the Lifesavers. These men have developed a highly coordinated and voluntary system of lifesaving, a precise pageantry in ceremonial display and uncanny brilliance in handling boats which they race through towering waves.

Not an hour from these surf beaches are areas of primitive bush with birds, beasts and flowers to match. The gentlest of the animals is the koala bear. Fastidious to a degree, he will eat only the tenderest leaves of one among all the hundreds of varieties of eucalyptus available to him. And there are goannas with blue tongues, snakes and venomous funnel-webbed spiders.

Winding through much of this landscape flows the Hawkesbury, the river which reminded Trollope of the Rhine. But the oysterbeds along its banks are marked by delicate stakes in a rhythm more Chinese than European. On a breezy day, the scent of orange and guava blossom bursts across the dark water from the fruit farms.

Yet another five hundred miles north again, and we come to Brisbane. Once a feared prison camp, now a pleasant sub-tropical capital, this is a city almost without chimneys. A great number of the houses are built on stilts which protect them against termites and allow cool air to circulate beneath the living room. A morning bus ride from your hotel will bring you to a rain forest where giant orchids bloom almost out of sight on a ceiling of interlacing boughs. A completely hollow, lace-like tree reaches to the sky, its construction inexplicable unless one knows that a parasitic fig has slowly strangled its host which crumbled, leaving a paper cut-out, ten stories high.

In the shops of Brisbane there are tropical fruits — mangoes, paw-paws, granadillas, custard apples. Choosing between the excellent barramundi fish and fresh crab, one begins to think of the Great Barrier Reef. "Now I have got this far I might as well go a little farther," you rationalise. And, indeed, a thousand miles pass easily on a very pleasant cruise north to Cairns, a convenient point for starting all explorations of the Reef. One of the simplest ways is to take the boat which leaves every day for Green Island, only a few miles from the mainland. At low tide a new world is exposed, a bumpy plain that is the living coral reef. To overturn any rock is to expose a brilliant microcosmos.

At night, armed with flashlight and shod in protective heavy boots, one can walk across the reef observing living shells trailing their diaphanous mantles, spotted snakes, octopi, fish marked with turquoise, scarlet, indigo and black stripes, and small voracious sharks. Far back, out of the black night, is a gleam of light from the hurricane lamp. Once out on the reef after dark, all sense of distance and direction is lost. Take a watch: tides wait for no man.

Perhaps D. H. Lawrence should have the last as well as the first word. In 1922 he wrote: "But Australia would be a lovely place to lose the world in altogether. I'll go round it once more — the world — and if I ever get back . . . I'll stay."

136   *Bikkhu Monks, Ceylon* ROLOFF BENY 1970

overleaf: Golden Gate Bridge THOMAS SENNETT 1973

HAITI AT MARDI GRAS

by JOHN GIELGUD

Jean-Paul met us at the airfield, a huge good-looking negro speaking slow meticulous French, dressed in an American-cut suit of powder blue with gold threads in it. We purred along through Port-au-Prince in his white roadster. First there were only huts, then a huge market place, a fantastic walled cemetery with towering obelisks, and streets lined with colonnades of square stucco pillars. Outside the undertaker's two elegant hearses, white-carved, white-plumed, stood with empty shafts, like Oliver Messel coaches in a theatre property-room waiting to take Cinderella to the ball. Up on the hill, in the residential quarter, steep narrow little houses with pointed corrugated-iron roofs, and fretwork balconies in brilliant colours, perched silent in the blazing heat amid high palm trees and thick blossoming foliage.

It was not until midday, twenty-four hours later, that we first heard the drumming, and the carnival tune which hardly stopped during the whole of the next three days and nights . . . a gay, melancholy little tune with a haunting and irresistible rhythm, always accompanied by a regular drum-beat to which everyone sang and marched and danced. We had been driving down an apparently empty street when suddenly we came upon a little group of six or seven men. Some were playing drums and pipes. The tallest men were dressed as brides. They wore white masks, with rosebud lips and blobs of carmine on the cheeks, and large caps with streaming veils. They marched along, holding up their long white dresses with one hand, and painted paper sunshades with the other.

There was no shoving or jostling as we stood in the street to watch the big procession pass; and two hours later, when the last of the floats had gone by, there was no litter as in European cities, no trampled flower-beds or broken chairs, no cartons, papers or cigarette butts. The carnival costumes were all simple and cheaply made, but beautifully worn, and designed *en masse* to create the maximum shock effect of line and colour. Two hundred men were in pale blue, with turbans and large earrings, two hundred others in steel helmets covered with gold and silver paper. The Haitian girls were beautiful, with crowns and wreaths on their dark hair, perched high on thrones and pedestals, bowing gracefully and blowing kisses to the crowd, who applauded wildly as the men dragged them along in the huge decorated cars. Between each car a hundred maskers jumped and sang and danced, and occasionally encouraged one another with swigs of rum. The sun blazed down. The bands played continuously.

At night the open-air café was crowded with people who had been in the procession. Their costumes still looked fresh and unsoiled, and they still danced indefatigably. Sleep was impossible. All night the drums went on beating, and still the little groups of masked people kept bursting into the hotel garden, whacking out the carnival tune, screaming and leaping. Next morning we drove up into the mountains, thirty miles away. But even in the smallest villages the Mardi Gras was not forgotten. Tiny children ran out of the huts and raced along beside the car, masked and dressed fantastically, turning cart-wheels and trucking for our small change. Some older men soon caught up with the children and began to dance. We bought bouquets of flowers which they pressed on us, done up in tight bundles like Victorian posies. As we got back into the car, the headman, his face bound in a muslin scarf, posed for us: standing on the edge of the cliff, a bouquet in his hand, his huge false stomach stuck out, his legs wide apart, grotesque and unforgettable.

Goreme Valley, Turkey BARRY LATEGAN 1971

MY SORT OF CANAL

by E. ARNOT ROBERTSON

The more I read about the world's important canals, like Suez or Panama, the more I long to get away on a weedy, neglected, moorhen-haunted English one, say the Oxford, which runs through sleepy Banbury, where the famous cakes come from, past Aynho, one of the loveliest villages in this country, to join the Grand Union at Napton. And I shall, too, in about a fortnight, when my husband and I start taking our small motor-launch from Teddington up to the Nene, near Northampton.

"What's Nasser got that I haven't got? The wrong canal, mate, that's what! Ought to be put in charge of the Welsh section of the Shropshire Union. Couldn't do it a mite of harm. It's falling to pieces anyway." This excellent reflection came from one of the narrow-boatmen, the few remaining commercial users of that vast network of inland waterways which seemed to be doomed altogether, a little while ago. There are two thousand four hundred miles of canals in the land, or there were; only about two-thirds are still navigable. The railways bought them up at the turn of the century, when they were crowded and prosperous, and deliberately let them fall into decay, afraid of their competition. I know just how reed-choked and water-starved the Welsh section of the Shropshire became — we went from London to Llangollen, via Birmingham, on our last canal holiday, and we towed, punted, struggled for days through floating reed which the wind jammed together into solid obstruction under innumerable bridges. But now there has been a change: it is not often that something which has been allowed to become disused wins back its popularity: every year, though, more and more people like ourselves are discovering what a magnificent summer playground lies neglected at our back doors. The most unlikely places are linked by inland waterways, Tewkesbury to Brentford, Stafford to Warwick. The recent petrol shortage, and the present congestion of the roads, have given the canals a fillip too. Trade is looking up a bit and the locks (high time! The gear is rusty, extremely heavy, and we have to work the gates and paddles ourselves) are actually being repaired. Even the Welsh Section is being re-organized to let a reasonable flow of water through the "flight" where it breaks off from the main Shropshire Union.

A "flight" is a series of locks so close together that they open, with back-breaking effect, one out of another. Nature puts rivers, inevitably, at the bottom of the scenery, where there is bound to be a restricted view: but man runs canals along the sides of hills, so that for a good part of our trip to the river Nene we shall be floating along looking down over a wide stretch of country, on one side; and in many places, where the canal is double-embanked for miles, on both sides. (It was a staggering engineering feat, the building of the canal system in the last century, not with the mechanical grabs, bulldozers and theodolites, as it would be today, but just by armies of chaps with wheelbarrows, and a good eye for country.)

Occasionally the view is altogether too unrestricted for my liking, where the canals are slung, like long tanks, across gorges on tall viaducts. There's an impressive horror of a place over the river Dee, about six miles from Llangollen, where there are not even any railings on one side to break, for the eye, the 160-foot drop on to the rocks below, round which the river swirls. If you suffer from vertigo, as I do, you drive across, your hands clammy on the steering wheel, trying not to look at the unprotected edge of the

138

canal, which of course is about on a level with your feet, so that there is nothing but space all round you. I am told the view is lovely: I have been across four times but have never seen it except accidentally out of the corner of my eye.

The only other patches of distress are the tunnels. Perhaps someone inclined to claustrophobia as well as vertigo is not ideally suited to life on English canals: it's a great tribute to our inland waterways that I love them all the same. At blessedly long intervals (thank goodness there is only one tunnel on the way to the Nene) a canal disappears into a black hole in a hillside, and we follow it, I doing my clammy act again. Some of the tunnels are over two miles in length. There is not even a glimmer of light to be seen from the other side of the hill for what seems like hours, but is probably only minutes: then a tiny point of brightness appears, and we steer on that. The roof, of brickwork which has not been repaired since about 1860, is always dripping with water; cascading with water in fact, in the places where there were once vent-holes to let in light and air. These have all been choked for years with vegetation, and in the thick blackness the brambles growing overhead let down long, trailing dead fingers which softly touch your face as you pass.

The warning that one of these worse-than-useless vent-holes is close ahead comes by an increase in the splashing all round in the blackness; but in our boat, anyway, no-one can cower in the cabin for shelter while in a tunnel: a bit of canvas has to be held carefully over the acetylene lamp perched on the bow as a headlamp. If that ever went out in a tunnel, and I emerged at all, it would be mopping and mowing with frenzy. The roof is so low, which adds greatly to my mental discomfort, that men lying on their backs on the deck of a narrow-boat could "walk" their craft through, in the days when all canal traffic was horse-drawn: if you flash a torch upwards you can still see the footworn grooves in the roof. While the boat went through the tunnel, the intelligent old trace-horse ambled over the hill, usually by himself, along a railed path, to meet the boat at the other side. (I wish I could do that.) Nowadays the motor-drawn craft, in couples, tandem-wise, go blinding through with electric headlamps lightening the gloom, and think nothing of the tunnels at all. (I wish I could do that, too.)

The brightness of the world on the other side seems almost unbelievable, always.

Dusk is the loveliest moment of the day. Then, as a rule, the wind drops, and when the surface of the water becomes absolutely still, swallows in companies swoop down to achieve that breath-taking triumph of precision flying, drinking at full speed on the wing: I never tire of watching this, nor the rest of the wild life which comes in the evening for water. Charming, clumsy hedgehogs lean too far down and fall in, and have to swim till they find a piece of broken bank low enough to let them climb out. Because these are the quietest places in England, the banks of the little-used canals have become the haunt of all the shyest things left in the land: badgers, foxes, adders, the occasional rabbit (unsuspected by those who believe they have abolished this pest-to-them, but pleasure-to-me!).

When night falls the swans, decorative enough by day, take on a new dignity. At all hours they drift past us as we lie tied up to the bank. Grave and moonlit, they bend those gracious necks of theirs to peer in at us through the long windows beside our bunks, meeting our eyes from a distance of about four inches. The procedure is almost invariable: they drift on, shaking their heads, as though it were hard for them to believe that any sight as awful as we present, horizontal, wrapped up in sleeping bags, had really been seen on their canal. Then they come back for another look, just to make sure. And go on their way again, shaking their heads once more, convinced of our repulsiveness. Swans, even small cygnets, rarely seem to sleep at any time of the day or night for more than a moment or so at a time, head under wing.

"J.D. loves B.S." "L. don't love no-one but G. for true." On the old, old uprights of the lock gates, and the vast beams, made out of whole chestnut trunks, which act as handles to swing the locks open, there are messages from one narrow-boat to another, usually written in tar on whitewash. Narrow-boatmen nearly always marry girls from other canal families, because the life in the tiny painted cabins is very hard for women; a boatman's wife requires tremendous water-skill, best learnt in childhood, and if you get a girl from the land it is the accepted belief that she probably will not stick it. "Gone for the alimony" is the terse explanation you get, all too often, if you ask what happened to that pretty girl from the local town whom one of the boatmen was rash enough to court and win, only a season ago. So that there is doubly touching quality about these love-declarations, set up for all to see, in youthful certainty that human emotions are as enduring as chestnut-wood and tar. The sad fact is that they are not, on canals or elsewhere. Tar is practically indelible. It is fifty years or more since many of the great lock-beams have been whitewashed: *does* L. still not love anyone but G. for true? I hope so, but can't help wondering. Even on my sort of canal human nature is frequently less admirable than the landscape.

But what an enchanting holiday lies ahead of us, unless anything unforeseen happens, or the weather is absolutely awful. We shall go at a snail's pace. In hilly country, where the locks are close together, fifteen miles is a good day's journey. We shall really get to know the country through which we pass. This is the finest antidote I have ever found to the normal pace of a town-dweller's life.

MADRID

by SIMON HARCOURT-SMITH

In my childhood we would often pay a visit to relatives on the Bay of Malaga. Yet we never seemed to break our long southward journey at Madrid. What with Aunt Amy's sea-sickness which, beginning at Victoria Station, lasted roughly until the Pyrenees, and my mother's fussing lest the drinking water had not been boiled, moving between London and Andalucia was an experience one wanted to cram quickly into the past. Even an excited little boy was in no mood for lingering . . .

The grown-ups never mentioned Madrid with affection. An artificial, soulless city, they said, like Washington or Canberra, boasting neither the flowery *Ramblas* of Barcelona, nor the sinister mysteries of Seville's half-Moorish slums.

All the more violent therefore was the enchantment of the rosy domes and of the great palace on its rocky plinth when many years later I first saw Madrid from across the Manzanares. In the high evening air (Madrid stands some 2,000 feet above the sea) the whole city seemed to glisten and sparkle just as it does in Goya's *Vista*.

In subsequent years I have never left Madrid without a pang, never found my pleasure blunted by many returns.

As one sits of a morning on the Gran Via watching the long-lashed girls sidle by, two by two in sharkskin suits almost as tight as their own magnolia skins, the Hemingway heroics of the Civil War seem no less remote than the heroic grumbling figure of San Isidro, guiding the Christian army through a Guadarrama blizzard to victory over the *paynim* at the frozen Madrid fort. Perhaps the winter lingered unduly in the mountains that year, for San Isidro's Week, when Madrid gives itself up for seven days solidly to bull-fighting, falls generally towards the middle of May. In Goya's time — and in Madrid Goya is ceaselessly at your shoulder — San Isidro's Festival also involved a fair that sprawled across the meadows on the opposite bank of the Manzanares. But this fair became a pretext for very free behaviour, and in one of those fits of prudery that seize Spain from time to time the disgraceful festivity was proscribed. Now there is only the bull-fighting in the *Semana de San Isidro*. But what bull-fighting! The finished talent of the tauromachic world concentrates in Madrid; the rest of the season's ordinary Sunday fixtures seem almost an anti-climax beside the pyrotechnics of that inspired week. It is as if the Centre Court Finals were to be played right at the beginning of the Wimbledon Tournament.

Philip II, it is said, would sit on his terrace at the Escorial, twelve miles or so away, and scan his new capital through a powerful telescope for signs of slackness in his Government offices. He may not have managed to prevent a princely languor from sweeping over the rest of his Castilian-speaking dominions, but throughout Madrid's three hundred and ninety-seven years, Philip's telescope has always seemed to be upon his capital. Only during siesta time, from about four in the afternoon till seven, do the turbulent streets empty. Then the traffic lights shut off, the fatherly police disappear — if there is one place in the world of which one can say without falseness "I think your policemen are wonderful," it is Madrid — and one can whizz down the empty boulevards at risk only to oneself and to the stray car that may come shooting round a fountain full of Spanish Gibson girls in stone, who would have been more suitable to the back of a 1,000 peseta note. For most of the other twenty-one hours in the day, the streets have always boiled and clanged. The rest of Spain calls the inhabitants of the capital *gatos madrileños,* for like cats they come particularly to life after dark. Perhaps it is the altitude which makes repose almost unnecessary. Many a visitor can boast of having gone sleepless the twenty-four hours through, but for a scant siesta, with energy undaunted and his thirst for pleasure unsoured.

A city you love but which is not your own holds for you, therefore, neither of modern life's twin ogres — no Bank Manager advising you to cut your coat, nor Inland Revenue Inspector enquiring where the coat came from in the first place. You tend to think of Madrid in perpetual spring — particularly if you are writing of it on an opaque English winter's morning — with the tulips of the Buen Retiro Gardens ranged in a floral Trooping the Colour around noseless statues of past Kings and Queens. You ignore the unctuous monotony of the Castellana, that Edwardian avenue which is the axis of modern Madrid, the Spanish passion for skyscrapers, the icy winds that can rip down from the Guadarramas, the power-cuts after a dry summer when your electric razor behaves like a roller-coaster, and the old crones surely invented by Velasquez who guide you with badly trimmed candles through the cavernous darkness of the Ministries. For the true lover of Madrid these drawbacks are but *grains de beauté* on a charming face. After all, who has not heard Anglophile foreigners speak with apparently sincere affection of our telephone service, even of the English Sunday?

The bustling vulgarity of the Gran Via — officially the Avenida José Antonio, named after the recent Spanish Ambassador's brother José Antonio Primo de Rivera, saint and martyr of the Franco *régime* — with its Spanish passion for modernity, can at least afford you a number of cheap and satisfactory hotels, where the twenty-four-hour service and the cheapness would put any English hotelier to shame. The other favourite quarter for good hotels is the area round the Castellana, among the foreign diplomatic missions. But if you have a little Spanish — *Madrileño* hotel servants are almost English in their reluctance to master foreign tongues — there are innumerable *pensions* or *residencias* to which you can commit yourself with confidence.

Madrid, and to some extent the whole of Spain, brings you a *douceur de vivre* utterly opposed to the polished refinements of France or the cynical subtleties of Italy. It is as if you have recaptured the innocent keenness of childhood's palate, when the water of a Scotch burn tasted more delicate and yet more decisive than does any wine of 1949 today. Rid yourself of the notion that because olive oil is used frequently in Spain, all Spanish cooking is greasy and fattening. Spanish food handled by a practised cook is a good deal less fattening than much of ours and far more stimulating.

Denying their favourite conception of themselves as the essence of moderation, English visitors either tend to react furiously against *Madrileño* customs and food, or become so utterly enslaved by them than no time is left for "cultural uplift". In the likely event of your taking to *gambas* and lunch after 3 p.m., don't let your new tastes interfere with your sightseeing; Madrid and its environs are full of treasures which you will subsequently upbraid yourself for neglecting. From sad experience I have found that it is vain to put off any of the sight-seeing till the afternoon; so emotionally exhausting can it be, that you will in any case need the restoration of a good lunch.

This is no place to harp upon the splendours of the Prado. If its scope be slightly more restricted than that of our National Gallery or of the Louvre we must nevertheless, I suppose, account it the finest picture gallery in Europe. But there are two treasures in Madrid which visitors too often pass by — the Royal Palace, and the Church of the Florida, which lies not far from its foot near the banks of the Manzanares. Perched high above a garden of greenery, curving walks, and grottoes in the Anglo-Chinese style, Juvara's Palace — undoubtedly his masterpiece, with its theatrical colonnades staring into space — suggests a gigantic set for *Aurora's Wedding*. And within is the last ceiling

G. B. Tiepolo executed before his death — the *Four Corners of the World rendering homage to the Spanish Monarchy* — a gigantic, enchanted pattern of negroes, Chinese, Red Indians and fauna that runs the whole length of the *Sala de los Embajadores*.

It was almost precisely at the moment of Tiepolo's death in Madrid (1770) that a violent young genius from Aragon, Francisco Goya, began to attract the attention of the *Madrileño* connoisseurs. His frescoes in the little Florida provide one of the most profound experiences that Madrid holds for the traveller of taste. Somewhat cynically they depict the miracle of a man being raised from the dead to identify his own murderer; and Goya's love, the famous Duchess of Alba, is supposed to figure among the group of *majas* who idly watch the scene from the base of the dome. All this is of less importance than the ferocious delicacy and speed that suffuse the whole composition, a style and a point of view which seem to foreshadow Manet's *Execution of the Emperor Maximilian* and through it so much of French Impressionism.

If its spell is to be profound, a great city must be hedged about with outside delights, pretexts for agreeable excursions. Here Madrid excels, with the added pleasure for us intellectual snobs that these outings are less commonplace than quick canters to Fontainebleau or Tivoli. Speed out towards noon down the long straight road that leads to Aranjuez, through air so luminous you could touch every distant monastery or oil storage tank. Across silver and olive hills, naked to the sun. Then suddenly you are dropping into the shade of the lush, gentle valley of the Tagus, to eat incomparable strawberries and asparagus on the river bank, as petals of shocking pink fall from the Judas trees to tickle your nose. Then feed your soul upon the dream-like room which Charles III panelled with *Buen Retiro* porcelain, or on the expensive rusticities of the *Casa del Labrador,* that workman's cottage encrusted with platinum. Then bump your way across country to Toledo, to gaze at El Greco's *Burial of Count Orgaz* in S. Tomé, upon Greco's own house, and the *Transparente* behind the cathedral's High Altar, perhaps the most audacious wedding of theatrical technique to religious mystery in the world.

Nobody will let you miss the Escorial. Why should you, when it contains Greco's *St. Maurice and the Theban Legion* together with a little-noticed treasure that is a great favourite of mine — the mitre of Mexico City's first Archbishop (c. 1515) made of Aztec feather-work? The thing looks grey enough at first sight, but if you run your finger gently against the tiny faded humming-birds' plumage, you perceive through the dust a heart-breaking intimation of emerald, pink and sapphire, and you feel some of that wonderment which beset *Conquistadores* when they set foot in those fabulous forests new as the morning.

Another day fork right from the Escorial road to La Granja, across the Sierra Guadarrama where the shepherds stand motionless as dead tree-trunks, and where boulders, from behind which you expect Carmen at any moment to emerge singing like billy-o, have instead been stencilled with advertisements for a firm of Madrid oculists. The little palace of La Granja glints pink and white, guarded by rows of terracotta sphinxes. Once, during the Carlist wars of 120 years or so ago, George Borrow saw wild boar come snorting up to the deserted windows. Now there is no sound but the murmur of the fountains, the tallest in Europe, which come faintly to you on the breeze with a scent of sweetbriar, and the chatter of the amiable sentry who is thankful to find a listener for his woes. Terrible moth-eaten old place, he says. Give him the Gran Via and all those new tall buildings. Nowhere in Europe are they building so high as in Madrid . . .

I/LAND OF RHODE/

by LORD KINROSS

Each evening, music, Greek and Turkish, blares from the radios in the cafés. Beneath the mediaeval battlements is a humble Greek tavern with walls of flaking plaster, and an uneven pavement of pebble mosaic. Here, under the glare of an acetylene lamp, within a circle of rickety tables, a young boy in shorts dances alone, with all the solemnity of innocence, in a slow, sedate Greek rhythm. A sailor claps for him in time to the music. A cook fans the embers of a charcoal brazier, grilling meat on spits for the men who sit watching him, talking and drinking as they do so. A boy on a bicycle, a man on a motor scooter, stop to watch. A bus goes by, its passengers turning to see what's on. Around the café rise tenements with lighted windows, insubstantial as a stage set. Flowers bloom in whitewashed tins; a bird perches in a cage on a window sill. At the windows, on stairways, at doorsteps, families sit, gazing downwards, relieved by the cool of the night. Children wrestle in the dust; a baby sleeps in a hammock; a woman sweeps out a room, giving on to the pavement, where a man lies ill in bed. The dance finishes. The dancer picks up his basket, hawks his peanuts among the crowd, goes on his way. Over all there looms, like a moonlit back cloth, the silhouette of a mediaeval city.

North of it, by the harbour of Mandraki, which the masters of the classical galleys called the Sheepfold, is a new quarter, modern and bright and a trifle theatrical, built by the Italians during the short-lived period of Fascist prosperity. Here, among gardens of pink oleander, with hedges of scarlet hibiscus, looking across to a mole where a line of red-roofed windmills marches out towards the lighthouse and the fort of St. Nicholas, is a sea front colonnaded in the Italian manner, with cafés beneath the archways; a modern church built by the Knights of St. John and a Palace of Justice and government offices built in the style of the Doges' Palace at Venice. The Italians turned Rhodes into a gay centre for tourists, producing, as it were, an *opéra comique* setting. They established a spa outside the town, at a spring traditionally associated with Hippocrates. Here tourists took waters which he was said to have recommended in the fifth century B.C., but which in fact were largely imported Epsom salts.

The island has a dramatic natural setting and a dramatic history. The continent of Asia runs out to the west with a flourish, flinging before it, like outposts, a galaxy of peninsulas and islands. This end of the continent has been known since Byzantine days as Asia Minor, a name appropriate enough to its interior — the bare Anatolian plateau

144

within the barriers of the Taurus range. But the coastal fringe is, rather, Europa Minor, a shore of Europe in Asia.

Here, beneath snow-capped peaks and scented foothills, are sheltered bays and long white beaches recalling those of the Western Mediterranean, but on a wilder, grander scale. Here, from earliest times, came the peoples of Europe: Greeks and Romans in search of trade, Crusaders in search of the Holy Land. Here today come people from farther west, in search of holiday pleasures. They come especially to Rhodes.

The approach to Rhodes from the sea is around the south-westerly tail of Turkey, the cape where the Greek city of Cnidus stood. Here, where a segment of rock curves sharply upwards, then breaks off abruptly, tumbling seawards, with the face of some corrugated, dome-headed lion, was the temple of the beautiful Venus of Cnidus, famed throughout the classical world. Cnidus and the opposite island of Cos each commissioned a statue from the great Greek sculptor, Praxiteles. Cos chose a draped goddess, Cnidus preferred a nude one — and thus captured the tourist trade of the age. Pilgrims, connoisseurs of beauty, flocked to Cnidus from all parts of the classical world to see the naked Venus with the "half-suppressed smile" on her lips, admiring, in the words of Lucian, "the delicate formation of every limb ... the harmony of the back, the wonderful fitting of the flesh to the bones, without too great plumpness, and the exquisite proportion of thigh and leg, ending in a straight line to the foot". His companion was so moved that he ran forward and repeatedly kissed the statue. The draped Venus, on the other hand, attracted few visitors to Cos, whose people were thus unable to pay the bill for her.

Today statue and temple are gone; but a harbour survives, its jetties and quays still substantial enough, for all their two thousand three hundred years. To the west of it an archipelago of islands dances away towards Greece, like a menagerie of mythical beasts. To the east of it stretches the Dorian promontory, where the early Greek colonists settled. The boat sails on through the Gulf of Symi, where sponge fishers dive down to a depth of eighty metres, retrieving not merely sponges but the occasional remnants of a classical statue. Finally, there emerges, rising straight from the sea, the blue, mountainous outline of the island of Rhodes.

It was a mediaeval legend that the Colossus of Rhodes, one of the seven wonders of the classical world, had once straddled the Grand Harbour with its gigantic legs. In fact it stood on a site nearby. Erected in the third century B.C., at the cost of three hundred talents (some seventy thousand pounds), it was a statue of Helios, the Sun God, the god of Rhodes, who bequeathed the island to his favourite nymph, Rhodon. A hundred and five feet high, it took twelve years to cast; its fingers were each as big as an ordinary statue. It was destroyed in an earthquake only fifty-six years later, but survived in ruins for nine hundred years more. Finally, in Saracen times it was sold as scrap to a contractor, who is said to have used nine hundred camels to load and carry it off.

The colossal scale prevailed at Rhodes. The city had been besieged by Demetrius, described as a second Alexander the Great, not merely with an army of forty thousand men and a fleet of two hundred warships, but with an immense siege-engine — a tower on wheels of oak, nine stories and 150 feet high, 75 feet broad and 25 tons in weight, needing 3,400 men to propel it. It overtopped the Rhodian walls, complete with catapults, grappling irons, battering rams, and draw-bridges, a top floor which was a nest for archers, a floor beneath it with water tanks, serviced by pumps and hoses made from the intestines of cattle. Despite its aid, Demetrius failed to become master of Rhodes. It was from the ultimate sale of this and the remaining war material that money was raised for the erection of the Colossus. Under its aegis, Rhodes became, with its command of the sea, the capital of a rich commercial empire.

Little today remains of the classical city but a number of statues in the museum, among them a Venus raised from the bottom of the harbour, her features worn and softened and encrusted by the action of the sea water. The Rhodes of today is a mediæval city, like some walled fortress of feudal France or Italy or Spain. Built by the crusading Knights of St. John of Jerusalem, after the loss of the Holy City in the thirteenth century, it fell into ruins during the Turkish occupation, but was restored by the Italians, after the First World War.

The weathered stone walls and bastions of Rhodes enfold its harbour in an austere embrace. Above it, dominating the city, is the imposing castle of the Grand Masters, once a fortress in itself, then a Turkish prison, then the seat of a Fascist governor, now an empty Gothic *palazzo* open to tourists, restored and decorated in Italian "period" style. Around it run two and a half miles of ramparts (originally built in the fifteenth and sixteenth centuries, and restored by Philippe de l'Isle Adam, with the aid of Italian engineers), their severity softened with lichens and wild flowers amid drifts of almond and peach blossoms.

Crusaders of all nations — England, Germany, Italy, Spain, France — once kept guard over these walls. In the steep, cobbled Street of the Knights, like some alley in a French mediaeval town, are their inns, their lodges, their hospital, stern in their stone façades, but relieved by leafy courtyards behind their studded doorways. Everywhere the Mediterranean sunlight has weathered and gilded the frowning stone.

Some of the churches of Rhodes lie in ruins — Gothic ruins unfamiliar in this Eastern Mediterranean landscape; others were turned into mosques at the time of the Turkish occupation, and survive as such. For within the walls a Turkish town still thrives, the slender minarets of the infidel rising above the rugged Christian battlements.

The Turks give a polyglot air to the city. The Greeks live side by side with them — Asia Minor Greeks whose families lived and worked under the Ottoman Empire for centuries. Smaller in number is a community of Italians who have remained behind, adding the leaven of a refined craftsmanship to the Greek and Turkish commercial lump. The Greeks no longer exploit the spa as the Italians did. But, in their rough-and-ready way, they have preserved the tourist amenities of Rhodes.

South of the city, roads encircle the island which is some forty-five miles in length. They wind through an undulating sunlit landscape, shaded by olives and cypresses, scattered with villages of flat-roofed houses, white cubes shining in the sun. Mountains assume gay, fantastic shapes, as they prance down to the sea, breaking the coast into an infinity of coves and inlets, fringed by smooth white beaches. Here are the classical relics of three forgotten cities: Kamiros in its valley, Jalysos on its mountain, Lindos on its glittering bay.

At Lindos the world of the Greeks and the world of Knights coincide. Piled up on a black mass of rock, above a clean white town, are the sun-gilt bastions of another Crusader castle. Within its battlements, relics of a rough mediaeval strife, there arise the slender columns of a Greek temple, built a thousand years earlier, in a more serene and graceful age. Beneath them, in the red-roofed, pebble-paved town, is the Greek world of today, alive and clean, welcoming the foreigner. In the church, its walls glowing with paintings, black, red, and gold, is a notice: "We pray the visitors if they please to give each his penny for god philanthropic." Pleased with the island, they seldom refrain.

I/RAELI DIARY

by JOHN ROTHENSTEIN

MANNES

South-eastwards over the Taurus Mountains, over red lakes which from the high-flying aircraft looked like pools of blood, over Cyprus, a dry leaf afloat on the bluest sea. Then I perceived what appeared to be a white thread suspended in the far distance between sea and sky. It was the line of waves breaking on the long shore of the Levant, stretching away northwards out of sight: Israel, Lebanon, Syria sharing this perfectly straight coast — but how little else!

"We're going to drive straight to Jerusalem," the man who came to meet me said — a breathtaking prospect for one who visits Israel for the first time. We drove across the sandy coastal plain; through Ramle, a small town entirely Arab in style: past dignified burnous-clad figures who sit on miniature donkeys as though they were thrones; past camels, crowds of children, soldiers in jeeps, everything in a haze of dust. The road climbed into the stony Judaean hills. Suddenly we came into a village of Arab houses built on a steep hillside, and a twelfth-century Crusader church. Feeling that the time had come for me to tread this holy and historic ground, I got out of the car. The church was in the care of an Arab who spoke French. Abu Ghosh (for that is the name of the place) was identified with Emmaus . . . but, he shrugged, there wasn't much evidence. There was a stone in the wall with an inscription referring to the X Legion. This genial sceptic doubted whether it really was the men of this legion who cast lots for the garments of the Lord.

Up to Jerusalem: the new city built, so far as I could see, entirely of white stone, with a complex of well-designed massive buildings, either already standing or else springing up, to form a kind of official acropolis.

Woken early by the sun, a fierce yellow ball like the sun Van Gogh saw at Arles, rising above the Old City. A cock crowed. Did it crow for me?

I visited the Bezalel Museum which houses a vast, miscellaneous collection particularly rich in objects of Jewish ritual, and a collection of paintings and drawings which includes a group of Pascin so fine as to compel me to revise my estimate of him. The director of the museum took me to see the series of some sixty-first-century tombs, carved out of solid rock, of members of the Sanhedrin, set in a beautiful garden; at least one of these has a fine classical façade decorated with acanthus leaves or pomegranates.

Access to the Old City being forbidden, I went up to Abu Tor, a high place which overlooks it. On my way I passed through one of the "Orthodox" quarters, a place of narrow streets where, in contrast to the informally dressed and robust generality of the population, walked men wearing black hats, some trimmed with fur, and black suits or loose-fitting long black coats and black stockings. Both they and the children, also

147

dressed in black, wore long side curls, and all looked pale. Many of the·men, I was told, were fanatics and fierce opponents of the State of Israel, regarding as blasphemy its foundation before the appearance of the Messiah.

There it was, the place most sacred to three religions: Calvary and the Holy Sepulchre just out of sight, and likewise Gethsemane, but the surviving wall of Solomon's Temple, the Wall of Lamentation, could just be seen; also, quite plainly, the Dome of the Rock from which Moslems believe Mohammed ascended to Heaven. What is there to say about these endlessly written-about places, down there in the shimmering heat? Nothing, except how melancholy it is that these most holy shrines of three great religions are no longer accessible.

That afternoon I drove northwards from Jerusalem towards Haifa. A few miles distant from it I stopped near the foot of the splendid Carmel range at Ein Hod, a deserted Arab village handed over to a group of artists. Were I a painter or a sculptor, I should find, sooner or later, the close proximity of others sharing my vocation distracting or worse. Therefore I want to Ein Hod prejudiced against the notion of an artists' colony. To me, artists, while they should not by any means be isolated from their kind, should be no more than a leaven. Israel, where a great majority of the artists have been brought up in the traditions of other countries and therefore have little in common, is the last place for an artists' colony. But if anything could have removed my prejudice it would have been this group of enterprising and lively painters — one of them an original Dadaist, with a pretty daughter nostalgically named Dada — sculptors and craftsmen, inhabiting the spacious white Arab houses perched on a steep side of Mount Carmel. They had built themselves exhibition galleries, studios, firing ovens, a common room and the like — they had extended their houses, they had made gardens. As I drove on to Haifa skirting the great Mountain, a huge wall of blackness now, I was charmed by what I had seen and heard, but my scepticism about artists' colonies lingered.

After a visit to Haifa's excellent museum of antiquities, I set out for Acre. The fortified sea-port has a various and momentous history, which still pervades its massive stones. In its history figure persons as diverse as Hercules, Jonathan, St. Paul; Richard I of England and Saladin (as its conquerors), and Napoleon whose assaults it successfully resisted. For almost two centuries it was the principal base of the Crusaders, and for more than four centuries it was entirely deserted. After walking along the massive ramparts — built in the eighteenth century on Crusader foundations — which surround the Old Town, and descending into the Crypt of the Knights of St. John of Acre — a great vaulted Romanesque chamber only recently discovered and now being excavated, which might have been designed by Gustave Doré — I was ceremoniously entertained to lunch in his house by a painter whose career whould have been extraordinary anywhere else, but was, I suspect, nothing out of the usual here. He was an emigrant from the primitive Yemen. Thinking to find the leisure to become a painter he became a shepherd on a collective farm, but this, he told me, was a grave mistake. Contrary to appearances, a shepherd's life calls for vigilance so constant, that, far from enabling a man to paint or draw landscape, it gives him little opportunity even to observe it.

Approaching Safad a splendid prospect opened out suddenly below: the Sea of Galilee, with Tiberias clearly visible on the near side, and on the far, the Syrian shore rising steep and tawny. Safad is an ancient town, the capital of Upper Galilee and set high on a hilltop. It was long the chief centre of Cabbalistic study, and the author of *The Zohar*, the basic book of the Cabbalists, is buried here. A last, aged Cabbalist is said to survive and I went in search of him from one splendid old synagogue, vaulted and white or blue-washed, to another, listening to the sonorous ineffably melancholy prayers and watching the old rabbis with their rapt expressions. But the last Cabbalist was not to be found.

There is a narrow passage giving entrance to Safad from the country, called the Passage of the Messiah; and an old woman was pointed out to me who had sat for ninety years at her window, which looked on to it, waiting for the Messiah. "What if He came when I wasn't there?" she asked her friends when they urged her from time to time to leave her vantage point.

Down past the hill on which the Lord delivered the Sermon on the Mount, to Capernaum and to the ruins not far from the shore of the synagogue where He taught. In spite of the bustle of pilgrims, Capernaum (now called by its still more ancient name of Kfar Naboum) retains a serene and lyrical air. Farther along the shore, near the traditional site of the Miracle of the Loaves and Fishes, a multitude of black goats, minded by blue-robed Arabs, were cooling themselves at the water's edge. To the places along the shores of the Sea of Galilee and to rural Cana, Nazareth provides an odious contrast. It is not too much to say that the thieves driven from the Temple have re-appeared in force in Nazareth: I saw accredited guides, hired at fixed rates, harrying visitors for tips, and attempting to extract "extras" in return for chips of chalk alleged to come from the house of the Holy Family.

From Nazareth, I went to Ein Harod, a *Kibbutz,* that is to say a collective farm. This is run in accordance with a rigorous discipline: the members of it own everything — except a minimum of personal belongings — in common, and do not use money, except for external transactions; all necessities are supplied in return for work.

Passing over Ascalon and Beersheba I flew down to Eilat, the new port at the head of the Gulf of Akaba. The Gulf offered a spectacle unlike any I had ever seen. To begin with, the sea was really blue — a far deeper and more brilliant blue than the Mediterranean. This wedge of blue is walled by diverging ranges of red, jagged mountain. On the left lay Jordan and in the distance beyond, the arid mountains of *Arabia deserta;* on the right, Israel, and not far away, Egypt. I first went inland up the valley which is a projection of the Gulf. Turning away from its white earth and scattered tamarisks into a region of red rock too hot to touch, and shaped as though by some crazy sculptor, was like turning from a real world into a nightmare. It is a fierce region where nothing grows and the only signs of life are the lazily wheeling, sharp-eyed vultures and an occasional huge crow. I walked upon the site of King Solomon's copper mine, and picked up two little fragments of slag from the site where his refinery stood five thousand years ago. After lunch I went out into the Gulf in a glass-bottomed boat. Beneath it I saw suddenly among the coral reefs something man-made and quite near the surface. It was a crow's nest of a sailing ship, and resting on the sea-bed was the ship itself, both hull and rigging intact and the bleached white, tinted the palest green by the limpid water, I have never seen a stranger or a more beautiful sight. Putting on a glass mask and snorkel I swam out into the sea, over the miraculous coral reefs, blazing white with "flowers" of sapphire and of scarlet, and among the darting blue fish. Swimming over a coral reef, which can grow so near to the surface that you think you may be scratched (or worse), and passing over its farther edge and seeing the sea-bed fifty feet below put me in mind of childhood dreams of flying over cliffs.

Israel today offers to the traveller the most exhilarating spectacle — a modern state with the latest techniques at its command, emerging with dazzling speed in a setting of the rarest natural beauty, and of unique antiquities, the discovery and study of which has become the chief national pastime.

/ICILIAN VE/PA

by ANDREW SINCLAIR

Swimming in the Gulf of Spezia, I felt dead Shelley's hand hold my left ankle coldly. Or so I said. And shouted to prove it. The red-haired French girl swimming with us was sceptical and talked of jelly-fish. But, later on, she showed us a bronze manikin, two inches of shaped corrosion which looked convincingly antique. She said it was genuine Etruscan. Local middlemen were selling them for a few hundred lira near the new excavations at Selinunte in Sicily. We were not sceptical. We left by our Vespa next day for the south.

It was late autumn and hot. So hot that we might really have seen Naples and died and got no farther, had not a xenophobic mob made their Neapolitan holiday happier by assaulting us with pigs' bladders, small sticks, burping whistles and pinches from behind. We fled at midday through windless Calabria, making our own wind on our moving Vespa. We could not stop. For the shade of the occasional tree by the road was always full up. If the tree was small, a man lay asleep in its shadow; if large, a man and his donkey. Those who owned scooters, however, left their machines in the shade and lay in the sun; machines are valuable in the south, men not so much. While, if two or three trees were gathered together, there was a bar to exploit them. Passing the three temples at Paestum, we drove over the mountains all night in the moon and reached Reggio the next evening.

By ferry to Messina, and quickly through the town; that is the best way to begin a Sicilian holiday. First stop down the coast road is the tea-shop of Taormina, where the English colony long ago brought its four o'clock habits. Lord Bristol reorganized one of his many hotels here, on the hill standing over the most perfect bay in the Mediterranean, where a sandy semi-circle split by a tongue of land and a small island holds the nibbling sea in its mouth. If the Englishman abroad attracts, stay here; it is his hotel from home. But if every prospectus pleases where only the known is vile, make plans to hurry past to Catania, only stopping to declaim a few phoney Horatian tags in the Graeco-Roman theatre in Taormina, which is the largest and the ugliest and the reddest in the island. Like the visiting Englishmen and me.

Etna squats off the road to the right, occasionally puffing. The fields grow cold lava. Racked rocks twist the imagination. All at once you see the hardness of Sicily in the bleak and bare and stripped light of the sun. The black, frozen-molten stones are set in the red earth against white dust; the primitive paints jar as sharply as the shadows cut short of life by the sun. For Sicily is a battleground, used to frequent destructions by men and nature. The Sicels held it and then the Greeks, the Carthaginians invaded and the Romans; they were followed by Vandals and Ostrogoths, Byzantines and Arabs. Count Roger won it for the Normans, the Swabian Emperors inherited it and the Angevin Kings and the Aragonese. Hapsburgs and Bourbons ruled there; even Lord William Bentinck and the English army ran the government for a few years. Garibaldi conquered it with his 1,000 men in 1860; the Allies conquered it with 160,000 men in 1943. The invaders have left their buildings and children and dialect words mixed up in the hot-pot of the island, which daily plays out its battles again in the clash of hostile colours on the ground, and the fight of the sun against the shadows.

The road runs across dry plains to Catania, where the Athenians made their base to attack Syracuse. The Greek theatre there is as much of a failure as their expedition and as fallen as Athens. The road, well surfaced now, hurries on to Syracuse; there you can plot out where the Greek camps lay and their walls and the hill from which their night attack recoiled headlong. In the National Museum a superb collection of remains and bald statues and pot-bellied jars mutely tells of the past, guarded by a frieze of seven gargoyles with lions' faces by the door. A great Greek theatre opens its ridged, upturned palate of white marble to the too-blue sky. It is worth sweating to the top of the amphitheatre under the high sun, for a fountain cracks the rocks in the pillared shelter there. Wet green moss from the stone, put on the forehead, scares away heat-headaches like frightened fish.

Sunning and winding ourselves on the spinning-wheeled Vespa, we made it through Noto, Modica, Ragusa, Vittoria, Gela, Licata and Palma to Agrigento and Selinunte. Then we realized why we had travelled so hopefully and so fast to Sicily for the arrival was even better than the hope. In Modica, late at night, stranded, finding the advertised hostel as yet unopened, we were put up by an ashamed Town Councillor, who thought it a personal insult that the promised amenities of his town should not exist. He bought us meals next day, guide-books and stockings and wanted us to stay a month. We could only stay a day. But Modica showed us the civilizations squeezed together cheek by jowl within the boiling bowl of its five hills. It has more Spanish churches and monasteries than any other town of its size in Italy; these surround an untouched Arab *casbah,* seemingly lifted from a Valentino film. The Church seemed to be the only local industry; but they were hoping for the new tourist trade to come, scattering dollars. This was one of the reasons for our rapturous welcome, although traditional hospitality was certainly their chief motive. For the Sicilians still are more exaggeratedly hospitable to the beautiful than you could believe. You only have to be a beautiful, blue-eyed blonde, which I am not, or to take one with you, to find the Sicilians open-handed to the limit of embarrassment. Their hands leap to their thin wallets or to the caress quicker than any prevention.

There are only three classes of travelling women recognized in Sicily: wives with husbands, sisters with brothers, and whores. Other subtler relationships are misunderstood. Therefore, touring girls must sport a ring and a protector. But wherever they go, the fantastic local worship of *la modela americana,* which is confined to slim girls and big cars, will surround them with free grapes, free drinks, free food, free stares and free offers of marriage. It is wonderful to be a foreign girl in Sicily, as long as there is male help within call.

As we scootered to Agrigento, the main road became full of donkey-pulled tubs mounted on wheels, bringing in the grapes. At night, a lantern was meant to hang behind them; but this was often hung in front, to keep the cart-driver company. Vespaing in the dark was interesting always — with tarmac suddenly changing to gravel, donkeys weighed down with hay and sticks, men all at once leaping up out of the murk, and unlit carts. Especially round Gela, the road became a farm-track; for the district is still that fertile region which made it the granary of Rome.

We stayed days in Agrigento, at one of the state-sponsored hostels, built in the manner of mock Viennese skiing huts, blown by some alchemy from the Alps. Five temples spot the hills round the hilly town, temples to Hera, Aesculapeius, Hercules, Vulcan and Concord, the one virtue the quarrelling gods lacked. Lying in the Temple of Hera at midnight, watching the stars make the sky a purpled pincushion of pricks of light, and a broken pilaster balance the moon precariously on its pointed end like a neon ball on a seal's nose, we knew why we had come and why the word "beauty" is banal against the sight of the Sicilian night.

We came to Selinunte, where nine temples lie in a spoiled scatter, an expanse of spirit in a waste of stone. A city of two hundred thousand people, it was razed to the ground by Hannibal, son of Gisco, in 409 B.C. Lizards run among the square miles of disjointed blocks of stone; also one tarred road. Two temples have been reconstructed, one badly with concrete additions. The wasted stones look towards Africa over the slight concave of the lens of the bay, that sharpens the Mediterranean air against the eye in an infinite exactitude. The sun sets there in a frame of shattered pride. The keeper of the temples is a sympathetic man, who killed leopards with a bow and arrow in Kenya, and hides depths of joy in the pocks of his brown face.

Our time was trickling away like the egg-timer sand we strained through lazy fingers on the beach. We set off again to see the most beautiful fifth-century bronze statue of all in an income tax office in Castelvetrano, and a fantastic Roman mosaic in Marsala, where springing leopards were caught for ever in a coloured net of mosaic squares. We slept in another government hostel in Trapani, a town of salt and ships, with more barber-shops than even bars; it stretches down the tentacles of its salt-pans and docks from the hill of Erice above like a polyped into the saltier ocean. On a foggy and cold and unusual morning, we climbed 1,200 feet up to Erice, where a perfect Norman fortress town is preserved by the refrigeration of the winds.

We descended with relief to the plains, which seemed almost cosy now, after the bleak heights. We went inland to Segesta which has the most singular temple and Greek theatre in the island. The theatre is at the top of a hill. You can hire a horse and ride there at the guide's pace, jogging upwards all the way, but, scolloped at the peak, lies the Platonic essence of the perfect theatre, the imagined Idea of Theatre realized. Its back-cloth is a sheer drop of hundreds of feet and the view of the surrounding hills, brown, red, forcing their attention upon you. The marble semi-circle of the seats rings you on the stage in an open claustrophobia, with the sky sitting like a hollow helmet on your head. A whisper carries to the limit of the seats.

So we went on to Palermo, and the ship to Naples. Palermo is an ugly town, but near it are the greatest mosaics in Europe, greater to the uninitiated than those of Ravenna and Istanbul. In the Capella Palatina and Monreale, gold glazes put the semi-dark to light, and the stylized figures and biblical scenes have a frozen motion that calms all restlessness to a willed quiet. There is time there to stand and stare; while the restrained charm of Roger II's *San Giovanni degli Eremiti* with its Arab garden and sugar-pillared cloister is the coolest of endings for a Sicilian trip, until the night boat to Naples takes the traveller and his Vespa back to Vesuvius.

Sicily is a juxtaposition of oppositions, black and white, red and yellow, old and new, poverty and wealth, the relic of invaders which overcame them all. There is no place where I would rather return.

BRUGES

by PAMELA HANSFORD JOHNSON

"Whether the tourist has only a few hours to spend in Bruges," goes the Guide, "or takes it as a holiday centre...." All wrong. In both respects, all wrong. A few hours in Bruges is like tipping one's hat in passing to Helen of Troy. And it is just through taking it as a holiday centre, a place to sleep in while tearing round a new bit of Flanders every day, that people miss the secret of it altogether. It is a tourist centre only in the sense that tourists scamper through it while "doing" Belgium. A few hours, an evening with the illuminations, perhaps a night or two — it is just no use. The point is to stay in Bruges and not move, for as long as you can spare the time. You won't need a car: a car is a positive nuisance, since it tempts the visitor to widen his horizons. In Bruges you walk, you sit about, you lose time — not waste it, simply lose it, like a handkerchief or pencil out of your pocket. It is the quietest place under the sun; to slip within it is to slip between the pages of a *Book of Hours*.

It was one of the world's great cities before the sea silted up and left it dry and thirsting on the plain. Its power and riches melted away. And in place of the merchants, the captains, the bankers, came the tourists who, by their habit of dropping in and out, left it inviolate: a tourist city less like a tourist city than any on this earth.

It is bounded by a bracelet of canals, with an inner mesh of waterways. When I first went there thirty years ago the place-names were French: Quai Vert, Quai du Rosaire, Rue aux Laines, Rue Nord du Sablon, Lac d'Amour: now it is the Groene Rei, the Rozenhoedkaai, the Woollestraat, the Noordzandstraat, the Minnewater. Despite a well-heeled, French-speaking *bourgeoisie* living a brisk social life of dances, tennis and golf, it is an obstinately Flemish city: if you ask a fervent Nationalist the way he will probably pretend he understands no French. "Quai Vert" might be a suburb of Omsk for all he cares.

Visiting Bruges for the first time, nothing is more charming (if impracticable) than to walk from the station to the Grand' Place, which takes about twenty minutes. The first impression is of a bright, gay, new suburb, with charming parks, geraniums, ornamental waters, an inn called the Watermill, and a general air-scrubbed liveliness. Go down past the inn: now it is reminiscent of the Backs at Cambridge. The red and white houses (most of them new) are garlanded with lawns running down to the river, and the willows trail in the stream. Further, now, into narrower streets, not so new, not so bright. The first wall-shrine: a metal Christ in a lantern, with paper flowers, His candle burning. Narrower still, and darker; the first step-gables. Humble windows veiled in queenly lace, heavy with grapes and vines.

The bells begin to ring from everywhere, whole tunes and broken tunes, big Bong Bongs, little notes fluttering along like lime-flowers on the wind. Turn a corner now,

153

and here it is: the full green beauty of the quays — Dyver, Rozenhoedkaai, Groene Rei, the boatloads of tourists chugging under the bridges, the man with the megaphone: and on the Quai du Rosaire, the most beautiful corner of all, the probing swans clustered together into a huge white rose. Over the rooftops is the octagonal tower of the Belfry, signpost of the city. In Bruges it is impossible to get lost. You are miles away from it, you think. You are tired. The bells sound bleak and distant. You make a Proustian turn round an unfamiliar corner and are checked by the thing itself: the Cloth Hall with the Belfry above, the Lion of Flanders flapping on the standards, black and crimson and gold.

The centre of this splendid square is a vast car-park, which is a pity. The green statue of Jan Breidel and Pieter de Coninck, the butcher and weaver who organized a successful revolt in 1302 against their overlords, looks small and swamped in a flood of big, glossy cars. The trams have gone, that once clanged over the cobbles. But still the Brugeois sit outside their cafés, listening to the carillon. They are cheerful and prosperous in this living town with which they have encrusted the past.

But they have protected the past pretty carefully. As in Venice, there are restrictive laws to control dangerous flights of fancy: neon-light signs and enamelled advertising plates are banned on façades within the periphery of the old city, and a shopkeeper contemplating a new awning must submit to the city authority a sample of the textile he has in mind. When they rebuild, it is with care. When the old Cranenburg palace fell down, the Brugeois built an honest replica: it looks much as it did when the townsfolk imprisoned in it Count Maximilian, and made him witness the torture of his minister, Lanchals, on the rack the latter had had the misfortune to invent. It is a café these days.

Now go along to the new Groeninge Musée Communal, which is near the exquisite paddock of Notre Dame, and see five rooms of the most wonderful paintings in the world, faultlessly hung: Jan van Eyck's *Van der Paele Madonna*; David's ravishing *Baptism of Christ,* with the pearl-faced women inattentively praying in the Courbet-coloured wood; Memling's *St. Christopher*; Bosch's *Last Judgment*; and again David, with his beautiful horror picture depicting the flaying of the judge who has taken bribes. Then go and sit in the paddock or walk about the town, and you will see, alive and alight, the faces these men painted: in a priest, the embarrassed Canon van der Paele: in the woman in the pastry-cook's shop, canny Margaret van Eyck: in the baker, the thoughtful, dedicated flayer of Sisamnes, no sadist, simply a man who thinks that anything worth doing is worth doing well.

What have *we* been doing, and what's the time? Time for lunch — somehow we have lost a bead or two from our string of hours and can't imagine where they have gone. Afternoon and evening stretch ahead. This is autumn, with the light solemn and the air still; the leaves are just beginning to fall from the limes. There is a carillon concert tonight, but that is all. The great event, the Procession of the Holy Blood, takes place in May; the pageant play is five-yearly, so we shan't see that again till August 1962. We have lunch (soup, *fondu au parmesan,* steak, pastries, fruit, cheese, for 12s. a head) in the Café Vanden Berghe and then we go to the Minnewater and the Béguinage.

The Béguinage is an open square of grass and trees, surrounded by small, whitewashed alms-houses of the late seventeenth century. In spring, when the daffodils are out, the sisters walk, singing a Latin hymn, in procession round the square and into the small chapel. Outside is the lake of grey satin, embroidered with swans and willows. You may, if you want to, throw a coin in and wish for a lover, then walk along the ramparts to the Port de Gand and down the Lange Straat to the Grand' Place.

At night you will see the illuminations, which are continued until the end of

September, and attend the *Son et Lumière* in the courtyard of the Gruuthuse. The Belfry itself is splendid on the indigo sky, its hard, serviceable, burgher's headpiece slanting backwards as if pegged upon the stars. In the Place du Bourg the wonderful town hall is a mass of little silver kings and noblemen, Tenniel chessmen carved in stone. All the finest buildings in this town are civic, rather than ecclesiastic; they were erected by the successful lords of the middle ages, businessmen, tax-gatherers, shippers, merchants. The palaces, streaming down into the floodlit waters, were the houses of patricians; the Cloth Hall of the Belfry, with its Shakespearian inner court ripe for the entry of an ostler with a lantern and news of Robin Nightwork, is the handsome seat of bosses.

If you dine, rather expensively, at the Duc de Bourgogne, perhaps the smartest hotel-restaurant in Bruges with the most enchanting site of all, you may gaze out from the terrace over the Quai du Rosaire to the fine seventeenth-century courtyard just off the Wollestraat, which looks Swiss or Germanic rather than Flemish. When I first went to Bruges, in place of the Duc de Bourgogne was a modest café with a little dancing floor; one sat for hours over a single coffee and danced to a mechanical piano. One was in love there. But if the place is different, the enchantments remain: the bell-haunted quietness, the swans glimmering in the dusk or swimming up sparkling through flushes of gold and silver light, the inevitable visitor leaning on the parapet opposite, looking out across the water.

Well, you say, so much for one day. But what about tomorrow?

Tomorrow you go to the Memling Museum and see the Floreins altar-piece, infinitely gentle, with the softness of velvet and fine wool; you see Saint Ursula's huffy little virgins being shot through with arrows. You visit the Gruuthuse Museum, which holds the domestic history of Flanders. You go on a motorboat tour along the canals: "Heads down, please!" under the bridges — and down they have to go unless you want them knocked off — under the bridges with their sour smells, both fresh and rotten, and into the open water again which smells of apples and the sea. Above are the fine, simple houses, and Jan van Eyck in green-bronze turns his back upon the oncoming boat. You can walk further along the canals after that, and find a pale blue house standing like a stern dream above a quay where the waters are as still as glass, untroubled even by the brushing of a willow tree. And then you can walk and walk, through the gabled canyons of the city under the canopy of bells, and then . . . You can do everything again, next day, any day, with the hours slipping unnoticed from the string till they are gone and you must pack your bags.

Bruges is a town for the contemplative, for people who like to sit about by water, who like to look at paintings, who like to read in peace and quiet, who like to eat some of the best and least fussed-about food in Europe without giving food too strained an attention. In Joye's, the pastry-cook's in the smart main shopping street, there are chandeliers, there is brocade, there are marvellous ices and a lovely air of harmless marginal greed. Bruges is a town with a lively, even a *chic* life of its own, which is, of course, no business of ours. The middle ages are for us. This town has a farouche and bloody history. Here, where these smart cars are parked, they tortured heretics and rebels, heated irons for them, blew them up with water. The men of Ghent came over to massacre the men of Bruges; on the following week there was a return match. They were extravagant people in their way: stolid and extravagant at once. There is a story of the architect of Notre Dame at Bruges, who when the work was completed looked up and saw that the spire was slightly out of true. Unable to endure the sight, to have his failure forced daily upon his eyes, he rushed up to the top of it and dropped off. It isn't a true story. But it is a true Flemish perfectionist story, nevertheless, and one likes it.

IRELAND

by CLAUD COCKBURN

A Dublin publican and thinker showed me the other day a novel type of map which he keeps locked in his safe. As I saw when I looked at it, he is right to keep it locked up. Wrongly studied, it could cause trouble to a lot of people that many of us know.

Specifically, it is a map of Ireland, with big-headed pins stuck in it — as in war. In this peaceful case, what the pins show are the movements and ports of call (social, cultural, scenic, and for fun) of these and those distinguished travellers from Britain and the United States who, over recent years, have from time to time landed in Dublin, walked into this man's bar, and told him, in the course of a drink or so, why they are in Ireland and what they aim to see and do and experience while ashore.

I looked immediately for the pin of a fairly public figure of my acquaintance who once told me that, when visiting Dublin on business rather than for relaxation, he makes it an absolute rule never to accept any invitation to lunch or dinner, never to agree to have a drink with anyone elsewhere than in the bar of his own hotel.

When I asked him why he said: "Because in this city, if you so much as step round the corner to have a cup of coffee with a man, you finish up four days later crooning Gaelic ballads on the ocean shore of the Dingle peninsula, with two friends you made in the course of a lunch party at the Russell Hotel, some café-society characters you picked up at a house-party in County Wicklow, some men who joined your little band somewhere in County Meath, who were going to show you an antique ruin but you all missed the road, and a Cabinet Minister who says he longs to be at his desk, but duty calls him to stay with you and help you and explain the general situation of the nation if that is what you would like him to do. Also you have bought a horse. Furthermore you have just telephoned your London office to tell your Chief to close up the joint and come on over and live".

And sure enough, there was this man's pin right in the middle of the Dingle peninsula. He had relaxed his rule, and the thing he had always said would happen had happened.

It was a little while before it occurred to me to look for my own pin. Being pin-plotted on a map by a thinker is something you suppose happens only to other people. But there I was, a blue blob, solidly tacked in between the salmon in the river and the long white sands of the sea at the mouth of the Blackwater.

My "progress pins" — showing how I got to where I was — had been taken out. The man figured I was there to stay, and the way I got there had lost news value. And in fact my specific, personal reasons for going there are of no general interest at this date. Suffice it to say that I was tired of living in England, could not go to the United States because the FBI thought me too red, and could not go anywhere beyond the Curtain because the Communists thought I was an agent of the Pentagon.

And these same facts brought a lot of dodginess into any plan one might have had for settling in France or Italy — just a small change of Government and you could find yourself uprooted and expelled for one variety or other of Very Bad Thoughts.

If this were the whole story it could suggest that one went to Ireland *faute de mieux,* and stayed on and on because there was no other place to get into but the soup. Not so — not even at the beginning, and still less so now. To conceive of Ireland as no more or less than a beautiful bolt-hole would be a dull misunderstanding of what Ireland "stands for" (as politicians say) in the Western world. No bolt-hole, but a place where a person is free to feel on top of the Western world instead of being overlaid by it.

It could be supposed that the resident might be stimulatingly aware of the flavour of Irish life, but that it would escape the briefly visiting traveller. The resident is seen as a character vegetating and appreciating; perhaps common-sensible and perhaps a bit cracked; but in any case living in an Ireland which the man who has to be back at Collinstown airport in a fortnight's time to take the Aer Lingus Viscount for home, cannot be expected to penetrate, or even see. And there are plenty of Ireland-snobs (a peculiarly powerful *genre* of snobbery) prepared to implant just that idea.

It is nonsense. With a minimum of careful planning, the traveller can arrange to see just as much of what is lovely and unique about Ireland as the resident. In the opinion of the Ireland-snobs such a statement is an abominable heresy. They will bob up here and there all along the route to inform the voyager that whatever he happens to have experienced or to be experiencing just at the moment is "not the real Ireland".

Dublin, they are, of course, perfectly sure, is not the "real Ireland". To hear them tell it, those two or three restaurants which are among the best in Europe, those horses running at the Phoenix Park or the Curragh in the unique atmosphere of an Irish racecourse, those parties, routs, fêtes and galas which can justifiably remind you of 1914, those furious intellectuals who can justifiably suggest to you 1984, those film stars, those copper and oil prospectors, those hordes of genuinely Irish stage-Irishmen — all these are not at all the "real Ireland".

Horrified at being victim of such a deception, our man gets into his car or locally-hired drive-yourself, and heads west. The road he travels is a first-class road, but it is also amazingly traffic-free. By dinnertime, unless he has taken time off to visit castle or shrine, he will have reached a point where there is nothing but deep water between himself and Manhattan. We cannot say that he is in the midst of scenes like nothing else on earth, because they are a little like Skye, and a little like north-western Spain, while they sharply remind you here and there of Transylvania. There is also, admittedly, a section which resembles nothing much except the Mountains of the Moon. But this isn't the "real Ireland" either. Press on.

By the time the traveller has done his deep-sea fishing at Westport, and moved southeast again through Killarney which the *cognoscenti* will not admit is scenically wonderful, and humanly uproariously comic, because that is what the clichés say it is, he will possibly have grasped that all this is the "real Ireland" after all, and will thus be in good shape to appreciate the city of Cork. A confusing city, of which Irishmen everywhere who do not come from Cork profess to be afraid. And it is a fact that while it reclines there between the arms of the River Lee, looking beautiful and a little raffish and a little tired, it is also a volcano of energy spouting out people who go out and take over great tracts of government and industry in Dublin, Pittsburgh and Sydney.

And to my mind there is no better wind-up for such a trip than the town of Youghal, 30 miles out of Cork to the east. This could be the absolutely best centre for a gentle or — if you are in that mood — brisk and hilarious investigation of the entire south coast; an area where the hunting, shooting, fishing and sailing, together with the swimming and the simple, shameless lazing about, are perhaps more thickly available than anywhere else. And Youghal even contains one of those indispensable real Irishmen who, whether you want to fix up some hours of total and much-needed rest and contemplation at the great Trappist Monastery at Mount Melleray, or fulfil your corny but admirable ambition to kiss the Blarney Stone in comfort, will take over your business for you. To meet Mr. Donald MacDonald is an experience in itself — like taking a trip through Ireland before actually starting. If anyone can show you the "real Ireland" he can.

157

THE
WEST INDIES

By V. S. NAIPAUL

WILLIAM

Fifty years ago you went to the Caribbean not for the sun but the sights. The travel brochures of the time carried pictures of ancient cannon in a ruined fort in Colombia. You were taken to Martinique to see a volcano that had erupted not long before and killed hundreds of people. In Cuba you inspected a cigar factory and were given a twelve-inch cigar. And you visited the Pitch Lake and the Botanical gardens in Trinidad. The biggest attraction was the *Big Dig,* the Panama Canal, which you were urged to see "before the water is let in." When there was no particular sight the brochures chattered nervously about the memorable impressions left by majestic trees, brilliant flowers and smiling people. But not a word about sea bathing. And the sun was mentioned only as something to be guarded against. A businessman in Panama, warning against it, claimed that he had the largest selection of Panama hats "in Panama or elsewhere". For the walk across the Pitch Lake stout shoes and parasols were also recommended. What, I wonder, would Frances Cornford have made of an Edwardian group, Panama-hatted, parasolled and stoutly shod, picking its way across the weeds, the hard uneven asphalt and the stagnant pools of the Pitch Lake?

In those days you went not only to the Caribbean, but also to the Spanish Main, and the travel agents described the whole region as "historic, fabled and legendary". Because Sir Walter Raleigh had discovered the Pitch Lake in 1595 and used the pitch to caulk his ships travellers were condemned to a whole day on that dreary spot which deserves at most fifteen minutes. Whereas only half a day was given to the entire island of Barbados which had nothing to recommend it apart from beautiful beaches and the tomb of Ferdinando Paleologus ("descended from ye imperial line of ye last Christian Emperors of Greece").

Today the Caribbean is simply sunny. The sights remain: squares and statues in Jamaica, Nelson's Harbour in Antigua, and outside the Royal Victoria Institute in Port of Spain, an anchor which might be the one Columbus lost in 1498. But instead of the ruined Columbian fort the brochures show people lounging on crowded private beaches, or dancing and beating drums under coconut trees.

Now, public beaches are usually deserted, except at weekends. And you are unlikely at any time to see anyone dancing under a coconut tree. But it would be unfair to condemn the region for that, since nowhere else in the world is such an effort made to live up to the travel poster. The costume of the Caribbean folk-dancer is well-known: tight three-quarter trousers, loose collarless shirt and perhaps a large straw hat with a ragged brim. This costume, which I suspect to be Mexican in origin, was unknown in the Caribbean until quite recently. But the posters insisted and, in the Caribbean, life imitates poster art. Today you can see the costume in any night club.

The West Indian is sophisticated and compliant. The outside world expects him to

158

have folk-costumes and exciting folk-dances. So in made-up costumes he does made-up dances to made-up gods. Very often he does them quite well and gets a booking in a New York or London night club. He may even be asked to dance at the Horniman Museum. Or he may get a British Council scholarship to study British folk-dances. This can have surprising results. In 1956, when I was in Trinidad, I went to an exhibition of made-up folk-dances called *Caribe Etrange*. The title puzzled me until I realized that it was some made-up French for "The Exotic Caribbean." The usual things happened. Drums were beaten. Dancers pretended they were picking cotton or cutting cane, I forget which. Men in tight three-quarter trousers rocked on bended knees, threw up their hands rhythmically, prostrated themselves and uttered strange sounds. On to this scene spun a ballerina, impeccably dressed. She spun very well until she became involved in the curtain and disappeared from our view. The drums beat, the curtain underwent some convulsions, then from a cocoon of curtains a puzzled face peered at us. The ballerina unwound herself and the show went on. According to the master of ceremonies the purpose of the dances was to exhibit the medley of cultures that had bred the Caribbean folk-dance.

The Caribbean is indeed a medley. The islands are widely separated and no island resembles any other. In Montserrat they talk with an Irish brogue. In St. Lucia and Dominica they speak a French patois. (They did in Trinidad, too; when the drive for folk-culture was at its height night-classes were given in this mangled language.) The population of Tobago is almost wholly Negro. In Barbados whites and Negroes balance one another — and Indians and Chinese are curiosities. Trinidad, on the other hand, is possibly the most cosmopolitan place in the world. Jamaica is poor but Trinidad is rich. With such variety it is easy to get a wrong picture of the West Indies, to see it as being only Jamaica, and the source of immigrants.

And now there is the vision of the "island in the sun". Mr. Harry Belafonte has told us:

> This is my island in the sun
> Where my people have toiled since time begun.

No one has protested at this preposterous statement. The aboriginal inhabitants were the Caribs and the Arawaks, both now unhappily extinct. The Spaniards killed the Caribs, who ate the Arawaks and sometimes ate each other. According to the authority quoted by Patrick Leigh Fermor in *The Traveller's Tree*, before a Carib was eaten he was permitted to make a speech. He told the diners that he had grown strong by eating many of their tribe and that by eating him they would in a way be eating their own flesh. Such a speech, if effectively delivered, could cast a gloom on the banquet. Then the victim was knocked on the head, spices were stuck into his body, which was tied to a pole and roasted over an open fire. Cooking was woman's work.

Calypsos existed fifty years ago, but no brochure mentioned them. Today it is hard to get away from them. Mr. Belafonte has, I believe, come out strongly against those manufactured in London and New York. He believes they make a mockery of a people's culture. Culture is too strong a word, but I do feel that the exaggerated success of the calypso has thrown this limited but pleasing — and wholly genuine — art into disrepute. It is not simply a jumpy tune with words that don't scan. The true calypsonian is a witty and scurrilous observer of the life of a small community. The policemen in a calypso tent used to be there not simply to keep order, but also to make notes. The calypsonian, who is Negro, makes fun of other races. He has a gift for the gibberish in Chinese, Hindi or German (a lot of this during the war). But more often he ridicules himself:

Chinese children calling me Daddy!
I black like jet, my wife is a tar-baby,
And still — Chinese children calling me Daddy.
Oh, God, somebody putting milk in my coffee.

He is direct and never sentimental. Here is a pre-war song about old ladies who go to dance halls:

Old lady, you mashing my toe,
Old lady, stop! It isn't so.
You crazy. Leave the people dance!
Read your Bible and give the young girls a chance.

Above all, the calypso is bawdy. Sexual encounters are described in elaborate metaphor, and the fortunes of the women of the town tirelessly chronicled.

It is a minor art, and an intensely local one. The best deal with local incidents, local attitudes, and local people; and the allusions can be fully appreciated only in Trinidad.

A long way to go for a small pleasure. But half the joy of a journey to the Caribbean is the getting there. Three years ago, after more than six years in England, I returned. "Into the Sun!" the ship's book-matches exclaimed. And the gradual change from temperate to tropical seemed indeed almost miraculous.

We left from Avonmouth. The sodden flats of the Avon Gorge were cold, depressing. At sea the winds were bitter and the sky was sunless. Then as the days passed the sun shone, more and more brightly, and the winds became increasingly kind. Butter melted, the salt didn't run so easily, fans were turned on and the portholes left open. The ship's officers changed into white, the swimming pool was filled, and ice cream was served on deck instead of warm beef tea in the lounges.

And then, waking up to a strange stillness one morning, we saw Barbados. The sun was not fully risen and a haze hung over the island. Every port framed a travel-poster picture: the high sky, the coconut trees rising from the low green island, the blue-green sea. Some boys were diving for pennies at the side of the ship. Under water the soles of their feet were luminous. When they came to the surface they looked up and smiled and looked away quickly, as though overcome by shyness. A woman said, "You see? The smiles are not exaggerated". Far away a fisherman was standing in his boat, a tiny black figure in the haze.

The cliché, I realized, was right. Driving around Barbados that morning — and taken inevitably to see the tomb of Ferdinando Paleologus — I thought that tropical vegetations could only be described as lush. I had forgotten so many things: the enamel brightness of the colours, the quality of the light, the depth of the sky, and the bigness of the leaves: the banana leaf, the bread-fruit, the wild tannia. Even the grass on lawns had this astonishing quality of lushness. This wasn't the tanned turf of England, but something wild and scrambling which looked as though it could easily shoot up overnight into a monstrous creeper.

About midday it began to rain, the stinging big-dropped rain that drummed on a thousand corrugated-iron roofs and in next to no time had the street gutters full and racing. This was the rain I had liked to walk in.

And having arrived, there was nothing to do. No museums, no important buildings. And yet for three months the eye was richly entertained, by light, landscape and people. It was always warm, seldom oppressive. The beaches were empty. Restaurants were good and interesting and inexpensive, and the Chinese food far better than the best in London. Tobacco was cheap, drink absurdly so. And what else?

One evening I went to *Caribe Etrange*.

MEETING AN EXPLORER

by ERIC NEWBY

"Look," said Hugh, "it must be Anstruther."

Coming towards us was a small caravan like our own. He named an English explorer, a remarkable throwback to the Victorian era, a fluent speaker of Arabic, a very brave man, who has twice crossed the Empty Quarter and apart from a few weeks every year has passed his entire life among primitive peoples.

For a month we had been on the march. We were all rather jaded; the horses were galled because the drivers were careless of them; the drivers had run out of hashish and tobacco and were pining for their wives; there was no more sugar to put in the tea, no more cigarettes and I was reading *The Hound of the Baskervilles* for the third time. It was not a gay party.

Anstruther's caravan was abreast of us now, his horses lurching to a standstill on the execrable track that is the only road through this part of the Hindu Kush. They were deep-loaded with great wooden presses, marked "British Museum" and black tin trunks (like the ones my solicitors have, marked "Not Russell Jones" or "All Bishop of Chichester").

The party consisted of two villainous-looking tribesmen dressed like royal mourners in long overcoats reaching to the ankles; a shivering Tajik cook, to whom some strange mutation had given bright red hair, unsuitably dressed for Central Asia in crippling pointed brown shoes and natty socks supported by suspenders, but no trousers; the interpreter, a gloomy-looking middle-class Afghan in a coma of fatigue, wearing dark glasses, a double-breasted lounge suit and an American hat with stitching all over it; and Anstruther himself, a great, long-striding crag of a man, with an outcrop for a nose and bushy eyebrows, forty-five years old and as hard as nails, in an old tweed jacket of the sort worn by Eton boys, a pair of thin grey cotton trousers, rope-soled Persian slippers and a woollen cap comforter.

"Turn round," he said. "You'll stay the night with us, we're going to kill some chickens."

We tried to explain that we had to get to Kabul, but our men, who professed to understand no English but were reluctant to pass through the gorges at night, had already turned the horses and were making for the collection of miserable hovels that was the nearest village.

"Can't speak a word of the language," Anstruther said cheerfully. "Still, it's not really necessary. Here, you," he shouted at the cook, "make some green tea, and a lot of chicken and rice — three chickens."

The chickens were produced. They were very old; in the half-light they looked like pterodactyls.

Soon the cook was back, semaphoring desperately.

"Speak up, can't understand a thing. You want sugar? Why don't you say so?" He produced a large bunch of keys, like a housekeeper in some stately home. All that evening he was opening and shutting boxes so that before the lids clanged shut I had tantalizing glimpses of the contents of an explorer's luggage — a telescope, a string vest, *The Charterhouse of Parma,* some fish hooks and the 1/1,000,000 map of Afghanistan.

After two hours the chickens arrived; they were like elastic, only the rice and gravy were delicious.

ON THE SLOPES

1929

The first skiers in Vogue looked not unlike the first aviators — helmeted, jodhpurred, putteed and booted, and, judging by the prose in those early days, the two activities were regarded as not that dissimilar if only because they both implied youth and adventure. "Then onto our feet we strapped once more our wings and set forth on our flight down the valleys".

By 1924, these aviators of the slopes had become "a joyous company of sport lovers that takes train for the mountains, secure in the knowledge that snow and ice will be there for their playground, that skating, skiing, luge and bobsleigh will occupy their sun-warmed days, and dancing, theatricals, and cheerful hotel amusements will fill the crowded evenings". They made for St Moritz with its Cresta Run and its Palace Hotel as if to some exclusive club (which indeed it was), to Wengen "another resort beloved of active spirits" and to other winter sports' centres "too numerous for individual description", creating as they went a social and seasonal alternative to the Riviera.

Within a few years the number of winter sport's destinations had soared and by 1934 "the call of the snows comes echoing over Europe, from Norway and Sweden, Switzerland, the Austrian Tyrol, the Dolomites, the French Alps . . . Any kind of skiing is a lot of fun but the negotiating at high speeds of intricately winding trails, cut through the trees, down the monstrous sides of mountains from peak to base, is a kind of skiing so full of good things that it is more like a religion than a sport".

Vogue announced in 1936 that a fortnight in almost any resort need cost you no more than £20, including pretty well everything you could think of and many things which you couldn't. The pure mechanics of skiing too had improved dramatically: "Until a few years ago the would-be ski runner spent hours of his holiday laboriously toiling up the Swiss mountainsides, in order to enjoy a few moments of the exhilarating rush of a downhill run. Now all is changed. The skier who still climbs under his own steam does so from choice. Others get themselves carried to the mountain tops on ski lifts and funiculars with such rapidity and ease that they are able to make several runs a day".

The war put the slopes out of reach for half a decade, while currency restrictions limited the possibilities for the other half. But the biggest problem facing post-war British skiers was the increasing popularity of the sport amongst Europeans who had taken over the slopes in their absence. "It seemed once that a strictly selective providence had reserved the sport of skiing, like much else, for the English. But with every major town from Grenoble to Gratz disgorging a cross-section of its citizenry onto the snows every weekend, it has become a real problem to find good and easily accessible slopes."
It was a problem that set the pattern for Vogue's ski coverage over the next twenty years — the search for new and exciting resorts, from Avoriaz, Flaine, Les Arcs and Anzère "new places on the ski circuit, the look of the future" to the High Tatras of Czechoslovakia and the powder wastes of Alaska. But wherever the location, and whatever the conditions, skiing remained Vogue's favourite holiday activity.

*"The creed of dressing appropriately was obviously invented
by someone indifferent to human suffering"*

URGUE 1927

"At St. Moritz—clever cut, harmonious colour schemes and novel garmenting based on a study of the practical needs of Winter sports characterize these stunning models. Chic, very Parisienne and absolutely comme il faut"

164

(*Below*) Miss Lavender Sloane Stanley (right) with Miss Daphne Watson, the daughter of Sir Geoffrey and Lady Watson, at St. Moritz

(*Below*) Sir John Latta goes for a spin with his son, Mr. Cecil Latta, on the rink at St. Moritz

(*Above*) Miss Betty Stoddard, of New York, comes to grief on the ski-ing slopes in a trial spin

(*Above*) Sir Hall Caine taking a stroll at St. Moritz

(*Left*) Miss Emilie Hoyt, of Chicago, ready for a run

(*Right*) Viscount Knebworth enjoys a quiet ski run across country

TOPOLSKI 1939

166

CRACKNELL 1966

THE SIXTIES

"Whether you travel luxury class or strictly economy, you can go further afield this year than ever before . . . free to range over vast areas rather than cover the main sights on the tourist beat with a given travel allowance".

Everything conspired to make the Sixties a great decade for travel. The war had so accelerated technological advance that by the late 1950's jets had become a valid commercial proposition — and with time and costs reduced even the most ambitious destinations were accessible. The need to structure one's holiday within a specific budget had been a major factor in the "package holiday" and the development of the tour operator who supplied a destination for an all-inclusive price payable in sterling prior to departure: "No matter where, one can be sent off like a parcel, carefully labelled, transported and delivered". In the early sixties, "Pleasures and Predilections" listed a selection of current tours and tour operators, from a Port-tasting holiday in Oporto to Painting in Calvi and an Architect's tour of Sweden and when President Eisenhower declared 1960 "Visit America year" the reaction was swift: "every travel agency worthy of the name has devised tours and holidays in the United States ranging from fairly stringent economy to sky's the limit luxury". The Exchequer added its seal of approval by increasing the travel allowance to £250 a year for holidays outside the Sterling Area and three years later increased it yet again to £250 a journey. No longer would it be a question of either a summer holiday or a winter holiday — or both on a budget. The only limit now was what you could afford. There was "Honolulu, well named the crossroads of the Pacific, 2,100 miles over the blue water (from America), a few days away by ship, a few hours by jet . . . Four hundred miles south is the island of Hawaii . . . a hot 2,200 miles south of Hawaii, Samoa . . . and the most colourful spot in the Pacific, Fiji with its tropical rain forests, peaks and grasslands"; New Zealand "the most surprising thing about it . . . it's diversity . . . take a car, camping and stopping and starting as you please"; the West Indies, "for the leisured and discriminating traveller . . . endlessly fascinating, largely because no two islands are remotely the same, either in landscape or atmosphere, and each forms part of a mosaic that takes alarming hold on the imagination and affections". "The recently completed trans-Canada highway stretches 5,000 miles from sea to sea and camp sites, with camping facilities, are spaced every hundred miles along the route . . . the wide-awake traveller will buy a second hand car on arrival for £160, drive it to the west coast, and be reasonably sure of reselling it there for £140". In addition there was Japan, Kashmir, Mauritius, Bermuda, the Bahamas, Malaya, Thailand, Mexico, Hong Kong, Australia, Ceylon, Ethiopia and "India . . . fantastic architecture, landscapes seductive or majestic, men and women always polite, often intelligent or beautiful, and an ideal winter climate. English is spoken everywhere, and living is less expensive for the traveller than in most countries. If so few of us are attracted by these advantages and enjoyments, the reason can only be prejudice due to lack of knowledge".

Destinations in Eastern Europe had begun to open up once more and Vogue welcomed in the new decade with a report from Scottish poet Hugh MacDiarmid from behind the Iron Curtain: "Czechoslovakia is a country rich in pleasure for the traveller and it is easily and inexpensively accessible to us. Moreover it has a rarity value not to be had by going to more frequented resorts — the best rewards of travel are not for those who follow each other like sheep through the same gap in the fence!" There was rarity value too in Poland "at the end of Europe" and in Bulgaria with its Black Sea beach resorts. "Up to the end of World War II the Balkans were one of the hottest sources of headlines, then the Iron Curtain clamped down and nothing more was heard. Now they are gradually re-entering the scene — but with a completely different face and one which will astonish the world.

"Bulgaria, always a fertile country and positively littered with scenery, is realizing herself. For the tourist, she has become more than accessible — highly desirable. Fine skiing mountains seen only by monks twenty years ago are getting lifts and hotels, golden beaches visited only by fishermen in pursuit of fish are being umbrella'd like any Lido. This is the communist Riviera. Designed in the first instance for the recuperation of workers from Bulgaria plants, its charms have now been spotted by other countries in the bloc. Gradually Westerners are getting the idea, the French and Swiss are arriving, and before long they expect us."

But not all experiences behind the Iron Curtain proved so favourable. On her return from "what is fast becoming a well-beaten track to Moscow and Leningrad" Loelia, Duchess of Westminster reported that in hotels "you are not allowed to use the stairs and therefore have to try and squash yourself into one of the quite small elevators that serve over thirty floors. In the evenings, before going to the ballet, if you are on a low floor you can wait over twenty minutes before you are able forcibly to insert yourself in the solid wadge of humanity which has packed itself in on previous floors". The advice from Edward Cruikshank, doyen of Russian Correspondents, "Don't go at all unless you really want to".

An endless source of fascination for Vogue in the Sixties was the Middle East and those destinations where "East meets West ranging from the now popular Morocco, the nearest country of the Orient . . . only a little over four hours away by air at a return fare which can be well under forty pounds", to the Lebanon, Egypt, Persia and Israel. In 1960 James Morris wrote of the Lebanon, "on the rim of the Arab world, on the edge of Asia, at the end of Europe, half Christian and half Moslem where all the passions and pleasures of antiquity seem still alive, and the very stones of the place, its tall mountains and its delectable coastline seem soaked in old delights". The following year found him in Cairo where "if you are sensitive to the present as well as the past, if you like your history on the hoof, then Cairo can offer you stimulations far beyond the traditional or the picturesque. She is not a graceful or a courtly city, not polished or serene, but standing there at the foot of the fabulous Delta, where Africa runs away into Asia — standing there astride her great river she emanates the excitement of power. She is a fascinating place, often bombastic, always argumentative, frequently abusive, sometimes vacuous, but she feels too big for petulance". Across the Sinai, Israel frequently featured where "the difficulty for the visitor is to comprehend it all, not physically, for it is a tiny country, smaller than Wales, but to accept the human experience which has made it what it is, the dreams born here and their betrayal". "It has every kind of diversity", wrote novelist Simon Raven, "geographically it varies from stark desert to luxuriant valley; among its people, it comprehends rich, unhygienic sheikhs, red headed monsters from the Russian Pall, and greedy beauties from Cairo or Marrakesh; historically it will show you relics of numerous cultures, Eastern or Western, and almost numberless

religious faiths. Nor is there anything unbecoming in a condition so various and un-
certain, for Israel, after all, is the borderland where East touches West".

Despite Vogue's unbridled enthusiasm for the exotic in the Sixties, destinations closer
to home were not forgotten. "For peace in the West, for simple pleasure, for high sweet
sunlight of the easy kind, for a sky one need never stop raving about, for people with
good looks and good manners, for temperateness and style in the idiom of day-to-day,
for rose trees and fountains and children, for the loveliest picture gallery on earth, for
late hours, sweet taxi-men and perfectly arranged pedestrian crossings, for lovely shape,
lovely cheap wine and, I think, lovely food, just give me Madrid . . ." Or why not
Sardinia "a unique island hovering between old-fashioned banditry and jets . . . this instant untouched". In spite of international talk about an island flooded with boom resort
money (the Aga Khan had arrived in 1961) "nothing much has happened, land had, of
course, been bought; not developed". Yet.

In 1966 the bubble burst, the British Exchequer drew in the reins and for the rest of the
decade the travel allowance was fixed at £50. "Now money is short and abroad is Ver-
boten." Vogue fell back on proven and financially feasible favourites. The Sterling Area
was re-explored, budget holidays re-examined — "How to get from San Francisco to
New York for £65" (you could buy the Greyhound tickets in London), while cruising
elicited some amusing recollections: "If you are ever shipwrecked, my dearest Laura . . .
do contrive to get the catastrophe conducted by the Peninsular and Oriental Company. I
believe other companies drown you sometimes; and drowning is a very prosaic arrangement . . . fit only for seafaring people and second class passengers. I have just been
shipwrecked under the auspices of P. & O. and I assure you that it is the pleasantest thing
imaginable. It has its little hardships to be sure; but so has a picnic; and the wreck was
one of the most agreeable picnics you can imagine". And once again there was Britain.
Amongst the numerous possibilities Vogue recommended a tour of "Poet's Country": to
Grasmere and Ullswater in the Lake District; to Dumfries in Scotland where Burns spent
the last years of his life and wrote "Auld Lang Syne"; to Ireland, Yeats' country north of
Sligo; to the Oxford of Shelley, Arnold, Wilde and Belloc; and to the West Country
where Coleridge dreamed of Xanadu. "In the atomic age we all dream of escape",
Vogue had said a few years earlier, and in the closing years of the decade that was all we
were able to do.

THE STRANGENESS OF ASIA

by PETER DUVAL SMITH

For me the greatest pleasure is any fresh reminder of the strangeness of the world. As far as travel is concerned, this rules out the Costa Brava, which is like Chelsea on Sunday morning; or Capri, where blue-haired ladies from Minnesota patrol the Piccolo Marina: or even Greece, now that the tourist coaches crowd the road to Delphi. Europe is finished for my kind of traveller. What is left? Fortunately there are the other four continents. If wonders are what you seek, allow me to recommend a journey in Asia: far away and expensive but literally marvellous.

The trip begins for most people in the bank manager's office. The second stage is reached at Kastrup Airport, Copenhagen, where you depart for Tokyo via the North Pole. This is the way to the East: don't take a slow boat to China, unless you enjoy drinking in bad company. On the polar flight you are racing the sun, with some odd results: in the last stages, lunch is served four times at intervals of two hours, yet you arrive at half-past nine in the morning.

The first necessity is to sleep off the feeling of unreality induced by such a journey. Being in Japan, one goes to a Japanese hotel. With their mixture of elegance and squalor, these places are an excellent introduction to the country. Beautiful to behold, they are not so beautiful to live in. Sleeping on the floor is a fine idea, until you consider the dust, the rats, the centipedes. These pests cannot be avoided in a house made of wood and paper and open to the winds. There is no furniture, so one has to eat off the floor as well. Nor is the famous Japanese bath all it is held to be, for on the coldest day one is required to wash before getting into the water. Then there is the fear of falling into the Japanese lavatory, a gaping hole inhabited by spiders and snakes.

This austere style of living is reflected in the food. The Japanese value the appearance of food more highly than its taste, and one eye-catching popular dish consists of nothing but cold boiled rice embellished with seaweed. For actual eating, I preferred the unique raw fish with green radish sauce, or a steak of Kobe beef.

The Japanese are highly Westernized, which is why we think them so clever and charming. Not much strangeness remains, except in the way they express their notions of the West. For instance, all the plaster models in the dress shops have corn-coloured hair, although there is no single blonde Japanese: and every Japanese girl wants plastic surgery to alter her almond-shaped eyes into the semblance of Audrey Hepburn's. Of course, some of the traditional sights are still to be seen. The Kabuki theatre is a wonder, and even more the puppet theatre of the Bunraku, where the hooded manipulators are in full view of the audience and yet appear invisible. Finally, no one should leave Japan without putting in a spell of temple-gazing in the old cities of Kyoto and Nara, which contain the finest sculpture in the world.

All the same, it is a joy to get to Peking, which is easily reached by boat to Tientsin and then by train. On arrival, go immediately to the Chin Shan, an artificial hill erected by the Emperors on the plain of Peking so that they could overlook their domain. Climb the hill and you will see what they saw, the towering red walls and jade-green roofs of the Forbidden City, an enclave fully a mile square, the most grandiose of palaces yet also the most human.

It is the only monument one can imagine living in. Now hail a pedal taxi and be taken to the Altar of Heaven, on the other side of Peking. Here is a long marble structure with, at one end, a small conical temple, the Tien Tan. It is a building as beautiful as the Parthenon.

From Peking to Hong Kong is three days by train down the whole length of China. During this time the mysteries of Chinese painting are explained to any traveller who looks out of the window. Those smudgy, unfinished, improbable landscapes are an exact description of the countryside of central China. Hong Kong has spectacular views, also good shopping and swimming. Otherwise it is merely an oriental Manchester: no strangeness there. Leave it soon and go to Macao, the Portuguese colony next door. The four hours' voyage is a miracle on a fine day, as the ferry-boat threads through the thousand islands in the mouth of the Pearl River. Unlike Hong Kong, a city of convenience, Macao has a personality. Asia and Europe meet happily here, and the Chinese mansions with their tip-tilted roofs appear perfectly congruent with the gay, terraced villas in the Portuguese style. There is nothing more restful than to sit on one of these terraces, drinking Portuguese champagne (fiercely iced, with a squeeze of lemon to cure the sweetness) and trying to count the sails of the fishing junks in the estuary.

Macao has a reputation for wickedness that is much exaggerated. It is true you can gamble here, but the thrills are mild indeed. In the Street of Happiness there is a sleazy casino where the Chinese play Fan Tan, surely the simplest of gambling games. A pile of counters is emptied on the table, and the croupier removes them four at a time. The game is to guess whether there will be one, two or three, or none left at the end. The gamblers sit round a sort of gallery overlooking the table and the stakes are let down in a wicker basket; in a higher gallery, opium may be smoked, and the sweet smell, like roasting chestnuts, drifts down to the game. If you don't wish to try the drug, at least you can eat nearby at the excellent restaurant that caters for addicts. Opium smokers have frail appetites and can stomach only a few delicacies. Chief among these are fried milk and a special preparation of salamander . . .

From Angkor one flies north to Vientiane in the small kingdom of Laos. One flies of necessity because there are no roads or railways, and the happy result of these bad communications is that Laos remains what Bali or Tahiti were fifty years ago: an elaborate, self-contained civilization indifferent to the outside world. For the same reason, high living is compulsory for most foreigners in Laos: because air carriage charges go by weight, caviar is cheaper than corned beef in Vientiane. You will find neither in the old royal capital of Luang Prabang. There is nowhere more peaceful than this isolated place: a village more than a town, river-girt, with untidy bamboo shacks lining an avenue of shaggy palms; on a small height a Buddhist pagoda stands, and the air carries the sound of chanted prayers and the soft resonance of temple gongs. All day long one sits contentedly on the verandah of the primitive hotel, watching the people go by, especially the Laotian women with intricate chignons of their own devising, wearing gay skirts embroidered with gold thread. Also in Luang Prabang one may see members of the extraordinary Meo tribe. These people are the opium growers of the world, and they come to Luang Prabang to sell their product. They never remain more than a few hours; they live in the mountains, and cannot bear heat.

Perhaps there is no place today stranger than Laos. Moving on to Siam and Malaya, and to Burma and India, we are in the orbit of Europe again. There is one heart-lifting experience remaining, this time a thoroughly contemporary one. Go to Delhi and take the Russian jet; fly over the Himalayas to Tashkent and Moscow. If you are tired of life, try sitting back at 40,000 feet with the second highest mountain in the world a few miles to your right and not very far beneath, and on all sides as far as you can see, nothing but ice and jagged rock. The steward comes round and it is caviar for breakfast. Naturally you call for champagne.

ZANZIBAR

by JOHN DAVENPORT

When we are young and think that we are going to live for ever — or at least for a century or so — we take time about our travel. There was time when I was an undergraduate to spend eighteen days going in a Dutch freighter to New Orleans; time to dawdle down from San Francisco in a Swedish one, stopping at all the Central American ports and enjoying the flamingoes of Panama. Those days are over — at any rate for me; and now one flies.

B.U.A., B.O.A.C. and East African Airways are revered names to me since I was fairly recently whizzed to Zanzibar, which I had wanted to visit since I was at my private school. It is one of those places that surpass expectations. Perhaps if one were stuck there against one's will it would soon pall, but for a short visit I can imagine nothing more exciting. The trouble is that exotic islands seen through a tripper's eyes inspire travel bureau prose. Even its earliest mention in history (A.D. 60) has a purple tone: it is called Menuthias in the *Periplus* of the Erythraean Sea. The Arabs took it in the middle ages; Vasco da Gama stopped by in 1499; the Portuguese drove out the Arabs in 1503 and built the massive fort. (I was ejected when I tried to look over it. It is now the Indian Ladies Purdah Club.) The Arabs regained Zanzibar in the early eighteenth century; it eventually became the principal market of the slave trade, which only ceased (officially) in 1873. Zanzibar did not become the capital of the Sultan Seyyid Said until 1832. Its great days date from then. But the whole feel of the town is of an older age — the magnificent brass-studded doors, the sea-going dhows suggest the Arabian Nights. It was Seyyid Said who made the growing of cloves compulsory in the island and its neighbour Pemba.

So much for the historical background. One can occupy oneself perfectly happily in the town for days. The mistake is to regard Zanzibar as a town rather than as an island. To get the full flavour of the place one must drive through the clove and coconut groves; stop in the delightful African villages; feel the soft monsoon coming off the Indian Ocean, and swim in it; lunch under the palms filled with golden weaver-birds. The vegetation is indescribably lush and flamboyant, but never strident, always harmonious — *luxe, calme et volupté*. The scent of the cloves can be intoxicating: yet oddly enough the whole effect of this small island — which only lacks a mountain to be perfect — is stimulating rather than enervating.

Zanzibar has been enjoyed by thousands of people in the past, going by boat from Mombasa or Dar es Salaam. The peculiar joy of going by air is that you get the shock of it by contrast with the Kenya highlands. Stay first in Nairobi, fly down to Zanzibar, and then back by Kilimanjaro for a longer stay in the immensity of Kenya, that perfect country, where only man is vile; and perhaps even he only temporarily so. It is not altogether improper to be unconcerned with the local politics. This is not meant cynically. The vast beauty of the landscape can in fact cause one to ponder profitably on the littleness of man. It is no good butting ignorantly in. Since I went to Kenya I have read a great deal of its past and present history, and of course before I paid my brief visit I was not totally ignorant. But I am glad I did not go there full of preconceived notions. Prejudice can sour the view. For my part I wished to try to recapture some of the feelings of the early settlers; to understand the dreams of Lugard and Delamere.

EGYPT

by JAMES CAMERON

Ah, Egypt! Cleopatra, of the alabaster brow! The timeless Nile, highway of history and the High Dam! Land of the Pharaohs and the Mamelukes, the jackal-headed Anubis and the great god Khnum, and the University Bridge and the Gaza Strip and the Immobilia Building and the Ermitage Bar; kebabs in the kasbah and hamburgers in the Hilton. Gone is the furtive figure in the frayed tarbush; come is the Sandhurst type in the well-pressed khaki drill. The Sphinx endures, to be sure, but there are other enigmas that most vigorously compete. For lo, much has changed.

If you want to get along well in Egypt, then a good thing to remember is that there is no such place. Egypt now officially proclaims itself the "Southern Region of the United Arab Republic" — thus removing with some acerbity the final shreds of bogus romanticism that had somehow survived several centuries of strictly dreadful malad-ministration. It was a very proper gesture. The Old Egypt of the Pashas, of the Wafd, of the unspeakable Farouk — that has been gone these eight years and more, universally unmourned. The S.R. of the U.A.R. may not sound so scriptural, but it is at least real.

I have known both these nations over a good many years, in a variety of enthusiasms, alternating between being expelled from the country one year and being a guest of the Government the next, being dined most cordially by a unit that shortly thereafter was attempting, with I am happy to say less practised ease, to shoot me through the skull. Between these convivial extremes I have had uncommon pleasure in the country that is surely one of the world's most misunderstood, and deliberately so.

Few British ever tried to know Egypt. Thousands of them, with baffled memories of base-camps and shoeshine boys, think they did, yet their impressions were almost always coloured with various resentments of compulsion. You went to Egypt (a) because you were posted there; (b) because your ship stopped over at the Canal entrance; (c) because you were writing some dreary Middle Eastern book.

All peoples respond to those who attempt to know them, the Egyptians perhaps more warmly than most, having had less of it. They have survived, after all, so many con-querors — Persians, Assyrians, Greeks, Romans, Turkish, British — they have longed for an identity, and they are at last in a position to exact it. When you find yourself in the urgent new modernity of Cairo remember that this is not the Egypt of the Khedives, or of Kitchener, or of the Eighth Army; it is the Southern Region of the U.A.R., and in the matter of Anglo-Egyptian relations their record is somewhat better than yours.

In Cairo it is vital to remember that here you are very nearly at the axis of all Western civilizations; on the site of the first of all the Babylons; one of the half-dozen most archaic and established cities in the world. Today it may somewhat remind you of Milwaukee, with suburban overtones of Stoke-on-Trent; it may not at first be easy to recapture the mysteries of the incalculable past when every Kuwaiti oil-sheikh seems to be investing in new skyscraper property and the *pièce de résistance* of Taksim Square is a wooden replica of a MiG. It is imperative, then, to succumb to tourism, and take a guide round the mosques of the old quarter. If you are pressed for time you concentrate on the Ibn Tulun Mosque, the Mohammed Ali Mosque and the Citadel, the El Azhar University and perhaps the Kait Bey Mosque. No one has yet found a way of by-passing the Muski, the bazaar, where it will require some strength of will not to have Dervishes produced to whirl for you, and where you will be enjoined to buy scents, silks, carpets, and the one infallible and undetectable aphrodisiac.

The tourist season, as they say, is from November to March, when there is possibly no climate in the world so wholly sympathetic. In the summer it is, frankly, on the hot side, and when the Nile is in flood, and surging north like a deep, vast channel of tepid cocoa, you can swelter. But the winter is the time; of the soft days and crystalline nights; then you will see the Coptic Places and the Babylon Fortress and the Hanging Church and the miraculous Mandura Tree, with wonder-working powers . . . and the Aswan Barrage and Independence Avenue and the Semiramis Roof and the wooden MiG and the forty-four Colonels; and where Egypt ends and the U.A.R. begins you will have a job to say.

To the visitor, to the native, to the trader — to everyone, indeed, except the repeating generations of soldiers who have merely fought over it — Egypt is one thing only: the Nile. This is something much more than the greatest river in the world. One supreme consideration governs every aspect of Egypt's existence: that fact that only three and a half per cent of its area is habitable by man. To fly over Egypt is to appreciate this in-delibly; human Egypt is a narrow green serpent crawling through enormous expanses of empty desert, a meandering strip of cultivation clinging to the source of its life: the river. Ten miles on either side, or sometimes five or even two, Egypt ends abruptly in the sand. There are half as many people in Egypt as in Britain, in a land four times bigger, but because they must live congested along this narrow lifeline of irrigation their density of population is perhaps the greatest in the world. There is no way of overestimating the significance of the Nile. It *is* Egypt; there is nothing else.

This is not a wholly obtrusive factor. The Nile will not intrude on those who go to seek the twilit evocations of Durrell's Alexandria. In Port Said or Suez or Ismailia you are conscious only of the Canal. Nevertheless, it would be an uncommonly lethargic visitor to Egypt who did not take the steamers *Memphis* or *Sudan* to Luxor, since this is perhaps the one place on earth where you *do* feel the shadow of six thousand dark and mysterious years. So much the more so if you are that much of an antiquarian to whom something is said by the extraordinary names like Ti, or Ptah-hotep. In that case you will go also to Saqqara, which is rather an adventurous hour-and-a-half's ride across the desert from Cairo, and has this simple and quite unchallengeable distinction: that it is the home of the oldest art on earth. The Step Pyramid, for example (and truly a hell of anti-quity it is), is not only the first pyramid ever made in Egypt, but is generally accounted to be the oldest stone building on the face of the world. It is necessary to make the most extraordinary adjustments in a country where anything younger than two thousand years before Christ is practically *art-nouveau*.

The ordinary Pyramids — those of Gizah, where the Sphinx is, whose outline every-one knows — are in fact a tram-ride out of Cairo. A car will get you there in twenty-five minutes. If you want to *climb* the Great Pyramid, it can be done. It is ferociously hard work. Moreover, it is worth remembering that while you may swelter in the sun on the desert base, it is usually blowing a gale on the top. You may well be glad to get back to the Mena House Hotel, where both the swimming-pool and the martinis are exceptional. By that time you will already have learned more than one can define here of the arcane and occult history of these extravagant pieces of masonry, of the funerary ostentation of Cheops or Khufu, whose 100,000 men worked for twenty years to build his fantastic tomb.

A VIEW OF FRANCE

by HAROLD HOBSON

For me, happiness begins at Calais. Even that rather desolate town, with its mean cobbles and the carillon that keeps one awake most of the night, gives my heart a lift, not because it is a gateway to splendid things — which it is — but because, simply, it is a part of France and as such it shares in that circumambient thing which is the best feature of France, the general sum of all its particular glories, namely the French way of life.

Thus to me almost any part of France is sufficient for contentment, for the French way of life goes on in every section of the country. I do not mean that there are not things in France on which I look back with particular pleasure. I am fascinated by the collection of pottery commemorating Queen Mary which Edwige Feuillère has built up in her apartment in the seventh *arrondissement*: I recall with surprised pleasure the luncheon in the Closerie des Lilas at which I found out that Samuel Beckett is passionately interested in cricket, and that what Jean-Paul Sartre and Simone de Beauvoir most prize as examples of English culture is the memory of Jack Hylton and his Boys: staggered by those mediaeval villages which perch on the top of rocks that rise perpendicularly out of the plain north of Marseilles: astonished by the vast abbey shining with light near Avallon: teased out of thought by the evidence of a vanished civilization at Orange: and soothed by the grandiose Second Empire buildings by the sea at Biarritz, which already begin to add a noble melancholy to their grandeur. But none of these things is as valuable as that to which they all contribute: which, as I have said, is the French way of life.

What are the characteristics of this way of life? First there is in it an instinctive determination to have everything in a condition of excellence. We have admirable parks in London, and at some times of the year we can eat in them more or less in the open air. And what miserable, sloppy, cheap, indigestible meals we provide in them, even in Hyde Park. All because, in food at any rate, we have no notion of excellence, and willingly ruin our insides for the sake of saving our pockets. But in the Bois de Boulogne the restaurants are among the best in Paris: and if the price is high, the surroundings are gracious, the service impeccable, and the experience of eating there, under the trees, by the side of the cascade, in the shadow of the glass pavilion, memorable.

This same desire for excellence is seen in the number of serious weekly and monthly magazines published in France. They are concerned not only with politics and literature and the theatre in the broader sense but with style. It is more important in France that Jean Genet writes exquisite prose than that he was a thief and a pervert. In the French original of *Irma la Douce* there was a scene in which the thieves had a nightly grammar lesson. One of them, who was lost in the mazes of parsing and analysis, peevishly said he didn't think French syntax was all that important. His companions shrank from him in horror, unable to imagine a being so low and degraded as not to regard syntax as important. This scene is not in the London version of *Irma la Douce*. It would have no point in London, where no one is in the least interested in seeking for excellence of style. But in France it illustrates a national outlook.

What I am trying to say is that there is a distinctive French atmosphere — brisk, intellectual, eclectic — which pervades the entire country, and makes it stimulating and agreeable. France is probably richer than any other country in specific splendours: Notre Dame, the Winged Victory, the Palace of the Popes, Versailles . . . she would still be the best of countries without any of these. She is sufficient in herself alone.

THE OUT ISLANDS

by SIMON HARCOURT-SMITH

Far below, the waters of this last, south-westerly expanse of the Atlantic are turned by the afternoon breeze into watered silk. One cloud that floats past my cabin window is a white, terraced Spanish castle: the next is a polar bear with outstretched paws to hug the plane.

The sound of the jets sinks to a secretive whisper. The loudspeakers boom their distorted gibberish that seems to say we land at Windsor Airport, New Providence, in twenty minutes' time. Now it is no longer a limitless stretch of loneliness; the vast Bahamian archipelago swims into sight.

South of Cuba and Puerto Rico, where the Lesser Antilles curve like a bow through the Caribbean, the islands are far enough away from each other to appear from the next-door shores as no more than vaporous dreams. But here in the Bahamas some three thousand cays of varying sizes are crowded into a few thousand square miles, so that you are hardly ever out of sight of land or coral. From six miles high the dark blue waters look for all the world like a jeweller's tray.

It was raining when I left London. Now, so few short hours later, the dazzling heat of the tropics hits me like a rock. Yet after all it is nothing beside some heat I've known — in the Libyan Desert, for example. And once out upon the coast road to Nassau, a cool breeze breaks through the hedges of sea grapes from the sea, engulfing me in a wave of well-being.

The garden of my house at Sapphire Waters boasts at least four different kinds of hibiscus (the old gardener calls them "high biscuits"), lizards drowse under the yellow awnings; when I bathe in the phosphorescent sea, hundreds of little fishes (the locals dub them "old maids") swim fearlessly and curiously round me.

Nassau, with its great hotels, is not for me. I love my temporary home by the sea, no less than the platoon of flamingoes that drill with a precision worthy of the Queen's Birthday Parade. But it is the Out Islands to the north which draw me; and so, one fine morning, off I fly in a rickety old Dakota to the island of Eleuthera where the first Puritan settlers wrangled furiously and tried to rob each other of precisely that Liberty which gave the place its name.

We come down on an airstrip round which bulldozers are uprooting whole forests of Bahamian pine to grow in their place winter strawberries and cucumbers for the Florida market. The forest blankets the breeze. Against the fierce heat of our brief stop we crouch, African-fashion, in the shade of the Dakota's wings. Then, on again to Governor's Harbour and the unexpected luxuries of the hotel called French Leave.

The sun is hardly up when I go down to the harbour. Above the graceful early nineteenth-century pink Post Office the Union Jack hangs motionless against a radiant sky. We cruise along the low coral shores to a headland renowned for its lobsters (they are really langoustes). We put on schnorkels and flippers, arm ourselves with harpoon guns and plunge into the translucent water.

Now, a few feet beneath the surface, I can see through my goggles that the coral is riddled with little tunnels about six inches wide. Most of them are just black holes. But suddenly from one of them come two pinpoints of light. They are a langouste's eyes. I fire, haul in my line, and soon a three-pound beauty is thrashing in the stern of our boat. But alas! I can't match the artistry of the two coloured boys with me. In a quarter of an hour they catch six langoustes against a miserable two for me. And, when I cook them, these Bahamian shellfish turn out to be as tender and delicious as anything to be found in European waters, refuting all the stories I had heard of how the warm Bahamian seas make a shellfish tough and dry.

There are islands everywhere, ranging from tiny rocks inhabited only by turtles and doves to places like Andros, a hundred miles long, Grand Bahama, paradise of American yachtsmen, the Abacoes which the tourist is only just beginning to spoil, San Salvador where Columbus made his first American landfall — all entrancing, entwined in hibiscus, encircled by white beaches and clear water that seems blue enough until you suddenly find yourself floating in the very Gulf Stream itself, and you realise what blue really is.

When the sun at last sinks behind Andros you can hear the giant rays take to the air and then crash back on to the sea with a noise of artillery; or the fast motorboats on who knows what mysterious errands that slip across the forty miles of sea from Castro's Cuba. In the shanty with a corrugated iron roof that is the local night-club a grizzled old stonemason, after a whole day's work in the cruel sun, dances the calypso by himself all night long in front of the band.

I go to a party where I am the only Englishman. Three singers appear — huge mother, slender doe-eyed daughter and a spidery drummer who is an old friend of mine. They are dressed in white with floppy local straw hats charged with flowers. They dance and sing calypsos of varying bawdiness; then, as the party ends, the young girl stands up straight, her dark face suffused with emotion. She looks me in the eye and: "God save the Queen," she says, saluting; "One Crown, one flag, one Empire!" I think of certain friends in London who would have sniggered and called her nuts; I feel at once proud and ashamed . . .

How flat Nassau seems after the Out Islands, the Gulf Stream, the fishing. There is no food in my house and the markets are closed, it being Sunday. But I go down to the wharves and buy conk, that huge shellfish extracted from curling shells of incomparable beauty, and the flesh of which you must beat with an empty rum bottle (nothing else, they say, is suitable) to make it tender. An old vendor of mangoes and okras keeps a barrow by the quay. He is singing hymns softly to the crew of a conk boat tied up close by. When he sees me, he comes back to serve me. He goes on singing softly.

"You like music, I see."

"Ah suttinly do, sah. An' shall Ah tell you why?" He comes up close to me and whispers: "Cos He who makes us all, His name is Music!"

TO THE ROCKIES AND ON

by NORMAN LEVINE

BAWDEN

My personal image of Canada hasn't changed too much over the past ten years. But I have seen the public image change considerably.

When I left Montreal, Canadians could still take seriously Sir Wilfrid Laurier's slogan: that the twentieth century would belong to Canada. And, over here, in England, I found that Canada was still regarded as a healthy, young, uncomplicated country, where you could send your son and be fairly sure that if he had it in him, in a matter of a few years, he would make something of himself. Part of this optimism was economic; the belief that Europe, after the war, would need Canada's raw material for a long time. But Europe recovered faster than anyone expected. And nuclear strategy by-passed Canada and her hopes of becoming a great world power. Even so, the public image of Canada continued to be one of optimism and blandness. Until the French Canadians began to draw attention to some of the cracks. The French Canadians are the only people in Canada, of any size, who have refused to become assimilated, and are largely responsible for keeping Canada different from the States.

To appreciate some of this you'll have to go to Quebec City and Montreal. Quebec is unlike any other city in Canada. It is French, it is isolated, provincial, living off its past. And its strength lies in its refusal to change. It is also a storehouse of Canadian history.

You can't walk down a street or go down a slope without passing a statue of Champlain, or an archbishop, or a general. Or through the high walled gate, to the Plains of Abraham. It is noticeably Catholic (people doff their hats to the priests). And, being built on a rock, the social divisions are fairly obvious. Upper Town is wealthy. It has its Grande Allée, fine houses, white grey stone, large lawns, and few people about. It has the slowness and the dignity of an old university town. Lower Town — down the slope, down the steps, to narrow streets that end in the water — is seedy, poor. And though there are more people about and numerous children play in the streets, there is, like in the Upper Town, a deadness, a coldness about it all. It hasn't changed much from what I remembered when I first went there twenty-odd years ago. Nor has it changed much from what Henry James wrote about it eighty-five years ago. "You strive almost vainly to picture the life of this French society, locked up in its small dead capital, and gradually consuming its principal, as one may say — its vital stock of memories, traditions, superstitions." I don't think anyone can hope to begin to understand Canada unless they spend some time in Quebec. And from there go out to the north and south shores of the St. Lawrence and see something of rural French Canada.

Montreal, although ninety per cent French, is very cosmopolitan. Every time I return to Montreal from England I am struck by the rawness of the place. The atmosphere of

180

violence. And with it an immediacy, an energy, that gives a certain excitement in living there.

It consists of two main streets — St. Catherine and Sherbrooke — running parallel, for miles, across the full length of the island.

You don't know Montreal is an island until you go up to some height and look out and see the light green bridges that surround it. From the docks it comes quickly upwards by a series of terraces to the mountain. And it is the mountain that dominates the city. Not by its height — it is little more than a hill. But when you walk by the docks, or in the business section, there is the wooded slope and the short stubby cross. And in the heart of downtown, at each intersection, you look up, and there it is as well. The other important street is St. Lawrence (or Main Street). One part of it runs through what is left of the Montreal Ghetto. While east of it is almost all French — poor French. There are men in berets and the most attractive women I've seen in Canada. The intellectuals dream of a few months in Paris and their opposite numbers in Westmount feel the same about London or New York. Montreal is also a good spot to go and see the Laurentians, especially in the magnificent decay of the fall when the leaves are in their brilliant colours.

There is no mid-west in Canada as in the United States. Between Ottawa and Winnipeg there are no large cities. There is rock, lake and bush. And north of the Great Lakes, various mining and timber towns. But from Winnipeg, through Saskatchewan and Alberta, you begin to get some idea of the continental size of the country. (You can put all of the British Isles in any *one* of these provinces.) You drive along a highway that is perfectly straight, mile after mile, past the same kind of flat landscape. I remember from my flying-training days out in the prairies: if we were lost we were told a simple way to find ourselves.

We knew the fields ran north and south to the horizon: the railways east and west. We'd go down low over a railway track and just fly on, over the rails, until we came to the grain elevator where we saw the name of the hamlet painted on it nice and big. You also get a sense of space in the west — the sky seems further away than it ever did in Europe.

Crossing the Rocky Mountains, you are aware that you're crossing some kind of frontier. And once across you're not disappointed. Vancouver is the most physically attractive city in Canada. It very much belongs to the Coast. The vegetation, the colours, the sea, the slow pace and the two mountain peaks with snow and black trees and green-grass slopes standing there close like an enormous pair of horse-blinkers. If you have a chance, go north from Vancouver — through some magnificent mountain scenery, then sagebush — to the Cariboo, to places like Clinton and Williams Lake. Small cow-towns that look like sets for an abandoned cowboy film. You will also see some Indians, and their reservations. And if you happen to be homesick you can make a short trip to Vancouver Island, to Victoria, and see how the English middle-class live in exile. Signs in the street say: "Old British Fish and Chips. Take some home." "Real English Tea." "Real English Trifle." Or: "A stay in *Olde England Inn* has all the charm of a visit to England itself."

And after you've been in the country a while you'll understand why Canadian (or North American) writers are so concerned with the physical world. Even today, you can be in the centre of Ottawa, right beside the Chateau Laurier, and look to the Gatineau Hills and feel that there is nothing between you and the horizon.

PERU

by AUDREY WITHERS

There is a contrasting landscape. The desert running along the 1400-mile coast is interrupted only by oases. The mountains, the Andes, including the whole country in their march from the Caribbean coast of Colombia to Chile, soar into snow-covered chains and peaks. The jungle, birthplace of the Amazon and the seemingly endless forests, is broken only by brown river coils. The climate varies extravagantly. On the coastal desert, there is an average of quarter of an inch of rain every year. The Andes support two extremes — a rainy season, cloudy and cold and another so dry as to eliminate cultivation. In the hot jungles, heavy rains can cause the rivers to rise twenty-four feet in as many hours. But, these Peruvian extremes create an ideal atmosphere for such incongruities as hibiscus and roses, frangipani and geraniums, pelicans and parrots, humming-birds and vultures.

The descendants of the sixteenth century Conquistadores, the mestizos, or half-breeds, all have the look of the Southern European. And the Indians, who form about seventy per cent of the population, still exhibit the characteristic Inca profile — the hawk nose springing from the forehead, the high cheekbones, which reveal their Asian origin. They are as small as mountain ponies and, like them, jog-trot at altitudes where whites must pause for breath. They have a withdrawn dignity, and their brown skins, black eyes and blue-black hair — which the women wear in pigtails — set off their handsome clothes.

The Spaniards, themselves, are anonymous in conventional Western clothes. The Indians are as brilliant as tropical birds. Each district has its costume, especially its own style of hats. In Huancayo, they wear hard white hats with high crowns and black ribbon cockades — very chic with their chiselled features. In the Cuzco district, the hats are shallow, upturned saucers in red and purple. The women's ankle-length skirts are in electrifying shades of red, pink, blue and green, and over their shoulders are draped squares of heavy cotton, woven in striped and coloured motifs, in which is slung a baby or produce for the market. Their cardigans are fluorescent red. The men's ponchos are handwoven in natural brown shades, with striped borders, and they often wear close-fitting caps with ear-flaps. Both the men and the women go barefoot, or wear the traditional sandals with thonged toe — widely copied in plastic for the beach.

The art of Peru, like their clothes, reflects the Indian's passion for colour and design. The Indian art was being formed more than 2000 years before the Spanish conquest. Their ceramic art was almost a substitute for the written language they never possessed. The ceramics are moulded into human faces and into people fishing, making war and love. Their ceramic description of disease was so accurate that medical diagnoses can be made today. Their textiles were among the finest the world has seen, with woven borders, all-over patterns of the greatest beauty, and laces and nets exhibiting techniques which astonish current experts. These art forms ceased to exist by the end of the sixteenth century. Nothing took its place. The Conquistadores were interested in other matters. The conquest, itself, was an early Gold Rush. The metal, precious to the Incas as an adjunct of the religious ceremonies when it was lavished on temple wall-plates and armaments, was as precious to the more worldly invaders who melted it down and shipped it in ingot-form to Spain. Ironically, the Spaniards often used it to gild the altars and pulpits of their churches — dedicated gold to the glory of God.

Some of the wealth remained. The richest Peruvians are rich on a scale unimaginable

182

KENNETT

in Europe. One single *hacienda* is the size of Belgium. The well-off live delightfully in homes still cushioned by many servants. The poor at the other end of the scale are alarmingly poor. Almost without exception, the rich are of Spanish descent and the poor are Indian. Between the two extremes, a middle class is pushing up.

The well-off enjoy all the benefits of Western civilization. The poor live, as they have for centuries, on mud floors, without water, sanitation or light.

Peru's most modern city is Lima, complete with modern traffic problems. Everyone rides, bumper to bumper, in anything with wheels, from Cadillacs to *carcochas*. In Lima, the old Colonial buildings are disappearing in the all-too-familiar pattern of progress — to make way for undistinguished office blocks. In the small towns and villages of Peru, however, time stands still. Bulldozers are slow to demolish either rural or urban slums. The Indians carry donkey-size loads on their backs, and, lacking transport, walk great distances to market.

The severe contrast between the Spanish and Indian way of life in Peru also exists in its buildings. The remains of Inca building in Cuzco and at Machu-Picchu have an extraordinary grandeur and simplicity. Unlike the Mayan ruins of Mexico, they are without ornament and rely for their effect on a superb use of masonry. Without knowledge of iron, or of the wheel, and lacking draught animals (the llama carries only 100 lbs.) they transported stones up to several tons in weight, and shaped and fitted them so perfectly without mortar, that today it is impossible to force the blade of a knife between them. Sometimes the blocks are shaped with perfect regularity into smooth courses; sometimes stones of every size and shape are fitted together; one example is the famous twelve-cornered monolith in one of Cuzco's Inca streets.

The Spaniards brought a baroque style whose special richness and fantasy carries the name *Churrigueresque,* after a Spanish architect of the time. The façades of the churches are sculptured into barley-sugared columns, scallops and canopies. The inner walls are lined with carved and gilded altars of extraordinary splendour — soaring to roof height and erupting into tangles of vines, pineapples, arabesques and cherubs. They support holy images dressed in velvet and satin, encrusted with gold thread. The contrast is best seen in Cuzco where the Spanish churches are often superimposed on the austere walls of Inca temples.

The beauty and strangeness of the Peruvian scene is composed of these contrasts. The unacceptable paradox is that of wealth and poverty. One hopes that this towering inequality will be ironed out leaving only the rich differences of the two civilizations. There should be for both a place in the sun of Peru.

THE CANARIES

by PADRAIC COLUM

On the islands of the canaries — one notices it as one goes up a mountain — there are no singing birds. The blue sky should invite a lark, but there are no larks. No blackbirds, no thrushes — not even a crow to give evidence of bird life. The canaries we've heard are the canaries we know — caged birds. A cock by a farmhouse crows. The house is roomy and modern, but the plough is pulled by an ox. The old-fashioned and the contemporary mix as we go up from modern Las Palmas.

And then I come on an exhibition of the old-fashioned that is as lively as it is pleasant. Water gushes out of the ground: a trough to hold it has been hollowed out of the rock; a shelf has been smoothed out, and there are chisel-made gradings. Old women, young women, little girls sit here, steeping clothes in the water, rubbing them against the gradings as against a washboard, and laying them on the shelf of rock. It is the time, the place, the function for gossip, and gossip is going on, entertainingly it would seem. A little girl asks for a peseta. She does not ask in a mendicant way, but as if she were saying, "You've watched a performance, so contribute something". When she gets a peseta she smiles engagingly; there is no clamour for pesetas from the others.

Here let me note that on the island on which I am sight-seeing there is a spring of enterprise. Houses are being built, roomy houses for farmers' families. Through some corporate enterprise, water is being brought up to the heights. Or maybe it is being raised from artesian wells. Results are profitable. There is a banana farm whose produce amounts to a thousand pounds per acre. The trees, close together, are pruned to low size, not as I have seen them in Hawaii, tall, in natural isolation, and bearing ripe fruit: it is arranged that they have one prodigious bunch of green fruit. Tomatoes are another profitable crop. There are small factories up in the hills.

But however contemporary they become and their earnings mount up, the islanders will never lose their feeling for bloom. Colour for them is a way of life. I go by hedges that are bushes of geranium, gardens by the roadside that have familiar flowers beside tall lilies, mimosa, oleanders. I look into a valley that was a crater. Above me, on one side are ledges of lava. Below are blossoming almond trees, smooth grass in which buttercups are larger and more golden than any I have ever seen, and the anemones more scarlet. And so I come to the roadway inn where I meet friends to drink the local wine. Here are outbursts of bird song. Canaries. Like our own they have been domesticated for generations. I read in a treasurable guide-book that has been written by one who knows English professionally if not intimately, "Actually the canaries from Atlantidas Isles has come to less, but these Islands is still the nest for its wild reproduction. To conceive and better the race of canario cultures association was undertaken, quite altruistic and integrated by Canarian patriotic people". This means the Islanders are becoming canary-conscious.

And now we are in the town of Teror. The pilgrimage to Teror is in September. I should like to be with the pilgrims. My book mentions, "shepherds of typical clothes leading their select sheep, the great variety of the exuberant orchards, the good cheese from the top of the mountain, the bunch of bananas, the silver industry from the bottom of the sea, the most graceful of trees, fruit, etc., etc." And there is the presence of girls "of unsurpassable beauty, adorned with the typical things of their regions, placed on the

Mount Kilimanjaro GEORGE RODGER 1973

overleaf: Abhu Dhabi JOHN COWAN 1965

coaches with flowers, or on the backs of camels, in the incomparable picture of the sky and Grand Canary". The mention of camels is odd, but the arid parts of the islands have or had camels. A Canary girl in the quaint and colourful dress of her district, mounted on a camel, would be memorable in a procession of pilgrims.

And this brings me to my distant view of the island girls, particularly the Las Palmas girls. That the islanders are proud of them is easily seen. They look cared-for as the flowers look cared-for. The little girls have always fresh dresses, their hair ringletted, little earrings. Growing up, they carry themselves with dignity and are apt to conform to type — well-shaped features, dark, large eyes, grave looks. They are in offices and factories: their dresses and hair-dos are as various as those of other European girls. As they come from Mass on Sunday they queue for American and French pictures. I fancy they have more perspective on the life cinematized than have movie-goers in other countries: their feeling for glamour is, I expect, on other levels. Their decorum isn't due to segregation. Teresa Garcia — I generalize a name — is allowed to sit with a boy friend on a promenade that I frequent. She is accompanied by a sister young enough to be bored by advances and retreats. At Mass she leaves her bench and kneels before the confessional (as in Spanish churches confessions are visible if not audible) and whispers through a grille to the priest in the box. There are five minutes of tragic attitude. Then she comes back.

If street names are an index to civilization — and I think that they are — Las Palmas is a civilized city. With the exception of a few for military or political personages, all the streets are named for artists — writers, musicians, painters, and this not only for Spanish, but for European artists, Wagner and Victor Hugo amongst them. There is one for Pio XII, and there is another for the anti-clerical Ibáñez. And how sightly the streets are in the vivid sunlight! They are clean: the houses have colour — white, white and blue, white, blue and pink. Trees are graceful: the coconut palms in their height and smoothness attain dignity, but in their beginnings are types of arboreal misery. The centre of the town is Plaza de Santa Catalina where the flowers and trees are so well-tended. I suppose that in a city where the bus fare from one end to the other is only three ha'pence, the cost of maintaining the flowers and trees is low; nothing withered is left here, nothing dull.

There is another side to the verdure and bloom that is so noted: the side of the island that is rawly volcanic, where the whole terrain is a slag-heap. Partly it is covered by the grey-green of the cacti, those broad-leafed immigrants that so heroically undertake the conquest of a land where there is no prospect for anything else. In this region one comes on cave-dwellings, actually inhabited caves where family laundry is lined outside the entrances. I wonder can these be an inheritance from the neolithic population that the Spaniards so ruthlessly destroyed? They were cave-dwellers; some of their women were left to the conquerors. Would a cave have been taken over as well as a woman? In these contemporary cave-dwellers is there any of the blood of the "Dog-eaters" for whom the islands were named? Be that as it may, the caves will soon lose their occupants. Houses are being built nearby and a progressive municipality will see to it that these caves will soon be merely archaeological.

From the caves to the beach, with its hotels and bars and international assembly, is no more than a journey round a small island. And what a beach it is! This is not the "tideless, dolorous island sea". It is what that famous visitor to the Canaries, Christopher Columbus, claimed to be admiral of, "the ocean sea". The waves coming to the beach are Atlantic, the sand is the fine firm sand of the Atlantic beaches. Bending round us are houses in the colours fancied by the islanders — white, blue, pink, yellow. And, relief from the colour, bare hills each side of the bay. Across the water, in the clouds, Fuji Yama. Actually it is Teneriffe, sixty miles away.

GREECE

by KATHERINE WHITEHORN

There is a certain awkwardness about the fact that Greece is now smart. It used to be simple enough: no one was prepared to endure Greek food, Greek roads and the heat of a Greek August without some pretty compelling reason for doing so: reasons which usually boiled down to the need to fight a war (like Byron or the Eighth Army) or the urge to be inspired by ancient monuments. This had an excellent effect on the tourist trade — such as it was — since people who come to look at monuments look at them and then go away again, whereas people who come to look at unspoiled local life effectively wreck the said life for good. The long eager line of classical scholars from Britain (panamas with brims turned down all the way round), earnest fraus from Germany (messy buns and ankle socks) or France (querulous complaints about the coffee) did nothing permanent to the scenery and possibly something to improve the commissariat — even Byron himself, dream as he might of shooting Turks, in fact spent most of his time doing a quartermaster's job organizing stores.

But now things are different, and plenty of people pour into Greece confidently expecting the glossy beaches, pretty little bars and a half-day tour of the Culture that got them by so well in Italy. Anxious to please, the Greeks get out brochures, direct them to the beaches and unwisely recommend the retsina; the beaches turn out to be covered with what appears to be cornflakes, the wine tastes of old violin bows and the buses run on alternate Thursdays; confusion ensues.

For all that, Greece is not going the way of the Costa Brava; and all credit to whatever bit of Greek government control it is that has restrained the building and controlled the prices of the hotels, refused building permission for shacks on the road to Sounion and ensured that the Tourist Police, police the tourist trade and not just the tourists. The Greek tradition of austerity applies to Greek hotels only in so far as they are superbly simple and clean, and they are generally cheap for what they are. Anyone who has noticed that all the hotels in Paris were apparently built in the same year, and thought wistfully, as they bang the moths out of the brocade and try to hang up a blouse on the splintered mahogany, how marvellous it must have been to be there in the year when they were all going up should try Greece now; while it is in *its* golden boom moment: give it another decade or so and the showers will have fallen a prey to the eccentricities of successive Greek plumbers, the beetles will have excavated their own Knossos in the concrete.

Greek food is not, to be frank, up to the hotels; but it is possible to come to terms with it. There are three ways of doing this. If you are sufficiently hard up you can simply resign yourself to living on yoghourt (superb everywhere) and the snacks they give you with ouzo and beer in profuse quantities, *free* — black olives, little meat balls, tiny fried fish, lumps of cheese (one place was so overcome by the amount of beer we ordered that they gave us fried eggs and chips, but I think that was exceptional). Or you cook your own: it is the practice of Greek cookery that is so revolting; like English, there is nothing wrong with the theory except perhaps their way of hacking up the meat which gives the impression of it having been done by a drunk with a pair of nail scissors. Or — the most practical way for most — you can stick to those tavernas that let you go out into the back kitchen and point; and then the meat balls in tomato, the stuffed vine leaves in egg and lemon sauce, the bowls of beans and stuffed tomatoes if you get them when they are hot can lure you into a belief that Greek food really is lovely.

Provided that you can eat and sleep in comfort, there still remains the question of what you go to Greece *for*. Of course, you *can* find the obvious holiday attractions: the ingredients that make Mykonos *Le St. Tropez d'Octobre,* the good beaches—and plenty of them are still less accessible and therefore more empty than you would dare to hope — the intriguing things to bring home (especially Turkish coffee pots, strings of big beads, Greek tunics but *not* Greek skirts), and national costume — though I always think Evzones sounds like the kind of thing dieticians say we don't get enough of. And there is glossiness at the Hilton level — and in Greece it is possible to appreciate such luxury for what it is really worth. If you come off a steamer at Piraeus at five in the morning after a fortnight on a particularly rugged island, and intend to get on to another in the evening for a further fortnight of the same, a day tossing back ice-clinking drinks with the air-conditioned music all about you, eating Greek food as it was meant to be and not as it generally is and stepping elegantly over the marble floors reminds one why people actually build Hiltons.

But to my mind it is a waste to go to Greece — which is, after all, a long way off — for things you can get in other places. Greece is never pretty — it is either hideous or beautiful. The Greeks are never gay and superficial, like Italians: they are either the salt of the earth or very surly indeed. But its very austerity is its trump card. The perfect antidote to bikinis and Martinis, too many screeching autoroutes and a surfeit of Madonna-hung vistas, are these barren rocks where civilization began.

To think of Athens as the place where these astonishing old men hacked out the principles of democracy, of the sea not so much as a bathing spot, but as the treacherous stuff that boiled under Odysseus' bow, of Sounion as the temple of Poseidon and not just a good beach; to remember Corinth as the Gay Paree of the Fifth Century, lacking in moral fibre but not in anything else, of Thermopylae as the last hopeless stand against an alien tyranny; this, to my mind, is the real reason for going there. One publicity man tried hard to get the Greek tourist office to drop all this stuff about views and roads and beaches and say simply: "Until you have stood on the Parthenon you are not a civilized man," and personally I think he was right.

Of course, the plan is open to objections. It would keep you out of most of the Peloponnese, on the grounds that the Spartans were so loathsome. You might prefer Byzantine Greece, too much of which happens at the end of hot slogs up steep mountains. You may have had a highly modern education which leaves you with too much homework to do before you can enjoy such a holiday. Or you may go with someone who thinks ancient Greeks were a lot of rogues, hates monuments anyway and radically disagrees with every word Professor Kitto* ever wrote. But even this gives you something to argue about over the ouzo; and I suppose it is a mark of the versatility of the place that such a one can be just as smitten with Greece as the most besotted classic.

ROME

by NORMAN ST. JOHN STEVAS

Some cities pull at the heart strings, like lovers they inspire rapture but they also make demands, and Rome is the most demanding of all. Once she has cast her spell, she never lifts the enchantments and one is permanently enslaved, condemned always to return with longing in a vain attempt to sound her depths. Not that Rome is the most beautiful of cities, Paris can lay a courtesan's claim to that, nor the most romantic, Venice carries off that palm, nor the most nostalgic, Vienna has the crown, and certainly not the most stimulating, New York wins hands down, but Rome more than any other has time and history at her command. Rightly she bears the title of the eternal city, the dust of monarchs, popes, emperors and dictators mingle in the soil, and still the fount of civilisation, law and religion, she flows like the Tiber timelessly on. The city is one great theatre of marble and brick where the play is life and only the cast is ever-changing.

Rome is at her loveliest in October when autumn touches her domes and palaces with gold, suffusing the streets with lambent light, while the branching plane trees by the Tiber drop their russet leaves. If you cannot visit Rome in autumn then go in early summer, in the latter days of May or the early ones of June, when the sun is warm and lifegiving but not yet fierce, and the Borghese gardens, still unscorched by the glare of July and August, are a variegated pattern of green, and the wild roses are blooming on the Palatine. Easter, of course, has its claims for pilgrims but it's really too early for Rome and, as I know to my cost, it can be biting cold.

The great setpieces, St. Peter's dome and Bernini's colonnade, the skyline saints of St. John Lateran, the crumbling crenellation of the Colosseum, the jagged outlines of the Forum are well known enough to everyone by sight or vicarious postcard so I will let them be, and dart off along some byways. My first call is oddly enough a graveyard, the cimitero acattolico, otherwise known as the English or the Protestant cemetery, which nestles around the base of the pyramid of Cestius, by the Porta San Paolo, one of the southern entrances to the city. The pyramid itself dates from the first century BC and commemorates a well-known tribune of the period of Caius Cestius. St. Paul's eyes must have lighted on it when he was being led outside the walls to execution. In its shadow live today a colony of those rake-like Roman cats who wolf down the spaghetti left for them in newspapers by benevolent old ladies.

I know of no place on earth more beautiful, more peaceful, more deliciously melancholic than this lovely plot of land, remote from the tide of Roman life and traffic which rolls noisily by beyond its walls, which shelters beneath its shady cypresses the foreign dead. Nearly all its inhabitants died in exile save for a sprinkling of Italian protestants, equally exotic in their way. Unlike the Catholic cemetery of San Lorenzo, far away on the other side of Rome, which paradoxically is a bustling hive of activity (Italians practise an extraordinary cult of the dead), this is a real place of quiet. Poets, sculptors, artists and diplomats lie here side by side; English, French, German and Russians are for once at peace: Goethe's son and Prince Yousopoff's father are curiously united in death. But the stars of the place are the two English poets whose names are for ever linked with Rome, Keats and Shelley, whose remains lie here. Through an aperture in the wall one can glimpse the grave of Keats with its bitter epitaph: "Here lies one whose name is writ in water." Next to him is his lifelong friend Severn, sent by Keats to find this last resting place as he lay dying in the tiny *pensione* off the Spanish steps. When Severn returned and told the dying poet that white and blue violets, daisies and anemones were growing wild on the graves, Keats was happy and said he "already felt the flowers growing over him." Further up the slope lie the ashes although not the heart of Shelley, which the flames of his funeral pyre would not consume and which was plucked from the embers by his friend Trelawney, who bore it back to England. Here amongst the broken columns and marble fragments covered by trailing ivy and honeysuckle with here and there a fiery red camellia, one can sit shaded by pines and laurels and myrtles and find a little peace. "It might make one in love with death," wrote Shelley, "to be buried in so sweet a place."

Away in the heart of the city in the Piazza d'Espagna one finds another memorial to the two English poets, the Keats–Shelley house, where Keats spent his last days. The simple, narrow room where he died with its pale blue ceiling and lime-washed walls can still be seen. The house itself stands by the Spanish steps at the foot of the church of Trinità dei Monti where the nuns sing vespers on Sundays and holy days in piping high voices. The house is packed with books and relics of the poets but is not so much a museum as a house of contemplation, presided over by a serene and charming deity, Signora Vera Cacciatore, who has been its curator for many years. During the dreary days of occupation she shuttered the windows and resolutely kept the Germans out and was rewarded on the day of liberation when she threw open the doors and found by happy chance the soldier sent to guard the house by the allied high command was a Keats scholar.

In Rome, museums and galleries can get one down. The Vatican museums are as splendid as the Louvre and equally debilitating. My favourite Roman gallery is the more manageable Villa Borghese, the home of Napoleon's favourite sister, Paolina. There she reclines, immortalised in marble by Canova, a pose of which she later became somewhat ashamed but it was times that had changed, not she. Canova's masterpiece can hold its own with the marvels of Bernini which stand nearby, while above on the *piano nobile* live a choice collection of pictures of which the highlight is Titian's iridescent allegory of sacred and profane love. Spare a moment, too, for the highly idiosyncratic collection of paintings at the Palazzo Spada near the Piazza Farnese, a gem of settecento good taste, with a splendid *trompe l'œil* garden gallery by Borromini. Pop in also to the Museo Romano at the opening of the incomparable Piazza Navona, where Domitian once staged his chariot races, and you will be regaled by the sight of one of nineteenth-century Rome's most agreeable curiosities, the railway train of Pio Nono with its open and closed carriages complete with papal thrones. The Quirinale is also well worth a visit, especially its magnificent chapel with an intriguing papal squint and its formal gardens. You could also tour Rome's thirteen obelisks starting from the magnificent specimen in St. Peter's Square to its homely and diminutive fellow creature, which is mounted on the back of Bernini's delightful elephant in the Piazza della Minerva. But I must stop. As Silvio Negro, one of Rome's great lovers, wrote: *"Roma, non basta una Vita,"* for Rome, a lifetime is not enough.

ABHU DHABI

by POLLY DEVLIN

The silence in Abu Dhabi is what I remember. The silence in the undemanding audiences with Sheikh Shakhbut and his two sons Sheikh Said and Sheikh Sultan. Sheikh Shakhbut is the ruler of Abu Dhabi, a man of enormous presence and great dignity. He is an autocrat, his word is law and is respected since he is wise and knows his people. His presence fills the room where he sits. He has the great kindness and the hospitality, the traditional courtliness of his race. His ancestors are the legendary, fierce, desert Sheikhs and their blood flows strongly in the Royal Family. His palace is a huge white shimmering building dominating the town of Abu Dhabi and in the room where he holds his audiences a great chandelier hangs from the ceiling and the traditional carpets have been replaced by chairs. There the Arabs sit in silence, talking only when they have something to say. No matter where he sits, the whole focus of interest is centred on the Sheikh. At Sheikh Said's house everyone sits on carpets, visitors, retainers, and huntsmen with Biblical faces and falcons on their arms. Sporadic conversation breaks out, an Arab speaks to Sheikh Said about something important but there is no small talk.

Each Sheikh has an aura of dignity — their heritage is in their blood, a heritage that means hospitality and princeliness as well as bravery and strength. Their manners are superb. The manners that come with an anticipation of a wish not the voicing of it — the fact that you are their guest means that you are honouring them. Their generosity is overwhelming, even embarrassing, since when you thank them they say simply, "It is nothing." This courtesy isn't the prerogative of the Sheikhs although in them it is brought to a high degree — it is in every man in Abu Dhabi.

The stillness of the desert. Those who knew it when there were no tyre tracks on the sand, and no generators to break the silence in the morning, think it spoiled. But my background was London so the desert, tyre tracks or not, pulled me apart. The sand that fried the feet and hurt the eye with a negation of colour, the quietness as I walked up a dune and down another. And then the roar of an engine and down a steep dune almost at the vertical, came a jeep packed with men clutching guns, their faces gleaming, the first half of a hunting party going out to hunt buzzards and hares with Roger Upton, an English falconer. In five minutes we were all sitting around drinking the spicy bitter coffee that always seems to be ready even if one is a hundred and fifty miles out in the desert.

The splendid shout from the tower, the calling to prayer left me shivering, for not all one's previous knowledge prepares one for the sound as it rolls across the sand. Arabia is tamed they say but how can you tame a desert land or tame people who have bravery, flamboyance, wildness and cruelty in their blood. If they have jeeps, they still use camels, if there are Lucky Strikes, there are still one puff pipes, and if one can buy ice-cream, one still eats traditional magnificent feasts laid on the floor as they have been for hundreds of years. There, they have taken the expendable things of the West, and made them even more expendable. If you want to get from one place to another in Abu Dhabi you drive there in a Cadillac as the crow flies and it doesn't matter if the gears grind and the sand clogs up the engine.

The colour and movement; the blue sky with a sun revolving, a sun that slaps off your skin, and off the buildings with an almost physical force. The sand glistening, white and brown, sweeping up to the white palace of Sheikh Shakhbut. The brown boats drawn up on a pink shore; walking down a road, three black-eyed children in peacock and purple dresses playing with bright balloons. The sunsets, red slashed with orange, over a dark sea. The grace of an Arab woman as she walks with a basket on her shoulder or lifts her hand in greeting. Women are in strict purdah in Abu Dhabi, are veiled from the age of twelve, and never take off their masks in public.

Abu Dhabi is a large sheikhdom; the town is on an island connected to the mainland by a narrow causeway. At the other end of the island is a jetty where the boats come in and where Sheikh Shakhbut's magnificent yacht is moored (it belonged to Prince Rainier before Shakhbut bought it). I went there with Sheikh Said one day to see some of the horses he had bought in Iraq being unloaded. The jetty was packed with people, cars, cranes and lorries. The boat with the horses drew near to the jetty and the Arabs and Negroes began to haul on the rope which would draw it alongside. As they tugged, they moaned a slow and desolate chant that rose to a tremendous exhilarating shout as the boat shuddered against the wood of the jetty. Everyone seemed insane with excitement — a man in a crane nonchalantly swinging his great dangerous machine, other men screaming orders, others countering them; but without any apparent organisation, without, it seemed, anyone actually doing anything, the beautiful, high bred horses were rolling ecstatically in the sand, and suddenly the jetty was empty.

We went for a drive after that. Across the sands to a fishing village. It looked deserted, boats on the shore, stillness everywhere. From one doorway a woman peeped and then was gone, a man walked slowly past and disappeared. They are a contained people, but never secret.

A hundred and fifty miles across the desert is Buramai, a province of Abu Dhabi governed by Sheikh Zayid, brother of Sheikh Shakhbut, a marvellous extrovert with a great sense of humour.

Before the oil was discovered that was to make Abu Dhabi one of the richest countries in the world, Buramai was the wealthiest province for it had that most precious thing, water. It's a huge oasis, a great circle of towns and villages with gardens and trees and rivers. I loved the bare beauty of Abu Dhabi island more. In the summer the Sheikhs move to Buramai to escape the blinding heat of Abu Dhabi island, and even when they aren't there, their palaces glitter with electric lights like massive carnival entrances. We went to Buramai immediately after a great feast given to us by Sheikh Said. We set out into the desert though hardly in the manner of Lady Hester Stanhope. We were going in cars and jeeps, but I was enormously excited, even though we had provisions with us and water and, more useful, motor mechanics. We got stuck in the sand twice and had to be pulled out and while the men were doing it we ate oranges and wandered up and down the hills looking from the corners of our eyes at the enormity of barrenness, the arid splendour under the sun. We took photographs and shot at a cigarette stuck in a beer can. Then, there were aspects of a day out at Blackpool especially in the raucous gaiety and shouts of laughter, but underneath there was a tension, anticipation, a kind of panic induced by the thought of the desert around us.

We came to Buramai in the hot dry night, our hair and eyes stinging with sand. On the last half of the journey we had been quiet, no more laughing, just minds thinking of water and rest. The streets of Al-Ain, the biggest town were wide, deserted, quiet. The desert at night is filled with a deep low murmur but here was the opposite of sound. We stayed in Sheikh Sultan's European guest house, surrounded by long, green gardens and a swimming pool. The next morning the sun seemed to swell the curtains with its intensity and outside on the balcony the interpreters and huntsmen and drivers and cook were shrieking at each other in Arabic. We drove to the Beau Geste-like fort where a squadron of the Trucial Oman Scouts have their headquarters. Most of the officers are

191

British, funny, charming, and we had a marvellous time with them. We stayed four days there, were joined by the falconers and the huntsmen with Roger, and we set out again for Abu Dhabi, some of us in the back of open jeeps, some in cars, all racing each other on parallel sand tracks for miles and miles and screaming balefully when one passed another.

All along the route men were working on the pipeline that will bring water to Abu Dhabi, unlimited water, for the first time in history and as we tore past they stared, smiled and waved. When I saw the causeway that leads to Abu Dhabi island I was stunned by my reaction. I had soaked extravagantly in the space and sun of Buramai but returning to Abu Dhabi was now like coming home.

We went to see Sheikh Said that night to tell him about the trip although he had often been in touch with Buramai by radio. He listened with his rare and disconcerting attention, sometimes laughing with a whole-hearted amusement one would not have expected from a man with such lonely eyes.

I loved watching the falcons being fed. Their feeding is a part of their training and it had a stately ritualistic primitive beauty, as if the birds and their keepers were following the complicated steps of a private dance. Each bird knows its keeper, each keeper has a special call. Three people are involved in the feeding of each bird. The keeper, the man who swings the bait to attract the falcon (the bait is the wing of some more unfortunate bird) and the man who walks to a point almost out of shouting distance from the keeper — a very long way in the desert. As the bait is swung the keeper gives his taut high call and the falcon is released, and at enormous speed, straight as a die, flies to the whirling wing, clutches it and lands smack on its keeper's arm. There is grace, speed, elegance in the moment, although sometimes there are embarrassing, unspoken times of failure as when a bird flies lazily upwards, studiously ignoring the whirling bait and fades out of sight. The keeper's call gets more frantic and less musical with every flap of the bird's wing towards the desert and freedom. But this is rare, and most of the beautiful and valuable birds stay with their keepers without coercion.

The night before we left (three weeks after I had first stepped out of the small plane into Abu Dhabi and another mediaeval beautiful world) we sadly said goodbye to a country and a people I had grown to love. We would come back, inch'Allah.

COWAN

192

BOLT FOR THE BLUE

by WILLIAM SANSOM

February fill-dyke is the worst month, dishcloth skies and the whole country a muddied sink with the waste stopped up. Much more than saturnine, bicarbonated January, it is the month for our formative thoughts to plan for one of the best dykes in the world, a sink filled with waters of lazy azure, pure and salt. Not only is the cloud-hating Mediterranean the warmest and kindest inland sea in the world, but it is richer than anywhere else in the remnants of those ancient cultures which have tried to make us what we would like to be. It is thus a sea rich in old architectures and manners, health, history. Difficult to beat. Lake Titicaca? Too high. The Dead Sea? Too low. The open Caribbean? Apart from the year's boundless, bonded sunshine, there's one month with a middling chance of Hurricane Harriet wrapping a Portuguese Man-o'-war round our toothpaste grins.

The Mediterranean is mild, can lose its temper, but quickly regains it. And one is soon back with the best moments — like the late slow slouch down to the restaurant on the quay, where the water laps black and eely gold. A marine smell of old rope and dead fish hangs about, a taste of some anis drink hangs on the tongue, the feet are cool in sandals. Warm night air moons about our light-clad torsos, and a white tablecloth says sea-food and wine, wine and ice and sea-food, sea-food and fruit and wine. A fish-boat put-puts out with the sound of a marine lawn-mower, its bright balloon of light flaring white. And could that be the titter of a *real* guitar somewhere? While a black castle or promontory continues to stand and stare out against the silver sea, and, closer, the Phoenician eye of a painted boat glares codlike, godlike as it lurches its lead against the quay. But now the wine — *"Ghiaccio!" "De glace!" "¡Hielo!"* and whatever the Greek is, say, "Ice".

Another great all-Mediterranean moment, equally refreshing, is at the other end of the day, at about 6 a.m. I well remember getting up at this most earthly hour one July on a small Balearic island. Hitherto, the village where we were staying had been notable only for its lethargies: a black priest asleep, sequinned with flies; dogs lying about like the after-battle dead; the sea scarcely bothering to move at all; goats and tourists munching, everybody else sweating behind blinds — *"¡Qué calor, qué calor!"* Yet at sunrise? The place was what is called a hive of industry. Women washing steps, children, clothes, anything they could lay their lathered hands on; men washing horses; horses walking about in the sea; the sea actually *moving,* showing off, turning pink and gold and blue in turn; dogs standing up and looking rogue turkeys straight in the eye; goats still munching, but now only the visitor sweating and snoring behind blinds. And over all this refreshing scene of multiple activity, the sweet cool air of dawn, the sense of another great day beginning, the morning of the world. While a fisherman cycled by blowing a conch-shell to announce his catch; and now and then an anxious eye glanced skywards as inch by inch the incendiary sun, the enemy, rose higher.

It is the same in cities. Cool morning and cool evening — these are the best times of day. The rest may be relegated to sweating francs and lire and pesetas and dinars and drachmae and dirhams and so on out of the baking visitor with his beach ball and nose-cap, harpoon and skis, martini and plodding guide-book. Yet this visitor is not to be decried, he enjoys himself no end — even if the temporary end is a touch of gippy tummy.

But if the black-eyed *langostina,* the secretive *cannellone,* the fennel-scented *loup de mer* have not got you down, then life at most levels can feel as good as it can be. Mornings in the Corsican maquis, cystus and wood-strawberry scenting the air, and a stroll down to the old Genoese fort and the spanking new yachts of Calvi. Or a morning's bathe on any old beach, from the rocks of Nauplia to the long bikini-fringed sands of Pampelonne, from the giggly little beaches of Giglio to the grey grit of the Costa Brava; the luke-warm bath of Hammamet, the civic pebbles of panama-hatted Nice: even on those beaches encircled by white new hotels already cracking, clairvoyants of earthquakes to come, where the parasols grow close as parking-meters and there are bars and skiing and flesh and an occasional faceless figure in skin-tight rubber, slithy frogman black and waspish yellow. But everywhere, quiet or loud, there is the same salt on the skin, the same wedding with warm water, the same sense of sun and health and ease and shade and ice to come. Even at Torremolinos.

For myself, apart from a number of secret desert beaches, I must confess a preference for pools. One can stretch out in clean comfort, properly propped up near some benevolent palm, and the equipment of books and glasses and such stays free from sand, tar, shrimplets. I well know the opposite — such as the small beaches round the suburbs of Marseilles, where under great villas and hanging gardens and white limestone cliffs the intrepid *nageur* must navigate through a flotsam beyond his wildest dreams, a slalom among sewage, among sodden crates and a bobbing of plastic bottles, a test for the snakiest of crawls. Better the clear Adriatic waters by Sveti Stefan, so salt-sodden you can sit on them, you need hardly move — yet they are clear as spring water and emerald, sapphire, amethyst in mysterious colour.

And other pleasures — beyond the bathing, the swimming? The hydrofoil trip from Athens to the lemon groves of Poros, or farther to rocky piratical Hydra, home of old sea-captains and new boutiques — that hydrofoil skims across the Aegean at just the right speed, not fast for such slow-moving islands, it is like motoring on empty roads before the war. Or the boat across from khaki Malta to green Gozo, and a drink at the Royal Lady, named not after Queen Victoria but an old ferryboat from Scarborough. On Malta itself what architecture and treasures the knights built and assembled will walk you off your feet — though afterwards there is still room to bathe on this brown island more African in aspect than anything else. But a short air-hop north of Malta lies Sicily, an island more taxed, but still for the passing visitor a floral and architectural delight. Best to go early in the summer, May, to get the full abundance of sub-tropical flower, than which I have seen nowhere a greater. It is astonishing. The usual bougainvillaea, morning glory, orange blossom and so on — but all twice as big and rich. It all makes a wry frame for the down-drawn Afro-Spanish faces, either sad or impassive, which top most Sicilian shoulders. The wedding of Arabic and Byzantine architectural motifs makes for miracles, too great to be gaudy, but as gilded and coloured and domed and tiered as one of the huge ceremonial Sicilian ice cakes: into one of which we may wish to plunge our red-hot feet at the green flash of evenfall. It is all so rich — with the various baroques of Noto and Syracuse to come; and so many superb Greek temples *standing,* not just lying about in irritant lumps; and the art nouveau salon of the Hotel Igeia at Palermo. And. And. And. Sicily is all Ands — so very rich beyond its poverty. Best take the five-day *pullman* tour — and afterwards fall slap in the siren sea and stay there.

Gibraltar? Bathing again. But a wonderful laugh in the town among side-whiskered Spaniards dressed as London bobbies, red Victorian pillar-boxes, Bombay merchants conning you from every tax-free shop, kilted Scottish soldiers passing mantillaed ladies on high red Andalusian heels, and these same ladies blowing their jazzy lungs out on the trumpets and saxophones of half a dozen ladies' bands playing in the evening cafés —

special entertainment, but *roped off*, for the port-lusty sailors. Many a graceful house of glazed Spanish tiles, looking like a balconied bathroom turned inside out; usually a sleek grey page out of *Jane's Fighting Ships* at anchor in the harbour; and, if you can be bothered, Europe's only colony of apes chattering and moping on the rock top.

Europe's only date palm plantation surrounds Elche, a boiling hot town along from Alicante, and famous for piping hot rabbit pie. But for stranger Arab atmospheres, cross to Morocco — and, veiled for sand and scorpions, meet instead a kind of Atlantic-blown Ireland with lonely camels browsing among the clover fields and white storks playing the swan. By the grace of Allah, no Irish rainfall. But Moorish gentlemen stride about in brown burnouses like a race of monks; though their dusky colleens are still mostly veiled to halfway up the nose — which gives to dark and lovely eyes the same dominance and wild mystery that once graced a white woman's ankle.

Tangier for bars and bathing and many an odd business. Better to strike south and above all see Fez, most mediaeval of all cities, a fantastic warren of a thousand narrow alleys and tunnels busy with a life not much changed since, say, the fourteenth century, even to a mound of dead rats I recently saw piled against an alley-wall. Dignified Moors ride through on Arab horses, kohl is sold in silver lumps, the tanners tan and the silver-beaters beat, the porters port their enormous loads and the students study in a number of beautiful and ancient Moorish university buildings. Manifold mosques. And millions, it seems, of minute shops, holes in the wall full of silks and scents; and millions of grains of rice for the unwary who order a couscous — the wary go for *pastilla* or sweet pigeon pie. And you may stay in a fine old Arab palace, now a hotel, in an orange-scented garden overlooking the whole of this great grey labyrinth, towered and minareted, within whose walls it is unwise, for once, to go without a guide. Otherwise, though you might not get hurt, you would surely get lost: a western sense of orientation is not enough.

And at the capital Rabat there march the blue-black — Mauretanian? Senegalese? — members of the Royal Guard uniformed from head to foot in bright scarlet, a sight to sore the eyes, but splendid indeed. And anywhere there might erupt a ceremonial charge of a half hundred or so bedouins on high camel-back firing rifles into the air. Farther south, the red paradise of Marrakesh, a blessedly flat city built on oasis ground, red walls and towers and palms against the near snows of the High Atlas . . . but this is certainly for spring, it bakes at a 100 deg. F. in summer. though there are the mountains to cool up in, and the Sahara and stranger cities beyond.

However — this is far from the Mediterranean, to whose warm and lazuli depths we must return — for what? A game of cricket on the grassless square at Corfu? Drinking zinzinber (ginger beer) in the long field — both relics of the English occupation? Or the ascent again of old Capri, now a suddenly reasonable phoenix risen from its hackneyed ashes, for here for once is a blessedly motorless place where you can still walk, stroll, saunter in quiet and comfort . . . unlike Ischia next door with its ferry-loads of Neapolitan Fiats arriving every half hour or hour. There are even traffic jams on the beaches in Ischia.

The Mediterranean tale goes on for ever . . . *calamares en su tinta* on the shrimp-encrusted marble pavements of Málaga? Oysters and a bottle of Grk on the equally marble but spotless pavements of Dubrovnik? Take in a Greek Island or two? *Do* Italy? Wherever you go there will be something different, yet the same old sun and sea and the sense, or at least the nonsense, that all's right with the world. And wherever you go you need not take a transistor — others have them.

MONTENEGRO

by FITZROY MACLEAN

To me Montenegro, or as its inhabitants call it, Crna Gora, the Land of the Black Mountain, is one of the most romantic and exciting countries in the world. Its history is an epic chronicle of war, rebellion and strife. Magnificent figures in their splendid national garb, the Montenegrins are by tradition warriors and heroes. In them the fighting spirit of the South Slavs, their pride, arrogance and violence of temperament, are manifested in a concentrated, an extreme form. For them. a warrior's calling is the only honourable one. "May he not die in his bed" is a favourite toast when a Montenegrin boy is christened. While, through the centuries, their Balkan neighbours succumbed one after the other to Turkish domination, the Montenegrins fought on in their mountain fastnesses defying their Turkish overlords and maintaining, under their Princes and Prince-Bishops, a large measure of independence.

It was thanks to Russian support against the Turks that in 1878 Montenegro was finally recognised by the Powers as an independent principality. "We and the Russians," the Montenegrins would boast, "make a hundred and eighty million men." Today it is one of the six Republics that make up the Federal Republic of Yugoslavia. In the last war, resistance came naturally to them. Their rising against the Italians in 1941 was the beginning of a guerrilla epic that was to last with savage intensity for the next four years.

The approaches to Montenegro are as dramatic as the character of its people. Thirty or forty miles to the south of Dubrovnik, the coast road, which is as beautiful as any in Dalmatia, comes to the Boka Kotorska, or Gulf of Kotor, a gigantic fiord bounded by precipitous limestone mountains rising abruptly from the dark waters of the bay. This immense natural harbour, which between the wars sometimes accommodated the entire British Mediterranean Fleet, was for centuries a hideout of pirates and sea raiders. Along its shores the road passes a succession of pleasant little towns with characteristically variegated histories, all predominantly Venetian in character, though with earlier Byzantine and Slav overtones — Hercegnovi, Risan, Perast and Kotor itself.

After Kotor the road branches. One fork continues along the Montenegrin littoral to Budva, Miločer and Sveti Stefan. The latter is an old pirate stronghold perched on a rocky island joined to the mainland by a causeway. The pirates have long since disappeared and the whole island has now been converted into a luxurious hotel. The visitors live individually or by families in the pirates' little stone houses, now provided with modern plumbing, and eat expensively and well out on a terrace poised high above the Adriatic. On each side of the causeway the white sandy shore stretches away for miles.

The other branch of the road starts to climb up the sheer face of the mountain in a series of breathtaking zig-zags to Cetinje, the old capital of Montenegro, offering to any true Montenegrin who may be at the wheel unrivalled opportunities to test his own and his passengers' heroism.

The view as you climb opens out to embrace an ever wider panorama of grey and black mountains clustering round the gleaming waters of the Gulf. By the time you get to the top, you begin to have an idea of what Montenegro is going to look like.

Cetinje is a small, not very interesting town in a rock-strewn plain surrounded by hills. Its two principal buildings are the old Palace and the new. The old Palace is known as the Biljado, after the billiard table installed by an early nineteenth century Prince-

196

ACKNELL

Bishop who was a keen devotee of the game. The new Palace is a modest Victorian villa containing some rather pathetic belongings of the former dynasty and a large number of yellowing framed and signed photographs of nineteenth century European royalties.

From Cetinje, it is only another thirty miles to Titograd, the new capital, built from scratch on the ruins of the little town of Podgorica, which, being a German 'head-quarters, was bombed to bits in the War. In Titograd the Montenegrins have fairly let themselves go. Never were there such Government departments, such multi-storey buildings or such elaborately laid out vistas, while the Grand Hotel Crna Gora with its hundreds of bedrooms has to be seen to be believed. Here in the evening, in one or other of the columned ballrooms, you may see ministers and generals mingling merrily with gnarled but magnificent-looking peasants in national dress, who have ridden in on their ponies from the mountains to see life and consume large quantities of sticky pastries, of which they are, it appears, inordinately fond.

But to find the real Montenegro it is necessary to go inland and northwards from Titograd to Nikšić and beyond, up into the real mountains in the direction of Durmitor, the highest peak of them all. At its foot lies Crno Jezero, the Black Lake, where Tito had his headquarters during the Fifth Enemy Offensive, at one of the most critical moments of the War. There can be few wilder or more inhospitable regions upon earth than this great tangle of mountains, forests and rock-strewn uplands, broken at random by sheer precipices of limestone falling sharply away to the beds of swirling torrents three or four thousand feet below.

From Titograd the main road to Macedonia runs northwards and eastwards through the mountains, skirting round the Albanian frontier to Andrievica. At the summit of the Čakor Pass, five or six thousand feet up, you look out in summer to distant peaks across high mountain pastures bright with wild cyclamen and foxgloves and buttercups. In winter the scene can be less welcoming. From the top of the pass the road follows the course of the Bistrica, a raging mountain torrent, on its way down between the towering crags and pinnacles and rock walls to the ancient town of Peć — an exit from Montenegro scarcely less dramatic than our entrance by way of Kotor and the Lovčen Pass. It was here, on our way through the mountains, that my son Charlie contrived, while fighting with his brother Jamie in the dark, to drop his Gladstone bag out of the Land Rover and over a precipice. It was returned intact to Lowndes Square by a messenger from Montenegro eighteen months later.

197

SLOW BOAT
TO THE BLACK SEA

by ANTONIA WILLIAMS

Mark Twain took a cruise to the Black Sea in 1867, "a picnic on a gigantic scale . . . sailing away with flags flying and cannon pealing". We set off last June with an itinerary splendid enough, skimming round the Greek islands to Ephesus and Istanbul, out of predictable Mediterranean blue and into silky grey waters and the ports of Trebizond, Sochi, Yalta and Odessa. Leaving from Venice one smokey wet green evening in the Adriatica's *Illiria,* small and white with the lion of Saint Mark stalking across the funnel and everyone cossetted from the start — flowers blooming in the cabins, impeccable service, deck space and breathing space for all one hundred passengers.

Then down the Adriatic in a warm grey haze to Corfu, green and lush with idyllic beaches and plump cacti bordering the road up to the Achilleon, the Empress Elizabeth's hilarious and very Germanic monument to classical Greece, now a casino bristling with one-arm bandits and daguerreotypes of nineteenth-century royalty. Corfu is oddly like Yalta with its prolific growth, summer palaces and faded imperial past. You can sit drinking ouzo at Costa's bar in the main square and watch Sir Frederick Adam, Regency British Commissioner who stands on a plinth outside his peeling Georgian residence surveying the local game of cricket.

All ports of call followed much the same pattern — the organised excursions, myths, facts and figures were there, and a charming Greek guide travelled on the ship. Or you could lie happily mindless in the sun on ship or shore. In Rhodes, bound by pale walls and windmills, stronghold of the Knights of St. John and Scandinavian tourists, we hired a small Fiat with white-fringed gentian blue canvas roof and plastic cane seats that left indelible impressions on my legs, and took a roundabout route over scrubby hills, through pines, platoons of downy boy soldiers and the Valley of the Butterflies, to Lindos. Its toytown caught on an eastern peninsula, you climb to the Acropolis on tiny donkeys, past whitewash, scarlet geraniums and black and grey pebble mosaics, to the great golden Venetian walls, dusty grass and solitary temple columns high above the dazzling dark sea. After that a swim and fresh fish at the beach restaurant.

There was no time to see Izmir (or Smyrna, far more evocative), but our guide left us in little doubt that it was still a great trading centre, keeping up a muezzin export chant of figs, figs, tobacco, figs, tobacco, all the way down the wide fertile valley to Ephesus. Here the temple of Diana has vanished, the sea has retreated ten kilometres from the port and the past is at peace — an enchanting, drowsy mixture of wild flowers and friezes, buzzing insects, broken columns and Turkish workmen in teatowel turbans, digging at the layers of civilization in a desultory way so as not to disturb the spirits of Alexander and Mark Antony. There's a mountainous forestry reserve nearby with restaurant, and tiny church where the Virgin Mary and St. John are reputed to have lived.

The Turkish coast and offshore Greek islands faded rocky, black and purple in the evening light, and early next morning the Dardanelles and Sea of Marmora closed in with ancient battlements crumbling on the skyline. Istanbul flashed past in two days — too short a time to see so complex a place. At first it was all crackling noise and heat, the

198

Egyptian spice markets and slave market, where they now sell flowers not women, the vast maze of the Grand Bazaar with bemused tourists buying antiquated remains and puzzle rings, and being conned with such charm. But the fat cat mosques basking blue on the hills, the silver grey wooden houses leaning over the Bosphorus, provide oases of quiet. And the Topkapi palace is one of the most beautiful places on earth. Through arches and trees, the Gate of Felicity, you reach endless inner sanctums, pleasure domes and kiosks, brilliant ceramics, faded embroideries, incredible jewels — the Sultan Achmed's braces, tossed up from a few emeralds and pearls big as phoenix eggs, whole walls in the cavernous kitchens covered in celadon Ming — and this is just a fraction of the original.

Moving from Golden Horn to Black Sea, the horizon turned to ink, and dolphins followed the ship all the way down the wild Anatolian coast to Trebizond. Within a few years the coast road will be finished and everything will change. Now Alexander Comnenus's Greek kingdom is a small forgotten, flaking plaster port — with no towers unless you count the American radar pylons on the hills. The ship docked, a small boy rushed forward with a shoeshine box, stopping in dismay when he saw the rows of sandalled and canvas shod feet, another with crewcut and ruddy cheeks rocketed a giant cold drink cart over the cobbles with a storm of lemon surging inside, and as our plan was to drive up to Sumela, an abandoned Greek monastery high in the mountains, every flashy finned 'fifties American taxi came clanking into town. The country is like the Tyrol, with beechwoods, sharp mountain streams and little stone farmhouses. There's a tortuous path to the actual monastery, caught under a rocky overhang, a bored Turk sits at the top and inside nothing but grubby crumbling ruins and faded frescoes with hearts and arrows. *Suleiman loves Fatima* scrawled across sad Byzantine eyes. Lunch was a picnic. The local dancing champions with wicked black mustachios and baggy black pants gave a joyous performance while we crunched pastry cornucopias stuffed with cream cheese.

Back in Trebizond the place to see is Aya Sofia, the most delightful, small Byzantine church that has done the usual Christian to Moslem switch and now stands pale and empty on its grassy headland over the coast road, the interior covered in naive frescoes, this time scrubbed clean as Sunday School and restored by a team from Saint Andrews.

When Alexei Leonov spun through space in Vostok II, he "admired the wide expanse of the Black Sea and the lace-work of its beaches". This whole length of Russian coast suits the fulsome brochure language — sanatoria set in greenery, parks and gardens running down to the sea with everything growing in disciplined profusion. The sanatoria, not just for mud cures, are massive boarding houses where the unions send everyone for their summer holidays. In Sochi, Georgia's main coast town, there are tea plantations, box and yew tree groves, and tamarisk lines the roads in candy floss clouds. We arrived in a tropical downpour which wrecked the impeccable sun statistics and embarrassed our guide, anxious that we should see The Pearl of the Caucasian Black Sea Coast at its best.

We drove from Sochi to Ritza, high in the Caucasus, in a great black Zim, past endless sanatoria and those ubiquitous metal poster frames that line all the highways and display exhorting muscle, or V. I. Lenin peering foxily into the traffic. People with broad, brown, incurious faces and dowdy print dresses wandered down the road. On the outskirts, the sanatoria changed to clear blue wooden houses with fretted gables and tin roofs dripping with vines. And halfway up the mountain there was a herd of cattle and water buffalo en route to their summer pastures, with shaggy dogs and swarthy Georgian shepherds, one wearing the traditional thick black cloak that looks as if the hanger is still inside. Ritza is a beautiful and almost unfathomable lake, heavy with mist and legend, and the local hotel, rambling, sky blue and wooden, has an Edwardian charm, with darkened hallways and potted palms. It was chilly, but the impervious Russians lunched on the verandah in their short-sleeved, shiny striped nylon shirts without a goose pimple in sight. We sat inside with the Armenian manager who appeared to love the whole world and drank vodka toasts to everywhere on earth. The food was superb — caviar, fresh trout and clear Georgian wine like sharp apple juice. Almost all the food in Russia was as good — scrunchy brown bread and stew, vast macaroons with lemon tea and heady Crimean brandy at a plastic and chrome hotel on Yalta's Lenin Embankment.

Yalta is jolly, nineteenth-century villa land, a balmy watering place despite the fact that much was rebuilt after bad bombing in the last war. Everywhere you drive there are little white-columned rotundas for view-admiring, rocky hills rise behind the parks and snowy hunks of sanatoria and the czar's summer palace, Livadia, is one of the solidest sanatoria of all. There's a lift cut through the rock so the Imperial family could descend to sea level with ease, landscaped gardens where the last czar walked for hours and had glasses of vodka waiting on tables set along the winding paths (and probably a servant crouched in the bushes to refill the glasses after he had swilled and strolled by).

Well worthwhile is a trip into the Crimea to Simferopol and Bachiserai where the Tartars made their capital in the seventeenth century, pushed inland by the Russians. The road runs down rich, rolling Apple Valley with fields misty blue with lavender or spotted pink with roses. The Khan's palace, though much restored, is highly decorative, with fretted wooden eaves and splendid contrasts — the original Tartar part with Italian painted ceilings, Russian painted walls and Turkish stained glass. Rooms were specially prepared for Catherine the Great, who came here on triumphant tour in 1794 when her armies had routed the Tartars, and she looks out from her conquering portrait with a very hardboiled eye. There are rooms depicting Soviet history with model factories and photographs of our Glorious Soviet heroes and heroines. And a Moslem cemetery with carved headstones deep in wild daisies.

Back in Simferopol, there was time to visit the local department store — shoddy but fascinating. I bought some exercise books and a white cotton kerchief with plum flock design like wallpaper. The girl behind the counter was filled with suspicion, but a dear old woman with shining silver teeth patted me all over and laughed and laughed as if I'd landed from the moon.

Odessa, not just a resort, is a plump and handsome burgher's town and port, wide boulevards lined with plane trees and solid ochre and grey stone buildings. Bloody revolution seemed a far cry from the massive Potemkin steps, a smug prosperity still weights the air.

The galleries are good (no Hermitage, of course), with the usual naive mixture of the best and the simply terrible. Glittering little sixteenth-century icons, splendid eighteenth-century portraits alongside Soviet History panoramas dripping with carmine and schmaltz. "This," said our guide, "is Modern Art" as I stood in front of an obvious, not to say representational, landscape. "You must stand back here and then you will be able to see what it is all about. It is a landscape."

Odessa was our last port before the return journey (a day in dazzling hot Athens, another in Dubrovnik and so back to Venice and London). Everyone climbed on board, past the soldier who had stood ramrod stiff all day in the broiling sun, and as the *Illiria* nosed from her moorings, a lady crane driver, in iron grey serge, black winkle-pickers and platinum beehive, breasted down the quay to her mammoth machine.

BORN
IN MARRAKESH

by CHRISTOPHER GIBBS

Beneath a scarlet pentacle and a sickle moon Ramadhan died and new year was born. At the Mamounia, Krupp mignons giggle in a wasteland of Moorish coffee tables, Madame Domenica Walter looks quizzically down at the dripping datura flowers, and Mrs. John Lennon up at the twelfth-century Koutoubia thrusting its faded peacock helm above the thrashing palms. In the courtyards of young Paul Getty, where Fès tile and palm frond tangle and flow from the dancing wand of the best dressed decorator in the world, William Henri Willis III, fireworks shatter, and among the flickers and the fountains, Madame Tazi and Madame Benjaloun, the beautiful daughters of General Mizian, vie with lovely Mrs. Getty in frenzied Totentanz.

Above the palms and the dusty aromatic souks of this huge market place hangs the long snow white line of the Atlas, where, halfway between heaven and earth, the Berbers roam, hunting the gazelle and scracthing a living from the pockets of rich red earth in the foothills and valleys, while their womenfolk, anchored by halters of amber to their spangled carpets, stitch, cook, and concoct magical philtres to keep their men from wandering away into the arms of the skiing houris of Oukaimeden. Beyond all this lies the scorching Sahara and the rain forests of Africa.

We travelled by ramshackle Hertz wagon north-east across the plains and into the mountains to Fès. Fès, the ancient university city of Morocco, means crucible, and many valleys pour their molten offerings into this honeycomb, walled about and pierced with castellated gateways. There is no room, no need, for motor cars in this crowded ancient place of mosques and medersas. Shops are at cool, subterranean street level, home life above them, and beneath, flat baked terraces strewn with carpets for lazing in the sun. Everywhere there are glimpses of fountains splashing below tiled mandalas, the sound of rushing rivers, the sight of the Holy praying in rush-matted courts beneath glittering chandeliers.

The Palais Jamai must be one of the most beautiful hotels in the world, built by a rascally Grand Vizier in the walls of the city, with tiled courts of palms, daturas, bananas, pools, fountains, terraces and its own private door into the heart of the souk. Monsieur Hadi, the manager, makes his guests feel as cherished and cosseted as they could wish, plies them with the delicious sugary treats for which Fès is famous (little dishes of Cornes de Gazelles, delicate almond stuffed pastry horns, will come with your mint tea). There are painted ceilings and furniture, tiled floors, pretty carpets, and views everywhere into the pulsing heart of the Medina. There are also official non-hustling guides who know and love their labyrinthine city; and out of term time, charming Fassi schoolboys, pining to use their gift of tongues and just as knowing about their ravishing home town. They will find you the excellent *majoun,* patterned with almonds and raisins, take you to the Haman, where dexterous masseurs pull you gently apart and put you lovingly together again, fresh and free, find you carpets and sandalwood, citron babouches and sequinned girdles, bind your paperbacks in crimson goatskin, twine you bouquets of mint and roses. I know no better hotel, and no city more beautiful.

ʃCANDINAVIA

by PETER VANSITTART

Scandinavia. Clichés flock like the devils of Götland. Venice of the North, troubling myths of gods burning, girls leaping Midsummer Fires, Herr Generals going mad in libraries; nude parties, Ibsen and Strindberg muttering, "People are Trolls". Crayfish joys under August lights; Nansen, Hammarskjöld, prophetic heroes; autumn leaves like a carillon as winds sweep the Sund, blackening our dahlias; smörgasbord and high taxes.

Democracy's at work in Folk High Schools, Co-operatives, realistic Industrial Relations, but I have no sociological natter save that Stockholm provides talking parrots for the lonely. Lastingly inexpert in the Thorwaldsen sculpture, Josephson paintings, Haanpää novels, I trudged under swimmers' suns, the stillness that of Rilke's poetry, Rilke who craved the wide North and wrote, "How they enrich the room, roses that come to settle there for a while".

Urban Europe loses identity as suburbs take over and intolerance stalks like a recruiting-officer. But in rock-islanded Stockholm one can still be lost in woods, a luxury already bizarre. Its Skanson Park, scattered with traditional-style homesteads, is like finding Worcestershire in Piccadilly. Northern cultures have not quite shed old France, imperial Germany. Rococo pavilions in city parks, galleries drowsy with imitation Cézannes, Sundays decorated with toy parades, elderly diners bandying *skols* and titles: "Mrs. Junior Lecturer Rydstrom".

People are eager to display their homes, vital citadels against winter. A Swedish Fru Professor, proud of Welfare, exhibited her chilly naked furniture, her plants polished like coffin-plates. "Peonies are gentle. Good citizens. I water the weeds, too. They also must have their chance." At Göteborg, old haven of ships and music, a girl offered paintings designed to collapse after two months, so that criticism had to come to terms with recollections. A Danish student played limitless tennis but insisted we kept no score.

Even in towns summer is silver with water, the reflected glimmer of masts, trees, statues. Water lapping our sleep, inducing strict, simple architecture. Mornings are individual, lively and flowing, as dream couples exclaim, "Let's" and set gay boats towards villas, islands, themselves. Smoothness is everywhere: in perfected shapes of boats, in silences, graded to niceties lost further south. Silence of a fisherman solitary under a red moon on a lake like a smoked glass; silence of an astrologer's waiting room; silence of midnight sun lighting an arctic birch forest with the rich tints of fairy-tale, blessed but uncanny. There I forgot to be tired; such play of light, such pagan irresponsible time would not recur.

The Baltic. Try Blidö, the Mild Island, scooped from the mainland by a giant and dropped in warm currents. Runic death-stones, antlers nailed to doorways, wooden churches with steeples set some distance off; red, peat-roofed hamlets, cross-shaped bread used against lightning. The rich from cities playing badminton and love. Late summer there of marvellous mornings for sailing seas still strewn with sunrise, already agleam with swimmers, and mediaeval figures smelting herrings on shore. Or in dense woods I bent for mushrooms, bilberries, wild strawberries, "old men of the earth," and was praised for courage. *Courage?* Snakes, they said, and courage departed. Waiting for autumn, watching storks grow and distance change blues to boulder-grey, I clutched last silences, and clichés stacked like vintage, not lulling but startling. Some can seldom be startled. In testing ourselves against silence we discover our essence.

RETURN VOYAGES

by ANTONIA FRASER

Where travel is concerned, I am an inveterate return voyager. That is to say, I am on the side of Proust rather than Stevenson. I have never been able to understand how Stevenson could think that it was better to travel hopefully than to arrive: for me the whole pleasure of travel lies not in the actual process, compounded as it is of every unpleasant word in the language from "delayed flight" to "excess baggage," but in the notion of return into time past. And after all the fascinating Proustian return voyage only begins when the tedious Stevensonian time of travel ends.

The pursuit of the past is a romantic pleasure open to any traveller. You can see Majorca as a summer paradise of sun and sea and rocks. You can also see it as the remote unknown Spanish island to which Georges Sand fled with her lover Chopin from the disapproval of Parisian society. Visit Majorca in the summer, see the remote high-up monastery where Georges Sand and Chopin lived, and at the same time read her own account of their life there, and you will enjoy an extraordinary sort of time machine travelling. Around you the sun shines, your life is happy, the wine is delicious, the sea is clear and blue. At the same time you suffer with Georges Sand — the barbarian Majorcans, so cruel, so uncomprehending to these uninvited geniuses on their island; the wine so rough to the palates used to the fine wines of France; the wet and misty hills so unsympathetic to Chopin's declining health.

In Beirut the contrast is even more marked. There is Beirut, international city of glamour and sophistication, and there is Beirut where Lady Hester Stanhope ended her days alone, dying in her palace, her servants fleeing from her in the hour of her need. One hot day in early May I was inspired to climb up to her tomb, avid for historical sensations, and full of admiration for this exotic flower of English womanhood. The sensation I actually experienced was the unexpected one of buckshot riffling through my hair. As I looked round wildly for cover, an Arab appeared from over a wall, waving a gun in his hand and shouting at me. I shall never know what he was trying to say. Was it, "A million pardons, Madame, your beauty unnerved me!", or more sportingly, "Sorry, old thing, I didn't know the gun was loaded" . . . in any case I lost my head completely and bolted down the hill towards Beirut, showing absolutely nothing of Lady Hester's intrepidity in the face of danger, and little indeed of her fraternal feelings towards the Arab races.

It would be idle to pretend, after an experience like this, that the active pursuit of history does not have its difficult moments. My worst failure was an obstinate trek out to the castle of Elsinore, finding myself in Copenhagen, and convincing myself that the inner mysteries of *Hamlet,* so long withheld from scholars, would be blindingly revealed to me, once I reached the cradle of inspiration. I was correspondingly mortified to discover in Elsinore a bleak stone outline on a windswept promontory and nothing more.

"Surely you were aware that Shakespeare had never actually been here," said my husband acidly, having endured the bus journey from Copenhagen with only moderate good humour.

Romantic researches, too, can go so far as to cast a blight over lively spirits. One summer holiday in Venice was completely shadowed by my inquiries into the history of Byron and his "last attachment," Teresa Guiccoli. Soon I was impelled to take a trip to

Ravenna to see the thing through, as it were, growing increasingly melancholy at the thought of the Guiccoli's love, Byron's growing indifference, their mutual recriminations, and her pointless sacrifices, both of her own happiness and of everyone else's. I might have had to follow on to Genoa, for Byron's final departure for Greece and death, had I not fortunately stumbled on Macaulay's cruel dismissal of Byron and the English public: "From the poetry of Lord Byron they drew a system of ethics, compounded of misanthropy and voluptuousness, a system in which the two great commandments were to hate your neighbour and love your neighbour's wife".

Feeling instantly ashamed of myself at having pursued Byron to Ravenna, I scurried back to Venice and contemplated the life story of Ruskin by way of correction.

A more full-blooded, more earthly image haunts Naples. Here I have thought of Emma Hamilton, the darling of the Bourbon court, beloved of the queen Maria Caroline, and of her first meeting with Nelson — the first meeting of a pair whose united image has haunted the world for the last 150 years. The ghost of Nelson also haunts a very different part of the world — the West Indies. For the house once occupied by the British Governors of Jamaica was also lived in by Nelson during his command there. I climbed up the little tower which he had built to observe the arrival of the enemy fleet. My guide pointed to an enormous tree at the end of the lawn almost out of sight, and certainly, you would have thought, out of earshot.

"Here Sir Hugh Foot would sit, when he was Governor," he told me. "He told his children to make speeches to him from the tower. Woe betide them if they could not make themselves heard to their father under the tree". It was an unexpected side-light on an English political family abroad, and now it is they, not Nelson, who haunt me under the bright West Indian sun.

The most purposeful pursuit of the past I ever made was also the most ill-fated. While in Ethiopia I became filled with a burning passion to track Rimbaud to Harar, the Moslem city where he lived for 11 years as a trader after he left France. I had read the life of Rimbaud by Enid Starkie, and considered a night alone in the hotel at Harar a small price to pay for the interest of the journey, just as the squire does not jib at a night alone in the chapel, in order to become a full-fledged knight. But my first attempts to tap the vein of enthusiasm in the inhabitants of Harar about their great poet met with no success.

"Rimbaud?" said one charming high-born lady, "Ah yes, I have met him last year in Addis Ababa at the court of his Imperial Majesty." Heavy-footedly I chose to explain that this was impossible and gave a short lecture on Rimbaud's life and work, with dates. To make amends, she graciously drove me all round Harar in her car to look for Rimbaud's house. After a good deal of discussion, and inspections as detailed as if I was about to buy a house in the city, we mutually decided to accept the next one as being Rimbaud's. I solemnly photographed a dwelling clearly not built earlier than 1930. The lady then whirled me away to see the tomb of Ras Kakonnen, which all along she had thought a more suitable object of tourism. We gazed away from the white marble monument over the city of Harar, amidst its surrounding hills.

"Your friend . . . the writer," said my hostess with a delightful smile, waving a white parasol, "I think he is happier now he lives in Addis. I think he did not like Harar very much. All those houses." And so she dismissed the search for Rimbaud.

A trifle disheartened by this experience, I ignored the true possibilities of searching after Richard Burton and James Bruce in Ethiopia — indeed my own travels into the interior were so like James Bruce's in hardship and comic adventure, that for once my sense of history deserted me, for I was altogether too obsessed by a sense of the present. But the African continent could be the richest of all sources to return voyagers. Tracing Burton's path alone would provide one with the travels of a lifetime, including not only

Ethiopia and his early journeys round Harar, but the later, more famous trips in East Africa, which culminated in the tragic quarrel with Speke, and Speke's mysterious death — all the more tragic because Burton was wrong and Speke right about the source of the Nile.

I do not suggest that every return voyager should necessarily track Burton to India, to West Africa, to Brazil, to Damascus — after all his restless spirit was difficult enough to trace during his lifetime. But I do at least recommend a visit to its last resting-place: his tomb at Mortlake fashioned in marble in the shape of an Arab tent, 12 feet square and 18 feet high with a pointed gilt star on top and a crucifix over the door. His widow described it — and who shall contradict her? — as "by far the most beautiful, most romantic, most undeathlike resting place in the world".

But let us admit it: there is one return voyage, irresistible to the average well-travelled introvert, which I have not mentioned. It is the prospect of a truly Proustian return voyage in search of oneself.

The Dordogne where one camped as a penniless and, more important, francless student — Verona and Vicenza first glimpsed at dawn searching for strong coffee after a night on a punctured lilo — Sicily, backcloth to an early poignant, shattered romance — Apulia, scene of one hot summer of happiness — how will they seem now from the vantage point of years? This is the sort of speculation which haunts every sentimental traveller. Which of us, at the prospect of seeing the house where we lodged for two years in a foreign town, first loved, first wrote, first discovered the Casino or the races, no matter what the discovery was, which of us does not drop the guide-book, abandon the projected picnic at St. Odo's birthplace and rush madly through the streets in search of the past?

Sadly, however, I have come to the conclusion that this is the one return voyage one should not make: it is infinitely more rewarding to concentrate on St. Odo's birthplace. It is not that one feels too much — on the contrary, far, far worse, one feels absolutely nothing at all.

The long, often tedious journey to the sacred spot is achieved at last; all too often one has difficulty in recognising it: "I know it had a green door because that cynical Madame V. used to call it the colour of hope . . ." "But darling, perhaps she has repainted it in the 15 years since you were here *au pair* . . ." And then what follows? The Proustian voyager will know the results only too well. The house is either much bigger or much smaller than you thought, depending inversely on whether you had stored it in your imagination as a palace in which you were a princess or a hovel where you were a slave. A new building of modern hue casts a contemporary shadow on an ancient neighbourhood. It all looks absolutely the same and absolutely different. In any case no ghost walks down the street, and the girl who was you 15 years before is as dead as the little yapping poodle you once exercised there.

Let us flee from such painful memorials and travel on blithely on the more cheerful route of impersonal past history. Let us accept the fact that Housman's "blue remembered hills" were after all a

> ". . . land of lost content . . .
> The happy highways where I went
> And cannot come again."

The return voyage should be made endlessly into the past of others, but never into one's own.

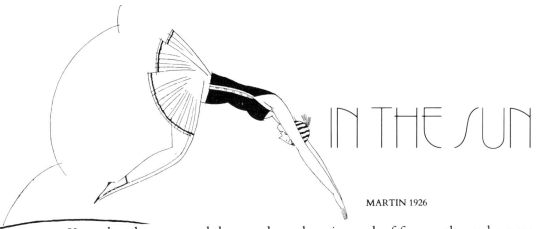

IN THE SUN

MARTIN 1926

Vogue has always pursued the sun, always been in search of fine weather and a more agreeable climate. There was Biarritz, glamorised by Edward VII, and King Alfonso's summer capital San Sebastian where, in 1916, "the smart world has thronged to forget the war for a few sunny weeks". When the Great War ended there were the more traditional summer resorts of Deauville and Le Touquet, and in winter there was the famous Train bleu south to the Riviera. But by 1923 a new generation had started to assert itself, creating its own fashions, setting new and more liberated patterns of behaviour and breaking away from such traditional and strictly seasonal restraints. "The world, they say, belongs to the young nowadays, and most notably is this true of the places by the sea at holiday time". Suddenly the days of San Sebastian's ox-drawn bathing machines were gone; gone, too, the crinolines, the taffetas, the hooped costumes. Instead, "along the sunny sands and in the blue-green wonder of the waves, the very last word in shortness of skirt, or trouser leg, bareness of back and multiplicity of sandal lacing, is to be seen". Though the older generation still made for the Riviera in winter it was no place for the young who now began to stay on for the summer. San Sebastian, the Lido, Deauville and Le Touquet were all very well for their parents in summer, but the Riviera was their discovery — and so was the sun. In 1927 Vogue investigated this new trend and for the first time ever, visited the Riviera in summer, making the journey south "on the Summer Train bleu . . . the little brother of the Train de Luxe that has carried the chic world to the shores of the Mediterranean winter after winter . . . a sort of concession to the handful of people who, in the last two years, have discovered that the beauties of the Mediterranean bloom for them under the summer sun". Amongst them was Meraud Guinnes. "I have spent my last two summers in Cannes and that has really spoiled me for the winter here. It is so much more fun here in July, August and September than in any other part of the year. Then is the time for the youthful and energetic and for those who love an out-of-doors life and we have a marvellous time. We practically live in bathing suits and coconut oil".

"Sunburn" — it was an emotive topic in the late Twenties, a subject of considerable discussion between those for and against this new development. On the Lido Beach Noël Coward observed with distaste that "every square inch of fine, powdered sand is dented and depressed by recumbent sun-blistered bodies", while skin specialists deplored "the recent craze for sunburn", and warned of exposure as costumes became briefer. But despite objections the craze lasted and although "fashion demands smooth white shoulders and arms even in the midst of the summer sun" Vogue reported that "the burners are even more numerous in 1928 than they were in 1927". By 1932 Cecil Beaton declared that "bodies must be brown at all costs", a colour now synonymous with health, vitality and youth, and fitting well with new thoughts on fashion. Within twenty years, "the marvellous aquatic costumes" of 1916 had shrunk to the barest minimum for maximum exposure. In 1951 the bikini made its first appearance — on the Riviera, where else? — and "in spite of the hopefully lugubrious announcements made by British and American beachwear people that it is doomed, the miniscule bathing dress is here to stay". And with it, Vogue's continued and increasing preoccupation with the sun — where to find it, winter and summer, and how to make the most of it.

FISH 1923

"The sea still yields up
its serpents, and it is
as well not to take
all seaside phenomena
too seriously.
There is for instance
the exotic professional
dancer who says
that he is a ruined
Russian prince;
well, he may be,
but then again—!"

DRYDEN 1921

FRISSELL

LE GUAY 1956   BÉRARD 1939

209

OFFIN 1948

KLEIN 1958

CHRISTIE 19

THE SEVENTIES

"770,000,000 people will be travelling 745,000,000,000 passenger miles by the end of the Seventies. Air routes change, flying times are shortened month by month, new airports and hotels open, and new airlines arrive to take more people further, faster".

Further, faster — no two words more precisely describe travel in the Seventies, and from the first issue of the decade Vogue's travel headlines were bigger and bolder, the destinations more exciting and exotic and the possibilities greater than ever before.

Vogue's travel coverage was both ambitious and optimistic, the first issue, for instance, featuring reports from Ceylon, India, Tokyo, Hawaii, the Seychelles and the Caribbean. It was the largest single travel feature ever, an appropriate start to a new decade.

Before the year ended Vogue had visited Timbuctoo "where the River Niger bends into the Sahara, the meeting place of all who travel by camel or canoe"; been to the "friendly isles" of Tonga "where 400 people read one copy of Vogue and where the government secretary has to stamp every page with an official seal"; to Mauritius "a tiny island with an eastern romanticism, and plantations, rivers, silver sands and coral reefs"; and to Zambia, with photographer David Bailey, on just one of many fashion and travel link-ups that became a regular feature of Travel in Vogue in the Seventies.

"Distances matter little", reported Vogue. "Plane services are frequent and reliable and the fare reasonable". It had never been easier to travel, physically and financially for, as the number of travellers grew, so prices fell, while ambitious tour operators, well entrenched in the holiday market, continued to produce ever more exciting packages.

Across the Atlantic, America was becoming the new Seventies attraction for Europeans, no longer a four-day cruise away, but a few hours by plane; no longer just New York and a splinter of land called Manhattan, but "3,536,855 square miles and no two alike, glaciers and deserts, great lakes, grand canyons, lowlands, madlands, badlands, bayous, swamps, suburbia, exurbia and more than 12,000 miles of coastline". In South America, Brazil became a tempting and feasible proposition, and if you hadn't been there, Vogue's advice was clear and insistent: "Fly there at once. Go straight to the Amazon and breathe deeply. You are surrounded by perhaps the richest plant life on our globe, and this river, that you should by now be canoeing on, has more water flowing out of it than the Nile and Mississippi put together".

Travel was global like never before — it was also total, demanding a kind of enthusiastic commitment. One no longer travelled to observe in Grand Tour style, one travelled to take part. "You don't move to Hawaii, you defect"; in India "to become initiated, one must participate"; and in Papua, New Guinea, Vogue's Travel Editor Peta Lyn Farwagi was " . . . amazed . . . astonished . . . hooked. I want to start all over again. I do not want to leave. After all, I've only met a handful or two of the tribes and there are two million people here, speaking 700 languages. I want to become an anthropologist".

Remote corners of the world, little known, rarely visited, became fashionable in what was soon a Seventies game of geographical one-up-manship. It was a time of discovery in the early years and anyone could be Christopher Columbus. Ever since Princess Margaret glamorised the Caribbean Islands during a tour in the late fifties, interest in the area had escalated. Apart from firm and lasting favourites like Jamaica and Barbados there was St Lucia "coming up fast"; Dominica with its "wild, virgin forests, mountains . . . and rivers in which the bathing is pleasant;" St Vincent with excellent sailing down the chain of islands known as the Grenadines and St Kitts "a waving mass of sugar cane with the most splendid fortress in the West Indies". Vogue recommended Tobago "if you are dreaming of a far-away beach for two where, on a moonlit night, you might even surprise the turtles lumbering up to lay their eggs"; or Bequia perhaps, "if you are young and vigorous, or middle-aged and active and your passion is the sea, sport-fishing, sailing and dropping anchor off a coral atoll, diving for lobsters, cooking them on a driftwood fire on a beach it seems no foot has ever trod before your own".

There was Bali; "a most giddying series of unfamiliar fragrances, where colours are extraordinarily bright and strong and where nature is at her most indulgent." Or another Seventies favourite, the Seychelles Islands in the Indian Ocean enjoying mounting popularity during the decade, though it was not long before Vogue advised readers "to take a trip there quite soon; the world is shrinking fast, travellers are greedy for yet more new scenes and, however carefully planned, tourism changes not only the place but the people and the trouble is they are not building any more islands".

The inevitable advent of mass tourism was the unacceptable face of travel in the Seventies. It turned primitive paradises into multi-million dollar resorts. "So tourism is coming to the Seychelles, it is inevitable. On Mahé within ten years every major beach will have its hotel and it is selfish to wish it otherwise; the islands and the people need tourism, not only to progress but to exist. But it is hard not to be sentimental and reactionary and wish it was not so", and those who knew the islands well bemoaned their sudden popularity and increasing accessibility. "When I heard they were building an airfield in Paradise I said 'Damn'," reported Athol Thomas.

But there were lessons to be learnt from other paradises that did survive discovery. Closer to home and certainly more accessible than the Seychelles, Sardinia "still belongs to wild things . . . though in a short decade, this last to be discovered, most naturally beautiful island of the Mediterranean has become the first successfully engineered larger-scale escape-resort . . . conceived in protest against the circus of the Riviera as a haven of clear water, clean sand and controlled privacy". Prices and careful packaging under the auspices of the Aga Khan ensured a more acceptable kind of tourism.

Africa attracted much attention during the Seventies. It was "the natural life, 2 million years of history and more animals than anywhere else in the world".

Equally popular — the Far East. Singapore was "the non-stop city"; Hong Kong "the super market place . . . that demonstrates so agreeably and excitingly the way to live a constant today"; while Malaysia, Thailand and Indonesia made even more frequent appearances in Vogue's Travel pages.

Vogue declared 1974 "the year to get up and go" and every year the pattern was repeated — to the North West Frontier and beyond, from the Hindu Kush to Kabul — anywhere so long as you went. "If you can appear on Djanet airfield neither Saint Laurent-clad nor crepe stilt-shod, adequately stripped of your customary Proustian melancholy; if you can subsequently bridle inopportune cravings for vitamin C in the shape of fresh oysters, do come and rove the Sahara with us", or trek the Karakoram range, or sail through the Galapagos Islands by schooner, or salmon fish in Alaska, ride through France, "skitabug" over grasslands, snow, beaches, shingle and mud flats and ski in places you'd never thought of: in the Lebanon, Morocco, Alaska and New Mexico. Global travel meant global gamesmanship, from tennis in Torquay to golf in Tobago; it meant holidays for families, for escapists, for businessmen, for pleasure seekers and purpose seekers; it meant long breaks and short breaks; cultural tours and mindless extravaganzas; European destinations and trans-world expeditions; it meant winter sun and summer snow; it meant whatever you wanted, wherever you wanted — farther and faster than ever before.

BRITISH LANDSCAPES

GLOUCESTERSHIRE   by POLLY DEVLIN

It was my friend Elizabeth Chatwin who first showed me a cowslip. She went on and on about this marvellous cowslip she had found in a field behind her house in Gloucestershire. That house! Rose coloured, with a shell canopy over the front door, the whole felicitous jumble of buildings lying under the edge of the hill and looking out over a valley of such exquisite emptiness you could hardly believe that Ozleworth (pop: 15) was just around the corner. The way she talked about this cowslip, and the measures she had taken to protect it, you might have thought that it was the great osprey itself, nestling in the bee orchis. I could not think why she was so careful about it, because where I grew up cowslips and primroses were thought to be the same thing. I could never understand those references in Shakespeare to "cowslips tall" and the crimson drops in the bottom of the flowers, and to their gold coats having spots like "rubies, fairy favours, in those freckles live their savours". What spots, how tall? I used to think gazing into the squat friendly and pallid countenance of a yellow primrose. (Curiously, the ointment made from cowslip petals was used in Gloucestershire villages to remove freckles and sunburn.) For where I was born in Ireland we never took much notice of wild flowers and scarcely knew their names. And then I went to live in cities and forgot about flowers. But now living in Gloucestershire my life and wild garden is a daily revelation, its abundance delights me, its beauty astonishes. It is like living amongst the Book of Revelations, in this lovely, louche county. Sylvia Plath was writing about somewhere else when she wrote about a county on a nursery plate, but I think, when driving through the small perfections of the northern parts of Gloucestershire, that she might have been writing about it. I live in the wilder, woodier south of the county, but even so there's not much savage and untamed about my country, except for some of its inhabitants, who look like centaurs when they are astride their hunters.

Often on clear, winter days, when I am on the edge of the great Cotswold escarpment, with my house hidden far below, I see the cream of the county in the distance (blue and buff if it's the Beaufort and yellow if it's the Berkeley) thundering to the edge of the precipice in hot pursuit of a fox. My heart thrills with the liturgy of the hunt then, streaming out against the graceful landscape, as indeed whose could not? I *do* think that it is the prevalence of fanatical riders and huntsmen and masters that has kept Gloucestershire intact. That great stretch of beautiful land, for example, which is Badminton, has always been held by the Beauforts, and therein lies the reason for its unfragmented and unsevered beauty.

I love Gloucestershire. I love everything about it. I love its snugness and its smugness and how all its inhabitants think they live in the prettiest county in England; and of course they do. I love the way the small towns lie crafted into their valleys, and it doesn't matter how often they are gazed at, or photographed, their peachy beauty still holds, unhackneyed to the end. The great tourist towns, I think, look more lovely in November when those famous golden tones take on a muted look, but the less famous towns are very beautiful too, they charm, and their names are melodious. I live in Wotton-under-Edge, and sometimes I telephone a friend in Shipton-under-Wychwood and the telephone operator bursts into tears. My nearest town is Chipping Sodbury, where the buses are called Sodbury Queens. I love the tumble of wool towns along the sides of the valleys. (A visiting poet once wrote, "O all the hamlets where hills and flocks and streams conspired to a language of waterwheels, a lost syntax of looms and spindles". Wotton, in fact, is short for wool town.

One could spend weeks in Gloucestershire and not even begin to exhaust its treasures, explore its histories, its churches, its staggering great houses, its famous gardens, its follies and monuments, gazebos, octagons and grottoes, its Chinese pagodas and Temples to the Wind. It seems to me that the gentry of Gloucestershire built a monument to anything that fell down, from drunken dukes to translators of the Bible, and they are scattered everywhere; they punctuate the landscape.

Gloucestershire has a flavour all its own, just as it has flowers all its own. The people still talk in a dialect that is broad and lively. Quite often when I query something the answer begins like this: "It was on this wise," and when they spill something they say they wasted it, and my daughters, egomaniacs like all children, start off all their sentences with Oi. "Oi love you," they say solemnly and one mustn't laugh.

Before I came to Gloucestershire the countryside was for me something like it had been for Sydney Smith — a kind of healthy grave where one always feared that creation might expire before teatime. But Gloucestershire is full of life and movement and vitality. Even the landscape seems to tumble away from crowned knolls and hills, towards plains and combes. Gloucestershire undulates toward vague and civilized boundaries, as its rivers thread their way towards leaner places.

CORNWALL   by A. L. ROWSE

There is a quite unexpected, and usually unrealised, diversity of landscape within the little land of Cornwall — sticking out into the Atlantic like a foot, some seventy miles in length and only twenty at most in breadth. It is almost wholly surrounded by sea; even the frontier with England is mostly water — the whole length of the River Tamar.

Most visitors coming into Cornwall come for the sake of the sea, the coast and the beaches, so they don't realise the variety and beauty of the landscape within. Especially if they come, as they mostly do, by A30 along the high spine of the county, across Bodmin Moor and Goss Moor, on through the bleak old mining country of Redruth and Camborne to the last uttermost peninsula, to Land's End.

Myself, a primitive inhabitant, one of the natives, I reckon there are more than half-a-dozen landscapes in Cornwall. In terms of cliff and coastal scenery alone, there are two or three. Addicts of North Cornwall will think first of the stupendous cliffs facing the Atlantic all the way down from Bude to Newquay. Some of these have a sheer drop of 700 feet into the sea — and how wonderful to look down on a summer's day from the churchyard of St. Gennys or above Crackington Haven to the heaving quiet of blue beneath. Still more, to confront the winter wind above Bedruthan Steps — sometimes I have been hardly able to stand against it — a wall of wind.

The south coast scenery is much quieter; we have good cliffs and headlands here, too, but of a more lyrical beauty, where the north coast is epic.

And what about the sand-dune country, the towns of Perranporth and Hayle, and around the lovely Padstow estuary? We have them too in the south — Whitsand Bay, Pentewan, Marazion.

There are three quite different coastal landscapes for you.

I love the inland landscapes no less, possibly even more. Tamarside, for instance: all that unspoiled country of exquisite river-valleys running down from Launceston to

Plymouth. As you go farther south the tide comes right up those valleys to Calstock or St. Germans, making lesser estuaries to explore, like the last and grandest of them all — the Hamoaze that divides Devon from Cornwall, Plymouth from Saltash.

And there are two great bridges — Brunel's 1859 railway bridge and the post-war road bridge — to tell you that you are entering a different little land on its own.

Everywhere the river-valleys are lovely. They are mostly on the south side — the Looe, the Fowey, the Fal and Helford. Those on the north, the Camel and Hayle, have another inflexion, barer, more sparse, with a paler, subtler colouring: those grey bent sedges, the willows like olive trees, grey-green, the tamarisk feathers over the wastes of sand!

My own secret love is for the edges of the moor: those parishes like Blisland or Northill where the bare moor tumbles down into good farming soil. An English friend of mine, mad about Cornwall, has pointed out to me how wonderfully the northern *massif* of Bodmin Moor looks, Rowtor and all, when you look back towards it south from St. Teath.

What a day in that country last summer! A cloudless day in St. Kew parish, standing on an old prehistoric barrow whence I could see five church towers, the pinnacles of St. Endellion pricking up like ears above the horizon.

What about the astonishing lunar landscape of the St. Austell china-clay country — in the moonlight, under snow? I once saw an *aurora borealis* up there on a snowy day. Or there is the last remote hilly Penwith peninsula — Zennor, Trencrom Hill, St. Buryan — so granity and strange, almost sinister with its longstones and cromlechs and stone circles:

"Home of the silent vanished races . . ."

To which we Cornish belong.

WALES   by GWYN THOMAS

Queen Victoria would allow no lamb but Welsh on her table, and our Welsh sheep have been snobbish about it ever since. I personally hold them in a kind of awe, and on my long, enchanted walks across the hills of my boyhood I would pause as they passed and give them a full, formal salute. The parts of Wales where sheep are, the high, ferny, quiet places, are the parts of Wales I love best.

Wales has no fat, broad plains such as you find in the Midlands and South East England. Our earth is puckered in a series of deep frowns of wonder and surprise, and in truth, history has provided us with many reasons for looking that way.

We were put down by the Normans, blown up by the pit-sinkers and bemused by a long line of witch-doctors and shamans in the fields of politics and religion. So much has happened to put us on edge in our strictly human relations that the apparent placidity of sheep has inspired in us a deep envy and respect.

Those witless, yellow eyes will never glisten with a wish to beat us hollow at the next Eisteddfod or to argue us into fuller support for the aboriginal Celtic language. I have not yet met a Welsh sheep that was not completely neutral in the matter of the Welsh-English controversy. I have heard North-Welsh chauvinists say that the sheep of Gwynedd bleat in a more guttural and thoughtful way than the feckless muttons of Glamorgan to the south, but I have my doubts.

The mining valleys of Glamorgan and Gwent have attracted the bulk of whatever attention has been paid to Wales over the years. Welsh fiction is as full of explosions as an average war, and when methane is not whooshing up a fresh disaster in our folk-tales, choral groups shuffle up the main street of the village to make sure the Welsh conscience is not left alone in too deep and tormenting a silence.

This is unjust. Between the valleys are the loveliest mountains of modest height in the world. Paths of the springiest turf wind through seas of fern. The resilience of this hilltop grass is remarkable. After hours of crouching ascent over the macadam and paving stones of the valley's hillside streets, one feels during the first loping minutes on the plateau's trampoline sward that one's legs have been given the super-normal thrust of the Six Million Dollar Man, the re-jigged human who outruns cheetahs and light aircraft on television.

Among the ferns, in all the spaces not occupied by lovers or people scrutinising lovers, moves the great, uncritical republic of the sheep. Watch a group of sheep staring down into a cluster of valley towns and you will read the message plain. They are waiting for us to go away. They never invited us and they think our ways peculiar. The ones who stray down into the streets have the impenetrable hauteur and calm of stage duchesses.

Legends abound of how urbanised some of the strays become. People travelling by bus ask to be put down, not at the next corner, but at the fourth sheep on the left. One sapient ram is said to have spent years hanging around a University Extension class on the history of military tactics, held at the local library and Institute, and to have set up instructional courses in self-defence among members of his flock.

At one sheep-dog trial he and his colleagues outwitted three sheep dogs, and it was the dogs, not the sheep, that landed up inside the corral, cowed, or sheeped. I strongly believe that when sheep lower their sights and wear wool as inferior as that worn by their human neighbours they will be given the vote.

Sheep blend perfectly with the grey rock that juts copiously from the Welsh hills. Walk the Pembrokeshire hills and the breath is constantly taken by a shock of delight as one sees the forms of sheep at rest among the cairns and cromlechs that stud those lovely places. Sheep and rocks have a venerable patience. There is, I am told, a sheepdog in the county of Dyfed that suffered a nervous collapse after weeks of trying to impose a servile obedience on a stone roughly the shape and colour of a sheep. A watching sheep died laughing.

Sheep would be good creatures to share the earth with. I think that if the Welsh had been given, in addition to sheep-ranges of the finest quality, a supplementary stomach enabling them to enjoy and digest ferns with as much relish as Queen Victoria put away her Welsh lamb, the Welsh could finally fling back their shoulders and sing defiance at inflation and time.

FIFE   by JAMES PILDITCH

I met a golfer once who had never been to Fife. Now, while a priest may never go to Rome or a Muslim to Mecca (or The Harley Street Clinic, come to that) and both live full, good lives, the golfer who misses Scotland — and Fife above all — is hardly a man fulfilled. The golfer who has never felt the eyes of unseen members of the Royal and Ancient bore into his back as he takes his first swing at St Andrews, who has never trembled before the Swilcan burn or Hole O'Cross, has trifled with his life.

Abundant though it is, however, golf is no more than a corner of the romance of this seat of ancient Kings. The Kingdom goes back a long way. You see religious stones weathered before Christianity came, tread ancient battlefields, pause where Robert the Bruce died. (When his body was found a legend was confirmed. As he asked, his heart had been cut out and taken to the Crusades.)

For those that can abide neither golf nor history, there are hunting and shooting, fishing and gliding and miles of beautiful country to walk in. You may get a tan in Fife, though it is more likely to come from the wind than the sun. Seldom far is good whisky and often surprisingly good food.

The Kingdom of Fife covers 500 square miles on the north shore of the Firth of Forth, the broad estuary that slices into the East of Scotland above Edinburgh. To the west is Stirling, with Dollar nearby. North is the Tay. On three sides there is water, 115 miles of coastline.

For 800 years people crossed by ferryboat into Fife. For over ninety years you have been able to take the train from Edinburgh, crossing the Firth of Forth on that famous cantilevered bridge, the engineering marvel that could be one of the wonders of the world.

More likely you will cross into Fife over the elegant new road bridge, a mile-and-a-half long, high, sweeping thing of beauty. You will know at once you have arrived. Fife is one place that when you are there you know you have travelled. It is neither homogenised suburban nor smartly rural. Though a new motorway cuts across it and a new town (Glenrothes) grows in the rolling landscape, Fife retains its independent, stern, "nothing without work" character. Gentler than the Highlands, less trodden than the Lowlands, not at all self-consciously pretty like Loch Lomond and the wild west coast, Fife is different from the rest of Scotland. It always was.

As if to stress this separation you pay a toll to use the road bridge. Fife, they say, is the one place you pay to get into and out of. But it takes a generous man to laugh at his thrift, and a Fifer is no exception. Indeed, if he could choose his own god a Fifer wouldn't know whether to opt for young Tom Morris, the youngest man to win the British Open (he won it three times and died aged 25, shortly after his wife, of, they say, a broken heart; his father, Old Tom, was the oldest man ever to win the Open), or to settle for Andrew Carnegie, a Fifer and one of the most generous men who ever lived.

Believing anyone could do it if he would only get up early enough and stop smoking, Andrew Carnegie amassed an immense fortune in America and showered it on Dunfermline where, in 1853, he was born. Parks, playing fields, swimming-pools, organs, libraries, a school of hygiene and more he gave.

Dunfermline is the first place you reach after the road bridge. You pass Rosyth, at one time the largest and best-equipped naval base in the world (Prince Charles was stationed there) and Pitreavie Castle, where the MacDonalds fought Cromwell's troops and seven sons bloodily tried to rescue their father, Hector. A thousand years ago Dunfermline was the capital of Scotland. Kings lived and are buried there.

Two, James I and Charles I, were born there. The Norman abbey (as well as Carnegie's cottage) is the thing to see. It was founded by an English princess. She had fled from the Norman invaders. For her saintliness she was canonised. Each year now a pilgrimage is held to honour St. Margaret. What with St. Margaret, Andrew Carnegie and King Robert the Bruce, who not only watched spiders but also beat the English at Bannockburn, it is no surprise to find in Dunfermline one of the few statues in the world dedicated to "Ambition".

North of the town it gets coal-miney. Turn east, along the shore an optimistic tourist board calls "the golden fringe," and you come to one pretty village after another. First is Inverkeithing. Though it has interesting old buildings (the town received its charter in 1165) and holds a Lammas Fair and has its own sporting event known as "the hat and ribbon race," what I like about Inverkeithing is the idea that it was the home of a Supreme Admiral of the Russian Navy. He was Sir Samuel Grieg. The house where he was born, in 1735, stands in the High Street.

Around the coast is the way to see Fife. On the way to Kirkcaldy (you say Kercoddy) you go through Burntisland and start to wonder about Mary, Queen of Scots. At Rossend Castle she found a French admirer, a poet, in her bedroom. There were lots of things to do about that. But she called a guard. The poet was tried (what would the charge have been?) and beheaded. "Adieu, thou most cruel and beautiful princess," he cried as the axe fell.

Kirkcaldy is the shopping centre of Fife. They call it "the lang toon o' Fife." Thomas Carlyle, who taught nearby, found the people "pleasant, honest and kind."

On round the coast is Wemyss, where Mary first met Darnley, and beyond is Largo. Lower Largo is a small cluster of a village, where a river runs into the sea and long silver beaches stretch. We stayed in a cottage where fishing nets were kept. Waves splashed against rocks below the house, curlews screeched, walkers collected driftwood. The cottage belonged to the local laird. Laird is a title he could do without. Though, even to this day, villagers pay him a tithe, he has to pay out far more to finance local services. He hunts in the hills behind Largo. A year or two ago, thinking he had a particularly good horse, he entered for the amateur Grand National. He won it. The huge gold cup is kept in the kitchen, over the sink.

The *real* Robinson Crusoe, a naval lieutenant called Andrew Selkirk, came from Lower Largo. The inn is named after him.

If Fife seems like a hard, man's country, go to one of the four golf courses around Largo. There faith is restored. One is called Lundin Links Ladies. Men may not enter the clubhouse. And, rumbled as the weaker sex, they drive off from in front of the ladies.

You cannot go far in Fife without a golf course, the AA hotel at Kingskettle lists twenty-two within fifteen miles. Nor, this is the delight of Scotland, are they costly. Forty pence gets you a game on some courses.

There is a wonderful links along the coast at Elie. The starter has an old submarine periscope in his hut, so he can see what is happening on each hole. James Braid, a hero who won the Open five times, came from there. Just along a bit there is a cave where Macduff hid from Macbeth. And the village where Lady Jane Anstruther lived. Modest as she was beautiful, when she went for a swim she sent a bellringer through the streets to warn off peeping toms. She had style. She persuaded her husband to move a whole village because it spoilt her view of a nearby loch.

Anstruther (where Robert Louis Stevenson lived while his father built Bell Rock Lighthouse) and Crail are more charming fishing villages. In Crail you can watch fishing boats in the tiny harbour, or walk by the roaring sea. You can visit the church where John Knox preached and touch a Pictish stone worn from sharpening spears more than a thousand years ago.

St Andrews, built of granite and slate, is a dour city. Rain sweeps in from a cheerless grey sea. The only colour, apart from the greens of you-know-what, is the welcome splash of scarlet gowns of undergraduates at the University.

Though it may be said to help, a knowledge of golf is not vital to enjoy St Andrews. (If you don't know anything when you arrive you assuredly will when you leave, so it is no matter.) There are the knitting mills to visit, where cashmere and Shetland sweaters may be half London prices. There is the old cathedral, rising gaunt against the sea. It is a ruin now. After a glorious period it became too costly to keep up, and was decreed the town quarry. You can see the ruins of the old castle and peer into the Bottle Dungeon, a dripping, dank hole cut down 24 feet into the rock and shaped as its name says, "In the place," says Knox, "many of God's children were imprisoned."

Though it is bang in the middle, you should end a tour of Fife in Falkland. There are two reasons. First, Falkland was a Royal Palace for 500 years and the heavy granite castle stands proudly still. Today it belongs to the Queen. Second, at the Covenanter Hotel opposite you will find one of the best meals in the Kingdom. Rob Roy quartered troops in the palace it is said. More usually, kings hunted boar and falcons in surrounding forest. A silent romantic air, particularly amid the swirling leaves of autumn, hangs over Falkland.

Pity the poor courtiers. When they fell out of favour they were sent a mile or two away to Freuchie. The sentence was, and you hear it still in Fife, "Awa to Freuchie and eat mice."

INISHERE   by DEREK MAHON

The island blazes with sunlight; the white sand gives off an almost Saharan glare. Where are we? The Tyrrhenian? The Aegean?

No, the Atlantic. To be precise, we are sitting off the island of Inishere, in the Aran group, at the mouth of Galway Bay, in the first week of April, before the tourists arrive. The ferry, the *Naeve Eanna (Saint Anne)*, carries only a dozen or so passengers this trip — a number of islanders, a handful of Irish-speaking schoolgirls from Connemara, a middle-aged American couple, a solitary German philologist. In the hold are a Volkswagen minibus, a bull, a bag of mail, Calor gas containers, crates of Guinness, and consignments of household utensils — kitchenware, lampshades. The *Naeve Eanna*, operated by CIE, the Irish transport authority, sails the twenty-one miles from Galway three times a week, wind and weather permitting, and calls at the three Aran Islands in turn — Inishere, Inishmaan and Inishmore, the main island, where there is also a small landing strip for the light aircraft that fly up from Shannon during the summer months. There is a dock at Kilronan, on Inishmore, but at Inishmaan and Inishere, with no natural harbours, the *Naeve Eanna* must anchor offshore for as long as it takes to unload passengers and goods — perhaps an hour, perhaps two. As we watch from the deck, strange shapes begin to move down the beach from the cluster of white cottages that make up East Village. They are like large beetles, shiny and black, with perhaps eight legs each; there are maybe half a dozen of them. When they reach the water they turn over, and we realise they are currachs, the tarred canvas island boats which will take us ashore rowed by small teams of men who carry them on their heads. All over the islands they lie, in rocky coves and vegetable gardens, at various stages of construction or decay. A Dublin tourist found the ruins of one half-buried in sand and started pulling the struts out for firewood; but an old man happened along and admonished him: "Ah son, don't be breaking boats."

He spoke in Irish, of course, for that is the language of the islands. (It wasn't always; in Synge's time it was English.) Most people can speak English perfectly well if they wish, except for some old women who have never really got the hang of it. But the Government gives a grant to Irish-speaking households which, together with the American dollars sent by emigrant sons, makes a useful supplement to the small income derived from mackerel and potatoes. Partly because of this artificially "pure" way of life, seemingly untouched by the commercialism of the mainland (the dance-halls of the Connemara coast to the north, the centrally-heated tourist "cottages" of Co. Clare to the south), and partly for reasons of cultural history, Aran has become a place of secular pilgrimage. Inishere has little to offer the culture vulture, except perhaps the memory of Orla Knudson, a Danish recluse who lived here until his death a few years ago, and wove traditional fabrics on a home-made hand-loom. Inishmaan, a wilder place, was Synge's island: here he forged the peculiar language of his plays by listening through a hole in his bedroom floor to the talk in the kitchen below. They say there hasn't been a fight on Inishere within living memory, the people are so gentle; but there's a fight on Inishmaan every Saturday night. Inishmore's claim to fame is that Robert Flaherty made *Man of Aran* there, starring the Dirrane family of Kilmurvy at the western end of the island. Beyond Kilmurvy is the prehistoric fort of Dun Aengus, an immense semi-circular arrangement of stones on top of a three hundred foot cliff that drops sheer into the Atlantic. Sea birds glide to and fro far below; the sea stretches away, becalmed by distance, into a remote oceanic haze. The next parish is Boston. Or perhaps this is the edge of the world.

I first read Lytton Strachey's *Elizabeth and Essex* on a train journey from Dublin to Cork, and encountered, somewhere in Tipperary, his magnificent description of the doomed Lord Deputy's first foray into the Irish interior: "The strange land — charming, savage, mythical — lured him on with indulgent ease. He moved, triumphant, through a new peculiar universe of the unimagined and the unreal. What state of society was this, where chiefs jostled with gipsies, where ragged women lay all day long laughing in the hedgerows, where wizards flew on whirlwinds, and rats were rhymed into dissolution? All was vague, contradictory and unaccountable; and the Lord Deputy, advancing farther and farther into the green wilderness, began, like so many others before and after him, to catch the surrounding infection, to lose the solid sense of things, and to grow confused over what was fancy and what was fact."

This is a classic statement of an undeniable phenomenon. To the Irishman himself, one would think, Ireland would be indisputably real; more so, indeed, than other places. Yet this isn't necessarily so. A rudimentary acquaintance with Irish literature — with Yeats, Beckett or Flann O'Brien — reveals that the Irish imagination is by no means as assured of the nature of reality as, say, the English. The peculiar quality of the light — always changing, made luminous by sun-showers and cloud-shadows — may have something to do with this. Also the sense of chronological uncertainty, in a country where history appears to be cyclical and everything happens several years after it has happened in the rest of Europe. The dual-language situation is a contributory factor, too. English is so often spoken with irony, as if the speaker acknowledged its foreignness and absurdity even as he uses it; and Irish with self-conscious pedantry, as if the speaker recognised that this is a dying language and his use of it absurd in another way.

But undoubtedly the greatest single factor in this metaphysical unease is the country's geographical position. As you approach Dublin, whether from the air or by sea from Holyhead (preferably a summer daylight sailing which can be delightful), it is im-mediately apparent that Ireland is not really a British Isle, but, like Iceland, a large island in the Atlantic Ocean, great tracts of which are bleak deserts of heather and stone. There are soft, richly cultivated parts, too, in County Dublin and the South East, but it's hard to travel in Ireland without being reminded (and this is both exhilarating and slightly frightening) of the implacable nature of Nature, and of the cosmic insignificance of mankind. Hence, perhaps, the Irish devotion to religion. Hence, certainly, the exaggerated gaiety and melancholy which the English think of as Irish "charm" and "madness." Hence, also, the Irish conviction of being special — that having survived for so long in this difficult but beautiful land, they and it must have something going for them. As J. P. Donleavy puts it: "No hell is under Ireland. They say instead, a dark daughter. The country at the end of the world. The oldest place."

CEYLON

by ROLOFF BENY

Ceylon has almost as many names as India has religions: Alexander the Great in 300 BC called it Taprobane; Ptolemy, who drew the first map in 139 AD, used the ancient names Simoundi, Salike and Silie-Vida, which later became Serendib, derived from the Sanskrit for "island of the cosmos"; then it was variously called Zeilan, Sailan and now Ceylon. In Sinhala, the language of the majority of the inhabitants, it is reverently known as Sri Lanka or "Sacred Island." But my favourite is that given by the first travellers from China which in translation is "land without sorrow."

We all know Ceylon is the tear-shaped island lying off the south-east tip of India in the Indian Ocean south of the Bay of Bengal and east of the Arabian Sea. Lovers of archaeology and followers of Buddhism have included Ceylon on their Easter itineraries for many generations, but today's travellers are beginning to realise that here lies a bite-size paradise island of totally independent excitements worthy of a visit anywhere from three days to three months — not just an extension of their "passage to India."

Touching down at the superb little airport of Katunayake, north of Colombo, you are immediately immersed in a total wonderland of coconut palms, luxuriant jungle, the air perfumed by a mixture of temple flowers, salt air, cinnamon and coconut oil. If time is short, I recommend avoiding Colombo altogether and setting out by car, even by bullock cart or on foot, in any of five directions. By road one can reach any one destination, whether on the coast or interior, in one day. But it is folly to rush through this spectacular landscape — fortunately one cannot since the narrow roads cut through plantations of cocoa, rubber, cinnamon, teak, and, of course, tea in the up-country, and you can rarely cover more than thirty miles in an hour. Every mile is like a village fair, replete with bare-chested men in multi-coloured striped and flowered sarongs, women in coloured saris which compete with the rainbow, naked children, bicycles, bullock carts, Buddhist monks swathed in togas of primrose yellow and saffron, cocoa brown and hibiscus crimson with lacquer begging bowls and palm leaf fans, and, of course, elephants carrying logs, bundles of sugar cane or just uprooting tropical philodendrons and ferns.

If you begin by driving about sixty miles from the airport to Kandy, you are also transported to the realm of the Kandian kings who, because of the dense, jagged jungle highlands, were able to resist the principal invaders until the 19th century when the British, more by cunning diplomacy than force, established a government agent and eventually built a residence for the Governor General called the King's Pavilion, a kind of Belgravia Square neo-Palladian townhouse set in an impossibly beautiful tropical park. Neither the Portuguese, who arrived in force in 1503, and christianised the fishermen and built churches along the coastlines, nor the Dutch, 150 years later, could penetrate this mountain stronghold where stands perhaps the most venerated Buddhist temple in south-east Asia, the Dalada Maligawa, or Temple of the Tooth, mirrored in a miniature, dream-like lake. Viewed from afar, this lake reflects like a blue-white sapphire (which is appropriate since the sapphires of all colours mined in Ceylon enhance royal treasuries around the world). It is enveloped by jade green jungles upholstering the slopes of amethyst mountain peaks rising tier after tier until they reach over eight thousand feet at World's End, where one can actually see the coastlines of the island in four directions.

If you are fortunate enough to be there in August, on the night of the full moon (which is always auspicious to Buddhists) and are prepared to endure long hours and the crush of thousands of islanders who camp in the city, you can participate for seven days and seven nights in a spectacle unparalleled in sheer pageantry by any in Asia. I cannot do better than to quote from my diary written on the seventh night of this event: "August 27, 1969 . . . in order to reach the head of the procession, I had to post myself thirty feet in front of the Royal Tusker called Raja, an elephant easily twelve feet high at his hump upon which is strapped the Golden Howdah which contains the Tooth Relic of the Buddha, bringing his height up to twenty feet; above this is held, on twenty-five foot bamboo poles, a batik canopy floating above this magnificent beast and supported by twelve near-naked men, their bodies gleaming with sacred coconut oil and the whole entourage flanked by iron baskets of flaming coconut husks. On each side of the great tusker are two supporting elephants. They are caparisoned in subdued splendour so as not to detract from the majestic trappings of Raja, who is covered from hump to toenails in yards of red velvet completely hand-embroidered and embossed in silver and gold thread with symbolic lotus, the sun and moon and the sacred bo leaf pointing in the four cardinal directions, while on the massive forehead there is emblazoned in pure silver the figure of Narilatha, the symbolic representation of the beauty of the female form cast in a vine and said to reflect an incarnation of the mother goddess Pattini, one of the four patron deities represented in the Kandy Perahera. Wherever Raja walks along the entire procession route, a white carpet is spread at his feet, and for a mere mortal to tread on this carpet is blasphemy . . . so while trying to take photographs, not getting too close to those ivory tusks, and not backing up onto three elephants immediately preceding, and dodging umbrellas, giant and always corpulent Kandian chieftains covered in jewelled hats, daggers, and wearing sterling silver shoes, requires a dexterity and certainly guts."

But don't be disappointed if you can't be there in August. The islanders, who are pre-dominantly Buddhist with a strong Hindu Tamil population, not to mention the Christian fishermen and the energetic Moslems, constantly entertain themselves with religious festivals which range in scale from Hindu weddings to Moslem country fairs; baby peraheras, which must include at least one elephant, when the full-bosomed ladies parade in white saris with white water-lilies in their ebony hair and carry a single lotus in their hands, Kandian dancers, naked except for beaded see-through vests and Greek evzone-like, starched skirts, and always the schoolchildren portraying in miniature costumes the many legends of Ceylon.

Another unique event to be contemplated only by those with the strongest stomachs is the pilgrimage to Kataragama on the south-east coast, where every conceivable degree of human penitence is exacted on the pilgrims' bodies, inevitably climaxed by fire-walking, which one must see to believe. For those with the sturdiest legs, there is always the almost vertical climb through the wilderness to Adams Peak, which is revered by all religions on the island. Moslems, legend contends, believe that when Adam was forced to leave the garden of Eden, he was made to stand for a thousand years on one foot on top of this 7,360 foot mountain, but later, joined by Eve, he settled down on the island to propagate the human race. The Buddhists consider the giant footprint at its peak to be that of Gautama Buddha, and in 1503 it was the landmark visible for miles out to sea which guided the Portuguese in their search for cinnamon.

Miniature the island is, but so rich on every sensuous level that one can only quote the Buddha himself: "I have directed you towards deliverance. The Dhamma, the truth, is to be self-realised." In other words, go and discover for yourself.

FIJI

by PETA LYN FARWAGI

Three hundred islands of every shape and size, like a jigsaw puzzle to last a lifetime . . . a nation that had to beg Queen Victoria to take them on as a colony in 1874. Pleasant to see, on the hot sunny day I arrived in Fiji, thousands of short-cropped Fijian and pig-tailed Indian children still happily carolling the marvels of Cession Day.

Geographically, from the moment Captain Cook and Captain Bligh recorded its existence, Fiji has been in a marvellous position. The crossroads of the South Pacific, it is the fanning out point for myriads of islands, such as Tonga, the Gilbert and Ellice Islands and New Hebrides, where mysterious sunsets blend with legend in the mind's eye.

On my first night after a 28-hour plane trip from London I collapsed to bed. The girl who came to turn it down giggled at finding me installed, asking, "Shall I talk to you? Are you lonely?" I lay there in a dream world as we exchanged day-to-day stories of our respective family traditions and habits. It was mostly one-sided but I went to sleep wondering if I had found the mythical islanders of the travel brochures.

I woke in the morning to the sounds of two tall young Fijian men leaping around the swimming pool under the pretence of cleaning it out. The job was eventually completed to the merriment of most of the hotel staff and the day had begun. In Fiji most things are a joke, there is always an easy smile, and most jobs can be turned into fun; but Fiji-time is the funniest joke of them all. The DC3 which takes you across the island generally leaves at the time it is meant to have arrived on the other side. Telephones are another victim. The system is up to date and efficient but the people running it have a gay lack of urgency. It might be something to do with Fiji's proximity to the dateline. After all, if you have just lost a day, why worry about an hour? Perhaps this too explains the sight of spaghetti and lamb chops for breakfast — it must be a bizarre but genuine attempt to please any person, coming from any direction, at any time.

The islands or island groups have their own characteristics. Viti Levu (Great Fiji), the largest, is 90 miles by 70 and houses the capital, Suva, and the majority of visitors. Reflecting the trends and differences, it is the melting pot of all the strains of Melanesian, Polynesian, Chinese, Indian and British. On the surface it is a colonial town, breeding beauty contest applicants, rugby players, maxi-skirted military bandsmen on the well-kept lawn at Government House. It is where the grand-sounding Queens and Kings Roads meet after the tortuous dusty ride across the island; where the mellow gold, yellow and brown colours of the north-west change startlingly with the climate into the red, orange, purple and green jungle extravaganza of the south-east — a kaleidoscopic experience which overcomes any primitiveness of the road. A division of another kind is less geographical and is the result of a misconceived idea by the first British Governor to import Indian labour to work the sugar plantations. He could not have picked a more unsuitable culture to mix with the indigenous one. Now there are 235,000 Indians and 195,000 Fijians, still living two different ways of life. In the north-west, near Ba, the Indians outnumber the Fijians three to one, as in the other sugar producing districts, giving rise to certain attractive paradoxes such as a shop called Lum Lock and Son, run by Chinese, crammed with Indian ritual pictures and occupied by Fijians drinking something called Imitation Orange Juice in a country where oranges and lemons abound; and sparkling white tin mosques next to pompous Methodist churches. It does seem strange that a religion so lacking in ceremony should have converted so successfully

226

a people who had a strong set of appropriate gods for every occasion; who buried men alive to give special power to their meeting places, and who practised cannibalism as a way of life.

Sunday morning sees a general turnout, best clothes are put on, the young men wearing their *sulus* — "mine is made of Terylene from England, Miss" — white shirts, ties and, if lucky enough to own them, carrying their winkle-picker shoes. In the majority of the proudly kept villages living is communal, all things belong to all men, and money is a rarely seen commodity. Near the coast they fish and grow all they need, in the hills livestock play a vital part. In Suva there is the chance to earn hard cash. For the visitors it is a duty-free paradise, glossy machinery stares at you from the windows of the Indian run shops: cameras, radios, binoculars and souvenirs so repulsive and plastic that they are fascinating (and you want to buy them). There is a food market where the crabs are sold in beautifully size-graded bundles, and mounds of bananas, paw paw, mangoes and pineapples compete for space with straw and basketware. Under a brilliant blue sky, tropical flowers fill the whole square with their fragrance. Behind, in the port, the copra boats set out for the islands and enormous visiting cruise ships dwarf the town, lending it a universal feeling. Colonial architecture is found mainly on the main street of the old capital, on the nearby island of Lavouka, but the Garrick Hotel and the South Seas Bank Corporation in Suva are from the same era, when men sat on shaded wood verandas, behind tall pillars and planned the future of the island they had come to. In the long gregarious Fijian evenings many of the hotels put on a Meke, a programme of emotive dances to tribal music, depicting the legends and military conquests of the past.

The other islands have different characteristics. Vanua Levu is part sugar plantation, part copra estate; the Lau group makes the best tapa cloth; Kambara is where the carvings come from and Komo dancing girls are national idols. The men from Beqa are the only ones who can walk on fire, and in Suva on the first Friday of every month they perform on stones especially brought from their island.

Seekers of a lazy, golden, shimmering and forgotten world have only to join a cruise or hire a boat and drift around the Yasawa and Mamanuca islands, sleeping on the boats, swimming off the fine white beaches or fishing by day and barbecuing dinner under a violet sky at night. This is really getting away from it all. The more gregarious could try the newly developed four-acre island, Toberua (*above*). Sixteen *bures* (exact replicas of the native homes on the outside and American luxury on the inside) look out to sea. Boats stand by to take guests fishing, over the coral reefs, on to an island which is a bird-watcher's paradise, and there is a standing invitation to the sacred island of Bau, where Ratu Seru Thakombau, first and last king, crowned himself in 1867 with a diadem of gold-papered wood and gems costing $4\frac{1}{2}$d. In the evening you just relax and listen to one of the staff singing songs from the islands, to the soft sounds of water and coco-palm trees.

MALAYSIA

by PAUL THEROUX

There is a sultan in Malaysia whose nickname is "Buffles" and who in his old age divides his time between watching polo and designing his own uniforms. His uniforms are very grand and resemble the outfit of a thirty-second degree Mason, but he was wearing a silk sports shirt the day I met him on the polo ground. The interview began badly, because his first question, on hearing that I was a writer, was, "Then you must know Beverley Nichols?" When I laughed, the sultan said, "Somerset Maugham came to my coronation. And next week Lord Somebody's coming — who is it?"

"Lewisham, Your Highness," said an Englishwoman on his left.

"Lewisham's coming — yes, Lewisham. Do you know *him*? No?" The sultan adjusted his sunglasses. "I just got a letter from him."

The conversation turned quite easily to big-game hunting. "A very rich American once told me that he had shot grizzly bears in Russia and elephants in Africa and tigers in India. He said that bear-meat is the best, but the second best is horsemeat. He said that. Yes!"

We discussed the merits of horsemeat.

The sultan said, "My father said horsemeat was good to eat. Yes, indeed. But it's very *heating*." The sultan placed his hands on his shirt and found his paunch and tugged it. "You can't eat too much of it. It's too heating."

"Have you ever eaten horsemeat, Your Highness?"

"No, never. But the *syces* (grooms) eat it all the time."

The match began with great vigour. The opposing team galloped up to the sultan's goal with their sticks flailing.

The sultan said, "Was that a goal?"

"No, Your Highness," said the woman, "but very nearly."

"*Very* nearly, yes! I saw that," said the sultan.

"Missed by a foot, Your Highness."

"Missed by a foot, yes!"

After that *chukka*, I asked the sultan what the Malay name of the opposing team meant in English.

The sultan shook his head. "I have no idea. I'll have to ask Abdul. It's Malay, you see. I don't speak it terribly well."

But there are Malay words everyone knows. There is *gong*, and *sarong*, and *mata-hari* (dawn), which are charming; and there is *amok*, which is terrifying. And though the customary greeting in Malaysia is *Salaam aleikum* (Peace be to you!), the Malays are capable of working themselves into a perfect frenzy. In a few short weeks of 1969, many Chinese were reported to have been killed in riots following a disputed election. On the other hand, there is a non-Muslim tribe in the southern Malaysian jungle which is completely pacifist: they have never fought or quarrelled with anyone and violence is unknown to them. They fit in quite well. In a country where a ruler doesn't speak the language well it is no surprise to find a primitive tribe of semi-naked pacifists. However, it was not that long ago that the now-retired headhunters of East Malaysia ate their last missionary.

Travelling through Malaysia I used to wonder who the real natives were. The Europeans I met called the Chinese natives; the Chinese referred to the Malays as natives, and the Malay phrase for the little jungle dwellers (who make a graceful living selling orchids and parrots by the roadside) is *orang asli* — "natives." There is a community of Portuguese in Malacca which claims to have been there for 500 years, and one is almost convinced. Malacca's pedigree is very long: there is an ancient Portuguese cathedral and fort, and Dutch civic buildings, and — notice the national priorities — an English club. In the Malacca antique shops you can buy furniture carved by "Straits Chinese" (whose food is probably the best in the country) 150 years ago and more.

The capital, Kuala Lumpur, is a convenient stopping-off place, and from there you can easily travel by train or road to the Cameron Highlands. Here, the air is as cool as an autumn day in England; below you, in Tapah and beyond, people are gasping in the heat and swatting mosquitoes, but you are thousands of feet up, in a temperate climate, where strawberries grow and beds need blankets and rooms log fires. There are country walks in the highlands, but you walk with a memory of danger: one day an American tycoon took a stroll after lunch and was never seen again. From the Cameron Highlands, the island of Penang is not far, and after driving the 100 hairpin bends to Tapah the train is a reward. First Class on Malaysian Railways includes a wood-panelled compartment which you have to yourself, with a comfortable bed, and at Butterworth you're woken by a man in a sarong with morning tea, a biscuit and a banana.

After the 1969 riots, American soldiers from Vietnam stopped coming to Penang for "Rest and Recreation Leave," and a local newspaper reported: "A survey shows that nine leading hotels, as well as 300 trishaw drivers and 200 'social escorts' will be affected." But Penang is rising again, and new hotels and holiday bungalows are being built on its Neapolitan-looking coastline. The food in Penang is superb, but eating habits tend to be unusual: the Chinese eat chicken feet and fish-lips, but are nauseated by Cheddar cheese; the Malays eat practically anything except pork (though during Ramadhan, the Muslim fasting season, they can be fined by the so-called "Religious Police" for eating in daylight hours), and in Indian restaurants one is given a scrubbed palm leaf as ceremoniously as if it were a warmed plate — it serves the same function.

The vegetation all over Malaysia is unearthly. Orchids grow wild, and because they do, carnations — duller, but much rarer — are specially coveted. Some trees (like the *Angsana*) grow three or four feet a year; there are "Chewing Gum Trees" and, on the slopes of Mount Kinabalu, pitcher plants the size of spittoons, which feed on insects; and importuning fig trees (*Ficus elasticus*), which attach themselves to other more docile trees and strangle the life out of them. My favourite Malaysian tree is called "The Midnight Horror" (*Oroxylum indicum*). Its leaves are so huge they look like branches, and its flowers — also quite large — begin to open at about 10 pm and give off a stench which by midnight is unexampled. Though this tree is used by the Malays for making medicine, no Malay would admit to an affection for it. I admired it from a distance, but bats are devoted to it. They find the odour of The Midnight Horror irresistible; they hang by the claws on their wings to the corollas and poke their noses into the flower's throat. The Midnight Horror might have been designed by Algernon Blackwood or Dracula: it is one of a half dozen trees in the world that are actually pollinated by bats.

The best things to do in Malaysia are the simplest: taking a £1 boat ride to an island off the east coast; getting an hilarious massage in Kota Kinabalu or an inexpensive feast of chili crabs in a fishing village on scaffolding and stilts in Kukup; buying a carved bargain in Malacca; swimming at Batu Ferringhi in Penang; spending a day at Trengganu, watching thousands of sea-turtles hatch their eggs on the beach, or really, just trading snobberies at a polo match with an agreeable sultan.

THE WHIRLING DERVISHES

by CLEMENT FREUD

When I got this pamphlet saying "Come for a visit to the Festival of the Whirling Dervishes in the heart of Turkey for £56.75" it seemed the answer to most of my problems. I had £56.75, had never seen a Dervish whirl, while the heart of Turkey was a location which had escaped me over the years.

The Whirling Dervishes, known as Mevlevis, are followers of the poet and mystic Rumi who died in the year 1273. The Mevlevis were outlawed by the Turkish authorities 50 years ago but permitted to whirl in public for a fortnight a year to mark the anniversary of the death of their founder. Hence this "festival" said the guidebook.

Apart from "whirling" (which entails rotating in an anti-clockwise direction) the Mevlevi pantheism involves the proposition that there is One Real Being which can be viewed either as God or the Earth, that there is no creation in time; the Divine Essence is unknowable, while in the sphere of reality there is no such thing as Evil. So there.

At Ankara airport a representative of Anglo-Turkish met me. He advised me against self-drive cars: "very expensive; ice on the road; poor signposting; wolves." I nodded eagerly.

As for the buses, he said . . . "they are slow, run only occasionally, are very full."

I told him that I could well imagine this.

Then, warming to his theme, he offered to let me make the 180 mile journey in his taxi for the bargain price of £20 . . . "very fast, non-smoking, reliable driver." I accepted and found that the driver did not smoke but he drove very slowly, passed other cars with his foot on the brake and flashed his lights at oncoming traffic until they slowed sufficiently for him to be able to shout insults at them.

After an hour and a half of this, we were passed by the fast, smart, half-empty Ankara/Konya bus — an event that filled the man with such gloom that he forgot to shout at the next six cars he had blinded with his headlights.

For the record, the road to Konya is good, well signposted, iceless and wolfless and we arrived only half an hour after the bus at 10.30 pm. The hotel had me booked in as M. SROYD, which suited me very well, and said that the dining-room was closed, which was less convenient.

Meals in Konya did present something of a problem, mainly because I spoke no Turkish and the Konyans spoke no other languages — though there was one restaurant in which the Turkish dishes were translated into French, German and English.

Following one item under the heading of *Yemetkin*, it was Cleopatra's Finger in English, *Doigt de Cléopatre* in French, *Turkische Mehlspeise* in German . . . Bemused, I pointed to it and ordered one; the waiter said it was off.

Breakfast was relatively simple. In the lounge of my hotel one opened one's mouth and made wild gestures as a result of which the waiter brought a glass of black tea, eight thick slices of fresh bread, a good pat of butter, very salty white cheese and a saucer of jam that had failed to set.

Then, for elevenses, there was half a street containing pastry shops. Konya is a bit innocent about commercial planning and there were, I discovered, one whole street of used car accessories shops, two hundred yards of a street containing fourteen chemist shops, a secondhand clothes street ending in a secondhand clothes square and a hairdressing salon street.

230

The pastry shops had front doors leading to the street through which customers entered, and back doors leading to heaven knows where, which admitted a constant flow of suppliers who raced in with trays laden with machine-decorated chocolate cakes, pastries, shortbreads, baclava and sweet biscuits.

For drink there was fruit juice, which is excellent, tea or Turkish coffee and, from a samovar, a hot, slushy, tapioca-tainted, cinnamon-flavoured milk drink which was only unpleasant if you were expecting it to be cocoa. The average customer drank a glass of this, consumed several pastries and a plate of biscuits and left with a kilo parcel of sweetmeals expertly wrapped. As there are no women in the streets other than fleeting yashmaked figures, shopping is done by men for men.

Main meals taken in my hotel, or elsewhere, usually consisted of a lengthy session with the menu and my dictionary . . . after which the waiter would gesture to me to go and look in the kitchen and choose from any of half a dozen dishes of greasy but well-seasoned and tenderly cooked meats and beans. As all food was pre-prepared, the average mealtime was about ten minutes for three courses — always served simultaneously!

There are in the main drag of Konya two tourist offices, one of which deals with tickets for the Whirling Dervishes. There is no queue, simply a gently pushing mass of people — with those not speaking Turkish, or seeming to be strangers to the country allowed to the front. Tickets were 20 or 30 lira — (60 or 90p) — with performances nightly, matinees on Saturdays.

The performance took place in the netball hall, opposite the football stadium on the outskirts of the town. The ante-rooms to the hall were filled with high-priced dispens-able gifts of the Presents-From variety: wooden spoons, shrunken heads, leather hats, keyrings and pottery vases. Also rugs. A number of courteous young men led people to their seats and there were notices urging people not to smoke and reminding them not to applaud.

The Mevlevis are a religious sect . . . and having been politically outlawed, they are now used by the Government of Turkey as a tourist attraction. Thus each performance is witnessed by 70 per cent deeply religious Mevlevis — and about 30 per cent flash-light happy tourists.

It begins with readings in Arabic and Turkish — presumably from the writings of the poet Rumi. Then come the musicians, performing on classic instruments that can have changed little in the 700 years since the Mystic's death.

There is a *Kudum,* a small kettledrum made of handbeaten copper, its rhythm guiding the whirling, the *Ney,* flute, a reed tube with seven fingerholes, the *Tanbur,* a long-necked lute, a classic Turkish instrument with 24 frets to the octave, the *Kemence,* a Turkish fiddle, probably the ancestor to the violin, whose nasal sound and glissandi add distinctive colour, and, finally, the *Kanun,* a plucked zither with 24 triple courses of strings.

After much talk and some music, the whirlers appear for the final 15 minutes of the two hour service. Dressed in tall hats that represent tombstones and cloaks that are shrouds, they observe the niceties of deep bows to their leaders and then, to the music of their players, try to elevate themselves towards the Divine Absolute. As they spin, their right hands turn towards the sky to receive the Grace which has traversed the heart and give it back to the world after enhancing it with their love.

"You are asked very strongly not to smoke and very very strongly not to applaud" says an English-speaking Turkish announcer, and when the whirling is over the seats of the netball court clear, frustrated chainsmokers light up and the American tourists re-open negotiations for unique guaranteed-silk carpets.

THE IVORY COAST

by GEORGINA HOWELL

I'd only been to Africa with Beau Geste. Rider Haggard and Karen Blixen, when I was given the chance to spend a weekend at a new hotel in the Côte d'Ivoire: not the name for a coast, but a country south of Mali, east of Liberia, west of Ghana and about 800 miles beyond Timbuktu.

Onto the plane to Paris, the first stage in the journey. To the wrong hotel. To the right hotel, the new Club Méditerranée, so big it's a city on its own. Every room is supplied with television, drink machine, fridge, plastic toothbrush, bathcap, bubble bath, an envelope printed *"Pour nos oiseaux."* Birdseed.

Next morning, to Orly and off. The DC-10 is enormous and I sit in a wide panel of seats in the aisle. Nine hours flight. We drive from blue-black stratosphere into a black cloud illuminated by flashes of lightning, as if someone inside is flicking a light switch on and off. We emerge from the storm, to black starlit night and land at Abidjan airport. When the plane doors open, it's like an oven that you've put boiling water in — hot steam. Out onto the tarmac and into the din of a tropical night, crickets singing at all levels. A few steps on, tearing off my cardigan, I hear drums. It's a rattling clashing rhythm, a circle of dancers around four musicians. The dancers are men in ragged sweaty crochet vests and mini-skirts, their wrists and ankles festooned with hundreds of tin can tops threaded on string, making a deafening crash with each shake. The musicians play drums and tomtoms with sticks of bent metal, an instrument like a big curved wooden xylophone and an ear-splitting rattle made of beads netted together over a hollow gourd. They reach a point of frenzy again and again. The women give them breathing space with a different sort of dance, an indolent spastic shuffle, babies sprawled sleeping on their shoulders. We wait in and out of the airport building, those of us susceptible to music and rhythm kept going by the dancing, the rest by gin. Eventually we get into the coaches, turn away from the electricity of Abidjan — down a dirt road into the black bush, and drive for another hour and a half. Every now and again, by the side of the road, a kerosene lamp flickers and lights up a ring of squatting figures, or there's a blaze where someone's burning refuse by the road. We pass a few shanty towns, and once a bar, just a refrigerator, a counter and a string of electric light bulbs under a thatched palm roof. In pitch dark the bus stops with a jerk and the engine dies. We are invited to get out. We stumble out into the arms of a frenzied crowd who are laughing, jigging about, singing, drumming and shaking hands with me. Everything is taken firmly away from us — where's my bag with my passport and all my money? Where's my hat and coat? We are danced onto a lightless jetty where we see a little fleet of old diesel boats bobbing up and down, painted African Queens. We are pushed on board, grabbed when we stumble, and sat down on wooden pews. The engine starts up and chugs us out. I ask the African next to me *"C'est la Mer? Un fleuve?" "Une lagune."* Now all the singing crowd who stayed with the boat and have been dancing a mamba on the roof, dive clothed into the water. The boats aren't going back tonight so they have to swim home. The air is like a Turkish bath on the black water, and the bank we are leaving is pure jungle: at least it looks like jungle to me, but it turns out to be a mangrove swamp. Not a light, not a hut, just a cliff of foliage. On the far side now appears a jetty lit by electricity, alive with a throng of dancers. There are sloping, palm-thatched roofs, emerald grass, orchids

232

Macchu-Picchu, Peru DAVID BAILEY 1971

overleaf: Ki River, China LADY ALEXANDRA METCALFE 1966

growing over tree stumps, palm trees growing from a clean sandy bank. We are seized upon, lifted like puppets out of the boat and propelled along in the middle of a welcome such as you may never know in a lifetime. Fully robed Africans dive into the water again in a burst of *joie de vivre*. Glasses of alcoholic fruit salad are thrust into our hands, decorated with rims of sugar and twists of paper ribbon. Like magic, all my possessions appear beside me. Less fortunate people are still trying to trace their cases. I escape to my room, I shut the door and suddenly I am in perfect quiet and cool, the only noise is the air conditioner, a sound like distant clapping.

When I wake up I feel quite different, although looking at the map makes me dizzy. I'm more than twice as far from home as Tunisia. If I flew the same distance in another direction, I'd be on the far side of the Urals. I'm as near the equator as Venezuela or Malaya. I begin to look about me. Les Paletuviers d'Assouindé is paradise, once you get there.

On one side there's the sea, rough and fresh, for strong swimmers only, tumbling onto naturally terraced blonde sand. No sand hoppers, flies or mosquitoes anywhere at Assouindé. On the other side, only 200 yards away, is the lagoon we crossed last night with its jungle bank. On the spit of land between is a park of grass shaded by palms, decorated with flowerbeds of painful brilliance. Sloping thatched roofs shelter an open dining-room, bar, shop, reception desk, ping-pong tables, nightclub and stage. There's a children's swimming-pool and a big one with water-beds. You can sit in the open shadowed dining-room watching lizards zipping up the palm trees while you eat the most delicious breakfast in the world off dark polished wooden tables with bunches of orchids in the middle. There are croissants and rolls, the excellent Côte d'Ivoire coffee, hills of fresh grapefruit and oranges, bouquets of bananas, fields of pineapples, baskets of mangoes, flocks of yoghurts and tureens of nuts in honey. For lunch and dinner there are hors d'œuvres by the ton, grills or lobster or other fish, soups, creamy puddings. Afterwards you can float in the swimming-pool. By midday the water has reached exactly the same temperature as the air which is a delicious sensation. I walk along the beach, first along the sea edge, then, from curiosity, along the palm fringe. An African couple are coming towards me, and being very short-sighted I think how exactly their swimming costumes match their skin. In fact, they're wearing nothing. Coming towards me now are four naked men. Losing my courage, I turn and head briskly in the other direction. On the far side of Les Paletuviers from the naked beach, there's a shanty town of bamboo and thatch. Two or three unpainted fishing boats are spread with indigo nets, and here is where the children swim. They come bounding out of the waves and run up to you shining with water, holding out hands like little black starfish for you to shake. The girls' hair is divided into immaculate chequerboards, each tuft tied in a puffball, or plaited into stiff snakes coiled with black wire.

The day subsides in stages. Some people drift off down the beach, others sink into the swimming-pool or stand up to their necks drinking and talking. I leave to spend the night at the famous Hotel Ivoire in Abidjan — two skyscrapers in a park of its own: you could be in New York. Next morning to the airport very early. They are selling enormous flowers like pink electric light bulbs on bean poles, but how can you get them back? To Conakri, a cracked, peeling, flyblown airport in Guinea, to Dakar, where a party of exhausted over-weight Russians are pausing en route to Moscow. I proceed to Marseilles, Paris and home. Hampton Court, where I live, and Abidjan are separated by more than distance.

NEPAL

by MARTIN O'BRIEN

Life at the top is not all it is cracked up to be. It is tough, gritty and thoroughly uncomfortable, a lip-splitting, foot-blistering, lung-tugging trudge at high altitude that demands masochism and fortitude in equal measures, and a constitution as sturdy and dependable as a pair of climbing boots.

So I'll say it now: I never made it. The country is Nepal, the shape of a stretched hide pinned between India and China, the mountains are the Himalayas, the greatest and most awesome range on earth. Fourteen mountains exceed 24,000 feet and hundreds more rise above 21,000 feet. Eight of the tallest peaks are Nepalese, including the highest in the world, known to Sherpas as *Sagarmatha Chomolongma* and to the rest of the world as Everest, Nepal's biggest draw.

The trek to Everest is only one of many trekking routes in Nepal, but it is the longest, the most arduous, and because of Everest, probably the most popular — more a pilgrimage than a trek. I started my journey at Lukla, a narrow turf airstrip that slopes sharply down the side of a mountain, about half-an-hour's flight from Katmandu. There I met the Sherpas who would be my companions on trek, chatted bravely with Chowtree, the head Sherpa or *Sirdar*, and experimented with the supposed ill-effects of altitude; I found I could still walk, talk, smoke and eat. At 8,300 feet, I was coping well.

That first day our party — consisting of three women, five men and a line of gym-shoed and barefoot porters — trudged slowly down to Ghat, one of many campsites located along the trail. Expecting only gruelling ascents, I became rather optimistic and by the end of the day was bounding along, only pausing to inspect the carved prayer stones stacked up as shrines along the trail, and to admire the scenery, as this height strongly reminiscent of the Scottish Highlands. Far below could be heard the dull rumble of the Dudh Kosi, a river we were to follow for some days before the real climbing began, its waters high, fast and freezing from the glaciers around Everest. Above, crows cawed and soared, and at every homestead grubby Sherpa children came running up the path to welcome us with cheers and shouts of *Namaste* — God be with you. The pioneer spirit was high.

That first night we camped at Ghat so close to the great river you could feel the ground tremble.

On trek everything is done for you by the Sherpas. For the first few days their help and care seem excessive, but by the time you start climbing you are grateful for anything. While the men look after the tents and baggage, the Sherpani girls build fires, cook meals and distribute early morning cups of tea that taste not unlike liquid wood-smoke — regardless of the amount of sugar and milk you mix in. It is a taste and smell you will become increasingly used to as the trek progresses. Every meal tastes of it and every Sherpa smells of it. Judging by the way they crowd around the fires at night, with their bare feet and hands literally thrust amongst the burning logs and their faces lost in clouds of smoke, it would be remarkable if they did not.

An average trekking day starts early and cold; warmth only comes once the sun is visible above the peaks. For the first hour or more, while the Sherpas break camp and load up the equipment, you will watch the shadow level crawl tantalisingly down the mountain side until it reaches you, at which point the sun breaks over the opposite ridge

234

and you stop shivering. It is possibly the best time of day, the sky clear and startlingly blue, the distant peaks above the pine line colouring from scarlet to pink to soft gold with the rising sun, the valley floor glistening with frost.

Each morning you walk three or four hours in single file along a narrow, boulder-strewn track, past small, stone-walled plots, through resin-scented forests where the ground is soft and springy with pine needles, in a series of "minor" ascents and descents rarely more than a thousand feet, but cunningly devised to irritate blisters, crick ankles and numb thigh and calf muscles. Lunch is a blessed relief blighted only by the thought of a further four hours trudge in the afternoon. Early enthusiasm soon wears thin.

Past the tiny Sherpa settlements of Phakding, Giphede, Gumita and Benkar the trail presents few difficulties, the only hazards the frequent and unnerving river crossings over rickety wooden bridges held in place by boulders and rope. Just watching the Sherpas, bent double under their loads and staggering over the roaring cascade, is enough to make you want to turn back.

At Thumbug, where the Dudh Kosi forks east and west, the trek changes dramatically. From here to Namche Bazar, the Sherpa capital, the route is near vertical, a three-hour continuous ascent of over 2,000 feet. Half-way up, you are told nonchalantly, you have your first view of Everest, so excitement spurs you on. On a fine day the view is ample reward for your exertions. Some ten miles ahead and 20,000 feet higher, almost hidden behind the combined bulk of Lhotse and Nuptse and literally peeping over the slanting ridge that runs between them, the pyramid peak of Everest aslant against a pale blue sky; sometimes a plume of white snow, whipped up by the wind, feathers out from the summit.

Physically and psychologically, reaching that look-out point was a traumatic moment. Up until then, I had accepted the inevitable blisters, the scratchy beard, the cold and the hardness of the ground at night, the aching muscles and wood-smoke tea. But at 10,500 feet and above, everything becomes a great deal harder. From here it is almost a continuous ascent. A 100 yard walk exhausts you, leaves you panting like a greyhound, tongue lolling, gulping at the thinning air; your lips start to split and chip like splintered planks; blood pumps through your veins and hammers in your ears; your face, your fingers, knees and ankles swell and puff; every footstep is a labour, every word a curse as you struggle upwards. You may experience spells of dizziness, a tightness in your chest, headaches, and every new symptom of your malaise you should carefully examine and compare with the textbook definitions of mountain sickness you have heard quoted so much at lower altitudes. At this height you need to take great care not to rush, not to over-extend yourself.

Most victims of mountain sickness will admit to going too fast, and ignoring the symptoms that lead to an attack. For many people a bottle of oxygen and a warm, log fire at the Everest View Hotel on Om Lhasa hill (at just over 12,000 feet the highest hotel in the world) rapidly settle such discomforts, while the view is added compensation: Khumbila, Tawache, Nuptse, Everest, Lhotse, Ama Dablam, Kangtega and Tamserku tower around you in a ragged line.

But for some of our party the hardship level had passed the acceptability point. One of the girls was gulping from an oxygen bottle, another had trouble keeping her cigarettes alight in the rarified atmosphere. And the men? We were prepared to accept the girls' decision. From here, only the brave continue, past yak herds and tea shops and water-driven prayer wheels to the monastery at Thyangboche, across the glacial scrubland of the Imja Khola and on to Pheriche, the last Sherpa village.

They tell of fine views of Everest from Kala Pattar at 18,000 feet, but, then, only the brave would know.

BHUTAN

by WILLIAM P. RAYNER

Hidden between the Indian subcontinent and the great land mass of China, Bhutan, the Holy Kingdom of the Peaceful Dragon, straddles Himalayan peaks that push twenty-four thousand feet into the air. It is a medieval land where a king rules by divine right and children don the cloth at age five. Men either join the army or the monastery — women pave roads or till the soil. All art is religious, and almost every product is hand-wrought. Entrance to Bhutan was forbidden until four years ago, and even now Western travellers only trickle in.

As there are no airports in Bhutan — though they have marvellous airmail stamps — the only way to gain entrance to this country is to fly from Calcutta to Baghdogra on the eastern frontier of India, and then to drive five hours across the Darjeeling plateau country, with its endless tea plantations shaded by acacia trees.

It was evening by the time we passed underneath the huge pagoda arch that marks the border of India and Bhutan. There can be no line so absolute in the disparity of its sides. The chaos and energy apparent in India suddenly yield to a Swiss-like orderliness and neatness. The plains turn immediately into mountains; the long-limbed, swarthy Indian is replaced by the compact, high-cheekboned Mongolian; and the traveller leaves one of the most densely populated areas of the globe and enters one of the least inhabited. Bhutan is the size of Switzerland, with one-sixth its population.

Passing through customs, we are presented with travel papers so official-looking they might have been designed in jest by Saul Steinberg. The formality of everything has a charm officialdom can rarely claim. As we eight are literally the only tourists in the country, needing to show credentials other than our white faces seems redundant. There can certainly be no mistaking us for Bhutanese: from the king on down, the population wears long, loose-fitting plaid *khos* (kimono-like robes). These are fastened about the neck and can reach down to the ankles for, at night, they are used as sleeping bags; but, during the day, they are hiked up to the knees and tied low about the waist by a cotton or woollen belt. The belts create folds in the robe in which daily necessities are stored. Among these necessities: tiny Lhasa Apso and Damtsi dogs that occasionally peek out from between ripples of cloth.

Our first glimpse of Bhutan comes the morning after Customs. At seven o'clock, our two drivers and our shy guide, Wandi Dupka, corral us into a waiting minibus and an Indian Ford to begin an assault on a road that will corkscrew over fourteen-thousand-foot passes. The route takes us through forests of semitropical ficus, mango, and banana trees that eventually give way to walnut, oak, holly, bamboo, and fir as the altitude increases. Giant one-hundred-and-fifty-foot rhododendron trees grow thick and, in the spring, they are said to shower red, pink, white, and yellow flowers. But there are flowers everywhere in Bhutan — and even the most humble cottages have neat little gardens of poinsettia, hibiscus, daisies, and climbing roses. However, as the road curls up the mountain and three-thousand-foot precipices begin to appear under the front fender, I lose interest in the flora and start wondering about the condition of the disc brakes!

The trip from the border to Thimphu, the capital, is only about forty-five miles as a crow flies, but it is about one hundred and fifteen miles as an Indian Ford makes its way over the tortuous macadam. And speaking of crows, these birds happen to be sacred in

236

Bhutan, since they spend their days repeating Buddha's holy syllables, *"ah . . . ah . . . ah."* Killing a crow is as great a sin as "slaughtering a thousand monks." But then killing anything is frowned upon by Buddhists.

After six hours of pressing my foot on an imaginary brake on my side of the car, we come upon the ancient Dzong of Simtokha, which marks the entrance to the capital Thimphu. Today the *dzong* serves as a language school for the study of *Dzongkha*, the Bhutanese language. Cities in Bhutan are little more than a cluster of houses surrounding the great *dzongs* that, for a millennium, have acted as administrative centres. The Tashiche Dzong in the Thimphu Valley has thick, sixty-foot-high walls of packed mud. These neatly whitewashed walls support a superstructure of carved timber stained in red and yellow and spaced with intricately carved windows.

Within the courtyard, where barefooted monks in maroon off-the-shoulder togas spend their day in prayer and meditation, there is a huge square tower housing the legislative chamber that meets each spring and fall. The walls inside the *dzong* are covered with tankas, those intricately painted mystic hangings that range from postage-stamp size to seventy or more feet high. The most incredible thing about the architecture of the *dzongs* is that they were literally built without architects: not one line or plan was ever drawn on paper. Also, not one nail secures the joints. In fact, most of the buildings in Bhutan are constructed without nails and employ the Chinese-puzzle principle of interlocking beams that reinforce each other.

Another striking architectural feature of Bhutan: the chortens or stupas — stone receptacles of varying sizes that hold religious relics. There is one such shrine in Thimphu that is a memorial to a recent king, and it has one of the most surreal interiors ever conceived. Upon entering, you immediately see a great glass cylinder rising three storeys high. Inside the cylinder: thousands of carved effigies of the elephant-headed god Chenreyzi. The god is represented copulating with a woman while, beneath his feet, he is stamping out evil. The "evil" is represented by doll-sized men and women, painted in Day-Glo colours, who are either writhing in agony or engaging in sexual gymnastics that would inspire a pretzel designer.

Each day in Bhutan brought some new excitement. Our last morning we take small mountain ponies and trek up to the holy-of-holy Tiger's Den, where hermits live and pilgrims come to worship in the wilderness. This spectacular looking lamasery, torn from bedrock, dangles precariously three thousand feet above a plain. Five hundred feet above the lamasery, a waterfall arches down and crashes before the entrance gate.

During our two-hour ride up an incline with passages so steep that the ponies appear to be standing erect on their hind legs, we pass forests of holly trees, mountain laurel, giant oaks whose naked roots clutch the granite cliffs . . . and on through stands of white pine and firs until we reach a point at which even the surefooted ponies can go no further. Here, we alight and hike the last quarter of a mile to the sanctuary, edging across, at one point, an eighteen-inch-wide path cut in the mountain face. To look down the sheer drop and see eagles soaring *below* you is a terrifying experience.

Legend has it that the founding guru of the lamasery arrived on this inhospitable ledge riding a flying tiger. However, our practical guide Wandi assures us that, in fact, it was built in the eighth century by Buddhist monks who cleared the area of dangerous tigers and pushed them back to the southern jungles where they remain today. Whatever its genesis, I shall never forget coming upon Tiger's Den for the first time and seeing its eight chapels with their walls hewn from the granite cliffs and covered with religious paintings — all set against the spectacular panoramic view of snowcapped Himalayan peaks. And everywhere: a majestic silence broken only by the prayers of hermits, the soft wind passing through the pines, the waterfall. It was like being in another world.

237

ROMANTIC CITIES

by WILLIAM GREEN

Italy is no stranger to visitors. Not even the brochures would dare say that her great cities are undiscovered.

Italy's cities, on the other hand, have a tradition that stretches back to the age of the Grand Tour, two hundred years ago, when the aristocracies would travel South to refine their minds and improve their manners. There have always been travellers in Italy — Canaletto painted for the tourist market — and they are an accepted element of the scenery. No visitor need feel guilty that he is trampling upon the delicate beauty of an unspoilt paradise. Italy's charms are hardy and perennial.

The romantic aura that haloes her cities also seems to be more than skin-deep. In the nineteenth century, poets made it a custom to run away and live, or die, in the peninsula's old capitals — Goethe in Naples, Byron and Wagner in Venice, Browning in Florence, and pretty well everyone in Rome.

Modern life has transformed all these cities, even Venice, but they have managed to retain the timeless atmosphere that marks them out from all others. There are many, very worthy cities where one would be glad to be and be busy; but in really romantic cities it is blissful to be doing nothing whatsoever. This, of course, is what attracted the poets, and all the other dreamers who have followed in their idle footsteps.

Naples is a familiar place, even on one's first visit. This passer-by tosses her raven hair coldly and proudly, just like a girl-friend one once had, and that untrustworthy-looking taxi-driver, with his pixie face, is a dead ringer for Chico Marx. The Neapolitan has all the things the Italian, especially the American Italian, is famous for — the lust for life, the vigour of expression, the wildness of gesture, compliment, and insult. Every conversation is conducted as a heated discussion, if not an argument. On the streets of Naples one constantly sees a curious gesture, that of the hands clasped together, as if in prayer, then wagged furiously up and down. It means "shut up and listen to me — it's *my* turn to speak." It is always ignored. A gathering of Neapolitans involves a babel of many voices simultaneously making their views clear.

Overcrowding seems accepted as one of the joys of life, and there is nothing very depressed about the happy-go-lucky slum of La Spacca, where the streets are so narrow that only a baby Fiat can squeeze through, and the buildings lean forward to try to touch each other at the top. Every day is a flag-day of flapping white washing, and every week-end a Cup Final. Small boys will employ any public lawn, church porch or terrazza that leaves room for the rebound to play football at five or twenty-five a side. Outside the rush-hour, they even use the roundabouts. Older small boys, to the age of twenty and more, take to driving their little motorcycles. They don't go anywhere in particular, just up and down an alley, or round and round the football game.

It is the people and the setting that makes Naples beautiful. Architecturally, there is relatively little of great merit. Most of the churches have had their finer details drowned in the flood tide of the Baroque era. Their interiors testify to that period's heroic, but vain efforts to make good marble look like flowing drapery, angel wings, or passing clouds of glory. In art, as in life, Naples prefers to overdo things.

In Rome, they are so much more subtle about it. Almost everyone has decided that he or she belongs among the patricians rather than the plebs. For Romans, this is still the capital of the world, and they like to ignore the fact that they are no longer masters of it.

The women strut, and the men swagger. It is a commonplace that Romans are well dressed. This is not true. They are overdressed, all of them, from the dandy doormen to the leather-jacketed traffic-cops, from the streetwalkers to the society beauties. It is easy to see this very early in the morning, when they are emerging on the stage, as it were, straight from the dressing-room. In the fresh light of dawn, when only the sweet-smelling cafés and the news-stands are open, and before the city plunges into the daily chaos of traffic jams and pavement squash, you can catch the actors unawares, a little rusty, and see through the whole, vain, delightful charade. By sun-set, however, when they all turn out for the street theatre of the *farniente,* their performance is polished and faultless, and you are once again persuaded that the people are what they pretend to be — elegant, disdainful, superior.

Like any great capital, Rome is a hard place to visit. A short stay reveals so little of the whole. The imposing grandeur of Saint Peter's Square, or Victor Emmanuel's huge wedding-cake monument, can be misleading. The real Rome is constructed of much more modest units, tiny piazzas, little churches. There is as much to see in the old areas of Monti or the Ghetto, as in the noble ruins of the Fora and the great meeting places of the Spanish Steps and the Piazza Navona. An aimless walk can be more stimulating than a tourist's mapped itinerary.

Rome is a place one would have to live in to appreciate fully. For all its ancient history it is very much alive. In the Vatican, devout pilgrims and nuns jostle with mere tourists. A stroll down the fashionable Via Condotti shows that all modes still lead to Rome. And the people remain among the most inventive on earth. It is a wonder to behold the daily resourcefulness with which they repack their millions of cars over every spare square foot of the city centre.

The English have a fatal weakness for Tuscany. It is lavishly beautiful to a degree that quite upsets our customary level-headedness. When the peasants tell of God coming down sometimes to stroll in the meadows round San Gimignano, we tend to believe them. After all, there are whole colonies of expatriates living contentedly in the old vineyards round Lucca and Castellina, so if God is an Englishman, this would be the perfect place for his afternoon walk.

It is strange that Tuscany should be so unsettling, when she herself hangs in such perfect balance. The province recalls the Renaissance ideal of the small city-state. The rolling countryside provided the stones, the inspiration, and the wine. The towns turned these materials into a matchless display of buildings, paintings and sculptures. The result seems to hold its breath, as if afraid to break a spell cast long ago.

This is so even in Florence. All the bustle and noise of its millions of visitors cannot disturb the peace of her cathedral dome, poised halfway up to heaven. The more accessible parts of the city, meanwhile, are defended from flood and Philistine by vigorous societies. They have, for example, recently blocked the construction of a Hilton hotel. It takes as much love to protect and preserve Florence as it took to build it.

It is satisfying to realise that Florence is still a city of private means, and not entirely dependent on its tourists. With all the students in numerous colleges and international institutions, it is becoming a sort of university town, combining the dignity of old stone with the liveliness of young people. Thus the city has found a fitting way to adapt to movement.

If only the same were true of Venice. Once the much-feared republic, and mistress of the Adriatic, this city has seen independence turn to isolation, and hospitality become a cynical prostitution of resources. Venice needs tourists as much as Disneyland does, and inevitably, one thinks of its canals and *palazzi* as matter for embalmment rather than preservation. We all know, too, that the latter are crumbling gently into the former, and that plans to save this most unique of cities from its own lagoon are as numerous and futile as projects to raise the Titanic. Yet, somehow, when one is actually there, three miles and a whole world away from the mainland, it takes no great effort of will to forget all this, or at least, to take a melancholy pleasure in the atmosphere of quiet decay that pervades the city. Venice is still the most completely romantic of settings, basking in the extraordinary light reflected off the canals, and moving to its own maladjusted time-scale.

All sorts of things will conspire against appreciation of the city — youths rev their outboards in case you may be missing the roar of traffic, gondoliers stick plastic flowers to their bark's prow and charge ridiculous prices for serenades, and herds of tourists will trample you to the ground as they play follow-my-leader — but none of these are important enough to spoil the mood. You remember that there is no other place to take a gondola ride, and very few with hotels that are really sixteenth-century palaces. And where else do you feel excited enough to do the things you thought only other tourists did, like feeding the pigeons in Piazza San Marco, commissioning a bad charcoal portrait of yourself, or having your picture taken by an old tripod-and-veil box camera that works very much worse than the Instamatic in your pocket. If Venice has a role, perhaps it is as the home of tourism, the originator of the whole phenomenon. It is a city of visitors, and it is hard to imagine actually living there, as one can so easily elsewhere in Italy. Even in winter, when the crowds are replaced by haunting, swirling mists, one is happier simply to come and look. The place is too unreal, and a short stay is usually long enough. One can always return. Venice is a dream that should recur at regular intervals, as the best possible antidote to a surfeit of reality.

Its buildings are the essence of the city. Of course one comes to look at paintings and observe the inhabitants, but it is the setting that gives them their sharp relief. Sir Harold Acton, who has lived there all his life, finds the city distinguished above all by its grace, its harmony with man. The river Arno and the hills around provide a just frame for buildings that are noble rather than grand. Similarly, the paintings and frescoes are complemented and enhanced by the tremendous variety of their locations — chapels, churches and cloisters, refectories, convents and monks' cells, palaces, great halls, private houses, tombs and secret passages.

Off the well-known tourist paths, many of these masterpieces are hard to find, and harder to get to see. *Chiuso per restauro* is a familiar sign, a pun juggled between "closed for repair" and "closed for lunch." Have patience, ring bells, demand at offices, argue, bribe, wait for weeks. It is always worth the effort.

by DESMOND MORRIS

The QE2 is docked at the newly completed Ocean Terminal, Hong Kong, a unique structure as if someone decided to build a new Harrods right in the middle of Southampton docks. Hundreds of glamorous shops packed together in ·the endless arcades, right next to the giant ship. Everywhere else in the world you step off the ritzy carpets of the great cruise liners and on to the harsh smelly shell of the docking sheds, with customs officials, police, workmen and whistles, barriers and officialdom. But the cunning Hong Kongers are shopkeepers right up to the water's edge. Within twenty paces of the gangway you are surrounded by exquisite displays of carved ivory (pity the poor elephants . . . there are 174 ivory dealers in Hong Kong), by beauty parlours, by tailors (I had a fine suit made to measure in forty-eight hours, and they thanked me for giving them so much more time than usual), and by shops crammed with gifts of every conceivable kind.

I could spend weeks here, exploring the maze of Hong Kong, but our ship-joining instructions demand that we stop our wandering and report to the main gangplank for boarding.

Staring up at the side of the ship, at very close quarters, is overwhelming. It looks more like a skyscraper that fell over and floated. The moment you step inside the image changes. The mood is strangely familiar from television. This is not a vessel, it is a spaceship. As we move out of harbour the feeling is confirmed. There is a whole world here — silent elevators, uniformed crew, long corridors, dark colours, bright colours, quiet voices over the intercom, the gentle hum of the air conditioning. We are not sailing, we are gliding off to take up our orbit in space again and, in three days, we will beam down in Japan. The sea is miles below us, there is no engine noise. Everyone is relaxed. The passengers give the impression of having nothing to prove. There are just over a thousand of them (and about as many crew) and this unique little village community is beginning to reorganise itself.

At each major port a few get off and a few get on. New faces appear at the next table in the restaurant, new greeting ceremonies are performed, new bridge partners discovered, fellow countrymen identified. There are small shoals of Japanese exploring with their cameras. They photograph everything. At a reception to meet the Captain, they pose in teams clinging closely to his vast 6 ft 3 in frame while their relatives crackle their little flash bulbs, and then they all swap round to do it again. It goes on so long that an aide has to arrange an urgent call from the bridge, to protect the Captain's valiantly persistent smile from collapsing with muscle-fatigue.

The Captain is a splendid man — a benign, holiday version of Jack Hawkins in *The Cruel Sea*. The rest of the crew have also clearly been chosen by central casting. They are exactly as the movies would have you imagine them. The waiters in the restaurants are perfect — slightly familiar and jokey in a Michael Caine way, but more efficient than seems possible. Our young son is brought a glass of milk at our first meal, just *before* we were about to ask whether he could have one. And the food arrives so swiftly. "The caviar," Magnus Pike had informed me a few weeks earlier, "is eNORmously good. You'll like that." I did indeed. It was the best I had tasted outside Moscow. At night the image of the ship changes and it becomes a Las Vegas Hotel, complete with a casino, night-clubs, cabarets, dancing, outrageous cocktails, and star entertainers. There is a different show every night and a different film as well, screened in a cinema almost as good as the Curzon. I must confess that watching *Star Wars* in a luxury cinema, in evening dress, gliding across the Pacific at thirty knots, has a certain appeal. It is foolish to be impressed, I keep telling myself, but . . .

It must be the breeding season for Jap choppers; there is a vast swarm of tiny helicopters hovering over the ship. What are they doing in such huge numbers, as we edge into Kobe for our first look at Japan? A pair of binoculars quickly tells us what we should have guessed — yes, they are full of men festooned with Nikons and Pentaxes, all clicking away in an orgy of exposed celluloid. Now we are touching the dock and a band in red tunics is playing ump-pah, ump-pah, and Kobe Queens in doll costumes and doll cosmetics are distributing flowers and traditional prints of Japanese mountains to everyone within reach. Now we are beaming down into inscrutable Jap smog to take a fiendish bus ride through impenetrable Jap traffic jam, while our guide gives us lecture about Jap pollution (yes, they really do wear surgeon's white masks in the street) and Jap inflation. We grind on, past the baseball arena and the MacDonald's Hamburger restaurant, up into the mountains behind Kobe to look at the view and our ship lying in harbour. But there is too much smog to see it, so down we come again in time to catch the rush of traffic converging on the harbour to see us off.

Perhaps Yokohama will be better? But this time we dock in the rain and mist, through which we can see 200,000 Japanese umbrellas, held by the faithful Yokohamans who have come to see us arrive and who must by now be having trouble with 200,000 light meters. More beautiful girls in traditional costumes trip puppet-like through the public rooms dispensing gifts — for each passenger there is a silk flower-posy and three packets of local cigarettes (to help keep up the smog-count?). Tonight it is off to glamorous Tokyo clubland, and we speed by the exotic Japanese neon signs, MacDonalds again, and there is Hon'able Southern Fried Chicken and, of course, beloved Coca Cola, and — my God it can't be true — a Berni Inn. Travel certainly broadens the expletives. But, to be fair, the Tea Ceremony was intriguing, and the Geisha Dancing following the traditional meal, squatting on the floor, was absorbing.

It is lovely to be back in the womb of the great ship again and heading out to sea.

Now we are off for a long spell, real cruising this time, halfway clear across the huge Pacific to Hawaii, and the ocean-village settles down to the important matters at hand, like what to wear for dinner. No, not the women — they have automatically brought enough to display a new costume every night — I mean the men. What has happened to the austere black of the male dinner jacket? It has almost vanished. Even the tropical white tuxedo is scarce. In their place parades a fashion show of gaudy male colours — dinner jackets in beige with brown piping, or green silk with black patterns, or black with silver flowers, or orange and blue tartan, or you name it. The "black tie" of the dinner invitation has exploded into colours to match or contrast with this new trend, and there is even a first glimpse of what will undoubtedly be tomorrow's male formal wear — the open-necked dinner suit. To get past head-waiters in future, this will have to copy the device I observed on the QE2. The fashion rule-breaker ensures success by making his open-necked formal wear twice as opulent as the neck-tied equivalent. The shirt is specially designed in pink with a black-edged, velvet trimmed frill, to match the pink and black velvet of the jacket. The tie-lessness becomes deliberate rather than casual and another of Society's little costume barriers falls. The man at the next table, my wife points out to me, has not worn the same dinner suit twice since we set sail . . . and he keeps this up for two weeks, always in colour harmony with his wife.

After dinner, decisions, decisions . . . should it be the latest Al Pacino movie, a game of chess, dancing to Joe Loss in one night-club, listening to Danielle Dorice and the Rob

Charles orchestra in another, playing roulette in the casino, listening to Max Jaffa in the Queen's Room, or playing millionaire bingo for prizes up to $1,685. Later, while we sleep, the ship's presses produce the *QE2 Express,* the liner's own newspaper, delivered under the door of each cabin every morning, in case we want to keep in touch with the ordinary world out there. In the morning air we surface to count the number of albatrosses following the stern. I marvel at the fact that they have been with us now for literally thousands of miles. Another 600 miles has slipped by since yesterday and I am tugged relentlessly from table tennis to swimming to mini-golf to shuffleboard by a stubbornly active young son who views relaxation as some kind of terminal illness.

The days merge into one another and just as I am about to feel guiltily hedonistic, there are the hills of Hawaii gliding past and a new bustle and excitement. There are no girls swimming out to the ship with garlands of flowers. Instead we are faced with a large building just beyond the dock, capped with the giant initials IBM. It is all much more like *Hawaii Five-O* than a paradise isle. But a taxi ride brings back the images of the past, with brightly coloured birds and impossibly large butterflies. Despite the way these islands have been wrenched into the twentieth century, the beauty and the atmosphere remains, just so long as you take the trouble to escape from the hula-dancing, night-clubland of Waikiki Beach. And the waters are so warm, the beaches so soft and inviting . . . I feel sure that I will be back one day, to explore the dozens of smaller islands, to lie in the sea and watch the fish rush past — the most exotic fish in the world.

We all hate leaving Hawaii and wish the ship's engines would break down. But it's over 2,000 miles to our next stop, San Francisco, and we cannot delay. The QE2 is more punctual than any airliner. After another blissfully unreal, orbital spell at sea, we wake early to gaze up at the broad span of the Golden Gate bridge as it passes overhead. Around us is a spectacular of small ships, including a fully rigged pirate galleon, an old paddle-steamer and the usual jet-happy fire-boats, squirting a multi-hose spray of welcome alongside us.

Soon, it is cable-car rides and strolls through Fisherman's Wharf and once again I fall in love with this most appealing of all American cities. Everywhere there seems to be music — a rock band playing in a city square, a group of strolling players in an arcade, a clown on a uni-cycle fooling around in the middle of a cross-roads, a quartet of bongo-drummers thumping away for themselves on a small beach. Unbelievably delicious shellfish on sale at every corner, and my favourite sideshow, the Automatic Human Juke Box, with twenty selections: simply drop in a coin, press the button and a flap comes down and up pops a small bearded man who plays — live — on a trumpet, the tune of your choice. One of the skyscrapers has been built in the shape of a tall, sharp-pointed pyramid — even the architects seem to feel the need to have fun here.

On board, there is a whole new crowd of younger Americans, and tonight, as we sail, it is an American cabaret with comedian Bill Crosby, who mystifies the British as much as Dickie Henderson puzzled the Yanks earlier on. Humour, most humour anyway, travels badly. Singers and dancers fare much better.

Time is running out now. It is such a short run to Los Angeles and our last breakfast before disembarking. Suddenly we are back in an airport again. What a crass way to travel. How boring, how impersonal. It is hard to leave that floating village. As the elderly Swiss lady said, standing in front of her ten tall trunks, trying to choose something stunning to wear for her last dinner on board, "You're never the same, after you've been on a cruise."

FAVOURITE HOTELS AROUND THE WORLD

Athens, Hotel Grande Bretagne by Lady Russell

The "GB" — thrill of thrills in my Athenian childhood, where the best ice-cream could be won only by braving the "Dardanelles," that narrow channel between the hotel's pavement tea-room and the chic café opposite where many a reputation was daily built or broken, between 7 and 9 pm.

Royal from birth, the "GB" was commissioned by King George I in 1862 as a guesthouse for his summer palace on Constitution Hill, then a rural area; Lampsa, the great chef was placed in charge of the "Royal Box" as it was later nicknamed. For over a century since then, the Petrakopoulos family have held sway here in the heart of Athens — both topographical and sentimental — a stone's throw from the old Royal Palace, now the Parliament. Headquarters for Dictator Metaxas, King George II, Churchill, General Scobie, Eden and Onassis — any plot, any multi-million dollar shipping deal, any wedding worth its orange blossom was hatched under the Edwardian glass dome of the great salon.

Over it all presides the Hall Porter, that benevolent despot who will procure for you at a nod a helicopter to take you to the top of Hymettus, or the Queen of Sheba's left earring—if he is your friend. Old Athenians still tell of the love-sick young British naval officer who became the Grande Bretagne's first streaker many years ago. Arrested stitchless chasing a beautiful elusive young lady on the upper floors of the "GB," the young aristocrat claimed immunity under a Royal Navy Regulation which states that an officer may remove his uniform when in pursuit of his chosen sport — the amorous hero was, quite properly, acquitted.

Barbados, Cobblers Cove by Dame Alicia Markova

I choose Cobblers Cove as my favourite hotel because there I get away from everything, especially the pressure of time, and completely relax. There is privacy in one's own spacious cottage, with good service and friendly attention. Guests are treated as individuals yet there is a pleasant social life if you want it.

An excellent chef makes good use of fresh fish, vegetables and fruit, cooking them in a variety of appetising ways before your eyes. Charming children bring beautiful shells and coral to your patio, pretending to sell them but really to sit and talk and to adopt you as their friend.

It is sheer delight to wake up to the beauties of nature, such as humming birds flitting from tree to tree, tropical flowers, white sandy beaches and clear blue sea inviting one to swim. Then to watch the hibiscus flowers close at night against breathtaking sunsets makes a perfect end to the day.

244

Bussaco, Palace Hotel   by Lady Longford

I came upon the Palace while researching for my book, *Wellington: The Years of the Sword* (Weidenfeld & Nicolson, £4.95). Upon this amazing rocky spine, towering up to 360 metres and 10 miles long, Wellington's Anglo-Portuguese army defeated Marshal Massena in 1810. Beside the hotel a museum commemorates the victory with life-size soldiers well up to Tussaud standards. The victory is celebrated again inside the hotel, where magnificent battle-scenes in coloured tiles are inscribed to "Lord W." The Palace was built on the site of the monastery which Wellington had made his HQ. His cell still remains, and the olive tree which he planted for peace.

Some seventy years later the Portuguese royal family chose Bussaco as their mountain retreat. Today the royalties have vanished, but not the peace.

Their Palace, converted into a hotel, is a "Manueline" fantasy of turrets, fretted arches, colonnades, and a crazy fairy-tale tower. A whole ghost regiment could march down the grand staircase. Perhaps it does. Around the Palace are ferny grottoes and waterfalls in 250 acres of seventeenth-century forest, planted by the Barefoot Carmelites.

I would not mind being a Barefoot Carmelite myself, for the summit is covered with warm basalt rock and pine-needles. You can lean against an ancient windmill and stare out over limitless blue mountain ranges. The brochure recommends two nearby spas as good centres for, among other things, "disintoxication." Personally I am happy to keep my intoxication with Bussaco.

Cap Ferrat, Hôtel Voile d'Or   by Alexander Walker

The Voile d'Or is like a perfectly ordered private residence where you sense your own behaviour is a source of pride to its director, Jean Lorenzi. That wonderful prospect from the terrace of the crescent Bay of St Jean satisfies my demand that every great hotel have an "outlook." It puts me in touch with how the Côte d'Azur looked before the property men arrived. You half expect to see Scotty and Zeida dropping in to have their revenge by living well. David Niven, who lives very well just down the street, does drop in: it's Margaret Gardner's "local," too: she has an apartment opposite. Rex Harrison and Gregory Peck give the guest list the distinction of a cast list, without your having to sit through the picture. Even Elliott Kastner has been so lulled by dining on salmon and fennel under the moon that the Big Deal at the other end of the line has had to wait. Armand, the sommelier, has come first three times running in his nation's palate-testing competitions. Do you wonder why I sigh with contentment at paying a bill that would make me wince anywhere else?

Costa Smeralda, Cala di Volpe   by Ronnie Stirling

I remember my first visit over seven years ago, standing in the bar, looking out to sea, at the almost surreal rocks, which make up the characteristic rugged coastline of Sardinia, and thinking that this must surely be one of the finest, naturally made settings in the world.

On entering the hotel for the first time, one feels a certain unrealism which must surely be attributed to the ingenious architecture of Jacques Quel. It is amazing that in mid-August, even though the hotel is fully booked, and the temperature outside is well into the 90s, there is still an air of peace and tranquillity. The Cala di Volpe has its own small private port and jetty for yachts. The view of the hotel on arriving back after a hot day's boating is the finest of any hotel I know. Food and service are of the standard one would expect in such a beautiful hotel.

Fort William, Inverlochy Castle   by John Siddeley

Hotels are like friends, you understand their faults and seldom notice their qualities. I travel a great deal and use hotels as places in which to eat sometimes, and sleep often, but essentially I am using the hotel because of business.

Inverlochy Castle is the only hotel I have visited where relaxation is total. Situated in Scotland outside Fort William, the Victorian castle has twelve guest rooms with bathrooms. It is like living in a dream home of one's own. You can switch off the motor. Mrs Hobbs, the owner's wife, and Miss Shaw, the family cook, are pilot and navigator; enter their magical world and time ceases to exist. Fresh linen, flowers, breakfast in bed, morning papers, hot water, a dinner gong, your own quiet corner in the baronial dining room, the food, oh the food, and time in which to eat it; the excellent wine list. Coffee in the drawing-room, quiet conversation and another day gone.

Hong Kong, The Mandarin Hotel   by Patrick Campbell

The hell of arrival at Hong Kong Airport in the middle of the night, jet-lagged, sand-bagged, covered with food, drink and cigarette ash, beset by touts touting in unknown languages for hotels, taxis, brothels and one another. Out of this pandemonium there surfaces a uniformed chauffeur who sweeps the luggage into the boot of a limousine and the wrecked travellers to the Mandarin Hotel, where flocks of snow-white gloves fly to open doors, to speed the baggage away, while impeccably dressed young under-managers with genuine smiles almost spoon the guests into their rooms.

The service of the Mandarin Hotel is so perfect as to seem unreal. Tiny Chinese servants whip travel-stained clothing away and it's back within a minute, crisp and gleaming. Room service arrives instantly with exactly what one has ordered — a miracle that doesn't happen in many hotels. In the roof restaurant, with the lights and ships of the harbour far below, simply superb Chinese food is served with the precision and elegance of a dance. And when it's time to go, a black Rolls-Royce, polished like a pearl, is there at the very door to drive you back into the gritty, bellowing world which, after the honeyed grace and efficiency of the Mandarin, seems to be unsuitable for occupation even by a dog.

Hong Kong, The Peninsula   by Michael Chow

The Peninsula is a rather squat, ungraceful building in Tsim Sha Tsu on Kowloon. It offers no wonderful views of Hong Kong or the New Territories; it cannot compete with all the fast services of the modern skyscraper hotels that have sprung up around it. The Peninsula does not compete. It doesn't have to, because The Peninsula is Luxury.

Luxury from a time when daily changing of the linen slip-covers for the Rolls' upholstery was mandatory; The Peninsula not only has the slip covers, it has the fleet of Silver Shadows to go with them.

To greet me, bellboys immaculate in white monkey suits and white sailor caps. To usher me into my bedroom, soft-footed corridor attendants appear from nowhere.

And The Peninsula has that delicious vulnerability that comes with being an endangered species. But for the moment The Peninsula can be all mine to possess and enjoy.

Istanbul, Hilton   by Ghislaine Lejeune

Staying at the Hilton you enjoy the city to the full while remaining blissfully oblivious of the language barrier! Built on one of Istanbul's seven hills, it gives you marvellous modern comfort with a difference. Sitting on the first-floor terrace, or the Roof Bar, you have a breathtaking view of the city's skyline, with its minarets and cupolas, over the Bosphorus and its ever-changing light. You can stay for dinner at the hotel, choosing between Continental or Turkish food — both equally delicious — or go to the Asian side of the city for dinner or to spend the day; the hotel will arrange it for you just as they will organise visits to museums, shopping in the Bazaar, a car or anything you wish. Then you can rest, lying by the pool in the middle of the most wonderful gardens.

Jamaica, Round Hill — by The Marchioness of Tavistock

It is very difficult to discuss Round Hill objectively — the two words to me mean happiness, warmth, luxury, excitement, beauty and a feeling that, having arrived, why ever leave. It is no good asking anyone, "Is Round Hill like so and so . . ?" Round Hill is like nowhere else — it is purely and simply itself. If you want to feel you are staying in your own home in the most exquisite surroundings, then go there. If you want to be surrounded by glamorous, elegant, amusing people and to have excitement every night, then go there.

The food is delicious and the atmosphere luxurious. Each house is owned by someone who has a shareholding in the hotel, so each is different, reflecting the personality and taste of its owner. For three months each winter I used to sleep on my balcony with the stars of jasmine, spices and hibiscus. Our boys still think of Jamaica as Paradise and all of us feel the same when we see a jet in the sky — will it fly over Round Hill later today . . . if it does, how I wish it would take us with it.

Jamaica, Sans Souci — by Leonora Lichfield

The perfect hotel, to me, is Sans Souci in Jamaica, with its privacy, unostentatious luxury, exquisite food, and service with a flashing smile. It is a pink and white confection curling round a small private beach, and an Italianate terraced garden full of scented trees, fountains and statued pools, drops to the sea. Private apartments and our maid to squeeze fresh oranges for a balcony breakfast, Croque Monsieurs equalling Harry's Bar, sunsets, birdsong, clean sea and utter peace. Perfection.

Jersey, L'Horizon — by Alan Whicker

The pink-granite-and-pines life-style of Jersey, a most beautiful and tranquil island only truly appreciated by cognoscenti, has sometimes been obscured by an undeserved Butlinesque image. Yet Jersey remains an adorable island with an agreeably gentle thirties atmosphere.

When you wake at L'Horizon you're faced by the great empty sweep of St. Brelade's Bay, with only a silhouetted rider or two on the golden sands beyond the pines, and a sparkling sea: one of the great vistas.

In the Star Grill overlooking that glorious scene I have relished some superb meals. One of the best was given by Patrick Forbes, of Moët & Chandon; as you can imagine, everything was accompanied and followed by, or drenched-in, champagne — and what could be better. Only afterwards did I discover a waiter had sloshed a large helping of the deliciously gooey Filet de Turbot Moët down the back of my Doug Hayward brown velvet . . . The fact that I still eat there shows how good it is.

London, The Dorchester — by Polly Devlin

The Dorchester has always seemed to me to be the epitome of thirties style sitting marooned in Park Lane like a big liner. I expect to hear the strains of *Begin the Beguine* played by a Palm Court Orchestra floating out from that odd entrance labelled Ballroom. Then I stayed there for a night not long ago and found myself in a room newly decorated by someone with a lovely baroque taste which exactly fitted the mood of the hotel. I had dinner in my room; the service was sympathetic and prompt. My coffee came within minutes of my ordering it and dinner was served in a manner that reminded me of a lush movie about the turn of the century. The Dorchester is a lovely place.

Los Angeles, Beverly Hills Hotel   by Quentin Crewe

The one thing I do not want from a hotel is that it should feel like home. There are those who reproduce that feeling all too accurately. There is a rim round the bath and the soap has nearly run out. The sheets are changed only once a week and there are this morning's crumbs in the bed. A light bulb needs replacing in the passage. At the same time I do like a hotel to have pretty curtains, more towels than anyone could need and an extremely personal (though not nosey) attitude.

The Beverly Hills Hotel is my dream. You check in and everyone treats you like a long lost friend. You go straight to your room, pick up the telephone and the operator says, "Can I help you, Mr. Crewe?" It is a simple enough trick, but it is lovely; and the Beverly Hills Hotel has many such tricks.

They are a bit pompous about ties and not always reliable about messages, but any shortcomings are compensated for by one detail. In nearly all American hotels, at about 7.30 a.m., your bedroom door opens and a face peers in. "Just checking," says the face, waking you up and leaving you awake worrying about what is being checked. That never happens at the Beverly Hills. They treat you with courtesy and believe (until proof appears to the contrary) that you are going to pay the bill.

Madrid, The Ritz   by Georgiana Russell

You could think of her as a woman, or a beautiful yacht, or a hand-made Bristol. There are many stories about her: the German general in the Second World War who committed suicide by throwing himself down the well of the grand staircase; the Duke of Windsor who always occupied the same suite on the fifth floor so he could look out onto Cerro de los Angeles, the geographical centre of Spain; the Maharajah of Kapantala who, in the '20s, held his wedding ceremony in her salons when he married the great flamenco dancer Anita Delgado.

They may all be apocryphal but one thing is certain — she is perfect. I refer, of course, to the Ritz in Madrid.

Built in 1910 in the best part of town, opposite the Prado, she has lost none of her Edwardian elegance; the magnificent carpets made by the Tapiceria Real de Madrid, the Louis XV silver, the chandeliers, ormolu and marble floors are all there. The service is fast, unobtrusive, the food excellent and the bar is still the favourite lunchtime rendezvous of Madrid's dowager duchesses.

The Ritz is one of the last of the Grand Hotels; not the largest nor the most obvious — just the best.

Majorca, Formentor Hotel   by Penelope Keith

Formentor gave me rest, peace and quiet when I most needed it. There are few English tourists and I can get away and remain anonymous. The service is wonderful and it's very comfortable without being over luxurious.

Marbella, Los Monteros   by Eamonn Andrews

I love going to Los Monteros — the place is marvellous, the atmosphere friendly, the surrounding countryside beautiful. To get to the beach you walk across green lawns, through orchards and woods. On the beach, there is a very good Beach Club with one of the best hors d'œuvres I have eaten, as well as a pool if you don't want to swim in the sea. There is another one in the grounds for those who don't wish to walk so far.

For the energetic there's sailing at the Port of Jose Banus, three excellent golf courses, and the Tennis Club where Lew Hoad coaches and will help you make your forehand drive a real killer. Or you can just sit and watch the many tennis tournaments.

The hotel itself is like a large Spanish villa with plants everywhere. The rooms are split-level, divided into sitting-rooms and bedrooms with lovely views. The service is excellent, the food very good, with fresh fish, exotic fruit and vegetables. It is a good place to take a family in the summer when the weather is hot. I also like to go in the spring to work when the weather is equally fine but cooler.

New York, The Algonquin   by Leo Lerman

Why the Algonquin? Because it is an oasis of Edwardian homeliness in the maelstrom of Manhattan. It sits on a mid-town, westside street, swirling with debris, on the scruffy fringe of the Times Square district — the calm in the eye of the Big City storm . . .

We go to the Algonquin for security, for continuity, for its legend. Once you go Algonquin, you almost never go anywhere else — at least not in Manhattan. It's Hamlet, the lobby cat, scrutinising the guests. It's the best coconut cake in the world, and the chicken pies. It's the tea-time tea. It's the after-theatre buffet — if you can get in. It's the Englishness of it all. It's the staff that last more than two weeks and become friends. It's the Bodnes, who own it, and son-in-law Anspach, who runs it to please . . . you see them constantly in the cosiest lobby in town. It's the feeling of intellectuality: at the Algonquin you encounter an ideal — not just a deal.

Paris, George V   by Jean Muir

I love grand, personally impersonal hotels. The George V is for me. I love the way it moved itself on from being an old grand hotel to a modern grand hotel and lost nothing in the doing. I love the new entrance — Aubusson, vast, sumptuous, opulent, un-ashamed, "age of extravagance." Great.

I love the Baroque tapestried salon I pass on the way to the lift. I love being Madame Mooeee all over the place. I love the vast seizième siècle red plush sofa on the 2me étage. It would take ten of me but I long for the day when I pluck up enough courage to ask M. Sonier if I could buy it.

I love the squashy comfortable beds; I must have slept in them all. I can hole up there quite happily for days; order dinner in bed — Omelette aux Truffles, Poulet de Bresse, Salada Verte, a little chilled Beaujolais, a Corbeille des Fruits which would make any Victorian wax artist turn in his grave with envy. All hail to M. Sonier and his staff. All hail to M. Forte to know that things that are great can continue being great.

Paris, The Ritz   by Cecil Beaton

The Ritz is like no other hotel in the world. Forget the prices. I love the way it looks. I love its smell. Managers, porters, waiters are overwhelmingly anxious to please; they respect one's smallest wish, be it seemingly unobtainable seats at the theatre, cars to Longchamps or Chartres, foie gras in the middle of the night, or just cleaning one's boots. Elegance, charm and comfort exude and pamper; food and wine are legendary. The head man will invariably know who has died, who is living with whom, what's going on generally, and will confide it to you. Each time you go he will keep you up to date. This being kept *au-courant* makes for an exciting, falsely intimate atmosphere.

After a stay at The Ritz one goes forth refreshed for life and ready to face the shocks of the outside world.

St. Tropez, Hotel Byblos   by Geoffrey Aquilina Ross

Elizabeth Taylor, I was convinced, walked the corridors of the Byblos, wearing an embroidered caftan and with her hair in curlers. It is that kind of place.

I was younger then, more impressionable, but only weeks before the Paris hairdresser, Alexandre, had taken it over for his son's wedding. Guests had winged in from all directions... the Windsors, de Ribes, Rainier and Grace by yacht from Monaco... the porters could talk of nothing else.

I've been back since, a beady eye open. The porters are discreet, they've seen it all.

The Byblos is St. Tropez' gem. Costly certainly, even on this expensive gilt coastline it is considered so, but it deserves the praises lavished for its understated Provençal decoration, its pool-side life. Outside, at first sight, it looks like an anonymous staid apartment house but from the playground around the pool you realise the building is like a horseshoe, trapping the sun, and staggered and painted in toning shades of beige to look like seven or eight typical Midi houses. Very cool, very simple, but, like St. Tropez itself, a good example of the ultimate in throwaway style.

San Francisco, Huntington Hotel   by David Harlech

In America the trouble is that small hotels tend to be scruffy and large hotels tend to have abominable service. The beauty of the Huntington is that it is small, immaculate, personal and with service up to the highest European standards. Add to that its position at the top of Nob Hill not 100 yards from the more illustrious Mark Hopkins and directly facing the only great private house to survive the 1906 earthquake, which is now occupied by the grandest men's club I have ever been in — the Pacific Union — and you have the reasons why I have nothing but happy memories of the Huntington.

Sidi bou Said, Dar Zarrouk   by Gayle Hunnicutt

Dar Zarrouk is a very small, old hotel hidden away in a tiny Arab village called Sidi bou Said on top of a hill overlooking the bay of Carthage. The village is pure white edged with deep sky blue woodwork and latticework in typical Tunisian style. One can wander through the tiny streets stopping occasionally to haggle in the souk or spend an hour in the town square drinking mint tea and watching the Arab world go by. In the evening, after a delicious Tunisian meal, part Arab, part French, with inexpensive but delightful local Tunisian wine, one can return and sit in a garden terrace filled with bougainvillaea, lemon trees, and night flowering jasmin. To me it is one of the most peaceful and magical spots in the world.

Singapore, Raffles Hotel   by John Hedgecoe

Raffles Hotel belongs to the days when the sun never set on the British Empire. Its rooms were filled with sea captains, tea planters and traders doing their multifarious deals, whispered behind whitewashed colonnades. The Empire has long departed but at Raffles the spirit is still decidely present.

Rudyard Kipling wrote that Raffles was the only place to dine in Singapore, and today it is still a gourmet delight to be transported back into more leisured times. It was here, in the palm court, with its huge fan-shaped palms, that Maugham wrote *The Moon and Sixpence*.

The dining-room, the Tiffin Room, is a marble-floored cathedral; its roof is three floors above. Bigger than most modern hotels, it has only 76 palatial suites, no single rooms, and the majority of rooms face on to the palm court. The bathrooms, dressing-rooms, bedrooms and sitting-rooms are all the size of grand monuments: stepping into this from today's compressed world, the sensation is one of vast space and even isolation.

To stay at Raffles is an experience and the staff make you feel that you belong to an older tradition of travelling that, alas, most people cannot share. Thank God!

Sydney, The Sebel Town House — by Hardy Amies

The Sebel Town House is not too large: ten stories. It is in the town, just near the delightfully wicked Kings Cross but at the same time perched on a hill above Rush Cutters Bay so that, from some rooms, you can see the harbour. The harbour's magic sparkles on all the buildings that line it. You must be near it to enjoy Sydney.

The welcome sets the key tone to a visit. The receptionists at the Town House always seem pleased to see you. Then, the second most important thing is the floor maid. I must have paid six visits to the Town House and Pat always seems to be there. The room service is swift and intelligent. There is a family atmosphere which I suppose is due to the fact that it is owned by a family rather than a huge corporation. The only black mark is the unreliable quality of the food, but I quickly counteract criticism with noting that the restaurant is open until two in the morning, a very rare thing for Sydney. My favourite bedroom is really a balcony suspended in a very tall room with windows from floor to ceiling. With great courage and openness of mind the owners are allowing me to decorate these rooms with my own colour schemes. I am going to enjoy spending February there, working just enough to pay the fare for Concorde and to dilute pleasure.

Torquay, The Imperial Hotel — by Edward du Cann

True, I have to travel a great deal. In two weeks I have made speeches in Blackpool, Brighton, Newcastle, Cornwall, Somerset and Glasgow. Yet I stay rarely in British hotels. I make it a rule to return home overnight whenever I possibly can. There is no place like home . . .

The one hotel in Britain I am always pleased to stay in is the Imperial at Torquay. It is outstanding in every way.

Its management is distinguished. Michael Chapman, who lives aboard (as sailors say), has a national and international reputation. It is well-appointed and comfortable. The service and the food are equally good. The gastronomic weekends are notable.

It has just about everything, from conference and business facilities to privacy. Squash, sauna, golf, swimming, or peace, perfect peace.

I am always at home by the sea, and in a way the Imperial is as pleasant as one's own home can be. It is built on red sandstone, typical of the West Country, typical of the warmth of the Imperial's welcome. Above all it is a friendly place.

Venice and Asolo, The Cipriani — by Lady Rupert Nevill

Surrounded by trees and gardens that float into the serene expanse of the great lagoon that stretches towards the distant Lido horizon, the Cipriani is large, cool and airy. You can breathe there after the crowded calli, and even swim or dance in the evening. The huge pool is an immense asset. To be able to bathe and sunbathe so close to the centre of Venice is unique and delightful, there can be no better place in the heat of the summer from which to mix sightseeing and relaxation. I have had delightful meals in the garden, piling my plate with delectable sea-food. Added to which, the journey across in the hotel's launch is free. What greater boon could a tourist ask for in Venice?

Cipriani in Venice has a sister in Asolo, which is a jewel in the crown of the hotel world. Small but roomy, immensely comfortable and friendly. The food is an exquisite experience, the management and staff superb. There is no problem too great, no trouble too much for them.

Cipriani Asolo lies in the heart of the Veneto, nestling on the toes of the Dolomites, surrounded by ravishing pastoral countryside. From Asolo you can visit the Palladian villas and explore the rich visual and intellectual harvest of the Veneto. Padua, Vicenza and Verona are all within easy reach. You can walk amongst olive groves, orchards and vineyards, ankle-deep in an astonishing tapestry of wild flowers; or you can contemplate the beauty of plain and mountain from the Cipriani garden, that paradise of bright green grass, pomegranate trees and showers of blue plumbago. A rose pergola frames the view across the valley towards a little hill, furnished so charmingly with a small stone fairy flanked by cypress. And beyond, more humpy little hills dotted with farms and campanile, threaded with belled cattle and winding lanes stretching away, as far as the eye can see, to Monte Grappe.

I can unhesitatingly recommend these hotels, but I must warn you they are expensive. You cannot enjoy such standards without appropriate payment. But because I have recommended something more than just standards in each of these cases, you will get that increasingly rare result, value for money.

Vienna, Sacher Hotel   by George Weidenfeld

First the location: ideal for the opera lover — just walk across the road and into the splendid marble foyer. Then the dazzling unpredictability of the rooms — each different in shape and size, but mercifully little in the elegance and the decor. The red bar with its exquisite menu (best boiled beef, sauté of brains and, naturally, the Sacher Torte), and nostalgic pianist; the Porter, a walking encyclopaedia and arbiter of manners and morals.

Yucatan, Hotel Cozumel Caribe   by Diana Rigg

Fifteen years ago Cozumel Island was completely undeveloped, no telephones, no cars, and one hotel. Then the Cozumel Caribe was built and now there are seventeen hotels.

The Cozumel Caribe looks modern, is modern, with such features as a false thatched roof adding a Mexican touch. All the rooms are suites — bedroom, bathroom, sitting-room — and all have a balcony overlooking the sea. In fact, all rooms face the sea. Service is excellent, food too — a mixture of Mexican and American. All the staff are Mexican and they will certainly teach you Spanish before you leave.

One feature of the island is the water: it is so pure that someone can go down 70 feet and you can still see him clearly from the beach. Swimming is safe: there is a reef half a mile out and the water is full of dolphins, so sharks keep their distance. There's marvellous deep sea fishing. The hotel arranges beach parties once a week complete with bonfire, balloons and rockets let off from boats. And you can take their Robinson Crusoe boat trip that takes in diving for fish and lobster and cooking them over a fire built of banana leaves on the beach. To complete the meal, coconut, pineapple and bananas picked on the spot.

The sun is strongest from May to July and even in winter around 70–80 deg. F. The sunsets are memorable with the sun seeming to go straight into the sea, often with a green flash, always with the sky turning a brilliant orange, then pitch black — there is no twilight.

WHAT NEXT - A GALACTIC PACKAGE TOUR?

by JAMES BURKE

Gilbert and Ellice Islands Oct. 15 2036

Dear Grandmother,

A week here, already! It seems like five minutes. The weather is perfect, the sand and sea and food the same. The mini-hotel is very comfortable. These Brazilians really know how to run a travel empire, though we did notice a tendency on the part of their computer to write the printouts in Portuguese first and PanAfrican second. Still, it's nice to know you are being looked after by your own people, isn't it?

The shuttle flight was, as always, a big thrill. We got to the launch-pad just in time to see the noon shot for Papeete go. Very spectacular. Mulele says the European pilots waggle their tail as they go past the top of the tower on purpose. I said if they did that with *me* on board, they'd soon be back in the land of their fathers living off a low-protein diet like the rest of the Europeans! But when our turn came, at 12.15, up we went like a bird — I must tell you that the Pacific from orbit is sensational! No matter how many times you've seen it. But it's *crowded* up there. Apart from all the old Russo-American stuff hanging about, we saw no less than *five* other tourist shuttles. Nairobi must be empty — and Rio, for that matter.

These new digifax computers the travel people have produced make everything so smooth: not a human travel agent in sight, all the way. We just dialled up the destination on the phone the night before we left, and out came the tickets. The shuttle terminals are all the same. Not like in your day. I don't know how you managed with the crowds, no air-conditioning, and all that religious ritual involved in getting on a jet plane. I'd have gone home in a huff. I mean, if they keep up the service you shouldn't have to wait longer than five minutes anywhere. Still — it can't have been easy for you then — before we put up our raw material prices. They must have made you feel awfully minority. Strange — we were saying last night in the lounge how neither of us could imagine anything *but* a white face behind the bar. The European staff here are quite efficient, considering. And guess what we saw on last night's submarine tour of the reefs! An American! Mulele says we can expect to see them more and more on the beaches now they've decided to come out of their ludicrous isolation. They'll just have to get used to it being us instead of their Anglo cousins!

We talked to *everybody* on the satellite the other night, lying out on the beach. They're really spread around. The Amins are in the Cocos Islands. The da Silvas are doing something crazy: driving the entire length of the Vietnam-Himalaya-Tehran freeway! And you remember that funny couple we met from Mogadishu? They're devoting all of their precious three months holiday to some social study of the old European holiday spots of the last century. They were saying Venice and Athens and Rome and Cordoba are all the same: crumbling. How sad the whites wouldn't take our offer to restore everything for them. Apparently the frescoes are peeling off the walls, and another bit of the Parthenon fell down last week. It's a shame. I'm sure our girls would have loved to

253

see some of it. I just know that by the time they're grown up Europe will be all the rage. But we're very happy where we are. That's another lovely thing about those computers. You can be absolutely certain there won't be more than ten or fifteen of you anywhere you go, even if you switch destinations at the last minute. I suppose it *has* meant the end of the desert island. There must be an Afro or a Brazilian mini-hotel on every island in the world, by now. Still, the vertical take-off jets mean no ugly airstrips, and the buildings are all styled into the landscape. But sometimes I long for a place where we can be alone. No hope of *that* any more! Though . . . who knows? Maybe Europe. Their birthrate's been going down for decades. They do say you *can* get away from it all in London and Paris, though nobody *I* know is quite ready for those "how the other half lives" jaunts they've started advertising in Nairobi.

I was thinking the other day — tourism may be on the way out, it's getting so easy to live where you like. Mulele says he could do all his work over the satellites. There are quite a few people already doing that in the China Sea islands. Wouldn't it be nice to be visiting friends all the time, instead of hotels. Just like the jet set of your day (what a quaint expression *that* was!) I hear a rumour the Americans have solved the fusion problem. Remember? Unlimited energy from a bucket of sea water? Do hope so. Otherwise it'll be no more holidays for anybody. I really do think we're getting a touch profligate in our use of fuel. Mulele reckons we've only got a generation or so before we're in the same boat as the Europeans. When we were at the South Pole last summer I was amazed by what that nuclear station had done to the place. All mod cons. I loved it. So empty. Thank heavens I don't need a suntan. That place would frazzle you — all the sunlight coming off the snow and ice!

Must stop and put some clothes on. Oh — that's something I forgot to tell you! Everybody — but *everybody* . . . is *wearing clothes!!!* It's really kinky. I must say I find it all a bit embarrassing — but Mulele says it turns him on, so . . . terribly risqué, though! Plankton fricassée and swordfish for dinner. I'm ravenous. Take care of yourself. The thought of coming home in nine weeks is unbearable. I must get Mulele to change his job and make a bit more money. You can't go anywhere *interesting* on a bank clerk's salary. And I do so want to make that trip under the North Pole icecap before the subliners get packed with those greasy *nouveau riche* Papuans. Lots of love from us both. Anene.

PLUƧ ÇA CHAΠGE

It is often remarked that the Twentieth Century is an age of easy travel. In fact, there is scarcely any more travelling to be done. The most ingenious brain must find it hard to contrive a novelty. It is clear that, in a hundred years' time, another Columbus will have landed on a star and initiated our conquest and moral improvement of the solar system. We shall appoint chaplains to Jupiter; Saturn will displace the Riviera; everyone will have his rocket, housed neatly in the garden, and the earth will lapse into a sentimental dotage.

From "The Problems of Modern Travel" by Robert Byron, August 21 1929

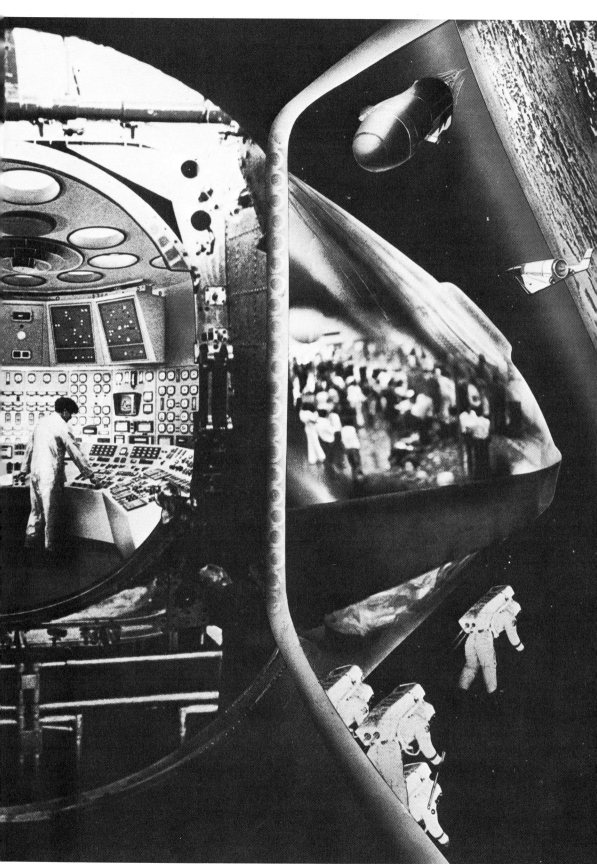